XENOCITIZENS

Xenocitizens

Illiberal Ontologies in
Nineteenth-Century America

Jason Berger

FORDHAM UNIVERSITY PRESS

New York 2020

Copyright © 2020 Fordham University Press

All rights reserved. No part of this publication may be reproduced, stored in a retrieval system, or transmitted in any form or by any means—electronic, mechanical, photocopy, recording, or any other—except for brief quotations in printed reviews, without the prior permission of the publisher.

Chapter 1, "Emerson's Operative Mood," previously appeared as "Emerson's Operative Mood: Religious Sentiment and Violence in the Early Works" in the Winter 2015 issue of *Studies in Romanticism* and appears here by courtesy of the Trustees of Boston University.

Fordham University Press has no responsibility for the persistence or accuracy of URLs for external or third-party Internet websites referred to in this publication and does not guarantee that any content on such websites is, or will remain, accurate or appropriate.

Fordham University Press also publishes its books in a variety of electronic formats. Some content that appears in print may not be available in electronic books.

Visit us online at www.fordhampress.com.

Library of Congress Cataloging-in-Publication Data available online at https://catalog.loc.gov.

Printed in the United States of America
22 21 20 5 4 3 2 1
First edition

For my parents,
Deborah and James Berger,

my sister and brother,
Carey Brunetti and Michael Berger,
with love and gratitude

For Sarah Ehlers and Jonah Berger,
who make home a living possibility

CONTENTS

Introduction: Xenocitizens   1

Part I   ILLIBERAL ONTOLOGIES

1. Emerson's Operative Mood   33
2. Agitating Margaret Fuller   58

Part II   ILLIBERAL ECOLOGIES

3. Thoreau's Militant Vegetables   101
4. Unadjusted Emancipations   153
   Epilogue: Care, *There and Now*   201

Notes   205
Index   279

Xenocitizens

INTRODUCTION

Xenocitizens

> [T]here is no such thing as an innocent reading.
> —LOUIS ALTHUSSER, *Reading Capital*

"Xenocitizen" might seem a peculiar term, especially in our current moment. Amid an era when neoliberal policies obliterate longstanding civic realities and a large portion of the U.S. population feeds on ever-new xenophobic and racist offerings, why appeal to the notion of *citizen* at all?

Instead of seeking civic origins or considering the "afterlives" of citizenship in the wake of neoliberalism, *Xenocitizens: Illiberal Ontologies in Nineteenth-Century America* attempts to move toward a positive abandonment.[1] Lauren Berlant and Lee Edelman suggest that Eve Kosofsky Sedgwick's term for "disrepair" is, in fact, "*abandonment.*" According to Berlant and Edelman, "[a]bandonment is when, in the scene of looking backward, one discovers that the end of sociality has come already and that there is nothing left to fear or constrain."[2] In our moment, sociality under the sign of liberalism has seemingly come to end—or, at the very least, is in dire crisis. *Xenocitizens* enters what is a wide field of responses to our present economic and existential precarity by challenging a shaken but still standing scholarly tradition based upon liberal-humanist perspectives. Through the concept of xenocitizen, a synthesis of the terms "xeno," which connotes alien and/or stranger, and "citizen," which signals a naturalized subject of a state, this book returns to the nineteenth century in an effort to uncover realities and, indeed, possibilities, that have been foreclosed by dominant paradigms that continue to shape our views about justice, tolerance, belief, and various demarcations of insides and outsides, including the separation of public and private spheres. Examining how crises in the antebellum years pushed writers to formulate alternative ontological and social models for thinking about personhood and sociality, I glimpse other citizenships—other modes of political ontology and, with hope, collectivity that arose during the throes of the mid-nineteenth century. Today, the old liberal-national model of citizen is not only problematic but also tactically anachronistic.[3] And yet, standard liberal assumptions that undergird the fading realities of humanist and democratic traditions often linger within emerging scholarly models that seek to move past them. The problems of our era, and our past, for that matter, demand that scholars push their imaginative and critical thinking toward new terrain.

It follows that xenocitizens are, by necessity, *illiberal*. By employing the term "illiberal," I intend to harness the negative Latinate prefix "not" but in a manner that connotes varying forms of non-identity with dominant modes of liberalism rather than a definitive opposition to them, even though such opposition is at times present. The concept of liberalism, and its manifold contexts, has rightly received much critical attention in recent years. While I will outline some of the major trends in this criticism, examining the vexed portrayals of both liberalism and neoliberalism, I want to begin for now with Lisa Lowe's suggestion that "liberal humanism is a formalism that translates the world through an economy of affirmation and forgetting within a regime of desiring freedom." In Lowe's terms, "Liberal forms of political economy, culture, government, and history propose a narrative of freedom overcoming enslavement that at once denies colonial slavery, erases the seizure of lands from native peoples, displaces migrations and connections across continents, and internalizes these processes in a national struggle of history and consciousness."[4] In the context of the United States, Gregg Crane locates such formal foreclosures within a constituent paradox at the center of American liberal democracy. For him, the early definition of certain races (*ethnos*) as outside the parameters of "citizen" reveals starkly how the "juxtaposition of identity-neutral norms of political and social coexistence and identitarian practice is a hallmark of American higher law constitutionalism."[5]

Since Aristotle, the concept of "citizen" has been buoyed by ideals about political civic participation (*politikos*) predicated upon various notions of "membership."[6] Historical reality, however, offers a different lesson: how expansive inclusion via shifting defined categories screens a myriad of systemic exclusions. As scholars in Indigenous studies, black studies, and feminist and queer studies have argued, such exclusions conveniently constitute the foundation for modes of extraction and appropriation, including what Jasbir Puar calls "debilitation."[7] Liberal democracy's outcasts often become, in this sense, forcibly in-cast (*Cherokee Nation v. Georgia*, section 9 of the Treaty of Guadalupe Hidalgo, *Dred Scott v. Sandford* . . .).

Instead of working along the familiar axis of inclusion/exclusion, *Xenocitizens* moves outward and alongside: pursuing examples where, in response to historical conditions, writers struggled to forge alternative conceptualizations of self and sociality. Consequently, in my formulation, the term "citizen" might be crossed out, designating a placeholder for alternate or para ("beside") constructions. Citing the types of foreclosures Lowe and Crane pinpoint, Frederick Douglass, in an 1853 speech, laments how U.S. laws rendered free blacks less-than-citizens. In his terms: "Aliens are we in our native land."[8] From the start, liberal democracy's promises were predicated upon necessary constituent failures. Aliens *are*—and it is this book's wager that future pathways out of our current political-economic predicament might come from starting here—where we have been all along.

Xenocitizens and its notion of the illiberal seeks to be a fellow traveler with various contemporary attempts to critique or move past foundational elements of the liberal tradition, especially those elements operating within and beneath neoliberal policies. At the same time, it might partially ally with more recent post-Trump attempts to radically reorient aspects of liberalism itself. For example, Charles W. Mills's *Black Rights/White Wrongs: The Critique of Racial Liberalism* (2017) sets out from the premise that contemporary scholars such as Domenico Losurdo are correct to argue that, despite its association with emancipations, liberalism has been a longstanding and active catalyst for various regimes of racial and economic oppression. Offering "racial liberalism" as a new rubric for a wide-ranging critique of liberalism's racial foreclosures, Mills attempts to "recognize these exclusions as theoretically central, admit their shaping of liberalism's array of rights and freedoms, and then confront the critics' case for discrediting liberalism all together with the defense's arguments for how it can nonetheless be reclaimed and redeemed."[9] In Mills's view, this critique might allow us to "pluralize liberalism into *liberalisms*," in essence producing "a self-consciously anti-racist liberalism" and thereby "correct[ing] the (anti-universalist, anti-egalitarian) distortions in mainstream white liberalism."[10] Working along a similar trajectory, Chantal Mouffe's *For a Left Populism* (2018) suggests that the 2008 economic crisis highlighted neoliberal contradictions and engendered "the populist moment," where both the right and the left have begun to produce new anti-hegemonic movements.[11] Advocating for the construction of a populist "transversal mode," Mouffe asserts that a qualified "left" perspective is necessary for addressing the challenges of the present.[12] "Left populism," Mouffe argues, "wants to recover democracy to deepen and extend it. A left populist strategy aims at federating the democratic demands into a collective will to construct a 'we,' a 'people' confronting a common adversary: the oligarchy." Mouffe hopes a new political alignment—calling for a "chain of equivalence among the demands of the workers, the immigrants and the precarious middle class, as well as other democratic demands, such as those of the LGBT community"—might "radicalize democracy."[13]

One must be nimble enough to forge alliances with such liberalisms while, at the same time, forcefully unsettling the codification of new middles that replicate aspects of previous liberal terrains or developing neoliberal formations. *Xenocitizens* hopes to build on, and perhaps productively break from, more recent studies of the eighteenth- and especially nineteenth-century United States that follow, in spirit, the welcome reformist impulses seen in Mills and Mouffe.[14] As my chapters demonstrate in various ways, if we are to radically alter liberalism, we must do so by at least passing through the emerging critical discourses offered by, for example, Afro-pessimism, contemporary Marxism, and some of the posthumanist work being done under the rubric of new materialism. Just as Cary Wolfe aptly describes posthumanism as coming "both before and after humanism," illiberal xenocitizenship might designate alternative formations or distortions of liberal realities both before these dominant orientations consolidated in the later nineteenth century as well as after they were transformed within twentieth-century neoliberal efforts that have paradoxically pushed liberalism to the brink.[15] Through examples of nineteenth-century xenocitizenship, I highlight the complex noise—slippages, foreclosed conceptualizations, and possibilities—surrounding contested terms and views amid a historical moment within its own specific crises. These examples might, in turn, provide a useful collective foothold for thinking innovatively about residual and emerging conceptions of sociality, including the traditional categories of individuality and collectivity, after our own era's postnational and posthuman turns.

The four chapters within this book form a discontinuous trajectory: working from the more ubiquitous locus of the individual toward systemic concerns with sociality and large-scale economic and ecological formations. Part I, "Illiberal Ontologies," reconsiders the work of Ralph Waldo Emerson and Margaret Fuller in an effort to present a new understanding of how selves are formed and activated via impersonal outsides. The types of loaded personhood gleaned in these chapters have significantly different compositions and stakes than those found within received Romantic conceptions of the individual subject as well as the modes of impersonality employed by contemporary Deleuzian-inflected studies of new materiality. Part II, "Illiberal Ecologies," takes up the work of writers such as Henry David Thoreau, Harriet Beecher Stowe, William Wells Brown, and Martin R. Delany, examining how political ontology and agency are transformed within complex material networks. Pivoting on Charles Darwin's notion that what we now call "ecology" designates an "economy of nature," these chapters depict how mid-century writers formulated, in response to varying forms of oppression and precarity, startlingly unique and unfamiliar material-economic models for existing and for leveraging change.[16]

Leveraging change is what Althusser has in mind, too, in the epigraph above. After stating that "there is no such thing as an innocent reading," Althusser feels impelled to "say what reading [he is] guilty of."[17] This guilt, which stems from Althusser's declared ideological and methodological interventions, does not, however, require absolution. Instead, his reading "takes the responsibility for its crime as a 'justified crime' and defends it by proving its necessity."[18] I want to invoke the dialectical verve Althusser imagines but flip the scenario inside out: to call attention to how reified liberal schematics and their systemic foreclosures undergird standard contemporary scholarship in the humanities, including this scholarship's trend toward fashionable essays that roll out arguments through various thematic and/or aesthetic gestures or via short mainstream thinkpieces. Against these trends, Bruno Bosteels builds on the work of Jodi Dean and, even more explicitly, Álvaro García Linera to embrace what he terms the "actuality of communism." This move to make Marxism the "untranscendable horizon of our time," which means, in Dean's terms, to view this "horizon [as] Real not just in the sense of *impossible*—we can never reach it—but also in the sense of the *actual* format, condition, and shape of our setting," has significant methodological and political ramifications.[19] To quote Bosteels at length:

> Far from remaining a utopian principle, communism would thus be what allows for the historical inscription of politics in a concrete situation. It is what operates in the space in-between the local and the

universal, the singular and the eternal, the interested individual and the disinterested subject of a cause greater than him or herself. In this sense, communism actually would be able to avoid the pitfalls of speculative leftism thanks to the triangulation of history, politics, and subjectivity enabled by the Idea.[20]

Scholarship following this trajectory would move toward a place somewhere between what Bosteels elsewhere calls "a true polemic" and "a genealogical work of counter-memory."[21]

In the remainder of this introduction, and in the book as a whole, I want to take seriously the injunctions that lie at the core of Bosteels's work. The next two sections of this introduction turn directly to the concepts of xenocitizen and ontology: setting the terms of engagement and conceptual terrain for the chapters that follow. I argue that in our historical moment what we need in the fields of American Studies and American literary studies is a critical account of *actuality without positivism*: an approach that, by resisting longstanding liberal humanist and positivist historical assumptions, illuminates both concrete realities and emergent formations. Such a perspective allows one to study the reality of partial or potential formations of xenocitizens in the antebellum United States. They are there, some in actual practices and spaces, others in theories or accounts of alternate political forms of being. Much like Marx's pioneering and digging mole, a metonym for a broader movement of "Revolution" in his discussion of the historical distortions of the English working class, I suggest we should push back into the antebellum period with an eye or, in this case, any hand or claw we might find. Or simply follow Thoreau, who found his head to be "an organ for burrowing."[22]

Xenocitizens

Cutting across various sites of the antebellum United States in order to present a new panoply of political experiences and alignments, *Xenocitizens* unsettles many of the ideological assumptions that have guided scholarship on the nineteenth century. The structural stakes of my chapters might be articulated, in part, using the terms that Étienne Balibar presents in *Citizenship* (2015), which traces the development of Western citizenship from the ancient *politeia* through modern variants of bourgeois civics. Balibar aims to rethink democratic citizenship by shifting our perspective on the traditional schism between constituent and constituted forms of power. According to Balibar, "It is the antimony lodged at the heart of the relationship between citizenship and democracy that has been, in its successive forms, the motor for the transformation of the political institution."[23] This foundational contradiction is especially apparent in modern bourgeois revolutions and assertions of citizenship. After all, as he points out, "bourgeois" and "citizen" were originally synonymous, with *burgher* connoting a "citizen of a free city."[24] In Balibar's narrative, the advent of modern liberal democratic politics in the eighteenth century established "equal rights" as a new universal, and this concept was predicated on the pairings of opposites, such as man/citizen and liberty/equality. In terms of the latter pairing, Balibar writes that they "are seen as two sides of the same 'constituent power,' despite the permanent tendency of bourgeois political ideologies (which we can generally group under the term 'liberalism') to confer epistemic, even ontological, priority onto the first term [liberty], making it a 'natural right,' to which the socialist tendency to privilege equality is a response." As a result of this central paradox, Balibar argues, the body politic is perpetually "incomplete," with forms of domination requiring various modes of insurrection in order to demand and institute new rights. This brings Balibar to the concept of *equaliberty* and his primary intervention: the need to "simultaneously [demand] equality and liberty," an assertion that "is at the root of modern universal citizenship" despite the hegemonic formations that have denied or displaced it.[25]

Building on Balibar's points, I use the term "xenocitizen" to designate modes of existence and agency that are shaped negatively by reified historical formations of political identity—which include modern notions of state citizenship as well as other interpellated forms of social being—and, at the same time, that are non-identical to and/or outside of these very boundaries and constructions. In *Plebeian Power* (2014), Álvaro García Linera notes how the concept of "citizen" has become welded to notions of the state, but that it is, on a foundational level, really about "the constitution of the collective self." According to Linera, this is a process of "intersubjectification" that is fluid and dialectical, with citizenship constituting a "*practice of citizenship*, . . . [a] will to intervene in the matters that link [subjects] to their fellow citizens."[26] And this practice indelibly shapes both the "*content and the form of political rights*." Although states and empires, in Hardt and Negri's terms, often control the rhetoric and structures that condition political realities, these realities are, at the zero level, constituted by the social relations among peoples and actants. Consequently, the practice of citizenship is at least potentially contingent and open. In a point that is essential to *Xenocitizens*, Linera states, "[C]itizen-power belongs to a space that is both narrower and broader than the space of the state, though it encompasses it." Linera thus accounts for the existence of "non-state forms of citizenship formation, or forms outside of state-circuits of political power."[27] In this light, citizenship might more aptly be thought of as a "community" in Jean-Luc Nancy's formulation wherein, as Alyosha Goldstein notes, "community is not a form of shared identity, 'common being,' or mutual understanding" but a "'being-in-common—with 'being' itself constituted in and as a relation."[28]

Following Linera's logic, the reduction of citizenship to state-sanctioned identity forecloses alternate sociopolitical realities and potentialities. George Ciccariello-Maher makes a similar point in his more recent push to "decolonize dialectics." Working in the lineage of Frantz Fanon and Enrique Dussel, Ciccariello-Maher argues for "an enrichment of anarchism [that] might result from loosening the formalist grip of 'the state' and embracing decolonization as a means of attacking the most powerful and essential hierarchy of our times—the ontological apartheid that renders some less human than others."[29] My effort is not to push for some new Jacobin institution, but, somewhat like Ciccariello-Maher, to promote new perspectives for resisting the historical powers of modernity. This effort begins by considering anew both the historical foreclosures of being that condition our present as well as alternate formations that have been forgotten or ignored.[30] Despite the fact that democracy has long been, in Timothy Mitchell's terms, "an engineering project . . . concerned with the manufacture of new political subjects and with subjecting people to new ways of being governed," there are, across the eighteenth and nineteenth centuries, many examples of non-sanctioned and non-state formations of identity and community.[31] According to Raúl Coronado, for instance, in eighteenth- and nineteenth-century Latin America, there were "different visions for imagining communities that did not necessarily have to lead to nationalism, of conceptions of rights and subjectivity that [did] . . . not genuflect to our now dominant account of possessive individualism."[32] In a different context, Monique Allewaert's work on the eighteenth-century plantation zone has been influential in revealing innovatively such possibilities: depicting how "looking at tropical ecologies offers ways to build stories about places and actors that archives documenting the citizen-subjects of print culture cannot." This includes, for Allewaert, a recalibration of ontological "theorizations of resistance" in the period.[33]

If Balibar is correct that liberalism itself stands in for "bourgeois political realities," then it is no wonder that, when one looks carefully at specific social and political experiences during the nineteenth century, events quite often exceed or outright complicate given ideological coordinates, even if these coordinates are in flux despite themselves.³⁴ The discontinuity within the era's liberal discourses and policies often manifested, on one hand, in very real exclusions, expulsions, enslavements, and occupations, and, on the other hand, in new and often desperate militant uses of this charged historical horizon. In 1829, for example, the North Carolina judge Thomas Ruffin ruled that the wounding of a hired slave did not constitute a crime because "the power of the master must be absolute . . . to render the submission of the slave perfect." Such logic has a long history in the West, rendering the slave, in Henri Wallon's terms, an "animated instrument."³⁵ And yet, abstracting a bit from Wallon's language, if Heidegger's famous notion of the broken tool illuminates the way a systemically normalized and ignored object or function appears only when it ceases to operate smoothly, then we might say that the antebellum United States' liberal landscape was strewn with such tools—tools many chose to see, to hold in their hands, and, at times, to hurl and weaponize.³⁶ Of course, in returning to Ruffin's rhetoric and following the lead of W. E. B. Du Bois, these "animated instruments" themselves fought back and resisted with localized rebellions of various kinds. They also collaborated directly and indirectly before and during the Civil War via what Du Bois calls a "general strike of slaves."³⁷ Similar to how Du Bois reformulates standard optics for viewing a nationalized civil war by revealing the unacknowledged forms of collective black resistance working amid regimes of antiblackness (in the north and the south), through the concept of xenocitizen I hope to pull discussion of historical citizenship proper below or outside received debates and discourses. In fact, as I hope is clear by now, this book is not about "citizenship" at all—but about the tortured and fertile landscape upon which exclusionary communities have been built in its name.

When making such structural and, perhaps, utopian claims about other forms of citizenship, one must not lose sight of the way historical communities, especially those shaped by modern national and colonial conditions, are predicated upon violence. For example, building on the work of scholars such as Saidiya Hartman, Nicole M. Guidotti-Hernández offers a compelling and uncompromising critique of citizenship as domination in the context of Mexico–United States relations, writing: "Citizenship plays a crucial role in the perpetuation of violence precisely because national membership, rights, birthrights, and state and local practices were often determined situationally." Although acknowledging scholars, such as Akhil Gupta, who view citizenship in terms of "split and multiple affinities," Guidotti-Hernández insists that "racialized, sexualized, and gendered subjects often are not viewed as full members of their respective communities or as full citizens of nations . . . and are more likely to be targets of physical, psychological, or discursive violence." She thus analyzes "the role of the nation-state (a legal and political entity) in forming national imaginaries . . . that perpetuate dominant narratives of national amnesia."[38]

Especially when looking at the nineteenth-century United States, a period in which the term "citizenship" was itself a contested concept with such tremendous stakes, one must foreground the violences that Guidotti-Hernández illuminates. It is in this era, for example, when the Supreme Court's Chief Justice Roger B. Taney asserted "the line of division which the Constitution has drawn between the citizen race and . . . the African race."[39] Citing David Kazanjian's work on Federalist-era monetary policy, Fred Moten explains how late eighteenth-century U.S. national financial structures had broader ideological goals pertaining to population control. Discussing James Madison's writing about the institution of a new tariff, Moten suggests such measures were a "national policy precisely because [they] promise[d] to transform . . . potentially plural and antagonistic 'constituents' into united subjects abstracted from their particularities and antagonisms and represented as formally equivalent units of national population—units [Madison] elsewhere calls 'citizens' who will engage in lively economic exchange." As both Kazanjian and Moten portray in different ways, such instantiations of abstract "unity" through economic citizenship allowed for the "disguised separation" of racial slavery, an institution whose appropriation of labor laid a foundation for the nation and whose anti-black ideological structures used blackness as a vanishing mediator for the construction and consolidation of sanctioned modern identities.[40]

By following Linera and others who call for a retheorization of citizenship in terms of non-state formations, collectives, and inter- or parasubjective constructions, I do not at all intend to diminish the staggering importance of studies such as Guidotti-Hernández's that attend to how systems of power effect and infect those "below the threshold of citizenship," to borrow Allewaert's phrase.[41] This is especially apparent in the nineteenth century, when the broader reality of what Achille Mbembe calls "necropolitics," or the way modes of biopolitics generated forms of social death for nonwhite persons denied political *bios*, created the conditions for what Russ Castronovo terms "necro citizenship." As Castronovo explains, this era saw racialized and gendered others caught in a "deathly logic of citizenship that sentenced [them] . . . to excessive and lethal embodiment" while an abstract notion of legalized identity reigned supreme.[42]

Indeed, in the nineteenth-century United States, socioeconomic oppression was starkly apparent in battles over the fate of chattel slavery.

Those seeking to end this longstanding institution faced the necessity of naming enemies, of drawing ethical lines in the sand, and, as Frederick Douglass famously demonstrated in his 1852 "What to the Slave Is the Fourth of July?" speech, of calling out the violence that liberal society smoothly maintained. As Kerry Larson points out, the term "liberal" was most commonly used in antebellum America in reference to religion—with "liberal Christianity," for instance, connoting a Christianity that was tolerant and accommodating, avoiding petty doctrinal intransigence.[43] In the nineteenth century, as today, the characteristics of liberalism Larson outlines crossed over into the secular realm, shaping the value of "diversity" (hence "pluralism") and "debate" (hence "agonism"). But what about the systemic violences obscured by the polite function of safe rhetorical norms and the half-truths of master signifiers such as "liberty" and "equality"? The violence not seen (willfully or otherwise) through lenses shaped by liberal fantasies is what Douglass calls out in his Fourth of July speech: not just that slavery *is* a violent problem, but that the means by which a liberal political sphere addresses itself (conceptually and rhetorically) toward this violence is a problem. Douglass asks, "Must I argue that a system thus marked with blood, and stained with pollution, is *wrong*?" After answering emphatically in the negative, he follows with: "What then remains to be argued?" He concludes by suggesting that "scorching irony" is now required, which includes the act of "pour[ing] a fiery stream of biting ridicule" into the "nation's ear."[44]

Such an odd blend of seemingly divergent ideological positions within the civic frame of a so-called liberal republic is, of course, not all that far from our own political landscape. Contemporary scholarly responses to neoliberal policies have inspired a rich array of studies of liberalism and its origins. Building with post–World War II shifts in economic thinking in the Mont Pèlerin Society and the Chicago School of Economics and breaking in the late seventies with Thatcherism (inspired by Friedrich Hayek) and Reaganomics (shaped by Paul Volcker and later Alan Greenspan), neoliberalism is, as David Harvey explains it, "a theory of political economic practices that proposes that human well-being can best be advanced by liberating individual freedoms and skills within an institutional framework characterized by strong private property rights, free markets, and free trade."[45] As the 2008 Great Recession brought home, these neoliberal practices and policies included widespread—and by now practically total—deregulation, privatization, and the decimation of publics and commons. Through international bodies such as the World Bank, IMF, and WTO, neoliberal policies allowed capital to expand rapidly through "structural adjustment" programs and austerity measures.[46] Earlier liberalisms and contemporary neoliberalism (the former, at best, offering various notions of "freedom from" institutional constructions that open up the space for democratic ideals, and the latter offering various notions of "freedom from" state and civic control that allow market forces to override all boundaries) share a historical base in the development of capital and its socioeconomic ramifications beginning, according to most accounts, in the early seventeenth century. Indeed, the structural adjustment policies forwarded by the Washington Consensus (operating under the aegis of the IMF and World Bank) tellingly synthesized traditional "liberal" tenets of openness, tolerance, and freedom with developing neoliberal financial policies. John Williamson's 1989 list of structural adjustment measures, for example, includes concepts such as "trade liberalization" and "liberalizing foreign direct investment."[47]

The historical and conceptual connections among earlier liberalisms and neoliberalism, however, are anything but continuous, and, as mentioned, the nature of these relations remains a charged topic with significant stakes. There are those, such as Amanda Anderson (*Bleak Liberalism* [2016]), who remain defenders of liberalism and offer various attempts to offset contemporary critiques of this tradition. Anderson argues that "challenges" to liberalism—described as "psychological, social, and economic barriers to its moral and political ideas"—may derive, at least in part, from *outside* of liberalism. This claim allows her book to pivot elliptically toward its primary consideration of the emotional toll rendered by attempting to adhere to embattled liberal ideals. By examining the "bleakness" of such liberal positions, Anderson seems to suggest that this tradition is somehow "thickened" (aesthetically and otherwise) and, by implication, more relevant or tenable.[48] To the middle-left of Anderson, a number of contemporary scholars are attempting to counter the forces of neoliberalism and right-wing responses to it via revisionist or activist reinvigorations of liberalism. In their own ways, each of these scholars asserts a break within liberalism—either one to come in a necessary future (as with Mills and his notion of purging liberalism of its racist historical structures) or as a constituent rupture that has already occurred, often with the advent of neoliberalism (such as Eva Cherniavsky referencing the "divorce" between capitalism and democracy, Dawson Barrett calling the era of neoliberalism a "post-liberal America," and Mouffe asserting the difference between "political liberalism and economic liberalism")[49] Further left still, scholars and writers continue to engage neoliberalism via the perspectives of

Marxism and other emerging materialist approaches and practices not aligned with the traditions of liberal-humanism or the horizon of recognized "politics" per se. For example, Achille Mbembe asserts emphatically that "[i]t would be a mistake to believe that we have left behind the regime that began with the slave trade and flourished in plantation and extraction colonies."[50] In lieu of imposing a definitive fissure within liberalism, and offering something of a staged schematic for what Cedric Robinson calls "racial capitalism" and what Fred Moten terms "racial state capitalism," Mbembe conceives of the development of modernity as a series of "three critical moments" related to capital and "the vertiginous assemblage that is Blackness": the Atlantic slave trade (1500–1900), "the birth of writing near the end of the eighteenth century" (essentially the creation of republican-liberal political idealism and its attendant revolts and revolutions), and neoliberalism.[51]

Coming amid the second critical historical moment noted by Mbembe, the antebellum era saw many of the dictums produced by liberalism's ideological agenda reifying, including a longstanding process of culling and renarrating aspects of the *ancien régime* for various Enlightenment agendas. The ancient Greek concept of *demos*, fantasies of the Roman Republic, as well as subsequent Judeo-Christian institutional conceptions of civic and personal lives laid the foundations for socioeconomic structures that developed out of early seventeenth-century corporations (the Virginia Company was chartered in 1606) and later Enlightenment political revolutions. In Jethro Lieberman's terms, "western imagination" was seized by a "beguiling idea" nearly four centuries ago: "A just balance between disorder and repression could be achieved if the state withdrew from the business of imposing an ultimate good. . . . Liberalism . . . holds that it is not only possible but also morally proper to govern by refraining from decreeing ultimate ends, and that the state's only business is to prevent people from harming each other." Lieberman, however, quickly notes a central paradox in the early liberalism of the eighteenth and nineteenth centuries: the fact that "only in the state and by obedience to law was it possible to be free."[52] Although Douglass's Fourth of July speech was delivered before John Stuart Mill's humanistic master narrative *On Liberty* (1859), it is safe to say that by the early nineteenth century the western and southern transatlantic world had tacitly incorporated a whole host of liberal ideological assumptions about the economy, the state, and civic personhood. According to Stephen Holmes, the "core practices of a liberal political order" of this era and our own includes:

Religious toleration, freedom of discussion, restrictions on police behavior, free elections, constitutional governments based upon a separation of powers, publicly inspectable state budgets to inhibit corruption, and economic policy committed to sustained growth on the basis of private ownership and freedom of contract. Liberalism's four core norms or values are *personal security* (the monopolization of legitimate violence by agents of the state who are themselves monitored by the law), *impartiality* (a single system of law applied equally to all), *individual liberty* (a broad sphere of conscience, the right to be different, the right to pursue ideals one's neighbor thinks wrong, the freedom to travel and emigrate, and so forth), and *democracy* or the right to participate in lawmaking by means of elections and public discussion through a free press.[53]

Each of these apparently natural and commonsensical "practices," as Holmes calls them, obviously has a complex genealogy. So, too, does the overriding term "liberalism." Domenico Losurdo grounds the modern use of the concept in mid-seventeenth-century England, where the specific term—shaped by the Seven Years' War, the outcome of the Somersett case, and the subsequent rebellion in the North American colonies—acted as an adjective linked to any number of nouns (sentiment, government, commerce, and so on) connoting a quality of "freedom" and "tolerance." According to Losurdo, the term began being used as a noun when the author of an article in the *Pennsylvania Packet* published on March 25, 1780, self-identified as "A Liberal" in their case for the abolition of slavery.[54]

In the early nineteenth century, however, being a liberal meant anything but simply supporting a pro-abolitionist agenda. As Losurdo notes, race-based slavery "is not something that persisted despite the success of the three liberal revolutions. On the contrary, it experiences its maximum development following that success," especially if one looks at the case of the United States.[55] It should come as little surprise, therefore, that although many of liberalism's classic texts, such as Adam Smith's *The Wealth of Nations* (1776), frowned upon slavery as a premodern source of "economic stagnation," just as many have either outright supported slavery, especially in the colonies and newly formed republics, or questioned the ramifications of abolitionist movements.[56] Such notable liberal proponents of slavery, both weak and strong, included Edmond Burke (whose work was used by pro-slavery Virginians such as Thomas R. Dew), Benjamin Disraeli (who explicitly lamented the social and racial implications of the abolition of slavery, even after the U.S. Civil War), Lord Acton (who categorized abolitionists in England as "Jacobins"), and, yes, even the much-quoted Alexis de Tocqueville (who criticized slavery in principle, but balked when faced with the "dangerous" socioeconomic reality of abolishing slavery where it already existed).[57] This narrative gets even more complex when one considers the related widespread civic exclusion of the working classes (many of whom were, of course, people of color), which included indentured servitude of various kinds, an expanding population of the working poor, and developing prison systems that kept the dispossessed subdued via incarceration and indebtedness.

Through the concept of xenocitizen, I seek to explore nineteenth-century formations and positions forged despite, against, or asymmetrically within the complex liberal coordinates presented above. *Xenocitizens* situates itself in the liminal space, often coded as a limit, fold, or interference, within and without criticism that examines the operations of biopolitical power in the nineteenth century. By employing the aforementioned critical perspective of actuality without positivism, I hope the book will begin to reveal examples of actual and potential persons and collectives that have, to varying degrees, been foreclosed by historical conditions. It is no wonder that these realities have been shied away from or demeaned by contemporary critical paradigms. Xenocitizens, as I will show, are not necessarily good neighbors. Born amid imperialist regimes, xenocitizens spring from places and non-places, training their guns toward the centers of things. As such, they present the nineteenth century as what Antonio Negri calls, in a different context, a "plural universe," one that is surely at odds with the ideological fantasies of liberal pluralism.[58]

Ante-Ontology / Illiberal Ontology

Because forms of liberal ideology continue to so pervasively shape dominant paradigms of thought in the humanities and social sciences, my historical revisions must pivot forcefully within a number of contemporary scholarly discourses. The prefix "ante" in this section's title references forms of ontology that existed before modern liberal-democratic reifications of being were fully constituted—reifications stretching from the nineteenth century through the Cold War's varieties of consensus and biopolitics on to our own neoliberal moment and its affective and speculative scholarly turns. My book's frame is historical in this sense, asking what ways of political being, or perhaps being political, were present or shot across the sky (to employ the popular metaphor of the era) in the tumultuous years leading up to the Civil War.

In the following pages, I situate the primary arguments of this book within an overview of contemporary scholarly approaches that shape the critical terrain for thinking about ontology and history. These include topics such as personhood and paraontology as well as the promises and limits of developing new materialisms. By way of a caveat, it should be noted that there are significant pitfalls that accompany any invocation of ontology. According to Christopher Nealon, the popular critical trend of speculative realism "swaps in ontology for epistemology," rendering such work incapable of critiquing the sociopolitical realities of capitalism. Instead, these contemporary varieties of realism merely target a loosely defined notion of textual "scholarly self-absorption."[59] Bosteels offers an even more nuanced warning, characterizing the contemporary ontological turn as offering modes of being and existence that are "spectral, nonidentical, and postfoundational."[60] In Bosteel's account, even the dominant leftist ontological approaches fail to allow for any "determinant politics" to "derive" directly from ontology.[61]

By offering a new account of political actualities in the nineteenth century, I hope to reveal historical exceptions to Bosteels's important precautionary claims about ontology as well as contribute to contemporary humanities and American literary studies criticism that offers innovative perspectives on ontology. In the first volume of his trilogy in progress, *Prolegomena to Any Future Materialism*, Adrian Johnston offers a useful conceptual foothold for the type of analyses I provide in the following chapters. Although the critical aim of Johnston's volume, a self-prescribed negative move of clearing space within contemporary philosophy for his own model of "Transcendental Materialism," is largely outside the purview of my literary-historical project, Johnston's call for a "conflict ontology" is remarkably salient. The idea of conflict ontology stems from Johnston's broader push for what he terms "ontic impurity," an approach that attends to the "messiness" that lies between the ontological and ontic dimensions, realms that have been viewed traditionally as distinct.[62] Based upon this structural premise, Johnston posits "conflict ontology" as a supplement to Lacan's famous thesis of *"le grand Autre n'existe pas"* ("the big Other does not exist"). He writes, "[I]n the absence of every version of this Other, what remains lacks any guarantee of consistency right down to the bedrock of ontological fundamentals. Strife, potential or actual, reigns supreme as a negativity permeating the layers and strata of material being."[63] For Johnston, ontology thus has a constitutionally open or incomplete status and, as such, it is located, at its elemental level, in an indeterminate zone of "strife" and conflict.

Introduction: Xenocitizens

When we look at an era and space such as the antebellum United States, we see that historical forces and contingencies shape a complex and discontinuous political field, one that includes many more positions and experiences than various liberal thematic categories or genealogies have allowed. By using a spatial metaphor to posit an *outside* to accepted forms of civic belonging, I am invoking the radical possibilities of the "surround," possibilities that Fred Moten and Stefano Harney, in their discussion of black study, describe as requiring "self-defense . . . in the face of repeated, targeted dispossessions."[64] Within this framework, I am attempting to recast the ideological and conceptual terrain of nineteenth-century personhood—which is all too commonly romanticized and hence liberally co-opted in ever new ways. Throughout *Xenocitizens*, I follow scholars such as Monique Allewaert and Michael Snediker who use the term "personhood" rather than "subject" or, as implicated, "citizen subject."[65] All such terms have complex and, at times, vexed genealogies within the history of liberalism and its imperial projects. Nonetheless, as Allewaert avers, personhood offers a capacious rubric that might include the nonequivalent categories of subject, liberal conceptions of the person, as well as the emergence of "a range of entities that were neither subjects nor citizens."[66] According to Snediker, the concept of personhood might thus constitute "discursivity at its most local."[67] In tracing various foreclosed and forestalled modes of illiberal personhood in the nineteenth century, I also join scholars such as Alexander G. Weheliye, who challenges the imposed limits of dominant biopolitical discourses to reveal "the existence of alternate modes of life alongside the violence, subjection, exploitation, and racialization that define the modern human," and Lisa Lowe, who traces the residual modes of liberal domination in the nineteenth century, but also the *"emergent"* modes of being where "ongoing conditions like settler colonialism, colonial slavery, and trade" were "rearticulated in other ways through new practices." These new practices sprung, she adds, from "intimacies" that were retroactively archived by colonial powers as illicit or dangerous.[68]

As a wide range of contemporary studies of our neoliberal reality have shown, the always slippery category of person is, perhaps now more than ever, linked ineluctably to the production and reproduction of economic and social realities. Trapped within the confines of financialized becoming, any self becomes by default an "entrepreneur of the self."[69] Some scholars, such as Wendy Brown, decry convincingly how the economic policies of the past thirty years have yielded a crushing blow to democracy's radical expressions, going so far as to suggest that neoliberalism itself "is the rationality through which capitalism finally swallows humanity."⁷⁰ Along these lines, Mbembe argues that neoliberalism's production of and reliance on "structurally insolvent debts" generates a cruel historical torsion where "the systemic risks experienced specifically by Black slaves during early capitalism have now become the norm for, or at least the lot of, all of subaltern humanity."⁷¹ Others, such as Brian Massumi, offer a counter model of affective economic subjectivity, where the former position of personhood is revealed, within a neoliberal world, to be the *"bare activity"* of a feedback loop within capitalism's reproduction.⁷²

As I suggested earlier, despite the many changes within the function and status of the *homo economicus* since the last quarter of the twentieth century, there is a nuanced political and economic genealogy, discontinuous as it may be, linking the neoliberal self to earlier productions and formations of the so-called liberal self within various arrangements of capital's development. Christopher Castiglia's *Interior States: Institutional Consciousness and the Inner Life of Democracy in the Antebellum United States* (2008), for instance, argues that, "democracy is not dead or dying but misplaced." This misplacement, in Castiglia's historical account, begins in earnest with the late eighteenth-century U.S. disciplinary project he calls *"federal affect,"* which "recast[s] the bodily coercions of government as the apparently voluntary and internally managed orders of what Foucault calls governmentality, an interior state that is both consensual and self-managing."⁷³ According to Castiglia, the self thus becomes a "micro-state" whereby socioeconomic conflicts as well as potential responses to them are divested of social contexts by various seemingly impartial institutional democratic structures, resulting in a self that is both a dangerous site of passion as well as the proper locus for (self) management. Although this interiorization of conflict effectively limns democracy's potential radicalism, it creates, for Castiglia, a "nervous state" that includes "an archive of democratic aspirations that have been discredited or foreclosed" by history proper. Castiglia presents antebellum interiority as a site of "individual liberty and collective restriction," a place "where subjectivity and state interest blend into affective hybrids that create both the possibilities for independent critique and forms of self management that limit those possibilities."⁷⁴ Castiglia's historical account allows him to ultimately suggest that the ideological production of personal interiority in the eighteenth and nineteenth centuries continues to shape contemporary political landscapes: where such interiorities have, paradoxically, "been citizens' last resort in a world with less and less properly social life." In the book's epilogue, he argues that although such deployments of interiority (citing the civil rights movement and the AIDS Coalition to Unleash Power) have been "put to progressive ends," they nonetheless evidence the way "interiority has gained a monopoly over public discourse, making alternative structures of sociality . . . appear quixotic, dreamy, out of touch."[75]

In his closing call for a future "humanism without humans" and "democracy without interiority," Castiglia brings us closer to my book's historical agenda. *Xenocitizens* contributes to what is a wide scope of innovative contemporary studies that offer revisions of traditional biopolitical analysis by taking up various notions of ontology, personhood, and/or materiality. In recent years, scholars have rethought the concept of biopolitics by interrogating the anthropocentric foreclosures that the term "bios" imposes.[76] Working alongside these studies but in a different mode, *Xenocitizens* reconsiders the second half of the term "biopolitical," the *political*. The wager of the book is that doing so illuminates and addresses aporias within existing critical frameworks. In different ways, therefore, each of my chapters calls attention to the historical symptomatic nature of not only biopolitics, but also the assumptions of Americanist scholarship produced in the lineages of its critical age—this includes acknowledging the limits of post-biopolitical scholarship in its various forms.[77]

To clarify this claim, it is important to distinguish between politics, on the one hand, and the political, on the other. According to Lauren Berlant, who employs aspects of Jacques Rancière's work, politics connotes "the police, the arts of power," whereas the political constitutes a wider "domain and activity of dissensus on behalf of the parties of no part."[78] On one level, then, I am asking if and how dominant contemporary critical trends have, in their efforts to move past the delimiting aspects of politics proper, begun to abandon the domain of the political. In short, have we moved from an era of grand narratives to an era of sanitized grand methods? As I note at the outset, the financial crises of 2008 and, more recently, the advent of Trump's administration, have forced shifts within emerging scholarly trends. All of a sudden, the various highly aestheticized and theme-based turns to formalisms and materialisms seen during the years of Barack Obama's time in office are now undoubtedly feeling pressure to make returns to the political.

Along these lines, I am not seeking to generate a new brand of parahuman, but a new onto-story (to borrow Jane Bennett's term) of para-historical reality. My use of the concepts xenocitizen and illiberal ontology, therefore, has significant structural resonances with Fred Moten's argument that black existence is a "paraontology." What Moten and scholars associated with Afro-pessimism reveal is that the ontological ground upon which most contemporary theories operate is irreparably corrupted from the start—with the aforementioned racial foreclosures (among others) of the eighteenth and nineteenth centuries laying the groundwork for modern citizenship via liberal assumptions about being and identity. These liberal assumptions continue on today in strange afterlives within center-left theories and discourses, including various discourses claiming the status of apolitical or newly re-political orientations. From this perspective, liberal notions of ontology are not only delimiting, but unnecessary. Centered primarily around the writings of Frank B. Wilderson III, Afro-pessimism is, according to Jared Sexton, "a meditation on a poetics or politics of abjection wherein racial blackness operates as an asymptotic approximation of that which disturbs every claim or formation of identity and difference as such."[79] Consequently, Afro-pessimism aims to unsettle all dominant discourses relating to politics of identity, theorizing blackness as what Wilderson calls "a *position* of accumulation and fungibility; that is, as condition—or relation—of ontological death." Wilderson goes on to insist that, following Fanon, "though Blacks are indeed sentient beings, the structure of the entire world's semantic field . . . is structured by anti-Black solidarity."[80] The stakes of these positions come home in Moten's claim, based in the work of Nahum Dimitri Chandler, that "blackness is the anoriginal displacement of ontology, . . . it is ontology's anti- and ante-foundation."[81]

From his formative *In the Break: The Aesthetics of the Black Radical Tradition* (2003) through his more recent trilogy *consent not to be a single being* (2017–2018), Moten's work acknowledges the import of Afro-pessimism's critical assertions and, further, positions itself within a shared frame of a "common project." Yet Moten pivots away from Afro-pessimism's focus on social or ontological death toward Fanon's conception of "wretchedness."[82] Both Afro-pessimist scholars and Moten confront anti-blackness without recourse to transcendence or other existing positive categories. Whereas Wilderson and others privilege impossibility, Moten interrogates the possibilities of living within the reality of "exhaustion."[83] Moten suggests that because "blackness is prior to ontology" (including its "logistic and regulative power"), black life "shows up for political ontology as a relation of nonrelation or counterrelation precisely in the impossibility of black intersubjectivity." This is why, for Moten, blackness-as-paraontology, "must free itself from ontological expectation, must refuse subjection to ontology's sanction against the very idea of black subjectivity."[84]

As mentioned, in developing these arguments, Moten employs Chandler's work at great length. In *X—The Problem of the Negro as a Problem for*

Thought (2014), Chandler sets up the paraontological that Moten references by grounding the concept in specific historical conditions. He writes, "there is not now nor has there ever been a free zone or quiet place from which the discourse of the so-called Africanist figures, intellectuals, writers, thinkers, or scholars might issue." From the outset, Chandler links this lack of historical place or placeness to ontological concerns, suggesting that questions about the "putative Negro subject" have been consistently and inevitably entangled with underlying concerns over a "putative European subject"—thus presupposing certain well-known fantasies about being and essence.[85] Consequently, for Chandler, even the de-essentializing trends within and without studies of Africanist discourses fall prey to the imposed limits of the subject. Given this, one must "displace or attempt to displace" any and all problems of "pure being."[86] According to Chandler:

> A thought of the negative in this sense might still remain a simple stage in the consolidation of an original or destined being as a subject that would proclaim itself as absolute. What is at stake then is situated at a level somewhat more radical than the negative in general. Nor is it a matter of establishing a predicate of some kind. The originarity that one must remark in the situation of an Africanist problematic since the sixteenth century can emerge for thought only within an approach that attends to that within historicity and existence that would distend form in general, distantiate presence or its derivatives, disseminate any presumptive sense of being.[87]

Here paraontology becomes an actual historical otherness existing outside of and alongside positive discourses (of ontology and all accepted sociopolitics). And it has effects: "distend[ing]" form and "distantiat[ing]" presence.

Building on and extrapolating from Moten's and Chandler's work, I am interested in historical para-experiences: those related to the specific contexts of blackness and paraontology as well as other sociopolitical and material realities and possibilities that are foreclosed by standard ontological (philosophically) and liberal (politically/conceptually) assumptions. A relevant example of this type of work can be found within contemporary Indigenous studies scholarship.[88] Broadening our critical notion of personhood should include a reconsideration of humans and nonhumans, but also, according to Robert Warrior, the notion of place and location. Warrior cites contemporary indigenous resistance movements such as Idle No More and scholarly work in Native and Indigenous studies as "examples of the way personhood expands to recognize land, water, animals, and even the air we breathe as part of the matrix of relationships [Glen Sean] Coulthard calls 'grounded normativity.'"[89] Work by other contemporary Indigenous studies scholars has likewise asserted the lived stakes of resisting western and U.S. imperial models for existence and history. As Nick Estes explains, the Oceti Sakowin prophecy of Zuzeca Sapa, a black snake who stretches out across the land threating life, should not be viewed as an antiquated narrative but as the modern-day DAPL (Dakota Access Pipeline). According to Estes, such prophecies "are revolutionary theory, a way to help us think about our relationship to the land, to other humans and other-than-humans, and to history and time." Citing the historian Josephine Waggoner, Estes notes how "the word mi (water) is a combination of the words mi (meaning 'I') and ni (meaning 'being'), indicating that it also contains life." For the indigenous communities of Oceti Sakowin, therefore, "water is alive."[90] Estes's compelling work portrays in stark relief how indigenous notions of the biological, material, spiritual, and political ties among the land and the living remain a charged and threatening obstacle to U.S. capital. "Because Native people remain barriers to capitalist development," he writes, "their bodies needed to be removed—both from *beneath* and *atop* the soil—therefore eliminating their rightful relationship *with* the land."[91]

In their collection *A World of Many Worlds*, Marisol de la Cadena and Mario Blasier offer "political ontology" as a rubric for thinking about heterogeneous realities and antagonisms that western models distort or ignore. They explain how the experiences and histories of indigenous peoples push beyond "the modern onto-epistemic limits of modern politics." As such, their unique version of political ontology "operates on the presumption of divergent worldings constantly coming about through negotiations, enmeshments, crossings, and interruptions."[92] *Xenocitizens*' assertion of "illiberal ontologies" thus joins with, in its own way, de la Cadena and Mario Blasier's concept of "political ontology" as well as Moten's notion of paraontology in attempting to think ways of being and acting beyond limits imposed by existing paradigms. In short, just as the term "xeno" in many ways crosses out and opens up the category of "citizen," the concept of "illiberal" might ground historically and, importantly, modify the concept of "ontology."

My book's approach to ontology is, in this way, distinct from the approaches found in many contemporary literary-historical studies that take up the perspectives of emerging new materialisms. The rubric of new materialism holds together a diverse and discontinuous conglomerate of new approaches to materialism and material reality in the wake of what many of these critics view as the exhaustion of twentieth-century linguistic (textual hermeneutics, especially those relating to poststructuralism) and cultural (any variety of Marxism or other anthro-centered analysis) methods. For example, in their collection *The Speculative Turn: Continental Materialism and Realism* (2011), Levi Bryant, Nick Srnicek, and Graham Harman (scholars associated with object-oriented ontology) cite the "speculative turn" as a way to describe a developing critical purview that is a "deliberate counterpoint to the now tiresome 'Linguistic Turn.'" According to them, as opposed to the "repetitive continental focus on texts, discourse, social practices, and human finitude, the new breed of thinker is turning once more toward reality itself."[93] The noncorrelationist premise that a human can simply abandon discourse and the symbolic order proper for "reality itself" is less concerning for the arguments I make in the following chapters than the ideological and political assumptions that often sustain it.[94]

As Johnston's aforementioned work reveals, new materialism is anything but a united field. In fact, Johnston spends a good deal of time in *Adventures in Transcendental Materialism* attacking the "neo-Spinozist stances" of influential new materialists such as Jane Bennett and William Connolly. Echoing other left-leaning materialist scholars such as Slavoj Žižek and Bruno Bosteels who have criticized, on shared ground, the dominant Deleuzian-influenced track of new materialism, Johnston here portrays Bennett's immanent naturalist vitalism as representative of a "flat, even, and democratic first nature of weakly emerging not-quite-subjects."[95] For my purposes, Johnston's claim that this pluralist vitalism is overlaid with and promotes democratic ideological assumptions is most salient. According to Johnston, new materialists such as Bennett "admit that there is no direct, one-to-one link between ontology and politics" but their thinking tends to "[leap] this gap" in ways that promote liberal (my term) forms of "reformist micropolitics."[96]

Johnston counters new materialism's implicit politics by citing Žižek's incendiary line: "Do not expectantly await any acts from actants other than ourselves!"[97] While I agree wholeheartedly with Johnston's cautionary message, when considering historical responses to modes of domination, we might just as well ask who the "ourselves" are in Žižek's formulation. Johnston's structural fundamentalism may, therefore, foreclose the significant political purchases of studying historical actants (non- or not-quite-subjects). Indeed, a subset of scholars working in the direction of new materialism has offered innovative approaches to politics and important reconsiderations of biopolitical frameworks.[98] Elizabeth Povinelli's

Geontologies: A Requiem to Late Liberalism (2016), to note one example, demonstrates how the precarity of human life in an era of global warming causes "ontology... [to] reemerge as a central problem."[99] Along these lines, she suggests that "posthuman critique is giving way to a post-life critique, being to assemblage, and biopower to geontopower."[100] The last term, combining *geos* (nonlife) and ontology (being), is Povinelli's contribution to post-biopolitical thinking, a way of conceiving how power structures within late liberalism "maintain or shape the coming relationship of the distinction between Life and Nonlife." Very much in line with my own aims, Povinelli states that her book and its concepts are "meant to help make visible the figural tactics of late liberalism."[101]

I thus want to follow scholars such as Povinelli as well as Margaret Ronda, who argues that we should fully address the realities of the Anthropocene (the historical epoch where humans have become a geological force). Ronda points out, however, that we should do so by not merely celebrating and indexing non-human objects/actants, but also by taking quite seriously the need to examine new and transformed modes of human existence. In her words, "We might see anthropos and its related term anthropogenic... as words that speak to the nonidentity and internal estrangement that accompany this species-wide agency."[102] I want to add to this the historical dimension of reexamining the range of anthropogenic realties and possibilities that manifested in the nineteenth-century years of the so-called Anthropocene, an age that, since Paul Crutzen coined the term in 2000, has been seen by many to commence with James Watt's invention of the steam engine in the late eighteenth century.[103]

In setting up her argument, Ronda employs at length Bruno Latour's work and terms—a move that is common among contemporary scholars who employ ecological and/or new materialist perspectives. It is outside the scope of this introduction to fully address Latour's rich and varying work or its discursive reproductions, though my chapters will engage this latter work on a number of levels. But I want to suggest here that we should read his influential theses in the context of the political effects noted in Johnston's critique of Bennett (who herself frequently employs Latour's terminology). From this perspective, the Latourian universe is, at its best, apolitical (in the sense of outside the standard coordinates of sociopolitical schemas) and, at its worst, blatantly liberal in terms the historical plane of political antagonism. Although Latour's structural moves in *Reassembling the Social* (2005) and elsewhere might have the productive aim of recalibrating social critics' hermeneutical approaches by opening up ontology to a much wider field of relations—moving from a "science of the social" (which uses a symptomatic depth model to trace the social to underlying factors such as the economy) to the act of *"tracing of associations"* (looking at a wider possibility of *"other* types of connectors" besides "specific social forces")—it does so via specific historical and political ideological assumptions.[104] In this sense, Latour's pithy use of Margaret Thatcher's line "There is no such thing as a society" to set up his project should be seen as either no joke at all or as a perfectly formed Freudian one.[105] This is because throughout Latour's work, his theories engender a litany of formulations that emulate the type of democratic micropolitics that Johnston spies in Bennett's scholarship. In his more recent *An Inquiry into Modes of Existence: An Anthropology of the Moderns* (2013), to cite just one formative example, Latour includes a perhaps laudatory move of opening up a "regional ontology" and an "ontological pluralism." And yet, he playfully and figuratively assembles (to borrow a phrase he uses elsewhere) them via an "imaginary diplomatic scene" where, from the structures of what might be some grand future United Nations *qua* United Ontologies, "Moderns" would be "reunited" with various "others." In his words, "Moderns [would] *present themselves once again* to the rest of the world."[106] Another joke, it seems. But these figurative appeals to liberal structures bespeak historical, ideological, and political assumptions that undergird Latour's expansive project.[107]

It is no wonder, therefore, that scholars such as Peter Wolfendale refer to the type of "flat ontology" offered by Latour and other proponents of new materialism as "ontological liberalism." For Wolfendale, this liberalism pertains to the "contemporary concern with *comprehensive* ontological commitment," where we are "encouraged to account for the full range of possible objects of thought, experience, and explanation."[108] But in this critical mode, where, in Jason Moore's terms, "nothing necessarily causes anything else,"[109] we also find obscured liberal-political assumptions about relation itself. In a similar manner that Bosteels sees models of antifoundational ontology replicating the logic of capital's globalization and that Rachel Greenwald Smith observes the homologous relation between the "affective turn" and neoliberalism's realities, I am suggesting that many Latourian-based literary-historical inquiries foreclose inadvertently political antagonisms (and hence political realities) by promoting a certain liberal brand of political relation.[110] One might say hyperbolically, then, that many new materialists perpetually commit the pathetic fallacy solely on the plane of relations. In other words, in their laudable efforts to move past the limits imposed by biopolitics, many scholars have sought to abandon all vestiges of anthropocentric formulations, including the political, only to have them reemerge in the formal aspects of their models. I would venture to call this brand of thinking a varied mode of *syntactical anthropomorphism* as well as, more importantly for my interests, *syntactical liberalism*.[111] In the end, instead of offering a more radical option to this expansive scene (taking the position, perhaps, as a minority radical-left representative in Latour's diplomatic convention), *Xenocitizens* is after forms of historical alterity found in the political relation itself.[112]

In terms of scholarship on the nineteenth century, this book joins with contemporary studies of nineteenth-century American literature that seek to rethink assumed political and material realities established by Cold War–era scholars and, lesser so, by the biopolitical frameworks used by New Americanists. *Xenocitizens* thus allies itself with—taking up and struggling alongside—formative work by scholars such as Monique Allewaert, Branka Arsić, Colleen Glenney Boggs, Christopher Castiglia, Russ Castronovo, David Kazanjian, Lisa Lowe, Dana Luciano, Donald Pease, and Caleb Smith, among many others, that typifies a vibrant and discontinuous collective of critical political-historical inquiry currently shaping the field. In addition to works by such major critical figures, the field has seen a bloom of studies that rethink ontology based upon various strands of new materialism and, more commonly, that present historical appeals to period-scientific discourses. Books such as Matthew A. Taylor's *Universes Without Us: Posthuman Cosmologies in American Literature* (2013), Kyla Schuller's *The Biopolitics of Feeling: Race, Sex, and Science in the Nineteenth Century* (2017), and Cristin Ellis's *Antebellum Posthuman: Race and Materiality in the Mid-Nineteenth Century* (2018), for example, offer various innovative takes on ways we might reconceive of nineteenth-century materialist discourses. Especially in terms of the antebellum years, contemporary scholars have also offered an array of original studies of topics surrounding slavery as well as explored various ways nineteenth-century liberal society impacted forms of identity and experience.[113]

At the same time, *Xenocitizens* intervenes in contemporary scholarship that, on one hand, contributes to emerging thematic trends and, on the other, uses or promotes familiar liberal ideological perspectives when shaping its analysis. There is good reason that terms such as "unsettling," "impersonal," "materiality," and "dissent" are perfuming the breath, to borrow Edward Taylor's phrase, of scholars of the nineteenth century. Unfortunately, however, these important acts of unsettling sometimes merely introduce thematically and aesthetically novel covers for a plurality of liberal topics and perspectives. Consequently, when walking down conference hallways or through academic book exhibits, one cannot help but feel like a Benjaminian flâneur strolling amid the fashion district of the new intellectual arcades. I believe avidly that Edward Said was right to herald "other humanities," or the possibility of being "critical of humanism in the name of humanism."[114] And yet we must also add an essential political qualifier to this, one no doubt in line with Said's well-known notion of the "worldliness" of the critic: that being posthuman, in any of its varieties, does not necessarily establish a new antagonistic ideological-historical position (anti-humanist, anti-liberal, anti-imperial, anti-capitalist, and so on). In other words, Said's term "critical," in the phrase "critical of humanism," should be seen to tremble with the weight it must carry. As Cary Wolfe aptly notes, one of the structural hallmarks of humanism is "pluralization," and all too often studies that seek to further or capitalize on emerging critical trends can paradoxically exemplify Wolfe's cautionary point about how "pluralism becomes *incorporation*, and the projects of humanism (intellectually) and liberalism (politically) are extended."[115]

As such, each chapter of *Xenocitizens*, in its own way, necessarily runs counter to a number of prevailing liberal tenets that continue to shape scholarly perspectives used to understand the nineteenth century. Collectively, the chapters portray the nineteenth century as an uneven totality, revealing the reality of multiple, discontinuous, and, at times, potential political sites. The first part of the book, "Illiberal Ontologies," examines how the work of Ralph Waldo Emerson and Margaret Fuller offer unacknowledged and obscured forms of political personhood, forms of being that complicate a number of foundational assumptions about transcendentalism's relation to historical and political reality. Chapter 1, "Emerson's Operative Mood," reexamines Emerson's early thinking about the relation of the individual to universal Reason, revealing that Emerson's writing is philosophically consistent in its insistence that the human self is "operative" in form and function. Shifting our conceptual perspective from a traditional Matthiessenian notion of an "optative mood" to something of a Badiouian "operative mood" opens up new ways to consider how, across the early works, the Emersonian self is shaped by interactions with a religious and universal Other, or what scholars of Emerson, following Emerson's own terminology, often term the "impersonal," as well as the ways these interactions influence the self's relation to specific historical landscapes. Intervening in formative scholarship on Emersonian personhood by scholars such as Sharon Cameron, Branka Arsić, and Donald Pease, this chapter offers an original version of Emerson's political vision, one that finds in his theory of "religious sentiment" a model for the self that may reframe all of Emerson's corpus, in a double sense.

In Chapter 2, "Agitating Margaret Fuller," I offer a competing portrait of Fuller's brand of political citizenship. By examining Fuller's earlier work, especially her writings about music, a new version of her political and social views becomes visible. Across this work, she uses musical terminology to depict an original form of radical political agency and, further still, political ontology. I suggest that by examining the affective and formal elements of Fuller's thought, where various sounds, tones, and pulsations explicitly and/or implicitly mediated her thinking about material reality, we might better understand the complex dialectic she posits between the personal and the social. The stakes of this argument go further than merely revising the common historical narrative that sees Fuller moving from Romantic to radical forms of thought after her departure for Europe in 1846. Ultimately, I portray how Fuller develops a model of nineteenth-century political personhood that literary scholars and historians alike have yet to fully address.

Part II, "Illiberal Ecologies," builds on the first section's focus on personhood but turns even more explicitly to the material and social landscapes of the era, interrogating anew how radical writings from the period engaged with emerging conceptions of reality. Chapter 3, "Thoreau's Militant Vegetables," takes as its starting point contemporary new materialist approaches to Thoreau's writing, especially the work of scholars such as Branka Arsić and Jane Bennett. Complicating the Deleuzian- and neo-Spinozan-influenced forms of democratic vitalism attributed to Thoreau by this formative critical trend, this chapter traces a competing mode of materialism in Thoreau's thought, one that is inherently dialectical and, by all standards, illiberal. Building loosely on the speculative ecological work of scholars such as Monique Allewaert and Michael Marder, I argue that Thoreau's vision of nature in his early works is in many ways allied with his subsequent radical political pronouncements in the mid- and late-1850s. Through three sections, I trace the structural aspects of Thoreau's unique dialectical approach toward materiality and historical reality, examining the types of political ontologies and actants that emerge within these dynamic material relations as well as their specific stakes for antebellum society.

Finally, Chapter 4, "Unadjusted Emancipations," adds a consideration of the economic horizon to contemporary scholarship that examines the radical and, at times, emancipatory "entanglements" among slaves/ex-slaves and the environment. The chapter's three sections present a developing arc of what I call unadjusted emancipations, tracing various ways that slaves and ex-slaves negotiated and leveraged the period's systemic production of bad debts in order to distort or circumvent standard formations of emancipatory logic. The first section examines Harriet Beecher Stowe's *Dred; A Tale of the Great Dismal Swamp* (1856) in light of ecological-economic hermeneutics. In my reading, the interface between humans and ecology spied by scholars who study the parahuman closes with an unsettling interface between personhood and developing models of capital. The second section looks at the ways William Wells Brown's novel *Clotel; or, the President's Daughter: A Narrative of Slave Life in the United States* (1853) and his appended "Narrative of the Life and Escape of William Wells Brown" manipulate the era's production of bad debts in order to craft points of divergence from and within standard channels of emancipation. The third considers the titular character of Martin R. Delany's *Blake; or, The Huts of America* (1859, 1861–62) and how his "secret" moves throughout southern plantations in ways that radically compound. Reading the modality of this secret as a blurred Moten-esque push toward a fugitive sociality of bad debt, I examine how the novel presents innovative forms of resistant collectivity.

I am stirred by Christopher Castiglia's aforementioned call for "democracy *without* interiority." Yet, by doing without the ideological trappings of standard interiority, we consequently do without traditional notions of liberal-democracy. And in this move we enter the perilous and open domain of xenocitizens. In the following chapters at least, I hope to show that the potential for this ideal, much like the "beautiful bug" at the close of *Walden* that springs to new "winged life" after sixty dormant years within an apple tree table, has perhaps been with us for quite some time.[116]

PART I

Illiberal Ontologies

CHAPTER 1

Emerson's Operative Mood

Almost I fear to think how glad I am.

—RALPH WALDO EMERSON, *Nature*

Our Ralph Waldo Emerson *still* has two faces. The first, representative of his early works, is portrayed in an 1849 *New-York Daily Tribune* cartoon of Emerson swinging on an inverted rainbow, a mood reified by F. O. Matthiessen's claim that Emerson was a Neoplatonic optimist who epitomized the wishful longing of the "optative mood."[1] The second, representative of his 1850s turn toward political radicalism, is seen in Emerson's enthusiastic declaration while visiting the Charlestown Navy Yard, echoing out of time, it seems, from the lips of Lieutenant Colonel Bill Kilgore in *Apocalypse Now*, "Ah! Sometimes gunpowder smells good."[2] I want to suggest that these two Emersons share the same conceptual horizon—that the disengaged transparent eyeball Emerson peddling visions of the Oversoul and the gun-toting, blood-lusting Emerson collecting donations for John Brown's raid on Harpers Ferry evince an important and unacknowledged structural continuity.

The perspective I present in this chapter thus contributes to contemporary scholarship that seeks new ways of thinking about an "other Emerson." In their collection of the same name, Branka Arsić and Cary Wolfe suggest that they intend to follow the "vertiginous sense of (dis)location invoked . . . by Emerson" and aim to "induce a similar kind of dislocation" in their audience.[3] By arguing that the explicit political engagement of Emerson's middle period (the late 1840s through the 1860s) is a logical development of his earlier thinking rather than a marked departure from it,[4] I hope to create a similarly productive disturbance, offering a picture of Emerson's brand of political personhood that departs radically from Enlightenment and Romantic models of political ethics that continue to shape modern liberal-democratic assumptions about identity.

Several decades of scholarship have detailed Emerson's embrace of religious violence in the run up to the Civil War. These studies leave relatively unexplored the question of whether this embrace involved a real turn away from Emerson's earlier thinking on the subject. Given the predominant narratives of Emerson's life that stress his secularizing and liberalizing trajectory—and considering his abrupt return to religious and illiberal pronouncements around slavery in the 1840s and 1850s—it is easy to conclude that there was, in fact, a significant discontinuity.[5] This chapter, however, returns to Emerson's early work to argue that he maintained a core commitment to a form of "religious sentiment" that offered the structural means and justifications for violent interventions within historical reality.

A reexamination of Emerson's early thinking about the relation between the self and universal Reason reveals that Emerson's writing is philosophically consistent in its insistence that personhood is "operative" in form and function. Shifting our critical and conceptual perspective from a traditional Matthiessenian notion of an "optative mood" to something of a Badiouian "operative mood" opens up new ways to consider how, across the early works, the Emersonian self is shaped by interactions with a religious and universal Other, or what scholars of Emerson, following Emerson's own terminology, often term the "impersonal," as well as the ways these interactions influence the self's relation to specific social and historical landscapes.[6] Indeed, in her discussion of Emerson's conception of moods, Arsić departs from previous scholars by depicting the way exteriority and relationality (for a person is "'floated' into a mood by other persons or events") effect a constructive "discontinuity of personal identity."[7] Arsić's work has helped generate a newfound interest in thinking with and perhaps past Sharon Cameron's foundational thesis about the role of the impersonal in Emerson's thought. The implications of the type of "impersonal thinking" that Arsić discerns, however, have yet to be fully borne out.[8]

The continuity in Emerson's thought regarding religious sentiment and its radical effects has been obscured by the shifting rhetorical positioning of Emerson's writing, including its changing audience base across the antebellum years. Nevertheless, and perhaps more important, it has also been occluded by twentieth- and twenty-first century liberal critical paradigms of subjectivity and political action. As discussed in this book's introduction, liberalism has a long and vexed history, and it informs almost all nineteenth-century sociopolitical formations. As Christopher Newfield explains, in the twentieth century, "liberalism" "has stood for a consensus about the American left's need to assimilate its ideals to the ways of the center."[9] Quite obviously, this developing ideological perspective has influenced interpretive paradigms that have been used to analyze antebellum personhood as well as Emerson's political thought. For example, in *Transcendental Resistance* (2010), Johannes Voelz illuminates the limitations of New Americanist perspectives that have predominated since the Cold War and generated "totalized" readings of Emerson's politics.[10] Even more directly, perhaps, Kerry Larson's "Illiberal Emerson" (2006), offers a comprehensive overview of the manifold ways Emerson's early thought departs from eighteenth- and nineteenth-century liberal tenets. My chapter in many ways shares with Larson's work the desire to "pierce through an assortment of liberal pieties and assumptions in order to make ... [Emerson's] beliefs intelligible." It also, however, adds an important aspect of historical antagonism to Larson's adept analysis. Throughout his essay, Larson critiques productively what he deems as contemporary liberal misreadings of Emerson's thought (citing scholars such as George Kateb). Yet when he makes his penultimate move of counterpointing a Lockean liberal preference for self regard over forms of fanaticism with Emerson's own brand of self-reliance, Larson portrays Emerson's apparent inconsistency regarding the self, including his penchant for impersonality, in "holistic terms," where radical variants are synthesized and "the impersonality of character exhibits a unity."[11] I ask what happens when we abandon this grand scope for viewing the Emersonian self and argue, instead, that Emerson's portrayal of encounters with the impersonal often relate to specific historical events and acts, including modes of political violence.

I thus hope to return the Other to Emerson: presenting a new (perhaps redeemed) form of political personhood at the heart of Emerson's work. In the section that follows, I examine Emerson's early conception of "religious sentiment" in order to rethink the constitutive role of the impersonal within the Emersonian self. These contexts set up my subsequent analysis of how Emerson's early work prepares the stage for his embrace of violent political rhetoric and action in the 1850s and 1860s.

Godly Navels, Impersonal Persons, and Other Religious Sentiments

The political thought that scholars have noted in Emerson's work during the 1850s is characterized by a new emphasis on the relation between the individual and cosmic power. The radicalism in essays such as "Fate" (1860) is anticipated in journal entries from 1857, where Emerson discussed political agency in terms of destiny. This formulation is evident in "Courage," an essay based on an 1859 speech given shortly before John Brown's execution, where Emerson suggests, "If you accept your thoughts as inspirations from the Supreme Intelligence, obey them when they prescribe difficult duties."[12] For Emerson, such duties could be severe, as seen in an 1863 speech at Waterville College where he asks: In the support of "universal liberty . . . who would not consent to die?"[13] Oddly enough, the groundwork for this absolutist identity manifests in Emerson's optimistic and joyous condemnations of Christianity during the early 1830s.

When the twenty-nine-year-old Emerson mounted the pulpit of the Second Church of Boston on September 9, 1832, to deliver his resignation sermon, "The Lord's Supper," a scathing critique of the sacrament of the Holy Eucharist, he had a specific topic in mind: institutional knowledge. As the sermon reveals, what riled Emerson the most was the way the church shifted religious devotion onto the figure of Christ via the codification of a specific (and limited) form of historical memory. In looking at Emerson's comments on religion from this period—such as his thought, in 1832, that religion "is not something . . . *to be got* [,] to be *added*"—it becomes clear that the problem was deeper than merely how the church was using knowledge. On a more foundational level, Emerson wrestled with the simple fact that institutional knowledge was becoming the conceptual ground on which the church operated.[14]

The complexity of Emerson's critique might be further illuminated by considering it in the context of the historical transition, well underway in the nineteenth century, within the institutional relations between knowledge and power. The Unitarian church in the early nineteenth century, as well as the Harvard Divinity School that supported it, typified the way theoretical knowledge was located increasingly in the position of power.[15] Established in 1636, Harvard College began as a means to educate New England's ministry, but by the late eighteenth century, many of Boston's clergy "saw themselves as scholars."[16] According to Barbara Packer, this move toward codified forms of knowledge developed in a "spiritual marketplace" when liberals in New England Congregationalism began using "history to establish faith," eventually distinguishing themselves as Unitarians who believed in "*progressive* illumination." Focusing on philosophers such as Locke, they found a means to confront religious enthusiasts with "tolerant, rational patience."[17] At Harvard, Lockean principles were bolstered with the work of the Cambridge Platonists, who promoted an "ontology that treated moral truths as objectively real," as well as with the systematic integration of German Higher Criticism, which employed historical modes of inquiry to interpret scripture.[18]

This prevalent connection between religion and historical or theoretical knowledge clearly troubled Emerson, producing a function for knowledge that was a far cry from the province of scholar he championed throughout his career. Such anxiety is evident in Emerson's resignation letter to the Proprietors of the Second Church, where he makes clear that his "devotion to the cause of divine truth" had not ebbed; rather, he explains, he differed on the means by which this end should be pursued.[19] Nevertheless, his subsequent criticism of religion is predicated on a radical recalibration of social relations. At the close of the Lord's Supper sermon, for instance, he boldly claims that he will "love" Jesus "as a glorified friend" and follow him only inasmuch as he "would lead us to seek our own well-being in the formation of the soul."[20] In so doing, Emerson establishes a key structural tenet of his subsequent thought: the primary role of the self in relation to the realm of the soul.

Emerson's censure of institutional devotion in his Divinity Address is well known. Yet within his critique of religious social structures he posits a realm of experience that exceeds such a system's knowledge and "analysis," namely "religious sentiment."[21] Indirectly building on the work of theologians such as Benjamin Constant and Friedrich Schleiermacher, Emerson links this affective concept, which he posits as "the essence of all religion," with the "sentiment of virtue." Here, such sentiment "is a reverence and delight in the presence of certain divine laws" (77). According to Emerson, the "perception of this law of laws always awakens in the mind a sentiment which we call the religious sentiment, and which makes our highest happiness" (79). Thus, we see a relation emerge where an individual's "perception" of the divine Law yields a form of delight that, as in the case of Jesus's own experience, approaches a "jubilee of sublime emotion" (81).

As Wesley T. Mott has shown, the "moral sublime" has a deep intellectual genealogy for Emerson, synthesizing European thought pertaining to "sublimity, stoicism, and sentiment."[22] What's more, it appears in various forms in Emerson's early days as a minister. The parameters of this conceptual landscape are illuminated in Emerson's 1837 lecture "Religion."

As Emerson's opening makes clear, religious sentiment exists in a liminal space between the vaunted function of Reason and everyday human perception. This is because Emerson figures Reason as the "Universal Mind," an exterior agency located within us; consequently, "We belong to it, not it to us."[23] The individual, therefore, exists in an "antagonistic nature" toward Reason, garnering "virtue" only when the "individual Will" adopts the "dictate of the Universal mind." As Emerson explains in a later essay, "That soul which within us is a sentiment, outside of us is a law. We feel its inspiration."[24] And it is precisely here where religious sentiment enters. In the pursuit and acceptance of Reason, religious sentiment is fired: "[R]eligion is the accompanying emotion, the emotion of reverence which the presence of the Universal mind always excites in the individual" ("Religion," 84).

Although Emerson goes on to link religious sentiment to various forms of religious enthusiasms and "ravishment," he adds an important qualification. In his view, this "shudder of awe and delight" is not a result of direct alignment with Reason, but "attends the individual's consciousness of that divine presence." Consequently, the "character and duration of enthusiasm varies with the state of the individual from an extasy [*sic*] and trance and prophetic inspiration, . . . to the faintest glow of virtuous emotion" ("Religion," 90). This is perhaps why, in *Nature*, Emerson casts the "influx of spirit" in the future tense. No matter where one falls on the continuum of ravishment, the "axis of vision," shaped by the realm of the Reason, remains (in various degrees) non-identical to the "axis of things," our current perception of reality.[25] That is, the gap Emerson establishes at the opening of "The Divinity School Address" between the Universal mind and "imperfect apprehension" is not yet closed (77).

The space of non-identity between full Reason and current forms of perception is, in this way, foundational to Emerson's understanding of joyous religious sentiment. But the historical and ideological elements of this schematic should be emphasized. Emerson's criticism of the church's manipulation of historical knowledge is also an implicit criticism of how the church is not identical to its presumed source of power. This may be why Emerson categorically dismisses institutional Christianity in "Religion," arguing that "[a]ll attempts to confine and transmit the religious feeling . . . by means of formulas the most accurate or rites the most punctual . . . have hitherto proved abortive. You might as well preserve light or energy in barrels" (92–93).

In conjunction with this institutional criticism, Emerson pushes the bounds of religious sentiment, establishing an even more complex relation between the individual and Reason. In a journal entry from 1828, Emerson describes the relation between self and cosmic Other using the analogy of a child in utero: "[A] child is connected to the womb of its mother by a chord from the navel. So it seems to me is man connected to God by his conscience. God has given him a free agency[,] has permitted him to work his will in the world—doing wrong and right but has kept open this door by which he may come in at all times."[26] When read in the context of Emerson's subsequent notions of Reason, this passage provides a helpful metaphor for the odd relation he casts between self and Other. In Emerson's thought, this Other (God, Reason, Universal mind, Oversoul) is addressed via the internal modalities of the self. Consequently, the scene of questioning and criticism shifts to the plane of the self, or, rather, to the gap *in the self* between self and Other.

Emerson's subsequent thought from the late 1830s and early 1840s might be used to recalibrate his analogy that ties God to one's navel. According to Emerson's formulation, Reason is temporally incomplete: lacking on our side of the proverbial umbilical cord because—epistemologically speaking—we fail to fully align with its power. The statement that God "may come in at all times" should thus be read in terms of a temporal dimension. That is, though the modal auxiliary verb "may" appears to signify agency, it should, rather, be linked to the related notion of *possibility*. In this schematic, we are in, but not yet fully experiencing (one might use the Hegelian term "actualizing") what Giorgio Agamben calls "messianic time," or a "zone of absolute indiscernibility between immanence and transcendence, between this world and the future."[27]

Emerson's conception of religious sentiment as an animated link between the self and Reason developed in relation to a number of discursive and scholarly antebellum institutional discourses. For example, in returning from Europe in 1833, Emerson began shaping the conditions with which to capitalize on a developing lyceum system. This stage for intellectuals was an organized series of lectures, where theological and social discourses mixed under the façade of middle-ground public dialogue. This middle ground, as Stephen Whicher and Robert Spiller point out, was paved by Josiah Holbrook, a lecturer on and avid supporter of science.[28] It is, therefore, no surprise that Emerson's first four lectures on the lyceum circuit concerned natural philosophy, the forerunner of antebellum institutional sciences. Emerson's decision to ruminate publicly about science, however, was not merely based on a calculation of public interest. As scholars have noted, Emerson's inclination toward natural science was stoked in Europe, where he visited Paris's Jardin des Plantes and met with scientists such as Professor Amici in Florence (optical studies) and Professor Caldania in Padua (anatomy). Immersing himself in scientific reading during the years leading up to the publication of *Nature*, Emerson often reflects in his journals about a desire to tease out the connections between natural systems and spiritual truth.

Tracing the connections between various developing sciences and Romantic thinkers such as Emerson has been all the rage in recent years. And yet such studies often figure Emerson's break from institutional Christianity as an anterior prefix to his intellectual becoming through science's logic and methods. As Laura Dassow Walls states, "The church lost Emerson's trust by refusing to renegotiate the terms of truth even in the face of the new science, and so science itself, that continual and free negotiation by which the experiences of the many could be grasped in one law, became Emerson's new standard."[29] This is, perhaps, a slightly more modest version of Walls's previous claim that in his early work, Emerson "offered to America a new faith: science."[30]

Considering Emerson's early lectures as a whole, religion may be the institution that he is most concerned with overcoming, but his use of science is far from a total supplement. As I have argued, Emerson's break from the church was in part a rejection of the role of institutional knowledge. Though Emerson turned to the popular topic of science following his ministry's dissolution, it is important to note that he is not turning from the matter of "spiritual laws" to simple earthly matter. Rather, Emerson's early lectures and writings mark a loose constellation of concerns that include both. And what unites them all, what cuts across them, is a push to shift forms of institutional knowledge toward Reason.

Thus, it is important to see the ways in which Emerson's negotiation of scientific discourses includes a consistent level of critical distancing. This is where some contemporary historicist modes of inquiry—a number of studies that seek to examine how scientific discourses and models influenced Emerson—may inadvertently skew elements of Emerson's early thought.[31] What I would like to suggest is that Emerson's use of and departures from science are part of a broader apostasy from institutional religion—a bump up on the horizon of circles, if you will, where Emerson finds more discursive space but includes a similar focus on the role of Reason and a similar censure of institutional knowledge.[32]

Emerson's general view of the material world is laid out in his lecture "On the Relation of Man to the Globe" (1833). Citing the way "the history of organic nature" is found everywhere, Emerson explains that the world "is itself a monument on whose surface every age of perhaps numberless centuries has somewhere inscribed its history in gigantic letters . . . but so far apart, and without visible connection, that only the most diligent observer . . . can read them."[33] This social hermeneutical landscape is soon converted into a more familiar spiritual hermeneutical landscape: "But perhaps the most striking effect of the accurate adaptation of man to the globe is found in his love for it. The love of nature—the accord between man and the external world,—what is it but the perception how truly all our senses, and, beyond the senses, the soul, are turned to the order of things in which we live?" ("Relation," 44). In *Nature*, Emerson follows the model of Emanuel Swedenborg and refers to this "accord between man and the external world" as a "radical correspondence" (*Nature*, 19). Just as joyous religious sentiment springs from one's perception of the Other, "This relation between the mind and matter is not fancied by some poet, but stands in the will of God, and so is free to be known by all men." Moreover, this process is shown to mirror the movement of Reason, where "the universe becomes transparent, and the light of higher laws than its own . . . shines through" (*Nature*, 22). As opposed to popular empiricist models such as Victor Cousin's "Eclecticism," Emerson's early writings intimate repeatedly that nature is itself a material symbol for spirit, a symbol we at present only half perceive.

Despite the usefulness, to play on Emerson's own terms, of emerging scientific discourses, Emerson at times directly correlates the realm of science with the realm of institutional religion, arguing that "[e]very system of faith, every theory of science, every argument of the barrister, is a classification, and gives the mind the sense of power in proportion to the truth . . . of the traits by which it arranges." The "success of Phrenology" is, in this way, "a lively proof of the pleasure which a classification of the most interesting phenomena gives to the unscientific."[34] But as we see in Emerson's discussion of religious sentiment as well as in his frequent ecstatic revelry in scientific wholeness, this pleasure is conditioned qualitatively by the "proportion" of "truth" that a given system of classification yields. And, for Emerson, science offers a positive, but limited plane of experience on all fronts.

The benefits and limits alike that Emerson spied within modes of scientific thought are conditioned by the internal parameters of the development of "romantic science" in the early nineteenth century. As Jennifer Baker explains, the aforementioned discipline of natural philosophy was at this time undergoing something of a "second scientific revolution." In this transformation, "natural science, a broad rubric for the disciplines we now know as astronomy, chemistry, geology, physics, and biology, came to be understood as vocational, analytical, and sub-divided into fields of specialization."[35] Considering Emerson's criticism of the role of institutional knowledge within the church, it is no surprise that he would find new forms of institutional knowledge promoted by the sciences to be restrictive. The inherent distance between Emerson and developing sciences is at times set in stark relief. For example, Emerson often includes qualified warnings about science in the very lectures that praise its potential benefits. These include pointed quips, such as his claim in 1834 that "[w]e are not only to have the aids of Science but we are to recur to nature to guard us from the evils of Science."[36] In a journal entry logged the previous month, Emerson gestures toward the fact that such "evils" relate to the epistemological and hermeneutical limitations imposed by scientific inquiry:

> The Classification of all Nat. Science is arbitrary I believe, no Method philosophical in any one. And yet in all the permutations & combinations supposable, might not a Cabinet of shells or a Flora be thrown into one which should flash on us the very thought? We take them out of composition & so lose their greatest beauty. The moon is an unsatisfactory sight if the eye be exclusively directed to it & a shell retains but a small part of its beauty when examined separately. All our classifications are introductory & very convenient but must be looked on as temporary & the eye always watching for the glimmering of that pure plastic Idea. If Swammerdam forgets that he is a man, &, when you make any speculative suggestion as to the habits or origin or relation of insects, rebukes you[,] . . . he is only concerned for the facts,—[then I say] he loses all that for which science is of any worth. He is a mere insect hunter.[37]

Emerson here not only impugns the limits of classification proper, but also couches this criticism in terms of social relations, chiding Swammerdam (a seventeenth-century Dutch biologist) for forgetting "he is man." Consequently, Emerson is concerned not only with folding analytical atomization back into a Romantic wholeness but with amending the social conditions that inform such scientific perspectives. Attention to the social formulation of knowledge and truth is echoed in later works, as when Emerson argues that "[e]mpirical science is apt to cloud the sight, and, by the very knowledge of functions and processes, to bereave the student of the manly contemplation of the whole." The institutional context of such comments should be emphasized. For, in Emerson's view, "the best naturalist who lends an entire and devout attention to truth, will see that there remains much to learn of his relation to the world" (*Nature*, 39).

It is important to note that these criticisms of science are crafted after Emerson's visit to Jardin des Plantes in July 1833, an experience that prompted him to boldly declare—first in his journal and then in "Uses of Natural History"—"I will be a naturalist."[38] Indeed, Emerson's experiences in Paris, and his rumination on them in this first lecture after his return, provide the most formative example of how natural science relates to his conception of Reason and the correlative affective experience of religious sentiment.

Emerson opens the lecture with the example of "practical naturalists" ("a farmer, a hunter, a shepherd and a fisherman"), arguing that the agents of such applied interactions with the earth are "the true founders of all societies for the pursuit of science" ("Uses," 6). While such an organic model (anticipating his later theory of the "doctrine of use") undoubtedly seeks to Romantically ground scientific study in the lower-realms of "natural" labor, it also highlights a discrepancy between what science is and what Emerson believes it should be. And what it should be is associated immediately with aesthetic concerns ("beauty of the world is a perpetual invitation to . . . study" [6]) as well as notions of pleasure. In terms of the latter, Emerson posits, "The earth is a museum, and the five senses a philosophical apparatus of such perfection, that the pleasure we obtain from the aids with which we arm them, is trifling, compared with their natural information" (6). But Emerson includes an implied polemic within this discussion of this mode of pleasure, suggesting that the enjoyment of nature is greater when unhindered by various modern "aids"—aids, one might add, that include both mechanical and conceptual models. In addition, Emerson suggests that "the reasons that make this knowledge valuable to us" "will only disclose themselves by a more advanced state of science" because "we have all a presentment of relations to external nature, which outruns the limits of actual science" (7). Just as Reason's "grasp of the scepter" will occur after an eventual ascendency, Emerson figures science's potential in the future tense, following on the heels of our personal relations to nature.

As mentioned, all such concerns come to a head when Emerson describes his visit to "that celebrated repository of natural curiosities the Garden of Plants in Paris" (7). Though Emerson begins with the proviso that "except perhaps to naturalists only [he] . . . ought [not] to speak of the feelings it excited," his description of "pleasing walks" through the museum garden indicate that these naturalists are anything but institutional scientists (7–8). After noting the way a botanical cabinet renders the "natural alphabet" "more exciting and intelligible," for instance, he quickly subverts the analytical base of such knowledge, arguing that when one observes the parrot of the "tribe called *Psittacus Erythropterus*, . . . [y]ou need not write down his name for he is the beau of all birds and you will find him as you will find a Raffaelle in a gallery" (8). By placing the parrot in the milieu of art, Emerson not only fantasmatically re-contextualizes the experience of the natural world (a noted revision to his current environs), but he does so in a way that renders the institutional base of scientific knowledge irrelevant.

This aesthetic rendering of the natural world is more than a typical Emersonian tangent. In discussing the "specific advantages" of the study of natural history, Emerson creates a familiar ascending continuum that moves from the "lowest" gain of "health" to the intermediate benefit of "useful economic information" and on to the highest advantage of "the *delight which springs from the contemplation of . . . truth*" ("Uses," 10–14). Although Emerson does not employ the terms "Reason" or "Universal mind" (no doubt pandering to his Natural History Society audience), one should read this "delight" in "truth" within the context of his aforementioned discussions of religious sentiment. For, as Emerson explains, such delight stems from a greater vision, where "[e]very fact that is disclosed to us in natural history removes one scale more from the eye," and is attended by "keen gratification" and "new pleasure" (15).

This expansion of the eye's domain undoubtedly represents Emerson's cherished notion of a shift to intuitive Reason. As he suggests, this new knowledge is valuable not as a quantitatively growing empirical index, but as a qualitative transformation of reality: "The limits of the possible are enlarged, and the real is stranger than the imaginary. The universe is a more amazing puzzle than ever" ("Uses," 10). From here, Emerson goes on to cite his aforementioned theory of correspondence, which reveals that "not a form so grotesque, so savage, or so beautiful, but is an expression of something in man the observer." Moved by such "strange sympathies," Emerson voices the cited exclamation: "I will be a naturalist" (10). It should be clear by now, however, that this form of naturalist, one that reads the inner sympathy between object and observer as opposed to object and scientific designation, is a far cry from the institutional propensities that are beginning to dominate such discourse. Echoing his subsequent description of Reason's axis shift in *Nature*, Emerson writes, "Thus knowledge will make the face of the earth significant to us: it will make the stones speak and clothe with grace the meanest weed" (17).

Speaking stones may not be what members of the Natural Historical Society had in mind. In fact, this imagery replicates Samson Reed's discussion of the markedly unscientific notion of universal symbols in *Observations on the Growth of the Mind* (1826), where he suggests that "[t]he very stones cry out" and we would "do very well to listen to them."[39] It is this terminus that fires the process for Emerson—a process that both produces and is motivated by a distinct enjoyment. As he succinctly puts it in "The Naturalist":

> This passion, the enthusiasm for nature, the love of the Whole, has burned in the breasts of the Fathers of Science. It was the ever present aim of Newton, of Linnaeus, of Davy, of Cuvier, to ascend from nomenclature to classification; from arbitrary to natural classes; from natural classes, to primary laws; from these, in an ever narrowing circle, to approach the elemental law, the *causa causans*, the supernatural force. (80)

In a wonderful sleight of hand, Emerson here casts a passion for the spiritual—anticipating his subsequent claim that "[t]he use of natural history is to give us aid in supernatural history"—as the catalyst of early science's inception and aims (*Nature*, 18).

Given these contexts, we should, therefore, reframe Emerson's notion of *individualism* in this era by taking seriously his claim that "the highest prize in life is the perception in the private heart of access to the Universal," a universal marked by "impersonality."[40] Scholars have noted this charged relation at the center of Emerson's work.[41] Stanley Cavell, for instance, examines how self-reliance is less a quality of "possession" than the "exercise . . . of reception."[42] But where Cavell sees this openness to an outside as a positive constituent element of Emerson's variety of radical individualism, Sharon Cameron posits that it evinces a troubling "erasure of personality." In Cameron's view, there is a "deficiency" in Emerson's innovative portrayal of encounters with the impersonal: the fact that when presenting this rhetorical encounter there is a "missing sense of the person." Invoking the liberal ethics of Levinas, Cameron argues that Emerson is consequently and ultimately unable to address "the register of suffering" and, as such, he "does not take the responsibility a person should for his words."[43] Grounding this very relation in sociopolitical contexts, Christopher Newfield builds on New Americanist readings of Emerson's complicity in the development of capitalism, arguing that Emerson's thought gives rise to "corporate individualism," a form of subjectivity marked by submission to a dispersed corporate "system of forces."[44] In all these cases, one might ask what definitions of the individual and the personal are being employed and, in turn, what political horizons of meaning are being reproduced. By focusing on Emerson's specific fantasies about religious sentiment, this divided and incomplete subject is shown to operate within complex political coordinates and with various capabilities.

Emerson's conception of religious sentiment should be distinguished from both a traditional form of earthly passion—sentiment that, for Emerson, is "a private and tender relation of one to one" as opposed to a relation between self and Other—as well as from the conservative mode of enjoyment that is often championed during the early nineteenth century.[45] An example of the latter can be seen when Germaine de Staël, a writer with whom Emerson was familiar during his early years, argues that the "real obstacle to individual and personal happiness is the impulsive force of the passions, sweeping man away quite independently of his own will." Though de Staël is considering the context of the Reign of Terror in France, she shapes her views into a codified position where the "base of happiness" is "never being disturbed or dominated by any force stronger than the self."[46]

Conversely, Emerson's notion of religious sentiment correlates to the affective response generated by one's perception that received notions of self and reality are incomplete. "Happiness," therefore, does not reside within a homeostatic and balanced whole, but in a charged pursuit of that which exists in the negative space of reality. We can, in this way, begin to conceive how Emersonian optimism functions: an orientation toward the symptoms of an imperfect and incomplete reality is what allows one to enjoy shamelessly—for, in Emerson's view, Reason is the hidden cause of the given world's glorious incompletion.[47]

The development of "self-culture," a term Joel Porte links to William Ellery Channing's notion of "the care which every man owes . . . to the unfolding and perfecting of his nature," here takes the form of a joyous and anxious courting of the Other within.[48] As Emerson would have it, it is our own responsibility to wake from "the sleep of the Reason" and put ourselves in the position to perceive the Other's hail ("Religion," 94). In many of his early works, therefore, Emerson's conception of becoming is rhetorically less one of self-discovery and more one of obedience. In "Spiritual Laws," for instance, he suggests that "by contenting ourselves with obedience" to the "soul at the center of nature" we "become divine."[49]

We might, in this way, build on and depart from Stanley Cavell's point that, for Emerson, each "state" of the self "constitutes a world."[50] As Cavell notes, these worlds are not complete. This is because a "self is a process of moving to, and from, nexts." That is, "the self is always attained, as well as *to be* attained."[51] This Emersonian process of becoming, most directly addressed in "Circles," clearly aligns with the aforementioned relation between self and Reason. Yet Cavell's diachronic model doesn't appear to address fully the formative role of Reason as mediator. For, we might add, every attained self is constructed against its own current incompleteness—

and, in Emerson's view, this space, this gap, is filled by the position of the Other.

Shifting our perspective on the incompleteness of the Emersonian self opens up new vantage points for conceiving of this subject's political realities and capabilities. For example, Cavell elsewhere situates the aforementioned diachronic model of becoming within the political realm, suggesting that the "Emersonian event" effected by the topology of his writing is a "democratic successor" of Socrates's idea of a "city of words."[52] Consequently, Emerson is a "figure of democratic inspiration and aspiration" because his works create an expanding imaginary community via "countless identifications" between himself and his readers.[53]

But if we alter our view of the Emersonian self, if this self is not only divided irrevocably at each state of self-development but also shaped and charged by this very division, then the political grammar of the democratic Emersonian event must also change.

"Trust Your Emotion"

In returning to Emerson's 1850s radicalism, where Emerson employed various orthodoxies to embrace explicit forms of political violence, we need not push too hard to see a substantial link between his aforementioned call in 1859 to heed the "inspirations from the Supreme Intelligence" by "obey[ing]" their mandated "difficult duties,"[54] and his 1838 directive, amid his supposed era of "postreligious spiritual pluralism,"[55] to "trust your emotion."[56] Indeed, shortly before Emerson gives the injunction to obey divine and difficult duties in "Courage," an essay based upon his 1859 John Brown–inspired speech, he cites the notion of religious sentiment, suggesting, "Whenever the religious sentiment is adequately affirmed, it must be with dazzling courage." He goes on: "As long as it is cowardly insinuated, as with the wish to succor some partial and temporary interest, or to make it affirm some pragmatical tenet . . . , it is not imparted, and cannot inspire or create."[57] Here, Emerson's notion of religious sentiment is mobilized for a new and particular political end. But the structural affinities between this urgent and potentially violent position and his earlier joyous affirmations should not be overlooked.

Before tracing some of these affinities in Emerson's early work, we must acknowledge that Emerson does, at various moments in the 1830s and 1840s, espouse "peace principles" that might curb the type of extreme position he promotes in the 1850s.[58] For example, in "War" (1849), Emerson argues that "[i]f peace is to be maintained, it must be by brave men, who have come up to the same height as the hero, namely, they will carry their life in their hand, and stake it at any instant for their principle, but who have gone one step beyond the hero, and will not seek another man's life."[59] Quite obviously, Emerson modifies this view eleven years later in "Fate" (1860), an essay I will discuss shortly, figuring the "hero" as an unchecked force, where "[o]ne way is right to go: the hero sees it, and moves on that aim, and has the world under him for root and support."[60] In addition to acting as an apparent foil to Emerson's claims about peace, however, this later passage from "Fate" illuminates retroactively important aspects of Emerson's early thoughts on violence. By having the hero "stake" their life "for [their] principle" in "one way," Emerson brings, however vaguely, specific historical alignments and forces into the picture. One might ask if doing so complicates, or at least qualifies, the premise in Emerson's argument about peace. From the perspective of Emerson's early views, should one always desire peace? What if the present is defined by violent relations? In other words, Emerson often avoids praise for specific acts of violence in his early work, but this same work sets up relations whereby one might dutifully work to hasten an ideal development of humanity through whatever means necessary. When looking at early lectures such as "Politics" (1840) and "Duty" (1839), we see not only structures relating to religious sentiment linking early and later Emerson, but also unambiguous gestures toward scenarios where these relations might be placed within the horizon of historical and political reality—setting the stage, in a sense, for the political rhetoric on violence seen in the 1850s.

In "Politics," Emerson makes the perhaps predictable claim that we must "treat the state poetically." But this mode is quickly shown to include more than concerns of aesthetics proper. Using a historical approach similar to that found in his aforementioned criticism of the Lord's Supper and prefiguring claims made in "Self-Reliance," he suggests that institutions "are not superior to the citizen" because every aspect of an institution "was once a man." That is, "every one of its laws and usages was a man's expedient to meet a particular fact." Following this logic, Emerson concludes that all social institutions are, therefore, "alterable." This means that "Society is fluid": There are not "roots and centres but any monad there may instantly become the centre of the whole movement and compel the whole to gyrate around him."[61]

The discursive and, indeed, political radicalness of Emerson's "poetic" vision in "Politics" should be read in the context of his early thought on religious sentiment. By way of illustration, Orestes Brownson, an otherwise lukewarm ally of Emerson against conservatives such as Andrews

Norton, included a pointed critique of Emerson's definition of religious sentiment in his review of "The Divinity School Address" in *The Boston Quarterly Review*. Brownson writes, "He confounds the religious sentiment with the moral; but the two sentiments are psychologically distinct. The religious sentiment is a craving to adore, resulting from the soul's intuition of the Holy; the moral sentiment is an obligation, resulting from the soul's intuition of a moral law. The moral sentiment leads us up merely to universal order; the religious sentiment leads us up to God, Father of the universal order."[62] Quite clearly, Emerson's unorthodox alignment of these two modes bothered Brownson to the point where he dismisses their union as a confused conflation. Nevertheless, as discussed, Emerson's revision should not be seen as a simple error, or as yet another facile example of his supposed contradictory nature. Conversely, it evidences the construction of a new model of personhood and agency, where the "obligation" Brownson attributes to moral sentiment is linked to the agency of "God" found in religious sentiment. The result, for Emerson, is that we are not merely able to discern the laws of the existing moral or universal order; we are capable of contacting the author of the universe—opening up a perpetual potential for exceptions to all systems and realities.

This "poetic" vision, then, entails a way of seeing that involves a politics of potential—where a given codified reality might be interrupted at any moment by the eruption of a new paradigmatic center. Yet Emerson acknowledges the material and timely nature of both these actualities and possibilities, claiming, "Politics are real and must be treated really" ("Politics," 241). Although tempered in this early work, the space for and of political violence can be discerned in this relation between existing real social structures and, in Emerson's view, unfolding ideal developments of humanity. After noting the reality of politics, for instance, Emerson suggests that "the state must follow the character and progress of man" and, as a result, "the form of government that prevails is always the expression of what cultivation exists in the population which permits it" (241). He earlier notes specific historical examples, citing representative men of "strong will" such as Cromwell and Pitt who "for a time" force a given society to "gyrate around" their acts or views. Although he subsequently adds the higher plane of influence with men "of truth" such as Plato or Paul, who shape society "forever," the seemingly lower realm of temporary political strife obviously aligns, for Emerson, with grander and permanent principles. Consequently, Emerson argues that the "reveries of the true and simple are prophetic. What you dream and pray and paint today, but shun the ridicule of saying aloud, shall presently be the resolutions of large bodies, then shall be carried as Grievance and Bill of Rights through conflict and war" (241).

Here we see clearly how the relations involved in Emerson's writings on religious sentiment play out in the broader social sphere—with consequences that include political declarations and, indeed, warfare. For Emerson, this political violence is engendered by the aforementioned gap between existing and emerging social paradigms, but also by the distance between varying embodiments of truth in a given historical moment. The latter can be seen in Emerson's subsequent commentary in "Napoleon, or the Man of the World" (1850), where he figures Bonaparte as embodying the type of "strong will" needed to create a new social paradigm. According to Emerson, "Napoleon's stamp almost ceases to have a private speech and opinion. He is so largely receptive, and is so placed, that he comes to be a bureau for all the intelligence, wit, and power of the age and country. He gains the battles; he makes the code; . . . he levels the Alps; he builds the road." Although Bonaparte's power derives from his alignment with a broader principle, Emerson suggests that this alignment is only transcendent in the sense that the ruler "had in transcendent degree the qualities and powers of common men."[63] Despite the fact that this link with the dominant trend of social history—one Emerson identifies as the process of "subordinating all intellectual and spiritual forces into means to a material success"—affords Bonaparte the adequate force to wage war and level mountains, it is not, in Emerson's view, as powerful as an alignment with the higher principles associated with Reason. As Emerson laments at the close of the essay, "As long as our civilization is essentially one of property . . . it will be mocked by delusions" and "there will be bitterness in our laughter."[64]

It should be noted that in "Politics" Emerson does implore the reader to "drop violence," seemingly relegating forms of warfare to the less enlightened levels of Bonaparte's ilk (245). Of course, in his early work, Emerson is often cautious about the necessity of violence. In "Demonology" (1839), for instance, he discusses the lower-level insight of truth afforded by dreams and the resultant "terrible freedom" we exercise within unconscious fantasies, where "every will rushes to a deed."[65] But across Emerson's early work, and even more forcefully in his later 1850s writings, there is little hesitation when his discourse moves from the level of (terrible) personal freedom to higher social and cosmic levels. When it comes to historical and/or universal horizons, we find a consistent, though multiform, desire for the divine will to erupt and shape the present. Moreover, throughout "Politics," historical and conceptual examples of righteous violence abound. On more than one occasion, Emerson touches upon diffuse and systemic potential relations of violence, mentioning how "the appearance of character rebukes the state" (243). More important, in addition to holding up the lofty figures of Cromwell and Pitt, he closes the piece by praising a string of historical heroic stands, each linked to subjective violence in varying ways: "the fight of Leonidas or the hemlock of Socrates or the cross of Christ." These extreme sacrifices were noble, in Emerson's view, because they were governed by "the sublime idea of a most private and beautiful Right," an unmediated idea that "drove them to their act" (247). This schematic adds the important requisite of action to other similar comments on the liberating effects of the perception of truth that attends religious sentiment, such as in an 1841 lecture where Emerson avers: "Give the slave the least elevation of religious sentiment, and he is no slave."[66]

These connections among private intuition, a transcendent idea of "Right," and political action are even more pronounced in the early lecture "Duty." At the opening, Emerson cuts to his point, advising his audience at the Masonic Temple in Boston: "Consent to accept the place the Divine Province has found for you." Falling in line with his writings on religious sentiment, Emerson describes this acquiescence as entailing more than mere submission to a traditional conception of fate; instead, it includes making oneself the "passive organ of its idea." As in "Politics," this embodiment yields requisite material and social acts of courage. According to Emerson, "[W]e are now men and must accept in the highest mind the same transcendent destiny and not pinched in the corner, not cowards fleeing before revolution." Consequently, Emerson outlines how the perception of divine principles affects a "perfect obligation" to join what he terms an "almighty effort." And yet, although Emerson is precise when laying out his view that one should "obey piously to follow," he is notably vague about the conceptual link that supposedly leads from divine ideas to earthly obligations—the very structural space where we might locate the domain of social ethics. As Emerson would have it, such a move is natural: All you need to do is "place yourself in the full centre of that flood; then you are without effort impelled to truth, to right, and a perfect contentment."[67]

This link between truth and right becomes more complex later in the lecture. After defining "virtue" as "the spontaneity of the will, bursting up into the world as a sunbeam out of aboriginal cause," Emerson posits that "duty" is therefore "the endeavor of man to obey this light: the voluntary conforming our action to the whole." Put in other terms, "Duty is the application of the sentiment of virtue to the varying events of every day" ("Duty," 144). Such claims hinge on an ambiguous notion of "application," which includes an elliptical relation between the "sovereign instinct" of the light, on the one hand, and the contingent historical act of endeavoring to apply it, on the other. In these early works, therefore, two phases are clear: the influx or unfolding of the divine idea within the self and the resulting obligation for action that includes, by necessity, "new danger" (146). The latter point, of course, provides an interesting early rationalization of the place of political violence. In this context, the conceptual space where the input of divine ideas transmogrifies into the output of historical violence is paramount for conceiving of the politics of the Emersonian self.

Emerson's later essay "Fate" may be useful here, providing a rearticulation of Emerson's early thoughts on both religious sentiment and duty. In the middle of the essay, after building on themes familiar in his early work (pertaining to the way thought "carr[ies] the mind up into a sphere where all is plastic," a process linked to "the will of Divine Province"), Emerson comments on the "moral sentiment," a concept, as discussed, that he consistently and directly associates with religious sentiment. Describing this relation of "spiritual chemistry," Emerson writes, "[W]e can see that with the perception of truth is joined the desire that it shall prevail. That affection is essential to will" (15). Importantly, the vague relation Emerson posits in "Duty" between divine ideas and the historical "almighty effort" to "apply" them is here recoded in terms of a specific "desire" for such ideas to "prevail." In so doing, Emerson shifts the ground of the aforementioned relation between input and output, moving from a scenario shaped by concerns of epistemology and potential translation (discerning how a divine idea applies to specific historical situations) to one of pseudo-ontological leverage (supporting and joining a preexisting force). Moreover, this formulation of desire alters aforementioned fantasies linked with Emerson's brand of religious sentiment. Instead of joyously courting a partially perceived Other, we move further along on the arc of desire to a specific political longing for this Other's fully formed ideas to be realized in historical time.

In this light, the specific aspects of Emersonian duty are quite distinct from a traditional Protestant conception of duty as well as the modern democratic idea of the concept. In terms of the former, Martin Luther's commentary on Lot's wife, where "look[ing] back," or delaying the execution of one's duty, connotes a departure "from God's command" and an occupation "with other matters . . . outside one's calling," is representative of a broader schematic where one is impelled to close with a distinct Other based on a foreign moral and ethical injunction.[68] For Emerson, of course, the self is not an obstacle to be overcome in order to actualize one's calling; instead, it is the actual threshold, the actual Other misrecognized in the present.

This view also distinguishes Emerson's thought from more modern liberal-democratic varieties of duty, ideas that can be linked to Immanuel Kant's late eighteenth-century work on ethics.[69] On the surface, Emerson and Kant share the view that the core of subjectivity and, therefore, supposed free acts are linked to external or foreign forces. This impels both thinkers to view political events and violence through the lenses of extrahistorical moral paradigms. For instance, Kant comes quite close to Emerson's writing on historical events when he suggests that the global "spectators" of the French Revolution, in witnessing even its worst "atrocities," felt a "sympathy" with the rebels (including a "wishful participation"), a sympathy that has "no other cause than a moral predisposition of the human race."[70] Contemporary scholars have focused on the radical democratic potential in the universalist ethic involved in Kant's "categorical imperative" to "do our duty." According to Slavoj Žižek, the ethical autonomy of this scenario derives from the fact that, for Kant, "it is not possible to derive the concrete norms I have to follow in my specific situation from the moral Law itself"; consequently, "it is the subject himself who has to assume the responsibility for translating the abstract injunction."[71] As Žižek suggests, this scenario affords a radical aspect of freedom, where "I am fully responsible not only for doing my duty, but no less for determining what my duty is."[72] As noted, the ambiguity Emerson places between divine ideas and specific historical action in lectures such as "Duty" might be seen to allow for a similar level of autonomy.

There is, however, a significant structural difference in the way Emerson and Kant conceive of duty, one that yields drastically distinct forms of political personhood. As Alenka Zupančič explains, Kant upholds the "irreducibility of the Other," insisting that we are ultimately subject to this Other. But, for Kant, when one submits to this Other, a "crack" or inconsistency in the Other becomes apparent, "a crack in which [Kant] . . . situates the autonomy and freedom of the subject."[73] Accordingly, Kantian ethical autonomy derives from the fact that we are ultimately distinct from the pure domain of the Other (noumena)—existing in a space of freedom created, paradoxically, only when we approach the Other. Conversely, for Emerson, any semblance of ethical autonomy exists before, or, perhaps, in the passage toward the Other (the domain where religious sentiment comes into play). Once one connects with the divine idea, the "desire" to actualize this truth forms a totalizing structure wherein the individual, aligned with Reason, becomes a direct agent of a higher power. And because, in this process, the planes of historical time/traditional self and Truth/Other conjoin, then there is no ethical scene—no requisite space between self and any Other. In fact, in an anachronistic way, one might say that Emerson here dramatizes Benjaminian divine violence (the destruction of existing law during the emergence of new Law) from the impossible (emerging) focalization of Law itself. Unlike Kant's positivist explanation of why happiness and morality are absent from the scene of duty, where these concepts are intentionally ignored ("we take no account of them whenever duty is in question"), Emerson's fantasy includes a configuration where all moral experiences exist in an ambiguous umbra between self and Other.[74]

It would seem that Emerson's position might thus fall prey to Kant's critique of a traditional dogmatism that imagines direct access to the Other, where "God and eternity in their awful majesty would stand unceasingly before our eyes. . . . Thus most actions conforming to the law would be done from fear."[75] But, as discussed, Emerson's vision of duty plays out within a complex set of relations where the Other is accessed via modalities of the self. As a result, instead of "stand[ing]" before us and pronouncing laws, the Other and its injunctions are seemingly transformed into affective experiences born within us.

In the crucible of Reason, therefore, Emerson posits a form of political ontology that in many ways breaks from both previous and contemporaneous models of subjectivity and political ethics. In returning to Emerson's aforementioned claim in "Fate" that "with the perception of truth is joined the desire that it shall prevail" and that this "affection is essential to will," we might ask more pointedly *whose will* Emerson is speaking of. Emerson elucidates the preceding statement with the following passage: "[W]hen a strong will appears, it usually results from a certain unity of organization, as if the whole energy of body and mind flowed in one direction. All great force is real and elemental. . . . Where power is shown in will, it must rest on the universal force" (15). For Emerson, "will" represents an encounter with the divine idea, but on another plane, where one passes from the reception of symbolic truth (Reason) to an odd embodiment of universal force. In this short circuit, according to Emerson, "[e]ach pulse from [the] heart is an oath from the Most High" (16). That is, the will represents an alignment moving in "one direction" from the universal to the particular. This perspective might shed light on the aforementioned passage in "Courage" where Emerson suggests that "[w]henever the religious sentiment is adequately affirmed, it must be with dazzling courage" (138). In this context, courage is not necessarily associated with directing or executing an action per se, for all action is here impelled by a foreign force. Instead, it refers to the fortitude required to *maintain* an established connection to the Other, despite the historical and social consequences. The type of political violence that Emerson sanctions across his writing in the 1830s, 1840s, and 1850s is marked by a similar mode of negative content—where the permutation of action is shaped not merely by a human agent, but by the consequences arising from the encounter between this embodied force and the specific (imperfect) terrain of a given historical reality. Emerson's brand of personal and social transformation is thus formed through a radical recalibration of political personhood and a structural understanding of the resulting eruptions of specific historical violence.

Traditional notions of self- and other-directed violence as well as positivist historicist notions of social agency are, therefore, inadequate for conceiving of Emerson's depictions of political actions and their ramifications. The reading of Emerson presented here thus departs drastically from a number of standard perspectives that cast Emerson as a champion of liberal, democratic, and/or pragmatist ideologies.[76] But more than merely launching a polemic against liberal-democratic traditionalists, by offering a new framework for considering Emerson's early structural vision of personhood, I hope to bolster contemporary scholarship that endeavors to take seriously and on its own terms Emerson's complex negotiation of radical politics in the 1840s through the 1860s. For example, both Michael Ziser's "Emersonian Terrorism: John Brown, Islam, and Postsecular Violence" (2010) and Donald Pease's "'Experience,' Antislavery, and the Crisis of Emersonianism" (2010) offer rich accounts of the way Emerson's thought shifted dramatically in response to specific historical events surrounding slavery. According to Ziser, developments in the 1850s, particularly the Anthony Burns trial, "led [Emerson] momentarily to reformulate his beliefs into a properly postsecular recognition of the formal necessity of a new kind of religious orthodoxy and violence to effect political change within a modern liberal state." Ziser suggests that in this period Emerson "awoke from his secular-universalist dream to his historical and religious particularity."[77] Similarly, Pease argues that in "Experience" (1844) Emerson, based on the loss of his young son, presents an encounter with the "limits to how far his annulment of social bonds could be taken."[78] In Pease's account, Emerson as a socially aloof impresario of the abstract "genius" in "Self-Reliance" transforms, in "Experience," into Emerson as the thinker of social and historical limitations. Here, Emerson developed the "anti-slave" as a "figure of address" that rhetorically "correlated the historical trauma of slavery with the personal trauma of his son's death."[79] Ultimately, according to Pease, a historically inflected notion of slavery allowed Emerson to rethink the conditions and preconditions of freedom. "Before 'Experience,'" Pease writes, "Emerson left out the figure of his thinking who inhabited the space between the desymbolization of the symbolic order and the emergence of the different social order to which genius called him."[80]

By looking more closely at Emerson's early notions of religious sentiment, one can discern the structural outlines of the radical thought that scholars such as Ziser and Pease locate at the far end of Emerson's political transformations in the 1840s and 1850s. That is to say, undoubtedly Emerson's radicalized thought on slavery and political violence in this period emerged in response to specific historical events. Yet the pervasive scholarly focus on Emerson's political turn may occlude important structures of thought within his early work that already favored and conditioned the later disposition toward action. A consideration of religious sentiment reveals that elements of a universal-particular axis of thinking, one that effected an operative relation to the Other, was, in terms of Ziser's work, prevalent during Emerson's supposed secular early years. In terms of Pease's argument, it suggests that there may not have been as substantive a gap between "genius" and the "anti-slave" in the first place. I wholeheartedly agree with Pease's elegant proposition that "Experience" "effected a crisis within the transindividual discourse" that governed Emerson's earlier division between transcendentalist and reformer.[81] At the same time, I want to redraw this crisis as a process by which Emerson was convinced of the ethical need to focus on a given historical antagonism, and, as a result, he applied previous structures of thought in new ways and to new ends. Instead of a particular struggle for freedom replacing a struggle for abstract freedom, an ideological bifurcation that scholars such as Russ Castronovo have shown was certainly in play during the antebellum period,[82] we might see Emerson's early work delineating carefully the structural space for the figure that would become something closer to Pease's adaptation of Emerson's term "anti-slave." As I have shown, this figurative space is empty or, perhaps more aptly, incomplete in Emerson's early thought less because he was shooting for an abstract ideal and more due to the structural relations that shaped his specific conception of duty and action. The historical, critical, and ideological stakes within this shift are significant. By way of example, one might ask why a reading such as Pease's, which embraces Emerson's approval of righteous violence (to a degree) based upon Emerson's historical turn toward recognizing the "the plight of black folk,"[83] might sit more comfortably with a genealogy of Emersonian scholarship predicated upon liberal-democratic ideals than one, such as my own, that argues for a modicum of consistency across Emerson's early work and mid-century fundamentalism.

The two faces of Emersonian optimism that open this chapter, therefore, are anything but exclusive. Although cleaved by historians, these two faces close in significant ways when considered in the context of a fuller account of Emerson's thought on religious sentiment, personhood, and violence. The amalgam of these concepts is apparent in the seemingly odd grouping of sensations in "Duty," where, as quoted earlier, Emerson implores the audience to "place yourself in the middle of the stream, the stream of power and wisdom which flows into you . . . ; place yourself in the full centre of that flood; then you are without effort impelled to truth, to right, and a perfect contentment" (139). Yet, if this process is a shorthand formula for the courageous execution of will, what, we might ask, is the specific nature of this consequent perfect contentment? Put differently, how does it feel to be in an Emersonian operative mood?

The answer is readily apparent soon after in "Duty," where Emerson outlines a number of experiences that result when one aligns with the force of "good." According to Emerson, the "awful truth" that is produced in such a union will not be experienced in "any known . . . way"; it will "be wholly strange and new." Consequently, in this state, "[t]here shall be no fear" for "[f]ear and [h]ope are alike beneath it." So, too, we might add, are joy and optimism. As Emerson states, "We are then a vision. There is nothing that can be called gratitude, nor properly joy. The soul is raised over passion. . . . It is a perceiving that Truth and Right *are*" (143). By, in essence, splitting the Cartesian subject—where we can perceive without existence proper because Truth and Right exist for and through us—Emerson creates the conditions for an original type of political ontology. This ontological shift resulting from the historical person's interface with the cosmic "flood" can be thought of in affective terms as well. As Rei Terada explains, "[B]y *emotion* we usually mean a psychological, at least minimally interpretive experience whose physiological aspect is *affect*."[84] In this context, Emerson's proposition of "pure sympathy with universal ends" necessitates what we might call a "disjunctive synthesis," where one's affective (bodily) and emotional (psychological) modalities are incorporated into an "infinite force" ("Fate," 15).[85] What is left, it seems, is a pure "perceiving" of events and reality, where the self is, in political terms, a modal agent of the Other.

Perhaps we, much like Christopher Pearse Cranch's famous caricature, had this whole transparent eyeball thing wrong after all.

CHAPTER 2

Agitating Margaret Fuller

The men thought she carried too many guns, and the women did not like one who despised them.

—RALPH WALDO EMERSON, *Memoirs of Margaret Fuller Ossoli*

In Margaret Fuller's unpublished 1843 "Western Journal," she notes the disturbing effect produced by the reverberation of the falls at Niagara: "After a while the perpetual trampling of the floods caused my mind to be haunted by fears, such as I never had before." She goes on to explain that the fear engendered by this natural force evoked fantasies where "Indians came continually before [her] fancy stealing upon a foe with uplifted tomahawk."[1] Months later, when Fuller returned to this scene in her manuscript of *Summer on the Lakes, in 1843*, she modified the scenario, claiming that the movement of water yielded anxiety about a "foe" lurking nearby, imagining "naked savages stealing behind . . . [her] with uplifted tomahawks."[2] This simple shift holds more import than one might think. By envisioning herself as the potential victim of an attack, Fuller clearly adds a flare of racialized drama, one that partakes in the tomahawk fantasies of her era.[3] Fuller does more, however, than merely play to such sensationalism. By modifying the journal entry and casting herself as the besieged foe, she disrupts the original link posited among the aqueous force sounding in the falls' "perpetual trampling," her ambiguous role as a witness (or more) of Indian aggression, and the execution of violence.[4]

Critics have had much to say about the way Fuller embraced revolutionary violence while in Italy during the late 1840s, often citing incendiary lines such as the one, written in Florence in December 1849, where she admits, "I am not sure that I can keep my hands free from blood."[5] In the popular record, however, Fuller's political bloodlust during the Italian spring is commonly set against her earlier mystical Romanticism, figured as an infusion of foreign enthusiasm within a renowned blue-blooded New England editor, scholar, and conversationalist; or it is lost sight of in a sentimentalized narrative that dwells on her 1850 death, where she perished tragically in a shipwreck off of Long Island with her Italian husband and infant son. But in Fuller's perspective at the time, the potential for blood on her own hands stemmed from very real struggles afoot in Italy. For Fuller, these various struggles merged in a new type of patriot, one that "delighted in duty" and had begun to "develop unknown energy."[6]

It is precisely here that I hope we might begin to hear and feel, however distant, the "perpetual trampling of the floods" Fuller cited at Niagara. In Italy, this "unknown energy" is associated with the revolutionary Roman populace and linked to the "effectual service of the Universe."[7] Fuller imagined this service had begun to forcefully create a "New Era," where a longtime social "transition state" was coming to an end and "the power of positive, determinate effort [was] begun."[8] At the height of these later pronouncements, penned with the élan of a full-fledged revolutionary, Fuller drew from the musical analogies for social and political action that commonly appeared in her earlier work. In a dispatch from 1847, for example, she argued that "voluntary association for improvement . . . will be the grand means for my nation to grow and give a nobler harmony to the coming age."[9] The use of "harmony" as a descriptor for post-revolutionary socialist reality resonates with Fuller's writing from the 1830s and early 1840s, where she used forms of dissonant energy, such as the reverberations found at Niagara, to describe sociopolitical topics, often coding this array of energy forms using the tropes of music, sound, and other pulsations. This conceptual approach is seen again in Fuller's last dispatch, written shortly before her fateful return trip to the United States in 1850. Discussing the aforementioned birth of a "New Era," Fuller delights in the belief that revolutionaries of her generation were "heralds" of new political alignments and, hence, could be "happy in the thought that there come after them greater than themselves, who may at last string the harp of the world to full concord."[10]

By gesturing to the rhetorical link between Fuller's later and earlier thought, I am less concerned with outlining a specific genealogy than in restoring a political framework for looking at Fuller's early major work. Few scholars have taken seriously the ways Fuller's earlier thought establishes manifold connections between formal and musical aspects of energy and the incipient formation of a radical politics. Nonetheless, Fuller's early work itself establishes a radical mode of political personhood, one that is refined and developed within the lived historical moment of revolutionary Italy.

Across Fuller's earlier work, she depicts a form of radical political agency and, further still, political ontology that is shaped by extra-personal forces. I suggest that by examining the affective and formal elements of these forces in Fuller's thought, where various sounds, tones, and pulsations explicitly and/or implicitly mediated her thinking about reality, we might better understand the complex dialectic she posits among the personal, the impersonal, and the social. The stakes of this argument go further than merely revising the common historical narrative that sees Fuller moving from romantic to radical forms of thought after her departure for Europe in 1846. Ultimately, I seek to portray how Fuller offers an alternate model of nineteenth-century political personhood, one that undergirds all of her corpus to varying degrees. As Emerson suggests in the epigraph that opens this chapter, this type of formation troubled men and women alike, creating a social liminality that led Henry James to dub Fuller "Margaret-ghost."[11] And it is this nonidentity with modern liberal-democratic parameters of the self that has perhaps led contemporary critics—many of whom wittingly and unwittingly use standard humanist ethical and critical paradigms to understand Fuller's work—to overlook the original aspects of her conception of political personhood. Instead of viewing Fuller's calls for harmony in terms of a positivist vision of social cohesion, I argue that her brand of political ontology includes a dynamic material relationship between particular social alignments and transcendental truths. According to Fuller, the imperfect (unharmonious) relation between these registers engenders productive forms of physical and sonic agitation that spur specific political interventions.

The Italian Revolution and Its Paradigms

Scholars have noted a shift in Fuller's thought during the late 1840s, pointing out the way she takes a number of radical positions in her dispatches from Europe, including her embrace of American abolitionism (a movement she previously chided) and her various personal pronouncements of support for socialism and violent revolution.[12] In this light, Fuller's political views in the late 1840s are outlined starkly against the backdrop of American apprehension with political radicalism as well as Fuller's own earlier work, which has been seen as largely measured in regard to explicit political themes.[13] But her radical positions in the late 1840s were wholly allied with European political perspectives at the time, which yielded a number of revolutions and uprisings in 1848. While Fuller was in Italy passionately taking up the revolutionary "Risorgimento" banner, for example, the French were deposing Louis-Philippe and the German states were forcing their way toward a federation. As biographers have noted, Fuller's scholarly focus and tone shifted as early as 1844, when she left New England for New York and took up journalism for Horace Greeley's *New-York Daily Tribune*. This mode of professional "observation," to use Fuller's term, soon yielded experiences that significantly pushed her personal and political views.[14] Traveling across western Europe in 1846 with the Fourierist Marcus Spring and the liberal-minded Rebecca Spring, Fuller was exposed to the lingering Chartist movement in Liverpool and, when in London, began a formative relationship with Giuseppe Mazzini, an exiled leader of the Young Italy republican movement. While spending winter in Paris shortly after, Fuller met Adam Mickiewicz, the exiled Polish poet and activist who, much like Mazzini, challenged her to seek material outlets for her idealistic social views.[15]

Fuller's experiences in Italy from 1847 to 1850, however, most directly shaped the articulations of her later politics. The Italy Fuller encountered in 1847, a geopolitical and cultural space she had idolized to varying degrees since childhood,[16] was divided into nine competing states: with Austria controlling northern territories and, via influence, a number of weaker southern domains; the Catholic church lording over the Papal States; and various European rulers, such as Spain's Ferdinand II, claiming others. Beginning in the 1830s, the Young Italy movement's call for the unification of the country gained momentum. Things broke their way when, beginning in 1848, various skirmishes, including physical revolt in places such as Palermo, led to monarchical concessions favoring the Risorgimento cause and, under the leadership of Mazzini, the eventual establishment of an embattled republic. Fuller was privy to and involved in many of the political events from this period, including weathering France's siege of Rome in June of 1849, where she aided the wounded while her republican husband, Giovanni Angelo Ossoli, fought at the frontlines.

As early as the spring of 1848, Fuller had decided to write a history of revolutionary Italy, a manuscript famously lost in the shipwreck that took her life. Fuller's thoughts on the topic pervade her personal correspondence and her *Tribune* dispatches from the period, evidencing her developing radicalization. When Count Pellegrino Rossi was assassinated in November, 1846, for example, Fuller describes how a crowd gathered to sing "Blessed the hand that rids the earth of a tyrant" and deems the killing a welcome "terrible justice."[17] Indeed, Fuller reveled in the growing agitation in Rome, admitting to William Channing: "It is a time such as I always dreamed of, and for long secretly hoped to see.... Perhaps I shall be called to act." This notion of action is soon linked to warfare: "[T]here may be need to spill much blood yet in Italy."[18] Of course, Fuller at times censures previous overzealous political bloodletting, referencing in one dispatch, for instance, France's "false position.... with all of its baptism of blood." A few sentences later, however, she returns to what is a typical embrace of contemporary violent revolution: "[A]t this moment ... all things bode and declare a new outbreak of the fire, to destroy the old palaces of crime!.... Here at this moment a successor of St. Peter, after the lapse of two thousand years, is called 'Utopian' by a part of this Europe, because he strives to get some food to the mouths of the *leaner* of his flock."[19]

Fuller's focus on class disparity as an impetus for revolutionary action reflects her embrace of socialism in this period. In a letter from late 1849, she praises the news that Marcus and Rebecca Spring had spent time at the "North American Phalanx," and proclaims, "I have become an enthusiastic Socialist; elsewhere is no comfort, no solution for the problems of the times."[20] Fuller is thus afforded a material and social vision for the grand solutions she deems necessary. Underscoring the stakes of these propositions in an 1849 dispatch, she suggests, "It is vain to cry peace, peace, when there is no peace.... It appears that the political is being merged in the social struggle: it is well; whatever blood is to be shed, whatever altars cast down. Those tremendous problems MUST be solved, whatever the cost!"[21]

Radical pronouncements such as these are often set against rather than read alongside Fuller's earlier writing, even those that take up explicit social and political themes. The need to reestablish a political optic for viewing Fuller's early work is necessary, therefore, because contemporary scholarship often imposes a historical break, which casts her writing before Europe as predominantly mystical or Romantic. Even when this simple divide is not imposed, scholars commonly maintain the ideological logic that sustains it by using delimiting liberal paradigms when analyzing Fuller's thought.

The latter paradigms are apparent in formative contemporary scholarship on Fuller. For example, Jeffrey's Steele's oft-cited *Transfiguring America*:

Myth, Ideology, and Mourning in Margaret Fuller's Writing (2001) provides a productive examination of the ways Fuller's use of literary mythology and the modality of mourning related to her ongoing political engagements. Moving past Christina Zwarg's focus in *Feminist Conversations* (1995) on the "transitional modes" of Fuller's writing, especially during 1845–1846 when she embarked upon her journalistic career,[22] Steele avoids positing an "epistemological break" between Fuller's early and late work, offering a nuanced account of how Fuller sought to produce specific political effects. At the same time, the explicit political paradigms Steele uses to examine the ideological work of Fuller's thought limit his arguments. On the very first page, Steele makes the important point that the "heart" of Fuller's insight "lay in the conviction that selves, communities, and even nationalities might be transfigured by a spirit of reform." Right away, however, he restricts this impulse for multitudinous reform by connecting it to the specific ideological horizon of the "ever-elusive ideal of democracy."[23] The ideal of democracy might, of course, stand in as a variable for any number of potential real revolutions and resulting socio-political alignments. But Steele subsequently grounds this ideal in specific modern political contexts. After suggesting that Fuller refuses to locate the "sign of womanhood," and hence personhood, within "any single universalizing category," Steele notes that, consequently, her "literary experiments . . . anticipated in important ways our own struggles to theorize a diverse and multicultural society."[24] Steele thus anchors retroactively the "ideal of democracy" within Fuller's nineteenth century to a modern vision of a multicultural society. Doing so distorts Fuller's thought in a number of ways, including framing her many discussions of psychological and sociological "harmony" in terms of a straightforward desire to "restore social harmony and justice."[25] In what follows, I will push against this familiar and perhaps appealing reading. What happens when we refuse to privilege the ideal of harmony and, instead, take seriously Fuller's thoughts on the political agency lodged in forces and forms of a markedly unharmonious present? As I will show, refusing to fasten personhood to "any single universalizing category" was less of an embrace of a pseudo modern multiculturalism (means and ends) and more of an initial negative move of critique and preparation for the radical imposition of a new order (means alone).[26]

In a similar manner as Steele, Wai Chee Dimock considers Fuller's thought from the perspective of modern liberal paradigms, especially as they pertain to developing global models of analysis. Expanding the historical scale to planetary proportions, Dimock offers the compelling thesis that Fuller's work provides a "model of large-scale causation." According to

Dimock, Fuller's *Woman in the Nineteenth Century* uses the mythology of the past in new ways, creating "long-distance exchange" and, by default, new models of personhood that go beyond the "discrete unit" as well as "biology."[27] Extending the bounds of personhood and community to the far reaches of time might productively challenge inherent limits within dominant transnational paradigms, yielding any number of radically new interfaces. Dimock's reading, however, effectively flattens out such encounters, portraying more of a tolerant ontology of relation rather than the dynamic notion of "exchange" that she cites. This can be seen when she claims that "fallibility" is "what generates kinship across such long distances." Here, Dimock argues that mythological figures such as Isis appearing in Fuller's work exemplify an "absence" of "power, mastery, [and] efficiency" and that this absence renders such figures "durable and reproducible, bearer[s] of an attribute that can be predicated on many human beings."[28]

Dimock's model for a transhistorical community comes replete with its own ethical code, based on the "postulate that we have always made mistakes and will always make mistakes." Consequently, "[a]ll of us are obligated, by these mistakes, to face up to the burden of time as the burden of things having always gone wrong, and therefore the burden of a cry for repair, for mending."[29] In Dimock's hands, Fuller's work thus becomes markedly positivist: an ethical cry for an impossible mending of what *is* and what will always be. The logic of relation forwarded here clearly mirrors Steele's own modern fantasies of multicultural democratic reality—where units and groups exist in a relatively passive status quo through bonds of likeness and an implicit tolerance toward others who are perceived as different.

The political stakes of Dimock's reading become clear when she discusses what is a central literary symbol for Fuller: the sistrum. I will examine Fuller's writing on the sistrum, or Isis's "brazen rattle," at length in the next section. For now, I would like to note how Dimock links the "ragged energy" of the instrument to the past—its three tonalities representing a "replay of the drama of Osiris, Isis, and Typhon." In Dimock's view, this drama evokes "not only . . . resurrection, but also . . . death, [and] . . . frequent and unavoidable error."[30] Dimock connects this schema to the political realm by using Karl Marx's *The Eighteenth Brumaire of Louis Bonaparte* as a foil (like Fuller, Marx wrote for the *New York Tribune* in the 1840s). Discussing Marx's critique of the 1848 French Revolution, Dimock claims that he urged a "forward-looking revolution" to leave the "corpse" of the past behind, where, in Marx's terms, the era of Pharaohs (an ancient moment standing in for all history) is "defunct." According to Dimock,

Fuller has a different view, where the past, "[a]lways on the verge of oblivion, . . . [cries] out to be revived and, in that cry, [makes] of us obligated hearers."[31]

Dimock's reading might be questioned on two fronts. In *The Eighteenth Brumaire*, Marx may be skeptical about the role of the past in the present, but his critique is leveled at a specific relation: bourgeois revolutions' rhetorical appropriations of the past. By stating that the revolution of 1848 was a "parody" of 1789,[32] Marx is referencing the way a loss of revolutionary reality in the present is masked by donning the radical tropes and events of the past (past "ideals" and "art forms" aiding the "self-deceptions that they need in order to conceal . . . the bourgeois limitation of the content of their struggles"[33]). In this sense, true "proletarian revolutions" must shed this cover and come "from the future," which means that their "content goes beyond the phrase" and, as a consequence, they "criticize themselves constantly."[34] Many scholars, including those in the Frankfurt School, have shown that Marx often located this future in the past itself, where, to quote Adorno and Horkheimer, "[w]hat is at stake is not conservation of the past but the fulfillment of past hopes."[35] It is in this context that Marx argues for a *"ruthless criticism of all that exists,"* where "[i]t will become evident that it is not a question of drawing a great mental dividing line between past and future, but of *realizing* the thoughts of the past."[36]

This perspective on Marx clearly complicates Dimock's reading: where Marx proposes a dialectical relation between past and present instead of a one-dimensional diachronic orientation.[37] In what is a distinct twist of fate, this same failed 1848 revolution shaped France's decision to invade Fuller's republican Rome in 1849. But we should extend this critique to Dimock's commentary on Fuller as well. For Dimock, Fuller's present is linked inextricably to the past, but in a passive, one-directional communicative sense (as "obligated hearers"). If we look more closely at Fuller's early work, especially at her conception of the sistrum, a significantly more dynamic model of historical and political existence emerges.

"The Magic Sistrum . . ."

The joyful revolutionaries whom Fuller lauds in her aforementioned January 6, 1850 dispatch, revolutionaries "who may at last string the harp of the world to full concord,"[38] might not have realized that they were to take up an ancient and mystical instrument-weapon. Indeed, they were.

As Emerson notes in the collective memoirs Fuller's circle published shortly after her death, Fuller "chose the *Sistrum* for her emblem." He goes on to write, "And I know not how many verses and legends came recommended to her by this symbolism."[39] Although Fuller does not mention the sistrum in *Woman in the Nineteenth Century*, she includes in the book's appendix an excerpt from Thomas Taylor's translation of Apuleius's *The Metamorphosis, or Golden Ass* that provides a description of the goddess Isis and her rattle. The text portrays Isis emerging from the sea donning an ornate crown and a dark robe embroidered with glittering stars. Quoting from the appendix: "What she carried in her hands consisted of things of a very different nature. Her right hand bore a brazen rattle, through the lamina of which, bent like a belt, certain rods passing, produced a sharp triple sound through the vibrating motion of her arm."[40] Fuller's conceptual and political use of mythology, including her portrayal of Isis, the Egyptian goddess of fertility (here inflected through a Greek genealogy), is well-trodden scholarly ground.[41] I would like to argue, however, that this particular "brazen rattle" and its "sharp triple sound" has been overlooked by critics and historians, who tend to follow Emerson by treating the instrument and its effects as a mere literary trope.

In her aforementioned 1844 poem "Sistrum," Fuller describes the form and structural functions of Isis's rattle. The poem reads:

> Triune shaping restless power
> Life-flow from life's natal hour,
> No music chords are in thy sound
> By some thou'rt but a rattle found,
> Yet, without thy ceaseless motion
> To ice would turn their dead devotion.
> Life-flow of my natal hour
> I will not weary of thy power,
> Till, in the changes of thy sound,
> A chord, three parts distinct are found;
> I will faithfully move with thee,
> God-ordained, self-fed Energy
> Nature in Eternity.[42]

In the poem, the sistrum designates the material modality through which the poet orients her worldview. I use the term "orient" here as something of a socio-political pun, for the absent hand that moves the mechanism ("the vibrating motion of [Isis's] arm" in Taylor's translation) seems to be lingering at the edge of the page. In an unnamed poem written the same year as "Sistrum," Fuller describes Isis's cultural and conceptual passage from her previous iteration of Io, writing: "Io in Egyptian clime / Grows an Isis calm sublime."[43] And yet, Fuller had long been haunted by an Egyptian Other who, like the "restless power" of the sistrum, had anything but a calming effect on her. In an earlier journal entry (undated, 1835–1842), for example, Fuller recounts how upon falling asleep with one of her frequent migraines she "dreamt that the Egyptian, who has so often tormented me into the nervous headache, sat by my side and kept alluring a gigantic butterfly who was hovering near to rest upon her finger."[44] It is no stretch to read this female "Egyptian" as an associative form of Isis and the "hovering" butterfly by her hand as a sistrum-like energy. In the dream, the butterfly "flapped his crimson wings," left the Egyptian's hand, and "settled on the *left* side" of Fuller's forehead. As Fuller describes: "I tried in vain to drive him away; he plunged his feet, bristling with feelers, deeper and deeper into my forehead till my pain rose to agony."[45]

In "Sistrum," however, Fuller excises Isis altogether. As a consequence, the poem remains ambiguous about the rattle's locomotion, but it presents a clear dichotomy between the literal discord of the present and the harmony to come at some unnamed future moment (the production of a triadic "chord"). In one sense, therefore, the poem presents a typical Romantic longing for union with the Other. This is consistent with Fuller's writing from the era, which presents frequently similar fantasy scenes depicting the present historical world as somehow perfected and anointed through the agency of a spiritual realm. In a short poem from 1840, to cite just one example, she writes: "From this spirit land afar / All disturbing force shall flee, / Sin nor toil nor *hope*, shall mar / Its immortal unity."[46] From the perspective of this earlier poem, the message of "Sistrum" becomes a simple call for patience and faith.

But if one looks more closely at "Sistrum" alongside Fuller's other thoughts on the instrument, it becomes apparent that this lone "brazen rattle" may affect its own formative agency. In the unnamed 1844 poem where Fuller describes Isis's shift from Egyptian to Greek contexts, Isis is portrayed calmly donning her rattle amid the lowly masses: "The magic Sistrum arms her hand / And at her deep eye's command / Brutes are raised to thinking men / Soul growing to her soul filled ken."[47] The logic of future harmony evoked in "Sistrum" shifts here into an epistemological register, where Isis's perspective provides scaffolding for man's intellectual expanse. A similar schematic can be seen in her unpublished journals from 1841 where she writes, "I crave one all transforming thought to make them again living to men as intelligences acting upon nature."[48] Taking seriously the explicit capacity of this "transforming thought" to "[m]ake again living," we find a pivot for rethinking the concept of movement in Fuller's "Sistrum."

If we bracket the manifest call in "Sistrum" to wait for the arrival of eternity, just as the poem brackets the celestial hand that supposedly propels the rattle, we discern a secondary focus on the rattle as an object-instrument. The state of waiting for and desiring the ideal thus transmogrifies from a passive religious longing into an active and repetitive animation, and this movement is aligned elliptically with the "self-fed Energy" from "life's natal hour." Read in this way, "Sistrum" provides a scenario that is antithetical to the vision in the aforementioned 1840 poem where, with the arrival of the ideal, "[a]ll disturbing force[s] shall flee." It is now, in the now, the disturbing forces themselves that offer power.

The poem, of course, is rather vague about why the sistrum may generate such dissonant energies. One possibility is that the rods produce frequencies that fail to render a harmonic effect, perhaps composing a group of pitches that do not fall within the tonal parameters of a proportioned triadic chord. A more compelling scenario is that all three of the rods may produce the same pitch, thereby preventing the sistrum from creating the required tonal differentiation of two or more thirds. In either case, Fuller calls for a new intermediary increment or augment that might retune the poet's present. This is no small feat for Fuller, requiring something approximating Benjaminian divine violence within the symbolic "laws" of musical tonality.

And yet, because Fuller links this tonality to kinesthetic forces associated with the body, adding something of a material ontological component to Kant's belief that "attunement (*Stimmung*)" is the basis for aesthetic experience,[49] the stakes appear to be even higher. There is a long Western tradition of ideological fantasies that associate musical tone with metaphysical and material realities, including notions that modifying the basic tonal system might yield troubling results. For example, Elizabeth Eva Leach points out that fourteenth-century music theory (a precursor to the era of tonal music that Fuller was part of) had a difficult time thinking about the ratio-based mathematical need for smaller increments than tone within the octave. This smaller step became known as the semitone and was a useful contrapuntal element as the century progressed. Nonetheless, theorists in the era remained uneasy about its use. Johannes Boen, for instance, argued that "if there were an intermediate string" within the evenly divided monochord, "its sound would not constitute a degree compared with that of the other strings, since up to the present such as sound has not given pleasure, at least when produced by us, who stand by the diatonic genus (about the song or harmony of the heavenly bodies and angels or birds we do not know how to guess)."[50] We might see Fuller, coming from the opposite direction, toying with a similar structural difficulty in "Sistrum": calling for a new intermediary increment or augment that yields for earthly ears the "harmony of the heavenly bodies."

Focusing on the materiality of tonal configurations, we might consider more closely the ontic and ontological elements of attunement within Fuller's "Sistrum." In the present of the poem, the sistrum is not attuning one to the ideal realm (fantasy of Other) or to the reality of the poet (as evidenced by the fact that the poet must "faithfully move with thee"). Instead, it appears to connect the poet to a mysterious materialized realm that is at once beyond and within the poet. Although Fuller notes in an 1833 journal entry that her "mind is not to be influenced through the pores of [her] skin," here an animated sensual reality with uncanny connections to the body is clearly supposed to influence the poet on a number of registers.[51]

It is in this context that the modern psychoanalytic notion of the drive might be useful for examining the specific form and function of this strange mechanized energy. In discussing the historical development of Romantic-era music, contemporary scholars such as Slavoj Žižek have used the theoretical conception of the death drive to discuss a conceptual shift in the "ontological status of music."[52] According to Žižek, music in this era was no longer viewed as a mere accompaniment of a given message, but as bearing a "deeper" message of its own. Žižek suggests that in the nineteenth century, music generated encounters with the "Uncanny: no longer the external transcendence but, following Kant's transcendental turn, the excess of the Night at the very heart of the subject (the dimension of the Undead)."[53] This "undead," the "inaccessible excess" and "flux of *jouissance*" at the center of the subject, is, of course, the death drive.[54] Many scholars have noted the ways that Freud's speculative descriptions of the death drive are misleading. In 1920, Freud outlined a form of "ego-instinct" that is "beyond the pleasure principle" and associated with longing for a return to the "inorganic existence" of "death."[55] As Lee Edelman explains, however, the death drive should be thought of in more structural terms, constituting "the name for a force of mechanistic compulsion whose formal excess supersedes any end toward which it might seem to be aimed." Consequently, "the death drive refuses identity or the absolute privilege of any goal."[56] There is a significant difference, therefore, between desire and drive. A person becomes a "subject of the drive," when, in Todd McGowan's terms, "the subject experiences the path of desire as an end in itself rather than as way of seeking something beyond that path."[57]

This psychoanalytic notion of the drive, along with its other common qualities (the compulsion to repeat, the excessive and uncanny animation of materiality, and so on), provides a means to reconceive the structural relationships at play in Fuller's description of the sistrum as well as her other writing on related forms of energy. As Emerson wrote of Fuller, she "felt in herself a tide of life, which compared with the slow circulation of others as a torrent with a rill. She found no full expression of it but in music."[58] But Fuller did describe this torrent of sonic energy, or, to borrow Žižek's phrase, this "musical Thing" in other ways than through direct references to music.[59] For example, in a letter from the early 1840s to an unnamed friend, Fuller describes the "Daemonical" in a manner that clearly has stakes for the form of energy that she notes in "Sistrum" as well as her aforementioned descriptions of Niagara:

> It may be best understood, perhaps, by a symbol. As the sun shines from the serene heavens, dispelling noxious exhalations, and calling forth exquisite thoughts on the surface of the earth in the shape of shrub or flower, so gnomelike works the fire within the hidden caverns and secret veins of earth, fashioning existences which have a longer share in time, perhaps, because they are not immortal in thought. Love, beauty, wisdom, goodness are intelligent, but this power moves only to seize its prey. It is not necessarily either malignant or the reverse, but it has no scope beyond demonstrating its existence. When conscious, self-asserting, it becomes (as power working for its own sake, unwilling to acknowledge love for its superior, must) the devil. . . . Yet, while it is unconscious, it is not devilish, only daemonic. In nature, we trace it in all volcanic workings, in a boding position of lights, . . . in deceitful invitations of the water. . . . We speak of a mystery, a dread; we shudder, but we approach still nearer, and a part of our nature listens, sometimes answers to this influence, which if not indestructible, is at least indissolubly linked to the existence of matter.[60]

Fuller initially describes this force's "instinctive" quality using the symbol of "gnomelike . . . fire within the hidden caverns and the secret veins of earth." Literally grounding this agency and "work" within subterraneous caverns, Fuller evokes the structure of the sistrum and its attendant energy. Among Fuller's unpublished papers is a transcription of Thomas Taylor's translation of Plutarch's writing on Isis and Osiris. This includes a description of the sistrum where Plutarch suggests that the agitated parts of the instrument correspond to the four elements. According to Plutarch, there are only three rods because the fourth element, fire, is sublunary fire, a form of earthly fire that is a product of celestial fire, and, as such, its pure element is missing (incomplete within the earthly realm). As a result, this lower form of fire is located within the cavities of the other elements and, hence, within the instrument itself.[61]

Both daemonic fire's gnomelike "hidden" work and the sistrum's mechanized agitation are constituted, in part, via a material play between absence and presence, a relation that is foundational to the drive. Drawing from Edelman again: "[T]he death drive marks the excess embedded within the Symbolic through the loss, the Real loss, that the advent of the signifier effects."[62] Todd McGowan unpacks this process a bit, writing, "The signifier imposes itself on the subject as a cut on the body, and this detached body part becomes the libido, the source of the drive in the subject."[63] Because this lost body part can never be retrieved, the "drive continually returns to and repeats the experience of loss."[64] It is this direct relation to loss that pushes the drive into the aforementioned zone of "mechanized compulsion whose formal excess supersedes any end."

Throughout her passage on the daemonic, Fuller presents many examples of the material nature of this type of force. The "deceitful invitations of the water" and the mysterious power of "volcanic workings" elicit our "dread" even as, or perhaps because, part of us "answers to this influence." It is clear from the passage that such foreboding impressions arise because this all-too-familiar power is beyond the symbolic realm of "[l]ove, beauty, wisdom, goodness," moving "only to seize its prey." Of course, this force's association with the metaphoric hunt might place it squarely within the mode of traditional desire. But Fuller quickly adds, "[I]t has no scope beyond demonstrating its existence." Thus, its prey is less of a fantasmatic object of desire than a material means for repetitive self-generation. This is why Fuller suggests that this force is the "devil" when conscious and daemonic when unconscious—for it is quite literally beyond the scope of symbolic ethical concerns (being neither "malignant or the reverse"). Operating in a manner consonant with the death drive, this dissonant amoral force engenders, in Fuller's view, "fables of wizards, enchantresses, and the like," beings who are linked so closely to their sources of "power" that they are "scarcely good, yet not necessarily bad."[65] As Fuller explains, "They draw their skills from the dead, because their being is coeval with that of matter, and matter is the mother of death."[66] Indeed, in a passage evoking the sistrum, Fuller writes in her journal, "I have a great share of Typhon to the Osiris, wild rush and leap, blind force for the sake of force."[67]

In *Summer on the Lakes*, Fuller suggests that one of the reasons we respond to such a force is that it relates to our own bodies and experiences within earthly time. In the guise of "free hope," Fuller exclaims, "I would beat with the living heart of the world, and understand all the moods . . . of nature. I dare to trust to the interpreting spirit to bring me out all right at last."[68] The structural similarities between this declaration and the propositions voiced in "Sistrum" are quite apparent. Instead of the shuddering dread seen in Fuller's discussion of the daemonic, here, as well as in "Sistrum," we joyously close with the beating heart of the world—the physical symbol of the drive *par excellence*. The distinct difference in tone and tenor might be attributed to the fact that these latter encounters offer only a temporary alignment with this force. Consequently, the act of living on the planet with "hope" seems to demand a precarious and careful coalition with this amoral material force, where one becomes for a time what Fuller terms, in the context of Frederica Hauffe, a "nerve-spirit."[69]

"Sistrum" thus offers something of an ontological manifesto and, as I'll go on to argue in the following sections, a political-ontological manifesto. In bracketing Isis's trembling hand as well as the future moment when the ideal chord will transform existing reality, Fuller calls for an interlude in which one should, somehow, move with the force of the "brazen rattle," a force I have here associated with aspects of the drive. The result is a paradoxical, albeit sound (if one can forgive the pun), structure that might resemble the form of a *divested prayer*.[70] Fuller's proclivity for all varieties of mythological and metaphysical fantasies is well documented. And in her early writing, particularly, we see her taking the agency of Christian prayer quite seriously. In a journal entry from 1833, for example, Fuller records the following prayer: "Blessed Father, nip every foolish wish in blossom. Lead me *any way* to truth and goodness; but if it might be, I would not pass from idol to idol."[71] Even in this early Christian plea for heavenly grace, Fuller seems to open the door to various earthly means for spiritual ends, save, of course, for passing along a chain of inauthentic materialized religious fantasies. Even here we perhaps see the logic of the sistrum beginning to churn. Although Fuller elsewhere notes that part of her admiration for Goethe stems from his ongoing belief that "nature could not dispense with Immortality,"[72] a position that she admits gave her courage to contemplate the "subject of metaphysics,"[73] her writing in the early 1840s portrays her grappling progressively with not only the means ("any way") of intellectual and spiritual improvement, but also the experiences of the present—what we might call the *mean*time.[74]

"Sistrum" outlines a divested prayer in the way it keeps the structure of prayer—orienting oneself fantasmatically toward the coming ideal (here as chord)—but suspends this direct desire within a backwards move into the mysterious agency of the rattle's drive-like motion. Via the sistrum,

Fuller crafts a scenario whereby one has both the hope for a distant amorphous law within the realm of desire and the negative pulsive force of the excessive and the particular found in the drive. Perhaps this rather odd short circuit might be thought of as existing somewhere between desire (belief in the reparative agency of a lost object) and erotics (a mode, in Elizabeth Freeman's terms, that "traffics less in belief than in encounter, less in damaged wholes than in intersections of body parts").[75] The two foundational elements of time and distance will be crucial going forward in my analysis of the politics of being that results from this formation. From this perspective, Fuller's temporary embrace of the sistrum's movement can be seen as not only a bracketing of the future, but also a rejection of the present. As opposed to a Wordsworthian "spot of time,"[76] the renovating use of spatio-temporal memories, Fuller here literally feels backwards into an alternate material reality—opening herself to the non-now of the sistrum's energy.

As we will see, this movement has significant repercussions for Fuller's conceptions of social reality: both its discontents and its potentials. The following multipart section, "The Electric Sistrum," keeps "Sistrum" as a frame and develops a contextual consideration of two major related topics: electricity and music. These linked sections establish foundational aspects of Fuller's thought on materiality and historical forces, and they extend a consideration of the sistrum to *Woman in the Nineteenth Century* and Fuller's other writings. The final two sections, "Distributive Harmonies" and "The Magic Sistrum Arms Her Hand," pinpoint Fuller's unique structural logic with regard to material discord and harmonics, arguing that Fuller's weaponization of the sistrum's energies constitutes a unique and unacknowledged mode of historical agency.

The Electric Sistrum

In an 1841 *New-York Tribune* review of Anton Schindler's *The Life of Beethoven*, Fuller portrays her era as "vast, flowing, [and] of infinite promise." The middle term, "flowing," is soon explained in more detail: "It is dynamics that interest us now, and from electricity and music we borrow the best illustrations of what we know."[77] Because Fuller viewed her age as a historical moment marked by a "steady unfolding of certain thoughts," where burgeoning modes of science yielded "a perception of universal laws and causes" and the arts, especially music, were likewise "in a rapid state of development," standard positivist and symbolic models were inappropriate for the realities of a transformation that she both observed and desired.[78]

This is perhaps why the registers of electricity and music were so appealing to her. These physical modes, which share a relation to the material elements of frequency and energy and, as such, figure prominently in the era's developing scientific and spiritual fascination with the unknown, aptly represent the amorphous "dynamics" that Fuller had in mind, dynamics that are clearly at stake in her conception of the sistrum.

It is no wonder, therefore, that the link Fuller posits between electricity and music has clear historical precedents. The experiments that Thomas Young and Augustin-Jean Fresnel carried out between 1801 and 1827, for example, championed an undulatory theory of light, which viewed light as arising from vibrations and, in turn, was "based upon an analogy with sound."[79] A similar conception of energy currents informed Franz Anton Mesmer's development of magnetic *baquet* therapy (what become known as mesmerism, magnetic sleep, or simply animal magnetism). As scholars have noted, Mesmer was passionate about music, hosting a number of musicians in his family's mansion on the Danube, including a young Wolfgang Amadeus Mozart, who, in 1768, performed an opera, commissioned by Mesmer, titled *Bastien und Bastienne*. As Adam Crabtree explains, however, Mesmer's preoccupation with music "was as much medical as aesthetic." His doctoral dissertation assessed the "resonance of animal gravity in living things to musical harmony," and his clinics used music within the treatment process.[80]

Fuller had her own personal and professional associations with both the electric therapies of mesmerism and the various musical events in antebellum Boston and New York. In terms of mesmerism, Fuller had a longstanding fascination with the occult, and, as Deborah Manson notes, her specific interest in mesmerism developed between 1837 and 1845 when she sought treatments to relieve headaches and backaches stemming from spinal curvature. While living in New York in 1844, Fuller published a review of a book on mesmerism, began seeking mesmeric treatments from Theodore Leger in an office near her employer in the *Tribune* building, and attended a number of mesmeric events (which she dubbed "our new Ecstatica"). One such event at her friend James Clarke's home featured "*Mesmeric* experiments," as Fuller termed it in an invitation letter to Ralph Waldo Emerson, with the famous clairvoyant Anna Q. T. Parsons. (Emerson, being Emerson, declined the invitation.)[81]

Fuller's relation to music had even deeper roots. Although she was never a professional musician, Fuller had lifelong ties to music: practicing piano as part of her daily routine in her youth and, in the 1830s and 1840s, attending a myriad of musical events in Boston, New York, and Europe. The experience of listening to various oratorios, symphonies, and orchestral works as well as enjoying performances by touring musicians such as the German concert pianist Ludwig Rakemann, the English singer Joseph Phillip Knight, and the world-renowned Ole Bull and Henri Vieuxtemps had deep impacts on Fuller that went beyond mere artistic appreciation. In Boston, Fuller first heard Beethoven's work in its full presentation, including *"Adelaïde"* (Opus 46) and the complete symphonies. Beethoven's symphonies, especially, would remain Fuller's most cherished musical compositions, but in New York she encountered an even richer musical environment, with the respected Philharmonic Society of New York's orchestra drawing international talent. Amid New York's transatlantic musical scene, she was exposed to a vast catalogue of classical music, including works by Bellini, Berlioz, Mendelssohn, and Listz. As Ora Frishberg Saloman points out, these various experiences prompted Fuller to develop both aesthetic and social commentary on the musical scenes that she experienced; in all, she wrote seven pieces on music in the *Dial* between 1840 and 1844 and twenty-nine articles on the subject during her tenure as a reviewer for the *New-York Tribune*.[82]

Considering Fuller's writing on the related concepts of electrical energy and music thus offers a way to more completely conceive of the structural logic that undergirds the form of experience Fuller had begun to present in "Sistrum." The remainder of this section will take these topics in turn, illuminating the broader conceptual contours that give shape to Fuller's political vision in *Woman in the Nineteenth Century* and beyond.

Electricity

Although the 1844 poem "Sistrum" is ostensibly about the sound and motion of the instrument, Fuller links the drive-like "restless power" of the tool to both the "life-flow" of the poet's "natal hour" and an explicit type of "God-ordained, self-fed Energy." In the nineteenth century, there was a preponderance of discourses about energy qua electricity—many of which were, according to Justine Murison, "literal and material, not just metaphoric and descriptive." Despite the fact that a number of scientific inquiries studied observable occurrences of electric energy in nature (such as lightning), a varied notion of a more amorphous "electrical body" proliferated in the middle and later antebellum years that attempted to describe "a force within the body that was both invisible and material."[83] One might think of Whitman's "body electric" or Emerson's reference to Reason's fluid and transformative agencies. The sistrum's "power," "flow," and

"Energy," therefore, render the instrument, quite literally, an electrical one. In doing so, Fuller orchestrates a conceptual way to present, via a singular material modality, the tenuous and open ontological relations between self and Other as well as the spatial-temporal relations between here and there.

This very same electrical aspect circuits and, perhaps, short circuits through *Woman in the Nineteenth Century*. The book itself, evidenced by its initial polarized albeit positive reception, might be characterized in the same way that Fuller describes the self-fashioned persona of Miranda within its pages, evincing a "strong electric nature, which repelled those who did not belong to her, and attracted those who did" (262). In the book, Fuller directly links the potential radical and multifarious agency she saw in modern humans, and especially in women, to this electrical force. After counterpointing the "genius" of the poet, which is called upon in the creative act in lieu of a "god," to the "intellect," a "cold" faculty that is "ever more masculine than feminine," Fuller synthesizes dialectically the bifurcation by suggesting that the intellect, when "warmed by emotion, . . . rushes toward mother earth, and puts on the forms of beauty." This brings Fuller to a central aspect of her book's thesis: "The electrical, the magnetic element in woman has not been fairly brought out at any period" (302). Importantly, the place of "woman" "in" the nineteenth century is one of immense potential (affective, aesthetic, artistic, and political)—potential that is, on account of its electrical modality, trans-temporal but also directly linked to and shaped by, in a negative capacity, the specific delimiting ideological horizons of the moment.

To back up just a bit, Fuller does not present women's electrical functions as an exclusive property of gendered being per se. As the book's preface makes clear, the historical unfolding she envisions for the nineteenth century relates to "man" in general. In her own words: "By Man I mean both man and woman: these are two halves of one thought" (254). This logic gives rise to her now famous claim that the "great radical dualism" of man and woman is, in fact, a dynamic where both aspects are "perpetually passing into one another. . . . There is no wholly masculine man, no purely feminine woman" (310). But there is, in Fuller's view, a significant gendered difference in how people relate to and function in the world—especially in the ways they are oriented toward and by various categories of power.

Throughout *Woman*, Fuller uses a wide scope of examples and analogies—from Cassandra's plight in Greek drama to the contentious role of women in the French Revolution to the multifarious connections between the condition of women in the United States and the oppressed state of slaves—to present the historical and ideological suppression of women. Her focus, however, seems to be less on delineating a coherent genealogy of historical oppression (the causes of woman's current condition and propensities) and more on revealing how various historical realities are marked by a disjunctive relation between specific social conventions and the internal powers associated with women—the effects of this long-standing antagonism yielding, in the nineteenth century, a new possibility for recalibration and revolution. In Fuller's account, this variegated antagonism produces a distinctly "unhappy present" for women of her moment due to the fact that they often "see too much to act in conformity with those around them." And this disjuncture commonly leads to critical views about their mien or conduct (where "women's quick impulses seem folly to those who do not discern the motives") or a more general angst about their seemingly foreign powers (where "[t]hose, who seem overladen with electricity, frighten those around them"). Although Fuller plays with the simple materiality of such encounters, with women's electric nature at times yielding physical "*hérissé*," or the static bristling of body hair, in their male counterparts, the primary social conflicts engendered by this constitutional divide are shown to stem from concerns of hermeneutics, if not epistemology. As Fuller notes, the magnetic element present in women renders their "intuitions . . . more rapid and more correct." According to Fuller, "You will often see men of high intellect absolutely stupid in regard to atmospheric changes, the fine invisible links which connect the forms of life around them, while common women, if pure and modest, so that a vulgar self do not overshadow the mental eye, will seize and delineate these with unerring discrimination" (302). Women's relation to the electrical element thus affords the ability to discern vast networks of relation, causes and effects, which the myopic perspective of reified patriarchal society (personified here as a "vulgar self") naively overlooks or, as we will see, willingly ignores.

Under the term "Femality," a concept borrowed from two articles published in the *New-York Pathfinder*, Fuller develops her description of a woman's particular faculties of perception. According to Fuller, "The especial genius of woman I believe to be electrical in movement, intuitive in function, spiritual in tendency. She excels not so easily in classification, or re-creation, as in an instinctive seizure of causes, and a simple breathing out of what she receives that has the singleness of life, rather then the selecting and energizing of art" (309). A woman's function is, therefore, related to the modality of "flow" invoked in the "Sistrum" poem—for as Fuller goes on to note, "In so far as the soul is in her completely developed, all soul is the same; but as far as it is modified in her as woman, it flows, it breathes, it sings, rather than deposits soil, or finishes work" (309). Here Fuller describes a mode that, to modern readers at least, might better recall the twentieth-century French post-structuralist notion of *écriture féminine*, where language and perception don a bodily and excessive surplus that resists dominant symbolic structures, than a nineteenth-century transcendental-materialist fantasy. (Indeed, the rhizomatic logic of the Deleuzian conjunction "and . . . and . . . and" certainly approximates Fuller's notion of a breathing and singing that resists the predicative and phallic depositing of soil.)[84]

In this important sense, Fuller's notion of the flowing function of femality, which can be seen across her early works, should be viewed as an ideological modification of predominant nineteenth-century views about what Justine Murison terms the "open body." In her detailed account of the political stakes of "nervousness" and anxiety in the period, Murison portrays how nineteenth-century medicine viewed the body as a dynamic system that was in constant interaction with its environment, producing a materialist and psychological view of the nervous system. Prevailing terminology about nerves and nervousness included, according to Murison, discourses about "animal electricity" and mesmerism, concepts that "conflate[d] spirit and matter."[85] In *Woman in the Nineteenth Century*, Fuller not only wrests this discourse from conservative scientific commentators of the era, such as Caleb Cushing's claim in the *National Magazine and Republican Review* that female mesmeric experiences were the result of male influence (via the mesmeric "magnetizer") or "nervous diseases,"[86] she largely removes it from the realm of medical discourse all together. Although, as mentioned, Fuller notes and discusses mesmerism in the context of medicinal effects and rewards,[87] here and elsewhere she uses the concept of electrical functions to portray the tension-wrought relationship between women's particular and supernumerary functions of being or perceiving and society's delimiting social realities.

Examples of this type of social critique abound in Fuller's works. In her 1840 composition "Autobiographical Romance," for instance, she opens by praising her father's "sagacious energy," which was shaped by New England society, only to censure such institutionalized and patriarchal powers in her discussion of Greek literature. Recounting the hours she spent studying Greek language and culture (a topic Timothy Fuller had promoted with her since her youth), Fuller writes, "The force of feeling, which, under other circumstances, might have ripened thought, was turned to learn the thoughts of others. This was not a tame state, for the energies brought out by rapid acquisition gave glow enough. I thought with rapture of the all-accomplished man.... A Caesar seemed great enough. I did not then know that such men impoverished the treasury to build the palace."[88] So much for sagacious energy, it seems. Though yielding a potent "glow" of "energy," such modes, structured by existing imperial society, often diminish both public and private resources in the service of the powers that be.

At times Fuller appears to naturalize the relations and formations that surround femality, such as in an undated and unpublished journal entry where she writes:

> A year ago I wrote this in my journal
> I thought while the child is in the womb it grows to its perfect form, but breathes not yet. So soon as it emerges into freedom, its lungs begin to play, and it is a living body, an individual in its species. A little longer it grows and develops the organs of its mental being; they begin to play as it breathes in air from the great sea of soul, and becomes a living soul, (a person in the universe) the breath of life the breath of soul animate this being, working with harmonizing laws, till (after this stage has long enough endured) the body can no longer hold together and her soul disengages itself into the electric element.[89]

Although this idealist fantasy includes an important aspect of materialism, where the human body acts as a host, in a sense, for the creation of the soul via the simple act of breathing in air from the "great sea of soul," it departs from period Romantic-materialist notions of the topic that are more social in orientation, such as John Keats's conception that the world is a "vale of Soul-making," wherein the spirit is "created" and schooled via experiences and suffering on earth.[90] But the naturalized divide offered in Fuller's account, one that finds the soul coming into its own only after breaking with the outgrown biological platform of the body, is often reworked in Fuller's early writing, depicting a sociological import not necessarily found within Keats's vision. Here, Fuller suggests that the formation of the soul via interaction with "the electrical element" and a requisite break with a lower or previous reality might occur within historical time.

This historical dynamic is apparent in *Woman in the Nineteenth Century* when Fuller notes the anxiety that women's electrical affinity produces in prototypical men, imploring, "Yet, allow room enough, and the electric fluid will be found to invigorate and embellish, not destroy life" (302–3). Debunking common and erroneous accounts of the deleterious sources and effects of this power, Fuller suggests that it is not "the agency of one human being on another" (as with mesmerists) that allows a person to enter "the trance of Ecstatica," where one is essentially "*over*-flowed with thought"; instead, this state and its effects are "produced . . . direct[ly] from the spirit" (303). Consequently, Fuller suggests current illnesses and weaknesses (where women are "easy victims both of priest-craft and self delusion") stem from the fact that society has not allowed women's electrical nature to "invigorate" all of their faculties.

As Fuller shows in stark detail in her *Summer on the Lakes* account of the plight of Frederica Hauffe, where a young German woman descends into a "disembodied life" within a mesmeric spiritual state, the limiting effects of social pressures and expectations can have devastating results for some women (89). Certainly, according to Dr. K (the physician whose account Fuller draws upon), Hauffe had an "extreme irritability of the optic nerve," which, in his opinion, "was probably a sign of the development of the spiritual in the fleshy eye." Yet, as Fuller subtly presents, Hauffe's "electrical susceptibility" takes an extreme and unbalanced turn precisely when, in her nineteenth year, she was "betrothed to Herr H." (84).[91] Sinking into "dejection" (84) and confined within the domestic duties attendant to a wife, she "was obliged hourly to forsake her inner home, to provide for an outer, which did not correspond with it" (86). This imbalance leads Hauffe into a reactionary flight toward a "magnetic state" and an "excessive activity of the brain" (88–89). As Fuller argues, "She needed, not only a magnetizer, not only a love, an earnestness, an insight, such as scarce lies within the capacity of any man, but also what no mortal could bestow upon her, another heaven, other means of nourishment, other air than that of this earth" (93). For Fuller, therefore, Hauffe's inability to find tenable recourse for the social limits imposed upon her, or, put differently, her lack of available political utopian thought, leads her to a dejected fantasmatic state whereby the "ghosts she saw were projections of herself into objective reality" (94).

A superficial reading of this account of harmful imbalance might lead one to think that Fuller, in turn, desired a traditional notion of harmony—a term that was bandied about in the era's Romantic circles and that appears quite frequently in her various writing about electricity and music. Indeed, scholars often present Fuller's desire for social harmony as, in Steele's aforementioned argument, something of a standard contemporary liberal desire to "restore social harmony and justice,"[92] or, in the case of C. Michael Hurst's reading, a personal journey whereby the "maintenance of . . . intra- and interpersonal harmony" via "being brought back to the body," will yield "harmonious interrelation between individuals."[93] This latter view was a very real belief in the eighteenth and early nineteenth centuries across a number of discourses and ideological perspectives, establishing what James Delbourgo terms a reformist "electrical humanitarianism."[94] This hybrid mix of materialist and religious approaches to forming social programs can be seen, for instance, in Mesmer's establishment of the "Society of Harmony" or in the domestic theories promoted by Catharine Beecher's *Letters to the People on Health and Happiness* (1837), where the troublesome gap between the mind and the body created by domestic work is addressed via appeals to personal harmony. According to Lora Romero, Beecher "design[ed] her postpatriarchal pedagogy to heal this gap through the harmonious development of all of the faculties (an economy of the body)." Yet, as Romero shows, this program—with its roots in nineteenth-century discourses about female hysteria (where females' ills stem from a "disruption of the integrity of the animal economy")—is predicated upon a limited critical framework, thereby preventing thinkers like Beecher, and her sister Harriet Beecher Stowe for that matter, from conceiving of "the subject in any relation to the political."[95]

Although Fuller's work clearly intervenes within these discourses about harmony and electricity, it also carries on an eighteenth-century republican tradition where, in Delbourgo's terms, "Languages of electricity . . . became critical as a means of debating the agency behind enlightenment politics."[96] In other words, Fuller's thoughts about the harmony of electrified bodies often surpass common concerns with the personal, the bodily, and/or the metaphysical and, instead, implicate directly the deep structures of historical power that shape society. For Fuller, harmony becomes a dialectical category, a conceptual placeholder, where competing political, historical, and trans-temporal or atemporal emergent truths interfere with one another. This is why Fuller is able to name harmony as, in a sense, *the* limiting ideological impediment that women face at present. She writes, in an aforementioned passage in *Woman in the Nineteenth Century*, that women who "combine" the electrical element with "creative genius" face an "unhappy . . . present" because, quite simply, they "see too much." And this sight renders them unfit "because a harmony, an obvious order and self-restraining decorum, is most expected from [them]" (302). On the heels of this claim, however, Fuller offers a competing and utopian construction of harmony, where, if women's "intellect was developed in proportion to the other powers . . . [,] [t]hey would, then, have a regulator. . . ." She continues: "It is with just this hope, that we welcome every thing that tends to strengthen the fibre and develop the nature on more sides. When the intellect and affections are in harmony; when intellectual consciousness is calm and deep; inspiration will not be confounded with fancy" (303). While the former notion of a simple balance (where a developed intellect acts as a "regulator" of electrical impulses) reeks of conservative period fantasies à la Catharine Beecher, the latter emphasis on an attendant and related historical revolution (where "inspiration" would hold more import than the current category of "fancy" allows) should not be overlooked. In this scenario, the developed intellect's "regulation" would presumably work with and respond to a heightened level of electrical agency as opposed to merely negating it. As Fuller writes at the close of the paragraph, "Then, 'she who advances/With rapturous, lyrical glances,/Singing the song of the earth, singing/Its hymn to the Gods,'//will not be pitied, as a madwoman, nor shrunk from as unnatural" (303). Quite literally, then, Fuller's positive form of harmony occurs on the far side of a significant symbolic and cultural ideological shift, where the visions and the songs of an "unnatural" madwoman would be recognized as God-like heralds.

In this context, Fuller's notion of "ravishing harmony" takes on a new resonance. Earlier in *Woman*, she describes a desired state of harmony foretold by the drift of history. In this case, she imagines that if "every arbitrary barrier [was] thrown down" and women were afforded the same rights a men, then "we should see crystallizations more pure and of more various beauty." She goes on: "We believe the divine energy would pervade nature to a degree unknown in the history of former ages, and that no discordant collision, but a ravishing harmony of the spheres would ensue" (260). This passage aptly presents Fuller's structural vision of historical change. Although she is conspicuously vague about the modality that would force social barriers down, Fuller follows with the rich imagery of historical crystallization. Just as the ideal relationship between the sexes is a dynamic engagement where "they are perpetually passing into one another . . . [f]luid hardens to solid, solid rushes to fluid," for Fuller, history itself is a dialectical process of becoming in which new formations are born from the interaction of varying and competing parts (310).

Although the standard concept of polarity, which was pervasive in the work of Coleridge, Emerson, and Fuller's beloved Goethe, informs many aspects of Fuller's thought, her concept of ravishing harmony moves away from a logic of pairing, however fluid, and toward a more dynamically constructive notion of cathexis—where, using Julia Ward Howe's example, instead of a crystal forming a bifurcation of light, we get something like the formation within time of new conceptual and material crystallizations.[97] Such a move is not necessarily a radical departure from her Romantic antecedents—in Goethe's novel *Elective Affinities*, for example, he presents the way chemical affinities between various people might override and, hence disrupt, existing marital boundaries—but it does shift emphasis toward the way the reality of polarity might interact within a given historical horizon to create new social structures and new modes of being.

Fuller's focus on dialectical change can be seen in the journal she was writing while revising *Woman in the Nineteenth Century*. It was at this time that she developed the symbol found in the book's opening pages: two overlapping triangles, one dark and one light, surrounded by the *ouroboros* (a snake biting its own tail), and the entire edifice projecting light outward onto the page. The image undeniably presents the power generated by polarity's logic—a pictorial presentation of ravishing harmony as, in the terms of one of Fuller's recent biographers, "radiant unity."[98] But, following Fuller, this radiant unity should be seen to have significant historical effects. In her journal, she explains the image in poetic form:

> *Patient serpent, circle round*
> *Till in death they life is found,*
> *Double form of godly prime*
> *Holding the whole of thought in time,*
> *When the perfect two embrace,*
> *Male and female, black and white*
> *Soul is justified in space,*
> *Dark made fruitful by the light,*
> *And centered in the diamond Sun*
> *Time, eternity, are one.*[99]

Here we certainly see our share of polarity, but this interface is shown to create a sublime actualization. When the "perfect two embrace," "the whole of thought in time" transmigrates from the ideal realm into existing "space." The result is an event, in the Badiouian sense, where within spatial and historical reality "[t]ime [and] . . . eternity . . . are one."[100]

The previously mentioned *Pathfinder* article that Fuller sampled in order to develop her concept of femality is, therefore, not far off the mark when it calls women the "harmonizer of the vehement elements" (*Woman*, 309). It is just that Fuller radically pushes this concept of vehement elements outward from the body and its systems and into broader conditioning social and political networks. Just before she quotes the *Pathfinder*, Fuller writes, "For woman, if, by a sympathy as to outward condition she is led to aid the enfranchisement of the slave, must be no less so, by inward tendency, to favor measures which promise to bring the world more thoroughly and deeply into harmony with her nature" (309). We might say that Fuller, therefore, is calling for a new and reinvigorated Hauffe (turning

Hauffe on her head, as it were)—for a type of woman that can put pressure on infelicitous and unjust social structures in order to move them toward change. Consequently, if, as I have argued, ravishing harmony offers a model of historical intervention and interruption, then Fuller's subsequent calls to "[l]et her work as she will," "[l]et us have one creative energy, one incessant revelation," and "[l]et it take what form it will, and let us not bind it by the past to man or woman, black or white" should be taken with the full political import they deserve (311).

Music

The dynamics at stake in electricity's relation to bodily and social harmony are even more profoundly pronounced in Fuller's many writings on music. Here, the components and implications of "ravishing harmony" come to full form. As mentioned, in her review of Schindler's *The Life of Beethoven*, Fuller suggests that the medium of music was currently "in a rapid state of development," and, along with electricity, its formal relation to "dynamics" allowed it to "open up new realms of thought."[101] This sentiment stays fairly consistent across Fuller's entire writing life: where music, a "universal [medium]," represented "the divine Urania who, hallows, guides[,] and answers the thoughts of Man"; where Beethoven, a composer whom Fuller followed devoutly, was nothing less than a "god of modern music"; and where various sounds, tones, and pulsations explicitly and/or implicitly mediated her thinking about personal and social relationships.[102]

The sistrum is everywhere present in such moments in Fuller's writing, even in the most saccharine ruminations on celestial harmony. At the same time, Fuller's developed discussions about harmony, tonality, and sociality allow for a more complete understanding of her thinking and, therefore, her political imagination. It is important to note how Fuller's conception of harmony and its social effects take shape within the context of a historical shift within continental music and its criticism in the first half of the nineteenth century as well as Fuller's specific interactions with the developing musical scene in Boston and New York, especially through her role as an arts reporter for the *New-York Tribune*. For example, as Ora Frisberg Saloman points out, the renowned Romantic work of composers such as Beethoven occurs during an era that witnessed increasing interest in forming hybrid musical genres and forms, and this is especially apparent when one looks at the growth of "intermediate opera genres" in the 1820s and 1830s. Such compositions and productions, such as new genres like the *opera buffa*, *opéra comique*, and *comédie larmoyante*, "sought to mirror the diversity of human experience by mixing styles," especially by incorporating dramatic elements. According to Saloman, this new "juxtaposition of opposing styles" can be seen in works such as Hector Berlioz's *Benvenuto Cellini*, which aspires to enact Victor Hugo's theory of dramatic aesthetics, where, in Hugo's own words, "the harmony of opposites" was the best artistic representation of nature.[103]

The dramatic notion of a "harmony of opposites" might also stand in nicely for the diverse musical scene in Boston and New York in the 1830s and early 1840s. As Irving Lowens suggests, critics affiliated with the Transcendentalist movement published approximately 183 pieces on music in journals such as *The Dial* and, even more frequently, *The Harbinger*. Such critics included the influential John Sullivan Dwight, the professional musician Elam Ives, the sculptor and critic William Wetmore Story, the future assistant secretary of war Charles A. Dana, as well as a score of other amateur authorities such as Christopher P. Cranch, George W. Curtis, and Albert Brisbane.[104] According to Saloman, while Dwight strove to review musical works in what Fuller termed the "comprehensive" stage of judgment, judging works via their own technical laws, Fuller remained primarily at the border between the autobiographical and aesthetic levels of concern. Although she championed many aspects of the burgeoning musical arts, she was at times critical of the choices made by venues, "call[ing] it 'semi-barbarous' to mix different kinds of music for commercial gain and ask[ing] concert directors to arrange carefully the genres of music to be performed with attention to balance to be achieved."[105] Such concerns might recall the views of Fuller's aesthetic idol, Goethe, whose interest in the way an audience received a concert led him to stridently oppose a performative disruption of music, viewing it as a "disturbing secondary phenomenon."[106] Instead of viewing Fuller's criticism of venues' practices as a mere aesthetic lament, however, one should keep in mind that her aim on such occasions was often focused on reforming the physical and programming quality of concerts rather than on upholding standard aesthetic norms per se.[107]

Many of Fuller's materialist interests in music and its glorifying effects are evident in an 1845 *New-York Tribune* review of the virtuoso Norwegian violinist Ole Bull. In Ole Bull's hands, the "violin seems . . . a living companion, the counterpoint of himself." Here it is not the musical score that delights but rather the physicality of the playing, where simple balladic airs were "transfigured, made celestial, by the pure tone of his instrument." Fuller imagines that as Ole Bull plays, his "lyre answers him like a female friend—a bride!" And yet, as with her discussion of personal harmony and polarity, she locates this dualism within Ole Bull himself, suggesting that the instrument "is himself, but a second self." As one might expect, Fuller adds an essential final step to these mounting relations, where the interactions between the self and the material non-self of the instrument engender a dialectic of timely becoming or, at least, a potential break with and from the present: "[H]is gestures seem, oftentimes, to express that he listens for it, and that, if awakened by himself, he knows not, except in hope, what he shall awaken."[108]

Fuller moves quickly to the affective and indeed social ramifications of Ole Bull's music, reporting how, after hearing the concert in question, she was "thrown into a particular frame of mind and led to understand peculiar crises in life." She expounds upon the "nature" of this revelation by way of a poem that she wrote the night of the concert. The similarities between this poem and her verses about the sistrum are extremely telling. Here Fuller opens with a description of Ole Bull's playing that evokes Emerson's concept of "religious sentiment," as discussed in Chapter 1. The sounds of the violin act as a hopeful and rapturous bridge between the present world and the ideal realm: "It came,—the first high, heaven seeking strain!/I knew those monumental thoughts again,/When o'er the buried hopes of early days/Pure marble tablets I had hoped to raise." The second stanza moves to the quieted reality produced by the necessary failure of this first gesture, marked by a "second, sad, impassioned strain." According to Fuller, this desiring melancholic state soon "[yields] itself to fond delusions's tide" and "[curses] the hour ever it was born." Lastly, Fuller moves to the third option or, rather, to what is largely a placeholder for a third option: "But where is the *third*—O artist sad and wild,/O where is the strain, thou dear and ardent child,/That shows me how to rise from the abyss." And she closes with the impassioned apostrophic plea: "O God! at least the barren third restore/Without that one help I can bear no more."[109]

As in "Sistrum," the present in the concert-inspired verse is marked primarily by the absence of a "third" "strain" that might offer a direct connection to the celestial sphere and, in turn, raise the poet "from the abyss." Although the initial "high, heaven-seeking strain" might approach the type of harmony Fuller has in mind, evoking, as it does, romantic and youthful visions, it remains, in the end, foundationally incomplete. Where though, one might ask, is the pulsing energy of the sistrum? Indeed, in lieu of chordless "sound" of the sistrum, we get various modes of a "strain"—a unit of music associated with the production of melody. As Fuller notes in her article "Music in New York," melody is a distinct part harmony, acting as "the *heart* of music."[110] Consequently, although the raw "power" of the sistrum's repeated movement and tonality remain distinct from the two contexts of strain found in Fuller's Ole Bull piece, there are important similarities, especially if one considers that a strain is often repeated in order to construct melody and is here associated with the pulsing organ of the heart.

The two poems, however, appear to differ significantly with respect to the emotional effects of generated sounds: "Sistrum" finding solace in moving with the tones offered here and now and the Ole Bull piece closing with a desperation that borders on crisis. I would like to suggest that what we find in the Ole Bull verse is a reflection on the potential material and historical consequences of faithfully moving, as Fuller puts it, with the sistrum. In "Sistrum," the poet remains contented within what I have called the movement of a divested prayer, but it also leaves off there. What happens in the "particular" room, in the "particular" town, in the "particular" region where this movement occurs? In other words, although the subjectivity of the poet in Ole Bull reaches a breaking point in terms of being able to endure the present state of things, what if the state of things in "Sistrum" might be feeling a similar strain (pun intended)?

Fuller explores the lived consequences of these themes in her discussion of Thomas Crawford's statue *Orpheus and Cerberus* in *Woman in the Nineteenth Century*, a statue Fuller viewed after the Boston Athenaeum purchased it in 1840. As in her Ole Bull poem, Fuller references the alienated state of U.S. society by suggesting that although Americans popularly used the adjective "Orphics" to describe their writing, they have largely failed to develop a "musical apprehension of the progress of nature." As such, the "strain" of Americans' work is not "warmed by the fire which fertilized the soil of Greece." In Fuller's hands, therefore, Orpheus becomes an apt "desired image" for a progressive era that is not yet fully conscious of its own potential. As she explains, Orpheus was a "law-giver by theocratic commission" who "understood nature" and "made [it] move to his music." As opposed to the undulating patience of "Sistrum" and the strained desire of the Ole Bull poem, here Orpheus himself is able to move the earth with his music—his "faith in the power of the celestial harmony that filled his soul" radically crowding out fear of "death [and] hell" (250–51).

But it is the self-authored poem about Orpheus that Fuller inserts into her discussion that perhaps best outlines the musical-social ideal fantasy that she had in mind:

> Each Orpheus must to the depths descend,
> For only thus the Poet can be wise,
> Must make the sad Persephone his friend,

> And buried love to second life arise;
>   Again his love must lose through too much love,
> Must lose his life by living life too true,
>   For what he sought below is passed above,
> Already done is all that he would do;
>   Must tune all being with his single lyre,
> Must melt all rocks free from their primal pain,
>   Must search all nature with his one soul's fire,
> Must bind anew all forms in heavenly chain.
>   If he already sees what he must do,
> Well may he shade his eyes from the far-shining view. (252)

In the poem, Orpheus's ability to "move" nature is grounded in a specific historical context. According to the opening lines, this potential movement is predicated upon a requisite break with the present: physically, by literally descending; symbolically, by befriending an other (and perhaps Other) of the likes of Persephone; and socially, having to "lose his life" or, rather, his previous life above. Only then does Fuller move to the topic of tuning, describing the effects of Orpheus's lyre as a twofold process—where a necessary negative move of "melt[ing] all rocks free" is followed by "[binding] anew all forms in heavenly chain," which clearly entails a positive bridging of the previous gap between social reality and ideal truths.

This is, of course, the ideal moment that the poet of "Sistrum" awaits and what ravishing harmony anticipates. And yet, the poem stays true to its source by figuring these radical modes of tuning as future potentials—for the scene, mirroring Crawford's statue, depicts Orpheus just after lulling the fierce Cerberus, guardian of the underworld's entrance, to sleep and shading his eyes, in Thomas Crawford's own words, "as if to gather together the little light" that remains as he descends.[111] What are we to make of the fact that this heroic act will, here, fail? That Orpheus will, as we know, turn back and lose Eurydice? I suggest that Fuller recasts the ideal double act of Orphic tuning and binding. Strictly following the scene, the act of tuning becomes a downward movement into the body of the earth and into enemy territory. Here, Orpheus's celestial music interrupts and interferes, in a sense, within the coordinates of his present, coaxing Cerberus to sleep and arming him on his descent. But it never quite wins out. Indeed, rocks remain rocks, impossible walls between Eurydice and any potential rebirth within earthly time.

The broader thematics of this reading are borne out in Fuller's next paragraph, where she modifies the Orphic scene by arguing, "[T]he time has come when Eurydice is to call for an Orpheus, rather than an Orpheus for Eurydice: that the idea of Man, however imperfectly brought out, has been far more so than that of Woman, that she, the other half of the same thought, the other chamber of the heart of life, needs now to take her turn in the *full pulsation*...." (252, emphasis mine).[112] In this context, the poem's terminus in future failure does indeed act to emphasize, perhaps even bracket, the way Orpheus's powers function within the process of attempted tuning—powers that manifest most directly as historical and social agitation (literally and figuratively). Unlike the anxiety found in "Sistrum" and the Ole Bull verse, where the poet longs for a missing tonal/social harmonic, Fuller's discussion of Orpheus points to the irreparable need for sistrumatic energy, here "full pulsation," within the existing social body. By reversing the directionality and gendering of the Orpheus mythic scene, Fuller locates the originary pulsive force, a force linked to and moving toward complete harmony, as the action of agitation and antagonism within the present, within the darkness of the underworld, and within women. Indeed, according to *Woman in the Nineteenth Century*, the time of the sistrum had arrived.

Distributive Harmonies

A consideration of Fuller's various notions of electricity and music begins to establish an important structural element of her social conception of harmony: that there is an immanent and physical link between the ideal realm of harmony and the present historical experience of various pulsations. The final two sections of this chapter examine the significant ramifications of this foundational relation in Fuller's thought. As I will show, these earthly pulsations (ranging from bodily energies to Beethoven's symphonies) are a distributive effect of distant forms of harmony. Furthermore, because these earthly pulsive effects are linked directly to harmony, they have a charged, even ethical, relation to the present—where they not only, on a zero-level, agitate the current imperfect state of both the body and the body politic, but also implicitly and explicitly push toward requisite socio-political change.

If, as I have suggested, Fuller's notion of ravishing harmony turns the over-charged and excessively spiritual Frederica Hauffe on her head, it is not merely because Fuller's variety of agitation occurs within the timely sphere of social reality. It is also because, for Fuller, there is a direct material link between the ideal (at times spiritual) realm where pure harmony purportedly resides and the various pulsations that are felt and heard in the present. Fuller describes this link in manifold ways across many of her texts. Her aforementioned claim, repeated on a number of occasions, that music is the highest and still developing medium for expressing the rapidly advancing historical progress of her age aptly hints at this connection. Her beloved Beethoven becomes something of an Ur-figure for this relation, standing at the vanguard of the material-symbolic human experience of the ideal. In her view, Beethoven "is felt, because he expresses, in full tones, the thoughts that lie at the heart of our own existence, though we have not found means even to stammer them as yet."[113] Here, Fuller creates something of a hermeneutic sensorium that stretches out across a continuum. On one side, we "feel" Beethoven's "full tones" but are unable to ideate this experience within the given formations of meaning. On the other lies Beethoven's music itself, and although such tones are not directly said to represent or, more accurately perhaps, align with the form of ideal harmony, Fuller certainly appears to suggest that they approach this reality.

This same logical schematic appears in Fuller's earlier romance "The Magnolia of Lake Pontchartrain," when the narrator's experience of encountering the god-like Magnolia, the "Queen of the South," is nothing less than a "revelation." Invoking *avant la lettre* her description of the effects rendered by Beethoven, Fuller describes how, upon encountering the flower, she "stood astonished as might a lover of music, who after hearing in all his youth only the harp or the bugle, should be saluted on entering some vast cathedral by the full peal of its organ." According to the Magnolia, however, this music can only be heard by the narrator; this is why the flower dwells alone, unable to "unite [her] voice with theirs in the forest choir."[114] Indeed, across a number of disparate writings about music, Fuller describes scenes where the historical and ideological terrain of the present shapes popular approaches to hearing and feeling harmonic elements, including the rather troubling racial and national hierarchies she uses in "The Celestial Empire," which juxtaposes Chinese music, marked by a "narrowest monotony" and constituting "nothing like anything else in the heavens or on the earth," with the "nightingale" tones of Ole Bull, tones that apparently fail to move a Chinese juggler in attendance because of an "Imperial Edict."[115] In all of these cases, there is a variegated divide between the material expressions of harmony and its potential ideal(s). As Fuller suggests in her journal, "not always do those who most devoutly long for the Infinite know best how to modulate their finite into a fair passage of the eternal Harmony."[116]

This lowly state, where society cannot or will not hear the tones of the absolute in the present (where, in Fuller terms, "oftentimes those who had ears heard not"), paradoxically, for Fuller, engenders the very need for music itself. That is, Fuller often frames this disjuncture between semblances of ideal harmony and its manifestations amid the crowd in hopeful terms—such as in her early "Mystical Experiences" reflections, where she recounts how she "would listen to the music of earth then raise [her head] and look straight into the secrets of the heaven."[117] This fantasy has all of the trappings of a familiar Romantic mysticism. Recalling Emerson's famous postulate in *Nature* that the "axis of vision," shaped by the realm of the Reason, remains non-identical to the "axis of things," our current perception of reality, Fuller appears to describe Reason's triumph via earthly music's ability to yield direct knowledge of the ideal.[118] Nonetheless, Fuller has a very different scenario in mind. As Emerson himself attests, Fuller "craved a larger atmosphere than [she] found; as if she were ill-timed and mis-mated." He goes on to suggest that she, as quoted earlier, "felt in herself a tide of life, which compared with the slow circulation of others as a torrent with a rill. She found not full expression of it but in music. Beethoven's symphony was the only right thing the city of the Puritans had for her."[119] Instead of an Emersonian distinction between self and Other that is internalized within the modalities of the self, Fuller is in discord (literally) due to the "ill-timed" (that is, misplaced) coordinates of social reality. It is thus apt that Emerson calls Beethoven's music the right "thing" for Fuller. In his own discussion of Beethoven's late works, Theodor Adorno argues that they "show none of that harmony which the classicist aesthetic is accustomed to demanding. . . . [T]he formal law of the late works . . . is such that they are not fulfilled in the concept of expression." He continues, "Beethoven's last works contain highly 'expressionless,' distant formations."[120] For Fuller, however, our experience of these expressionless compositions (causing us to merely "stammer") is shaped by the fact that we, ourselves, are the distant formation.[121]

Pushing the Swedenborgian (and hence Emersonian) model of correspondence more firmly into the material realm, Fuller imagines, in pieces such as "Yuca Filamentosa," that "the correspondence between the various parts of this universe are so perfect, that the ear, once accustomed to detect them, is always on the watch for an echo."[122] This "perfect" correspondence, one that sends echoes between the two positions, should thus be seen as something like a transversal linking various distant planes of reality. In an 1841 poem, Fuller allegorizes this spatial and temporal divide, telling of a band of "pilgrim angels" who were, it seems, accidentally pushed from a full and ideal world when they were drawn into a "wild cleft" that brought them downward through dark caverns. Lost in this lower world, Melodia was most affected by the change in environment. Playing on the poem's earlier thematic of the loss of the ideal, she laments, "Oh lyre once strung, how canst thou fail a note?" The failed note is the seemingly impossible loss of a full harmonic sound, one that was and is presumably still strung within the original world above. Such a concept of failure might productively revise the common mythical trope of mere loss. Instead of the total absence of ideal harmony, Fuller presents a modified, or, rather, stymied tonality, one that might remain latent within the existing composition of failure—if, that is, one has the correct perspective on totality. For Melodia, the initial effect of this failed note was an alteration to the "strain" of her "full-voiced . . . song," "[f]or the key-note was placed in other spheres / Whose echo her soul knew, but her ear missed." These other spheres, however, are soon shown to be materially linked to this lower world: "[L]o! a note sent back, vibration felt, / Startled her soul to sudden revelation, / And near her stood angel and her friend, / Receptive, bounteous, radiant, and profound."[123] In what might be something of ravishing harmony's Genesis 1:1, Fuller thus unequivocally posits that felt vibrations are the material echoes of distant harmony.[124]

For Fuller, therefore, it is as if two seemingly distinct planes (ideal harmony and earthly life) are linked across time/space via an indeterminate transversal. Creating a material tie between distant harmony and present discord, Fuller shifts the difference between the negative present and the utopian future from merely a quantitative impasse (one reality versus another) into a qualitative one (one discontinuous or, perhaps, divided reality). In other words, she dialectically shifts this gap, if you will, so that discord is not simply an absence of harmony tout court, but is harmony itself within the unharmonious conditions of the present.[125] Consequently, Fuller's material and spatial thinking should be set apart from Coleridge's strict division, in his *Specimens of the Table-Talk* (1835), between the effects of harmonic chords on sand, which form "geometric figures," and the sound of discord, which, in the same setting, produces movement "without any order at all."[126] In lieu of Coleridge's bifurcation between harmony and discord, a bifurcation also imposed by other U.S. writers considering the social effects of transcendental materialism, Fuller presents discord, itself, as a displaced effect of distant ideal forms.[127] In a sense, Fuller's view fills out fantasmatically the aforementioned sistrumatic functions of the drive: where the drive is a powerful and pulsive force precisely because it is a refracted manifestation of harmony, and this refraction is a byproduct of the limited and, indeed, negative horizons of specific historical and social formations.[128]

In these terms, Fuller's views on the materiality of harmony are quite relevant for various forms of speculative and vital materialism in contemporary criticism, critical perspectives that are increasingly being brought to bear on Romantic-era thinkers. In some ways, it is as if Fuller offers an earlier competing structural model to the one found in Timothy Morton's *Hyperobjects: Philosophy and Ecology After the End of the World* (2013). With Morton, vast and retreating formations, perhaps best characterized by the example of global warming itself, are at once all over us and our world (hence their "viscosity" in his terms) but imponderably large. In this positive model (one that, in essence, ontologizes a structural form of Kant's noumena or Lacan's Real via expansive historical-material objects), reality is recast productively as an "age of asymmetry," where "weirdness resides on the side of objects themselves, not our interpretation of them." Morton's position indeed shares with Fuller's a potential hermeneutic or, at least, affective link (via "perverse aestheticization," for example, such as in forms of "paramusic") between the human and the vast material objects that now shape our world. As opposed to Fuller's dialectical model, however, where the vast and palpably present material-ideal realm is conceived of in terms of difference (non-identical to existing social and perceptual horizons), Morton flattens out this difference by way of casting it as a by-product of our limited scale of perception. This move has significant political effects. Whereas Fuller's Romantic-era position holds that the experience of asymmetry yields a potential drive-like disruption of existing social structures, Morton's contemporary OOO-inflected perspective leads to an ambiguous and potentially static political reality within what he terms "*a charnel ground*."[129]

A similar dichotomy is found when one thinks of Fuller's schema in terms of Jane Bennett's model of vibrant matter. Invoking Spinoza's "conative, encounter-prone body" that "arises in the context of an ontological vision according to which all things are 'modes' of a common substance," Bennett offers an interesting take on the "agency of assemblages." In this Latourian riff on the vast electrical grids that crisscross the country, Bennett gestures toward a type of distributive assemblage that absorbs causality into a network or "heterogeneous field" rather than a "localized" site. Thus, like Morton but in a very different context, Bennett recasts human experience within a wide field of varying and related actants, which, in the end, complicates any notion of causality. Ultimately, her laudable effort to move ecological thinking past fantasies of environmentalism leads to a mode of political stagnation similar to that found in Morton's work, albeit from the opposite emotive direction. Instead of an unnerving encounter with the uncanny valley, as seen in Morton, Bennett calls for a Romantic openness to the universe. As Bennett writes, "I believe that encounters with lively matter can chasten my fantasies of human mastery, highlight the common materiality of all that is, expose a wider distribution of agency, and reshape the self and its interests."[130]

In terms of nineteenth-century thought, Bennett's model of vibrant materialism appears to inform Branka Arsić's reading of Thoreau's materialist views on sonic and musical reality. Although I will address these contemporary materialist models in relation to Thoreau's political thought in the next chapter, I introduce them here in order to set the stage, however sparely, for further defining the conceptual and political significance of Fuller's unique view of social harmonics. In discussing Thoreau's aim of experiencing a "pure materiality," Arsić suggests that Thoreau saw "matter [as] permeated by sonorous motions." Consequently, "[i]n Thoreau's ontology, *vibrant sound*, as the force of rendering corporeality, was thus elevated to something having the status of a being."[131] In this fascinating line of reading, Thoreau seeks to avoid all forms of ideation, and, hence, encourages one to "become deaf to harmony." Instead of chasing after fantasies of essences (distant or otherwise), Thoreau, in Arsić's view, perceives value as "'intrinsic to sound itself."[132] Arsić's version of Thoreau's thinking about music, however, is directly predicated upon both Philippe Lacoue-Labarthe's and Theodor Adorno's notions of *musica ficta* and, as such, moves quickly to the political sphere. According to Arsić, "The clear ear is de-sublimated by perceiving incoherent, ragged dissonance that cannot effect the political aestheticization of the subject's sensibility, that does not produce individuals fashioned by passions that overwhelm them, or masses exalted by the superhuman sublime." Thoreau thus becomes something of an anti-Fuller, in the terms I have presented: a peaceful and secular purveyor of modern liberal tolerance. Following implicitly Lacoue-Labarthe's censure of Wagner's supposed musical fascism and Adorno's criticism of Hegel's purported totalizing dialectic, Arsić casts Thoreau as a thoroughgoing anti-Wagnerian, where his decentered, non-ideational variety of sonic experience promotes a form of "'true bravery' . . . [that] consists in refraining from those 'resolute actions' through which one rather imposes a harmonious community of the soul."[133]

As opposed to the ontological and vibrant perspectives on materialism offered in Morton and Bennett as well as the Thoreauvian call for sonic liberal humanism we see in Arsić, Fuller creates a material-idealist model that unites the realm of the spheres with earthly materialism in a manner that agitates existing social coordinates.[134] In this context, Fuller's occasional references to a traditional idealist and top-down model for social and historical change, such as the 1844 poem where she recounts a dream where "the key-note of the special strain/Which must reveal the entire harmony" appeared to her,[135] are quite misleading. Instead, as she suggests in a journal fragment, "Man should be the key note to the universal harmony."[136] As with the case of Orpheus, this process begins with the "pulsations" felt here and now, where, as Fuller describes it in an 1840 journal entry, her own presence "fills [men] till they vibrate."[137]

"The Magic Sistrum Arms Her Hand"

Fuller's reference to vibrating men indicates once again that her conception of radical pulsations is far from the type of antirelationist energy offered in Edelman's contemporary notion of drive. Although Fuller's work takes up similar aspects of a negative extra-symbolic and extra-bodily energy, if we were to follow the future's arc of the archival grain, to twist Ann Laura Stoler's phrase, we might instead see Fuller's model (with all relevant caveats) more closely aligned with José Esteban Muñoz's constructive postulate of queerness as a future-oriented utopian ideality. For Muñoz, queerness "is not yet here," but "we can feel it as the warm illumination of a horizon imbued with potentiality." Queerness is thus a "desiring that allows us to see and feel beyond the quagmire of the present."[138] Within Dimock's planetary field, Fuller's nineteenth-century thought might thus present something of its own variety of ravishing harmony between the likes of Edelman and Muñoz: a form of negative energy and critique that is ineluctably linked, down to its materialized affective components, to a broader utopian and teleological movement. In this way, Fuller seems to share Paolo Virno's optimistic fantasy of positive negativity, where there is, quoting Muñoz on Virno, "a potentiality in negative affects that can be reshaped by negation and made to work in the service of enacting a mode of critical possibility."[139] As seen in Fuller's Orpheus adaptation, the lyre has both negative and positive movements, and these effects circuit back through and from the impasses and failure produced by imposed sociopolitical formations. This is because unlike the elegant materialist dialectic posited by Muñoz and Virno (where, much like certain strains of Marxism, a backward glance engenders a future vision), Fuller's future is at once now *and* not yet here. That is to say, for Fuller, we are already walking upon the groundwork of the future, for the echoes of a distant harmony move us at present and, somehow, propel us in a grand romantic-materialist circuit forward. And yet, there is tension and antagonism here. As seen in this section's title, a line borrowed from her early poem on Isis, Fuller imagined the sistrum as not only a "brazen rattle" but also as a weapon. In this sense, the vast material circuits linking historical time and ideal formations pass though and agitate very real living bodies within very real social structures.

From this perspective on Fuller's work, *Woman in the Nineteenth Century* takes the form of a referential weave of various political references (historical and mythological) as opposed to an abstract song of some orphic bard. In *Woman*, Fuller praises the blood letting during the French Revolution, that "strangely disguised angel," precisely because citoye*nne* was born via the broken necks of politicized women (252–53). This birth of a new universal through the bodies of particular women accords with Fuller's earlier idolization of the Roman character, where "[o]ne wants no universal truths from him, no philosophy, no creation, but only his life, his Roman life felt in every pulse."[140]

For Fuller, these localized pulsations have an immense fetch and, consequently, serious effects. After citing the fact that a "new manifestation is at hand," for instance, she moves quickly to a passage from Louis Claude de Saint-Martin that acts as a direct call for revolution: "The ministry of man implies . . . that he must be filled from the divine fountains which are being engendered through all eternity, so that, at the mere name of his master, he may be able to cast all his enemies into the abyss; that he may deliver all parts of nature from the barriers that imprison them; that he may purge the terrestrial atmosphere from the poisons that infect it" (*Woman*, 250–51). The reason this passage is, for Fuller, a "[strain] of prophecy" that "is not yet outgrown" is perhaps because St. Martin's 1802 text stems from the same historical horizon as her own—the same systems and logics of domination. Thus, pages later, after gesturing to an abstract moment to come when "all will have entered upon the liberty of law, and the harmony of common growth," Fuller states the crux of the matter: "It is . . . only in the present crisis that the preference is given to Minerva" (311). Just before this passage, Fuller presents Minerva (along with Vesta and Mars) as depicting primarily a "defensive" "animating power." Given the goddess's association with war and, according to Plutarch, Isis herself (and thus the sistrum), this defense is markedly and aggressively re*active*.[141] Fuller quite obviously had this context in mind when she penned "The Great Lawsuit" (1843) line: "New individualities shall be developed in the actual world, which shall advance upon it as gently as the figures come out upon his [Goethe's] canvass."[142] Her notion of advancing "gently" should not be read as simply advancing "peacefully," but, rather, as approaching and addressing the world easily or, perhaps, naturally—for although these figures may wreak havoc amid existing social and political coordinates, they are shaped by utopian possibilities and forces found within material historical reality itself.

Throughout *Woman in the Nineteenth Century*, this notion of the truth being "acted out," which includes the process of "love passing into life," is associated unabashedly with acts of violence shaped by militant fortitude (248, 254).[143] Fuller includes a catalogue of fighting women who forcefully interrupt or, in Fuller's term, "break through" existing delimiting sociopolitical barriers: from the Countess Emily Plater ("the heroine of the last revolution in Poland") to the Maid of Orleans (Joan of Arc) to Elizabeth I's "wide energetic life" and "courageous death" (265, 277). These figures had the ability to actualize, as Fuller puts it, "the birthright of every being," which is the "freedom, the religious, the intellectual freedom of the universe to use its means" (276). Due to this structural necessity of thinking the ideal in terms of a given negative historical terrain, Fuller often grounds her various abstract or aesthetic discussions of harmonic emancipation within specific populations and examples. This includes, of course, the timely cause of abolitionism, one of the primary "symptoms of the times" that links the plight of white women to southern slaves, as well as the recent annexation of Texas (275).[144] Fuller's thoughts on Texas aptly portray the historically loaded stakes of her grand vision. She writes, "[L]ast week brought news which threatens that a cause identical with the enfranchisement of Jews, Irish, women, ay, and of Americans in general, too, is in danger, for the choice of the people threatens to rivet the chains of slavery and the leprosy of sin permanently on this nation, through the annexation of Texas!" And she continues: "Ah! if this should take place, who will dare again to feel the throb of the heavenly hope, as to the destiny of this country?" For Fuller, the "throb of heavenly hope" is significantly threatened within the present, a present that is shaped on the national scale. Put differently, the "progress of history," as she terms it shortly after, is at risk due to specific nationalized and global forces linked to the institution of slavery. Thus, toward the close of the book, she incites her readers with a culminating localized (cosmically speaking) injunction: "Do you not feel within you that which can reprove them, which can check, which can convince them?" Indeed, she implores, "This cause is your own" (341).

Toward the close of the book, Fuller associates this tendency to be moved by ideal forces working within history, to be agitated and thus to agitate, with the youth of her era. "At present I look to the young," she claims, "[i]n place of an oath they should have a religious faith in the capacity of man for virtue; instead of a badge, should wear in the heart a firm resolve not to stop short of the destiny promised him as a son of God. Their service should be action...." And the name she gives to this movement, in a double sense, is that of "Los Exaltados," to which she affixes her own term: "Las Exaltadas." The "party abroad" that she references was a liberal coalition in Spain that struggled with Ferdinand VII after 1814 over his reluctance to uphold the Republican-inspired Constitution of 1812 and which came to power briefly in the early 1820s (333–34).[145] The specific history of this Spanish conflict, however, seems less important to Fuller than the name of the political party itself: connoting both "exalted" but also "over-excited," "excitable," and/or "extreme."

For Fuller, Las Exaltadas is surely the sistrum's collective: a party of the present for the future. As Fuller states emphatically at the close of *Woman in the Nineteenth Century*, this movement is at once personal and impersonal, timely and untimely, historical and cosmic. "I must beat my own pulse true in the heart of the world," she claims, "for *that* is virtue, excellence, health" (348). These pronouncements ring out in Fuller's subsequent *Tribune* pieces and other writings from revolutionary Italy. In her aforementioned last dispatch, titled "The Next Revolution" and written from a defeated Florence in January 1850, Fuller recounts the dark days of counter-revolutionary regimes, where "the worst men are in power, and the best betrayed and exiled." But she sounds a defiant and positive note amid the rubble: "[T]he struggle that is now to begin will be fearful, but even from the first hours not doubtful. Bodies rotten and trembling cannot long contend with swelling life." After evoking "Emmanuel," a term that Fuller uses, no doubt, in order to yolk the concept of messiah to socialist and republican revolutions via the act of prophecy (for the prophet Isaiah tells King Ahaz that the "Lord himself shall give [him] a sign" in the form of the virgin birth of "Immanuel"), Fuller pens a biting charge against specific adversaries: "Do you laugh, Roman Cardinal, as you shut the prison-door on woman weeping for her son martyred in the cause of his country? Do you laugh, Austrian officer, as you drill the Hungarian and Lombard youth to tremble at your baton? Soon you, all of you, shall '*believe* and tremble.'"[146] Here, it seems, pulsations do march in the streets after all.

What would it mean to think of Fuller not as a liberal-democratic heroine descending, with child in arms, into the stormy sea before she could see her dreams bear fruit in our distant neoliberal world but as, instead, emerging from it, donning a dark robe shot through with glittering stars and brandishing, in her right hand, her own brazen rattle?

PART II

Illiberal Ecologies

CHAPTER 3

Thoreau's Militant Vegetables

> We seem to lead our human lives amid a concentric system of worlds of realm on realm, close bordering on each other.
>
> —HENRY DAVID THOREAU, *Journal*, Volume 2

> Both the river and its banks are moving.
>
> —SUSAN BRIANTE, *The Market Wonders*

Both the river and its banks are moving. It's a line Thoreau might have liked. Not just because the Concord and Merrimack Rivers ran through his memory for years after his beloved brother John's death or because of the fact that rivers, themselves, were for him "a piece of wonder," a "huge volume of matter ceaselessly rolling."[1] But also because Briante's line effects something of a Thoreauvian scale shift: The river moves as water flows, the banks of the river move as the planet turns, and, in a simultaneous horizon of reality, capital and its numbers move (à la financial banks) under the aegis of the stock market. Here, all planes are in perpetual and interdynamic motion.

This chapter argues that Thoreau's writing offers something akin to this movement: an ecological loop dialectics. I use this concept to describe Thoreau's unique way of seeing specific places, ontologies, and matter in terms of complex interactions and entanglements among micro intra-relations and wider macro inter-relations. Thoreau's worldview offers a starkly original approach toward reality, one that includes models of causality and relation that depart in significant ways from a traditional western notion of dialectics as well as the various contemporary liberal rejections of it.

In 1853, while visiting his neighbor Minot Pratt, Thoreau imagined that the towering elm in his front yard, with its branches twisting upward "like vast thunderbolts," was nothing short of "Heaven defying—sending back dark vegetable bolts—as if flowing back in the channel of the lighting."[2] Such dark vegetable bolts, directed material effects engendered by and among loops and zones of relation, fit awkwardly within existing western liberal models. Playing off the notion of these "vegetable bolts," this chapter's title nods hyperbolically to the way Thoreau's conception of material and historical realities (loop dialectics) as well as the types of political ontologies and actants that are shaped by them (para-politics) have urgent stakes within antebellum society. These odd formations and their effects reveal a new Thoreau, one that is distinct from familiar portrayals found in contemporary scholarship and popular culture.

Building on the first part of the book, which focused on illiberal ontologies, especially their constitution via impersonal outsides of various kinds, the second part, "Illiberal Ecologies," shifts attention to broader material and political contexts. In this chapter and the next, I examine how political ontology and agency operate within and are transmogrified by complex material networks. By looking anew at Thoreau and, in Chapter 4, writings about ex-slave fugitivity, we begin to glimpse the precarious, half-formed, and always-embattled worlds at stake in this historical period as well as our own. The term "ecology" thus stands in for a wider array of relations than its modern scientific milieu allows. Following scholars such as Jason Moore, who turns to ecology's classical Greek root of *oikeios topos*, or "favorable place," to develop a critical perspective that reformulates "the creative and generative relation of species and environment as the ontological pivot—*and methodological premise*—of historical change," I am interested in offering strange and competing versions of nineteenth-century realities in the making (and unmaking).[3] In line with Darwin's earlier notion that what we term "ecology" is "an economy of nature,"[4] Moore suggests that capitalism is itself an "ecological regime," one whose "durable patterns of governance (formal and informal), technological innovations, class structures, and organizational forms . . . have sustained and propelled successive phases of world accumulation since the long sixteenth century."[5] Like Moore, I am interested in showing how this ecological regime is far from totalizing. Instead of privileging forms of multiplicity and indeterminacy, however, I hope to allow competing or fleeting ontologies the possibility of material effects that include an array of formations, fronts, and, at times, oppositional organizations, however minor or potential.

We might begin to discern the basic ground of Thoreau's material and political thought by looking in the sand where Margaret Fuller's body eventually came to rest. It was Thoreau, of course, who did just this: dispatched by Emerson in July 1850 to scour the coast and towns of Long Island where the *Elizabeth* had wrecked—to look for personal effects and manuscripts and news. Although Fuller's son's body had been found and buried, both Fuller's and her husband Ossoli's remains were missing. In a journal entry from around July 29, 1850, Thoreau pens a counterintuitively dispassionate account of coming upon Ossoli's coat and bones on the shore. The passages are couched within a rumination about the difference between the "actual" and the "imagined," where he comes down solidly in favor of the latter. "I find the actual to be far less real to me than the imagined," he writes. Going even further, he complicates the assumption that the actual is real, claiming, "I have never met with anything so truly visionary and accidental as some actual events."[6] As an example, Thoreau comments on the experience of finding Ossoli's coat:

> I have in my pocket a button which I ripped off of the coat of the marquis of Ossoli on the sea shore the other day—held up it intercepts the light & casts a shadow, an *actual* button so called—And yet all the life it is connected with is less substantial to me than my faintest dreams.[7]

Here, Ossoli's actual button—as an object—exists substantially in time and space, but this isn't, of course, the actuality that Thoreau is critiquing. What's missing or lacking is the "life it is connected with." The button's world, or, rather, the world it was once a part of, is only faintly connected to it now. At the same time, Thoreau's own dreams, although not parading before him, are a very real part of the way he experiences the present.

And yet, there is, perhaps, more to this weakened connection between button and "life." In a letter to Charles Sumner, Jr. from the same period, Thoreau describes when he first spied the bones on the empty stretch of beach. "There lay the relics in a certain state, rendered perfectly inoffensive to both bodily and spiritual eye by the surrounding scenery, a slight inequality in the sweep of the shore," he writes. The heap of bones is nonetheless "conspicuous": "It reigned over the shore. That dead body possessed the shore as no living one could."[8] Although the bones lord it over the space to some degree, this reign is clearly non-identical with the normal course of human affairs. What's more, for Thoreau, this para-state is engendered by the agency and effects (however merely aesthetic here) of the "scenery" itself.

The agency of the scene, as we might call it, is also subtly apparent in the aforementioned journal entry, where Thoreau offers an even bleaker view of the bones, writing, "There was nothing at all remarkable about them[.] [T]hey were simply some bones lying on the beach. They would not detain a walker there more than so much sea weed."[9] This latter reference to seaweed is not without import. In his writing on Cape Cod, Thoreau describes vividly the scene of a shipwreck—the brig *St. John*, full of emigrants from Ireland, had run into rocks off of Cohasset—the aftermath of which he and his companion Ellery Channing had witnessed in 1849. After offering a detailed account of dead bodies ("I saw many marble feet and matted heads as the cloths were raised, and one livid, swollen and mangled body of a drowned girl. . . ."), Thoreau turns his attention to the surrounding coastline.[10] He notes that amid the crowd concerned with the wreck, there were a number of men collecting valuable seaweed raised by the storm. Consequently, Thoreau reflects, "This shipwreck had not produced a visible vibration in the fabric of society." Soon after, he comes across an elderly man likewise focused solely on gathering seaweed. "It was the wrecked weed that concerned him most," writes Thoreau, "and those bodies were to him but other weeds which the tide cast up." Thoreau seems to have been swayed by this local perspective, noting, "I sympathized . . . with the winds and waves, as if to toss and mangle these poor human bodies was the order of the day. If this was the law of Nature, why waste any time in awe or pity?"[11]

I want to suggest that Ossoli's button and bones as well as the drowned bodies from the *St. John* fail to render adequately their own worlds for Thoreau because Thoreau believed so adamantly in the reality of the local given one. That is, for Thoreau, the world of the local maritime environment (winds and waves) and economy (seaweed gatherers) subsumes all foreign assertions of meaning and being. As Robert D. Richardson puts it, in Thoreau's account of the ocean in *Cape Cod*, "There is no salvation, there is only salvage."[12] But Thoreau's maritime coast is not merely the wild zone of Milton's chaos; it is also a specific wild zone: a real place with its own logos, of sorts, formed at the looping intersections of any number of worlds and systems.

If, amid the particular environs of the New England seascape, Ossoli's button is not magical, not even a proper remnant really, why does Thoreau commonly imbue other objects with such power? Take Thoreau's flute, for example, so often heard on the breeze in Concord's twilight hours, or the music box he played at the close of his sister Helen's funeral in June 1849. The answer relates to the fact that these material realities, or worlds as I have been calling them, do not just level and negate. Nor are they merely positive locations that leverage; they are also dynamic and asymmetrical configurations of time and space: quilting wide distances and collectives via a creative distributive agency. According to Branka Arsić, Thoreau had an intimate relationship with at least three music boxes in his life, listening to one of them repeatedly before Helen's death while his brother John was on his own deathbed. Following Thoreau's numerous writings about sound from this period, Arsić recounts Thoreau's notion of "the perfect time" of the music box: "Simply put, the listener's present—what Thoreau hears in any given now—always reaches him from the past, because sound needs some time . . . to traverse space."[13] In a similar fashion to the way that Wai Chee Dimock presents Fuller seeking to erect a "planetary" and material "long-distance exchange" among women in different ages or how Elizabeth Freeman calls for a queer and erotic bodily connection between the present and the archive,[14] Arsić recounts how Thoreau develops a theory of sonic materiality whereby sound, as an "acoustic strain," puts different historical moments in "touch." Going further, she depicts how Thoreau uses Orphic theogonies to conceive of this time as the "time of Chronos," a mythic time that "encircles the cosmos materially." Within this spherical configuration, the past and present never "pass," but those listening to the sonic medium can, themselves, transit between (52–53).

Coming back around to buttons and music boxes, we might say that whereas Ossoli's button is taken within the world of the maritime coast, the music box itself creates a material loop—its physical medium connecting itself and those around it to an alternate and existing reality. For Thoreau, then, the aforementioned "actual" is a pejorative concept because it represents a false and reified belief in a singular positive plane of existence. Shortly after the passage on the actual and imagined quoted earlier, Thoreau writes, "We are ever dying to one world & being born into another—and probably no man knows whether he is dead in the sense in which he affirms that phenomenon of another—or not."[15] In what follows, I want to show how these worlds upon worlds are not only nested in indeterminate and precarious ways, but also dynamically oriented and composed. Throughout his writing and career, Thoreau depicts loops of reality that are shifting and antagonistic, that redefine the local as much as the not local. Within this swerving multidimensional reality, Thoreau presents a new perspective on historicity and causality as well as the composition and agency of humans and nonhumans alike.

This chapter owes much to the spirit of Arsić's book: how Thoreau sought painstakingly and honestly to conceive of the world as an expanse, one that opened out into a seemingly impossible realm that touched his lost brother. In Arsić's hands, existence for Thoreau becomes something of a "bird ontology," with the self and the soul constituting "enduring yet self-modifying life" (161). This approach, however, casts Thoreau in a manner consonant with any number of dominant ideological fantasies within liberal modes of neoliberal being; it also updates a long history of studies that track various cadences of Thoreau's "withdraw" and negative political agency by focusing on a timely aspect of materiality. There is, in this sense, a foundational dissimilarity between Arsić's approach to Thoreau and my own: one that holds immense stakes for how we might think about and through Thoreau's work. At the risk of oversimplification, this divide centers on the fact that Arsić presents Thoreau as a non-dialectical thinker whereas I suggest he offers his own unique mode of historical and dialectical causality.

In *Bird Relics*, this ideological ground comes to the fore in a number of ways. In a section of the introduction to Part II titled "*Teleology*," for example, Arsić suggests that Thoreau's work "annuls the ideology of human exceptionalism." Her subsequent description of this departure from the anthropomorphic, however, reasserts a host of contemporary (human) liberal assumptions about relation and reality. In her terms, for Thoreau, "no living form is more accomplished than another, and life doesn't therefore unfold hierarchically and progressively but, more democratically, moves simultaneously in a variety of directions." In a conspicuous move, "democratic" relations here become a naturalized condition for the modality of "unfolding" life. Arsić goes further, adding to this *Demos Natura*, as we might playfully call it, a liberal aspect of ethics; for this "movement of life . . . charts an egalitarian network along which beings transform" (129). In Arsić's project, the qualitative nature of relation and material change thus has significant purchase for our understanding of Thoreau's politics, both in terms of subjects/actants as well as historically conditioned networks.[16]

One might go so far as to suggest that Arsić's readings are, indeed, formative because they do align so well with the wider contours of emerging contemporary liberal discourses within (explicitly) the humanities and (implicitly) many forms of interdisciplinary new materialisms. To note one central example, Arsić's presentation of Thoreau's distinct "vitalism," though carefully contextualized within the period's milieu of Harvard vitalists, such as Arnold Guyot, relies significantly upon twentieth century (Gilles Deleuze) and contemporary (Jane Bennett) perspectives on vitalism *qua* "transversal animation" (142). Though purportedly open and polymorphous, such varieties of vitalism are often liberal in their orientation toward form, relation, and history. Arsić is rather direct about this very point, setting up a rigid political schematic whereby dialectical totality is lumped with the likes of Nazis, on the one hand, ("At the heart of the biopolitics that culminated in Nazism one finds death, not life, in complete opposition to the vitalisms I refer, which were formulated in radical resistance to any hierarchization" [141]) and, on the other, Thoreau's supposed Deleuzian non-dialectical vitalism is associated with a positive notion of the "power of life" ("In Thoreau life individuates but without ever organizing itself into a closed whole, and thus it never itself becomes an individual, single totality" [123]).

In the end, the types of life, ontology, and materiality forwarded by Arsić's work all share the quality of being "continuous rather than interrupted" (*Bird Relics*, 137). In Thoreau and his moment, however, we might glimpse a different model of reality and relation just as, in our own, we might forward a different conceptual and political arrangement. In suggesting that Thoreau presents us with what I am calling loop dialectics, I am working along side scholars such as George Ciccariello-Maher who, in *Decolonizing Dialectics* (2017), acknowledges the imperial and violent past of western dialectics while, at the same time, calling for its political redeployment. In his terms, he seeks "a radicalization of the dialectical tradition while also opening outward toward its decolonization." He goes on: "This is a dialectical counterdiscourse that, by foregrounding rupture and shunning the lure of unity, makes its home in the center of the dialectic and revels in the spirit of combat, the indeterminacies of political identities slamming against one another, transforming themselves and their worlds unpredictably."[17] As Gayatri Chakravorty Spivak suggests in her own critique of Fredric Jameson's brand of historical totality: "[T]he epistemic story of imperialism is the story of a series of discontinuous interruptions, a repeated tearing of time."[18] Contra Deleuzians and liberal positivists, in Ciccariello-Maher's and Spivak's hands, "life" becomes a series of historical interruptions and dialectics constitutes a discontinuous series of totalities (on multiple competing planes).[19]

The stakes of shifting from Arsić's positive and continuous plane of self-transformation to a neo-dialectical possibility (existing both before and after the historical instantiations of dialectics Arsić eschews) has immense ramifications for our understanding of Thoreau. Scholars such as Stanley Cavell and, more recently, Shannon Mariotti have considered Thoreau's work in terms of dialectics, however broadly conceived, but these studies tend to focus on particular thematics of Thoreau's work. Consequently, they do not necessarily examine the fuller conceptual aspects of Thoreau's unique dialectical thinking or its material and political ramifications.[20] More generally, the sedimented layers of twentieth- and twenty-first-century scholarship on Thoreau tend to meld into something of the loamy and sandy railroad hillside that Thoreau takes such great pains to describe in the "Spring" chapter of *Walden* (1854). Like Arsić, scholars of different eras have sought to trace their own forms, or "lobes" as Thoreau calls them, often doing so by privileging a certain aspect of Thoreau's work, a particular generic or conceptual theme, or a certain thread or arc of this life. In the past half century, following the development of ecocriticism and environmental humanities in the 1990s, we've had Thoreau and "nature" (Lawrence Buell, David Robinson, et al.); with the continued institutional rise of STEM fields and their modes of positivist knowledge, there's been a renewed interest in Thoreau and science (Laura Dassow Walls, Robert Thorson, and so on); the formalist and literary crowds have long had their Thoreau, including a number of studies that focus on writing and especially Thoreau's journals (Stanley Cavell, Sharon Cameron, Theo Davis, and so on); and those interested in politics have offered readings of Thoreau's relation to historical conflicts through the lenses of various liberal models and traditions (Deak Nabers, Shannon Mariotti, and Larry Reynolds).[21]

The best of this scholarship offers ways across Thoreau's work and, at times, points beyond delimiting existing paradigms. For example, Robert Thorson's *The Boatman: Henry David Thoreau's River Years* (2017) privileges Thoreau's later scientific thought (Thorson fondly employs the phrase "my Thoreau" to describe the Thoreau of the physical sciences in *Walden's Shore: Henry David Thoreau and Nineteenth-Century Science* [2014]) by foregrounding Thoreau as "the mapmaker" and as a skilled civil engineer boatman.[22] And yet, this perhaps limiting optic acts as a nodal point that opens up a new way of thinking about the nexus between socio-political action and environments—where, in the case of his involvement with the "flowage controversy" of the Billerica dam in 1859, Thoreau's scientific aims are shown to be put in the service of an environmental activism that flirted with "vigilante justice."[23] Within recent scholarship, one finds glimmers of similar productive dislocations within and without familiar portrayals of Thoreau. In a collection commemorating Thoreau's two hundredth birthday, for example, a number of essays by scholars such as Lance Newman, James Finley, Susan Gallagher, and Lawrence Buell complicate previously imposed bifurcations within Thoreau's work to offer insightful reconsiderations of the links among Thoreau's political and environmental engagements as well as the relationships among *Walden*, his journals, and specific historical political events of the period.[24] This type of innovation can be seen, as well, in books such as Peter Coviello's *Tomorrow's Parties: Sex and the Untimely in Nineteenth-Century America* (2013), which moves explicitly past longstanding asserted impasses such as Sharon Cameron's claim that Thoreau's so-called "rage at the social" in *Walden* "suffers diversion from its own best subject: Thoreau's unmediated relation to nature."[25] Coviello charts a new path for thinking about Thoreau's social "disappointment" that "take[s] Thoreau's famous dissatisfaction with his fellow men to be part of a career-wide effort to imagine the domain of sexuality in alternate terms." This includes departing from "possessive domains of sexuality" and "inhabiting a unique temporality, one that renders the body at once out of step with modernity's sped-up market time and exquisitely responsive to the call of an intuited but inarticulate future."[26] Suffice it to say here that, like Coviello, I intend to offer a pseudo-tendentious cross-section of Thoreau's work via a structural vision that pervades many aspects of his writing and career. My claim is that, for Thoreau, the thickness of "now" is a dynamic and moving place that is both lived in and fought over; his toe never leaves *this* line.

This trembling and, at times, embattled now is a place, if we can speculatively call it this, that is cut across by various forces and effects. In the aforementioned journal entry where Thoreau ruminates about Ossoli's button and the "actual," he enjoins the reader to "[b]e not simply obedient like the vegetables—set up your own Ebeneezer.... Do not engage to find things as you think they are. Do what nobody can do for you—."[27] The previous notion of bold "vegetable bolts" morphs here into passive "obedient" string beans. I will show how this seemingly odd continuum is itself a symptom of a specific form of vegetal being in Thoreau's thought that includes an original perspective on ontology as well as a new field for political and historical actuality. Militant vegetables, as I call them, are not "simply obedient"; they are systemically oriented (effected and affecting) on multiple planes. By invoking the *Old Testament* Samuel, who erects a stone (*ebenezar*) to mark a military victory over the Philistines as well as to designate a potential limit of divine support ("Hitherto hath the Lord helped us"), Thoreau suggests that this pseudo- or para-obedient self should engage with material-historical reality via all means in order to, twisting Thoreau's language a bit, "find things as they are not."[28] For Thoreau, therefore, we must participate in making and realizing these other worlds.

Living intently amid various worlds necessitates that perception and, indeed, epistemology take on a heightened status. As Thoreau points out in *A Week on the Concord and Merrimack Rivers* (1849), one's "scheme," or the "medium through which [one] . . . see[s]," should not be colored by "tradition"; it should be constituted by "the frame-work of the universe."[29] And yet, according to Thoreau, this vast and abstract (however materialist) way of seeing is not always desirable. Even Jesus, in Thoreau's words, "taught mankind but imperfectly how to live; his thoughts were all directed toward another world. There is another kind of success than his. Even here we have a sort of living to get, and must buffet it somewhat longer." He continues: "There are various tough problems yet to solve, and we must make shift to live, betwixt spirit and matter, such a human life as we can" (73–74). Thoreau clearly replaces Jesus's metaphysical "world" with a historical and material horizon that is forged (and re-forged) in the loops between "spirit" and "matter." In both the Samuel and Jesus passages, *all* such possible worlds are precarious due to the specific historical forms and limits imposed by existing socio-economic forces. This precarity even touches the far reaches of the material universe. In *Walden*, stars are the "apexes of . . . wonderful triangles" where, perhaps, "distant and different beings in the various mansions of the universe are contemplating the same [star] at the same moment!"[30] Toward the end of *A Week*, however, Thoreau discusses how the bright and distant stars are merely "more waste land in the West,—star territory,—to be made Slave States, perchance, if we colonize them" (387). The stakes are clear: Wondrous apexes can easily shift into a one-way imperial encounter and the "various mansions" of strange beings might soon be converted into familiar southern plantations.

All of this talk of aliens might belie the fact that Thoreau's comments on Jesus ground the consequences of this worlding in terms of "human life." Nonetheless, earlier in *A Week* we see that this life, too, spans various forms of life, matter, and spirit (to employ his terms). In referencing the "poor Shad" with no "redress" for the ill-effects of the aforementioned Billerica Dam, for example, Thoreau declares, "Away with the superficial and selfish phil-*anthropy* of men,—who knows what admirable virtue of fishes may be below the low-water mark." At the same time, Thoreau posits something of a speculative political solidarity between humans and fish. He describes "countless shoals" of shad "turned adrift, and perchance know[ing] not where men do *not* dwell," waiting aimlessly at the mouths of rivers "[a]rmed only with innocence and a just cause." He then declares, "I for one am with thee, and who knows what may avail a crowbar against that Billerica dam?" (37). We've now come to a point where we can offer an early example of Thoreau's politics, or what I will call, in a subsequent section, his para-politics: a crowbar wielding human swinging from below the waterline amid "migrating nations" of fish.

Thoreau's fishy fantasy of a new counter-public's intervention is posited despite the wider-scale (forgive the pun) possibility that "[p]erchance, after a few thousands of years, if the fishes will be patient, . . . nature will have leveled the Billerica dam" (34). Even in this minor anecdote, we see Thoreau's historical and social thinking straddling the need for urgency and, perhaps, haste in light of negative historical contingencies as well as a wider consideration of seemingly diffuse forces and concerns. When viewed from the vantage of what I am calling the logic of loop dialectics, however, this is not a one-off or either/or affair. Instead, Thoreau might be seen to offer a more complex and fleshed out (material-historical) version of the dynamics among universals and particulars that I traced in both Emerson's and Fuller's work. If, for Thoreau, now is a potentially wide-ranging material loop (or braids of loops), then action (political or otherwise) includes the fulcrum of the manifest present as well as the gathering fetch of slow forces and violences.[31] Put differently, if the person or actant within these varying loops is intricately and intimately caught up in the material viscosity of complex realities in the making, then political *being* as well as *acting* entails, in part, putting oneself within the folds and fields of reality's loops.[32] This includes direct action à la wielding a crowbar or meeting personally with John Brown in 1857 to support the Kansas Relief fund's effort to raise money for weapons. As Thoreau says emphatically in "Slavery in Massachusetts" (1854): "It is not an era of repose. . . . If we would save our lives, we must fight for them."[33] As I have been suggesting, this mode of familiar direct engagement seen ever-so-clearly in the 1850s encapsulates and implicates, for Thoreau, more amorphous forms of action, including instituting inertia as a new model of politics—where one's "life" lends weight or, as he calls it in "Resistance to Civil Government" (1849), "counter friction" to aid one side of a grander historical-material antagonism.[34]

This unusual form of socio-historical ontology reveals in Thoreau something other than a liberal scientist, a liberal writer, a liberal activist, or a liberal vibrant new materialist. Consequently, Thoreau clearly has wider stakes for our understanding of the period. Instead of liberal takes on Romanticism's broader politics, such as Anahid Nersessian's notion that nineteenth-century Romanticism depicts a utopian mode of "restraint" that she calls "adjustment," with Thoreau we get something much closer to Martin Luther King Jr.'s call for "maladjustment."[35] In this dislocation, we find the fulcrum of Thoreau's worlds.

The following three sections offer a structural examination of Thoreau's worldview, building toward an original understanding of his various notions of political-historical reality. "Loops 1: Para-Realities" lays a foundation for these later topics by interrogating Thoreau's spatial understanding of place, spheres, and worlds. "Loops 2: From Nested Loops to Loop Dialectics" analyzes Thoreau's unique conception of how these material formations are produced and interact to shape historical conditions. And "Loops 3: Para-Politics, or, Militant Vegetables" examines the types of political ontologies and actants that emerge within these dynamic material relations as well as their specific stakes for antebellum society.

Loops 1: Para-Realities

Looping and circular formations abound across Thoreau's writings. In his 1852 journal, he notes in April, "[F]or the first time I perceive this spring that the year is a circle—I see distinctly the spring arc thus far."[36] Scholars might mark this as an early intimation of Thoreau's later obsession with empirically quantifying the seasons. I want to use it, instead, to set up a discussion of Thoreau's unique way of thinking spatially about time and reality. As noted, Arsić and others have tended to focus on the Greek antecedents of Thoreau's material and formal mode of seeing. According to Richardson Jr., for example, "The key to understanding what Apollo really meant to Thoreau is understanding that Thoreau, like his so-admired Greeks, perceived as *form* that which the modern mind understands as *law*."[37] I will take up the implications of this formalization and, indeed, materialization of law shortly. To start, though, we might begin by thinking of the above "circle" of the year in Thoreau's passage less in terms of cycles (presence and absence of natural phenomena) and more in terms of formal arrangements that include a whole host of objects, bio matter, actants, material-historical systems and forces, and so on. In the journal entry, Thoreau notes that this circle is composed of not only changing animal behavior, such as migrating geese, but also agricultural phenomena, such as cranberries washing up onto roads, and other forms of human material and symbolic networks, such as the wind carrying the sound of a "clock strik[ing] plainly 10 or 11. Pm."[38] In this sense, the whole of the year is a formation that, much like Caroline Levine's reinvigorated notion of *form*, contains various "arrangement[s] of elements," including "patterns of sociopolitical experience."[39] Put differently, we might ask what kind of "network imaginary," a term Patrick Jagoda uses to describe the "complex of material infrastructures and metaphorical figures" that shape understanding of the world, Thoreau develops across multiple texts and moments in his life.[40]

What becomes apparent right away is that Thoreau does not view this "circle," or any circle for that matter, as a totalized whole. As he writes in *A Week*, "[T]he universe is a sphere whose center is wherever there is intelligence. The sun is not so central as a man" (349). Although here donning a familiar Romantic anthropomorphism, Thoreau allows for a variable and varying "sphere" based upon centralized located perspectives. He goes on to write, "Upon an isolated hilltop, in an open country, we seem to ourselves to be standing on the boss of an immense shield." And he juxtaposes this vantage point to that of the embedded farmer "plowing and reaping," suggesting, "How fortunate were we who . . . had not renounced our title to the whole" (349–50). Of course, the hillside gazer owns, to play with Thoreau's pun, a type of "imperial eye" that many contemporary critics have noted in visual economies such as this.[41] We should not, though, lose the conditional phasing that establishes the scene, the "we seem to ourselves" postulate. That is, although the "isolated hilltop" view has purchase on a type of "whole," the scene itself offers other potential focalizations and therefore other constellations of visual totalities, including that of the laboring farmer or, perhaps, the potential views afforded from "distant mountains," the "shore of a lake," and villas on the horizon (350).

Thoreau goes further, however, than Emerson's well-known dictum to experience the world differently by merely "[t]urn[ing] the eyes upside down . . [and] looking at the landscape through your legs."[42] Thoreau moves at times beyond the scopic register all together when discussing various types of parallactic spheres related to sound and experience. For example, in his 1838 journal, Thoreau writes, "Each summer sound/Is a summer round."[43] This seemingly trite poetic line encapsulates a key element of Thoreau's spatial conception of what needs to be seen as realities, in the plural. In this case, each material sound offers a form of roundness that includes its own coordinates, both spatially and symbolically (even if non- or pre-discursive). This is why Thoreau mentions, in various ways, how the material universe itself can be thought of in terms of both simple and complex lived-in spheres. We see this in the first epigraph of this chapter as well as, for example, in *A Week* where the "world has many rings, like Saturn, and we live now on the outmost of them all" (384). The point is that Thoreau's universe, on the most elemental level, is one of variegated "concave" horizons of being and reality.[44]

There is, of course, a long history of spheres, orbs, circles, and the like in Greco-Christian thought. Peter Sloterdijk's "Spheres" trilogy *Bubbles*

(2011), *Globes* (2014), and *Foams* (2016) offers a recent and provocative account of this tradition. Although concerned exclusively with "human" experience and surely falling upon the organic conservative side of the political spectrum, Sloterdijk's work reinterpreting western metaphysics and materiality in terms of anthropological micro- and macro-spherologies offers a useful foothold for considering Thoreau's unique nineteenth-century experimentations with totalities. In *Bubbles*, Sloterdijk opens by shifting from familiar questions about "who" humans are to "where" they are. In a move that has implications for an understanding of Thoreau's thought, he claims, "We are in an outside that carries inner worlds."[45] Throughout the book, Sloterdijk offers a historical and spatial overview of the west's shifting conception of monadic (here spheric) realities. Moving from early metaphysical "inspired spatial communities" to the Enlightenment's destruction of traditional worlds and on to the post-Enlightenment's creation of prosthetic modes of "spheric security," Sloterdijk traces how global modernity and its precarious intimacies have been, literally, formed in geometric-conceptual terms.[46] In *Globes*, Sloterdijk telescopes out to examine further the ways in which micro "bubbles" in the west were created on a larger scale. Following how theologians and scholars after Plato struggled with two orb constructions, the "cosmological-immanent and the ontotheological-transcendent," Sloterdijk highlights modernity's various "wars of succession for the problematic centers of ailing totalities."[47] Finally, in *Foams*, Sloterdijk comes closest to the structures found in Thoreau, presenting our contemporary age as a "plural spherology" where "'life' unfolds multifocally, multiperspectivally and heterarchically."[48] In an era when the idea of a singular macro orb has "imploded," we find sociality organized spatially by co-determined foams or "co-fragile systems."[49] According to Sloterdijk, the bourgeois domestic interior Benjamin revealed in the *Arcades Project* should now be thought of as something closer to a malleable constellation of co-isolation within a "foam city."[50]

Thoreau's circles and spheres are anything but *sui generis*. In fact, as Laura Dassow Walls and others have pointed out, Thoreau's attempts to "read nature whole" passed through a litany of well-known western Enlightenment figures, including Goethe, Carlyle, Ruskin, Schelling, Humboldt, and Darwin. In Walls's narrative, Thoreau's variety of totality negotiates two dominant modes of thinking wholeness: "rational holism," which viewed the "mechanic-organic whole as a divine . . . unity fully comprehended only through thought," and "empirical holism," which "stressed that the whole could be understood only by studying the interconnections of its constituent and individual parts."[51] As I've mentioned, Walls's thesis is vested in promoting a Thoreau-*cum*-natural scientist, and she argues here that Thoreau sought to fold the former mode of idealism into a frame of empiricism dominated primarily by Alexander von Humboldt. According to Walls, Humboldt, who was Goethe's friend and an influential precursor to Darwin, offered Thoreau a period model for thinking that integrated various disciplinary modalities and promoted a "harmonized whole that emerged from the interconnected details of particular natural facts." For Walls, the Thoreau of the 1840s and 1850s was a "Humboldtian empirical naturalist."[52]

In this period, Thoreau was undoubtedly moving from a neoclassical model toward one informed by scientific data. In fact, he was officially employed by the naturalist Jean Louis Rodolphe Agassiz, a purveyor of European racial evolutionary exceptionalism who took a position at Harvard in 1847 and established subsequently his Museum of Comparative Zoology. Ironically, perhaps, while at Walden, Thoreau collected a number of animal specimens for Agassiz, including "seven perch, eight breams, four dace, two musk turtles, five painted turtles, and three wood turtles." In addition, he sent along a single mouse he had caught in his cellar.[53] Although Thorson attributes more influence to Darwin than to Humboldt,[54] both he and Walls portray Thoreau's thought during the 1840s and especially the 1850s as typifying what I would term geo-positivism and empirical-positivism, respectively. The former can be seen throughout Thorson's rich book, most blatantly at the outset where he equates directly Walden's physical basin to the "deeper causes" and "more general explanations" Thoreau was after. (Thoreau's circles end here with specific quantitative scientific knowledge that "[w]e now know.")[55] The latter can be seen in Walls's aforementioned neat binary between what amounts to idealism and empirical materialism, with Thoreau seeking to forge a new mode of something like materialist inductive reasoning.

Thoreau was certainly influenced by scholars such as Humboldt, especially his *Kosmos* (1845) and *Ansichten der Natur* (1859). As Sloterdijk shows, however, Humboldt's exact method of analysis and, further, the ideological implications of his thought are perhaps more complicated than Walls's account allows. Sloterdijk places Humboldt's *Kosmos* at the far end of a long historical shift away from older models of fixed heavens and planetary domes. Amid the Romantic era, Humboldt "had been given the mission of formulating the return from cosmic exteriority to the self-reflexive world of humans in exemplary fashion."[56] Paradoxically, given Walls's account of Humboldt's influences on Thoreau, Sloterdijk has Humboldt essentially moving from the material expanse of the universe into the interior of (bourgeois) subjectivity. In Sloterdijk's formulation, "The transcendental turn is the heart of Humboldt's description of the world, as well as the designs for philosophical systems among idealistic and post-idealistic thinkers." The term "transcendental" is employed here in a rather Kantian manner, for Sloterdijk posits that what Humboldt does is essentially ground earth conceptually as "the transcendental star that has become the determining location for all self-reflections." To quote Sloterdijk once again:

> When Humboldt brings the term 'spheres' into play, . . . he is naturally no longer speaking of the imaginary celestial domes of the Aristotelian bimillennium, but rather the transcendental 'spheres of perception,' which refer not to cosmic realities but to the schemata, auxiliary concepts and radii of space-imagining reason.[57]

Sloterdijk's short passage reveals that the inductive reasoning championed by scholars working in the tradition of the natural sciences is, in the formative case of Humboldt at least, predicated upon the functions of human reason. From this perspective, the empirical inductive reasoning that Walls and Thorson use as the bedrock (literally a smoothed granite "tectonic basement" for Thorson) of Thoreau's thought becomes much more historically and ideologically complex and, indeed, impure in terms of the fantasies of objectivity that traffic among the modern sciences.[58] The paradox here is that the Humboldtian empiricism Walls holds up to promote a Thoreauvian materialism may not be materialist enough given Thoreau's writings and aims. I am not suggesting that eighteenth- and nineteenth-century natural science and its rhetoric was not immensely formative for Thoreau or that it wasn't directly employed in his writing and thinking, especially as the 1850s wore on. But I am arguing that a certain mode of *historical* positivism often accompanies studies that use the disciplinary genealogy of the sciences to give shape to Thoreau's thought. It also necessarily renders either secondary or, at times, invisible the specific ways Thoreau's writing about worlds have direct cross-fertilizations for and with historical political realities.

By removing the various partitions scholars have erected within Thoreau's corpus and avoiding forms of historical and disciplinary positivism so common within contemporary scholarship, we begin to see the historical ramifications of Thoreau's conceptual thought more clearly. Understanding the "worlds" that Thoreau's circular and spatial formations yield requires an awareness of the "schemes," to employ Thoreau's term again, for "world" and, as Heidegger puts it, "worlding" that condition various twentieth- and twenty-first-century hermeneutic and anti-hermeneutic approaches toward these topics.[59] As Thoreau expresses famously in *Walden*, many of his townsfolk live their lives within false allegory of the cave-like interiors, willing to be "deceived by shows" and other "shams," while all along "reality is fabulous" (96, 95). According to Thoreau, this delusional practice is replete with phony spatial coordinates, where "[m]en esteem truth remote, in the outskirts of the system, behind the farthest star, before Adam and after the last man." Nevertheless, as Thoreau sees it, "all these times and places and occasions are now and here" (96–97). The concave rings and spheres where life dwells, therefore, are anything but static and definitively segmented. In addition to the slumber-inducing pomp of what we might call ideological fantasies, there is also, for Thoreau, the potential to move through and into the realities below and around. As he writes in the same passage: "My instinct tells me that my head is an organ for burrowing, as some creatures use their snout and fore-paws, and with it I would mine and burrow my way through these hills" (98). Although smacking a bit of the reason-based idealism Sloterdijk attributes to Humboldt, Thoreau here presents the world as a dynamic material encounter with other spaces and realities.

The various worlds that Thoreau encounters across his writings are, consequently, more dynamic than the "co-isolation" found in Sloterdijk's foam and more political (as is in having historical stakes for the states of existing life worlds) than the plane of scientific "knowledge" allows in Walls and Thorson. Instead, in his notion of place, spheres, worlds, and so on, Thoreau offers something closer to Elizabeth Povinelli's notion of "*hereish*," a way of thinking anew about the compromised relation between local and global in the modern world. For Povinelli, the geological catastrophes of the present force us to inhabit this new space/time of "hereish," and, in so doing, they shift conceptually our "object of concern . . . across competing struggles for existence, implicating how we conceptualize scale, event, circulation, and being."[60] It is precisely in this way and for this reason that I employ the term "loop" to re-characterize Thoreau's spatial, ontological, and, ultimately, political orientations. Although existing in a moment after the commencement of the popularly termed Anthropocene but before its manifest fallout,[61] Thoreau's own brand of "hereish" not only locates space within various configurations of *place* (different notions of local and nonlocal) but also animates these places via historical-material contingent affects and effects.

In his own work, Timothy Morton turns to the figure of the loop as a means for thinking about the modern "hereish" that Povinelli describes.

In Morton's terms, "Ecological awareness is weird: it has a twisted, looping form." He goes on:

> Ecological awareness is a loop because human interference has a loop form, because ecological and biological systems are loops. And ultimately this is because to exist at all is to assume the form of a loop. The loop form of beings means we live in a universe of finitude and fragility, a world in which objects are suffused with and surrounded by mysterious hermeneutical clouds of unknowing. It means that the politics of coexistence are always contingent, brittle, and flawed, so that in thinking of interdependence at least one being must be missing.[62]

To elucidate these claims, Morton offers a schematic of loop formations: There are positive feedback loops ("that escalate the potency of the system in which they are operating"), negative feedback loops (which "cool down the intensity of positive feedback loops"), "phasing loops" (loops that "come in and out of phase with human temporality"), and, last, there are "strange" loops ("in which two levels that appear utterly separate flip into one another").[63] Even a cursory reading of Thoreau's aforementioned burrowing head passage or his shad solidarity rumination reveals that Thoreau's notion of reality is very much aligned with Morton's conception of the "strange loop": where different locations and ways of being come into contact and, perhaps, transform one another. This, too, is Donna Haraway's main structural point in *Staying with the Trouble: Making Kin in the Chthulucene* (2016). Building on her previous analysis of multispecies relations, Haraway offers the Chthulucene, a combination of the Greek roots *khthôn* and *kainos*, as a friendly displacement of Anthropocene and as a conceptual "timeplace for learning to stay with the trouble of living and dying in response-ability on a damaged earth."[64] Much like Morton's zone of the strange loop, in this variety of place, "Natures, cultures, subjects, and objects do not preexist their intertwined worldings."[65] In an approach that is relevant for thinking about Thoreau, Haraway dispenses with longstanding assumptions about self-producing autopoietic systems and draws upon M. Beth Dempster's notion of "sympoiesis," or "collectively-producing systems that do not have self-defined spatial or temporal boundaries," to reveal a "looped . . . terran worlding."[66] Consequently, for Haraway, reality is composed "not at points, not in spheres," but among and along interactive lines.[67]

In his essay "Walking" (1862), Thoreau shifts his aforementioned notion of the circle or sphere into something much closer to Haraway's looping and perhaps braiding lines of interaction. Describing the common paths of his Concord walks, Thoreau writes, "The outline which would bound my walks, would be, not a circle, but a parabola, or rather like one of those cometary orbits, which have been thought to be non-returning curves, in this case opening westward, in which my house occupies the place of the sun."[68] As opposed to a circle's constant distance from a given point, a parabola opens up Thoreau's geometric analogy to various spatial and symbolic possibilities: such as an open symmetrical U-shaped curve or a three-dimensional conic curve, both of which remain open, closing only, within the Euclidian plane, at infinity. The point is that Thoreau conceives of his walks' "orbit" as being more complex than a simple circular return. As he mentions earlier in the essay, there are encounters and contingencies on such walks that alter both the route and the walker. In his romantic words, "We should go forth on the shortest walk, perchance, in the spirit of undying adventure, never to return; prepare to send back our embalmed hearts only, as relics to our desolate kingdoms."[69]

Using these historical and theoretical contexts, we might start to see Thoreau's worlds (geometric, cartographic, and existential) in terms of varying constellations of reality. After all, as we saw with music boxes and seaweed, Thoreau's worlds are both expansive beyond cognition as well as, at once, local to the microscopic. As he ponders in 1854, "Who placed us with eyes between a microscopic and a telescopic world?"[70] Thoreau's "prodigious and articulate fluency with the world of *things*," as Peter Coviello aptly puts it, is also a prodigious fluency with what we might call the networks of things.[71] In lieu of strict geometric circles, we might take Thoreau at his word and begin instead with the open parabola; following Morton, Haraway, and others, we might go even further and push to see how, for Thoreau, reality is *form*ed and constituted by looping planes. Our own conceptual walk, of sorts, from circle, to geography, to place, to looping realities effectively reframes Thoreau's specific ecological thought in terms that have tremendous stakes for issues of ontology as well as historical-formal politics. In terms of the former, we might return to Fred Moten's concept of "paraontology," a concept I outlined in my introduction that describes, in the context of black studies, modes of historically inscribed ways of being that exist despite, alongside, and, at times, against standard coordinates of being and acting. As such, in terms of the latter notion of historical-formal politics, Thoreau's various looping planes have historical-political effects if not aims (though, of course, these aims often exist). Caroline Levine employs Jacques Rancière's work to make a similar point about the politics implicit in form. She defines politics "as a matter of distributions and arrangements. Political struggles include ongoing contests over the proper places for bodies, goods, and capacities."[72] As mentioned in my introduction, scholars of the nineteenth century such as Colleen Glenney Boggs, Monique Allewaert, and many others have begun tracing the way such "arrangements" of "bodies" and "capacities" (including human, nonhuman, and their interference) have complex conceptual and political stakes in the period. If we place Thoreau in *this* world, we begin to see startlingly new aspects of his writing and, indeed, his relation to historical antagonisms and contingencies.

In the remainder of this section, I want to establish a variety of ways Thoreau presents this mode of looping para-reality. Here, Thoreau's loops will be discussed in terms of seemingly distinct places/worlds and/or the connections among such worlds, from his notion of houses, to places such as Mount Katahdin and fog-imbued ridgelines. This discussion aims to establish a baseline that the next two sections will complicate and put in motion: revealing the ways these planes are interdynamically situated and animated.

One of the most obvious structural para-realities in Thoreau's work remains his partially self-crafted house at Walden pond. Scholars such as Lance Newman have noted the concerted links among Thoreau's projects at Walden and local varieties of socialist Associationism taking place in efforts such as Brook Farm. According to Newman, Thoreau saw himself "engaging in a vitally important conversation with the utopian socialists there" to the degree that *Walden* "follows the logic of Association by articulating a moral critique of capitalist social relations."[73] Taking a different tack, in *Bird Relics*, Branka Arsić discusses Thoreau's specific construction of a pond-side home, presenting it as a "properly philosophical" exercise pertaining to "the art of living" and structures of subjectivity. Juxtaposing James Collins's shanty, the Irish railroad laborer whose home Thoreau purchases for materials, with Thoreau's eventual house, Arsić portrays the former as a traditional mode of architectural subjectivity ("isolationist," "perspectival," "ideational," "genealogical," and so on) and the latter as a new mode of existence ("rhizomatic," "nonperspectival," and "open") (295–304). I would like to place Thoreau's cabin somewhere between Newman and Arsić. Thoreau critiques capitalism throughout *Walden*, but he uses, at times, very different modalities than the Associationists commonly employed; what's more, the difference between Collins's Shanty and Thoreau's cabin may not be the difference between two distinct modes of subjectivity—less a "transformation," to use Arsić's term, and more of a modulation of bourgeois spatial experience.[74] If we think of the formation of Thoreau's new home less as a transformation away from Collins's shanty than as a *displacement* or even re-appropriation of it, then we begin to see how the house that was, as Thoreau deemed it, "all entry" offered a way for an antebellum bourgeois subject (however illiberal in Thoreau's case) to experiment in new and material ways with alternate loops of his surrounding environment (*Walden*, 132).

Thoreau presents the effects of his particular approach toward habitation in manifold ways. Well-known scenes in *Walden* recount how his home offered a number of open passages between himself and biological life of all kinds: from birds "flitting" through the house (111), to "bedding" with wasps at night (240), to mosquitos humming as they make their "invisible and unimaginable tour" through his rooms (88), to plants (sumac and blackberry vines) and various animals (moles, mice, and so on) breaking into his cellar (128, 141, 253). The beloved incompleteness of his home ("no yard!" [128]) thus blurs the standard constitution of inside self and outside neighbor, a blurring Thoreau praises aesthetically when he laments the completion of the plastering process, writing, "Should not every apartment in which man dwells be lofty enough to create some obscurity over-head, where flickering shadows may play" (242). In the case of the mosquito, Thoreau may not be able to conceive of the insect's world as it is in itself— here its circuit or the potential meanings of its humming ("itself an Iliad and Odyssey" [89])—but he does often seek to push beyond the limits correlationism had imposed within nineteenth-century philosophy and science.[75] He may not *know* the life or perspective of a squirrel, for instance, but he describes in detail an 1857 afternoon of *acting* like one in order to more successfully collect white-pine seeds.[76] Thoreau is not, therefore, merely attempting to forge new modes for thinking outside of the given human condition. Throughout his work, he takes a more materialist-systemic approach: putting himself in the position to experience new ways the world exists. Consequently, Thoreau offers his own antebellum speculative materialism, one that jumps from modes of impersonal thinking (which might leave "reality" as status quo) to modes of speculative being in the worlds, which has vast consequences for the formation of historical reality.

Moving closer, perhaps, toward Newman's interest in Thoreau's relation to Brook Farm, the various para-realities that Thoreau associates with houses often include forms of alternate sociality. In *Walden*, of course, the animals within and without the cabin's perforated boundaries are joined by other neighbors. These include, fantastically, the "former inhabitants" of Walden's surrounding woods, among them a number of ex-slaves. A similar airy potential for alternate connections arises, however fleetingly, in his description of ideal mountain homes. In his journal, Thoreau recounts how one such dwelling, high on a ridgeline in the Catskills, was so "equitable and calm . . . that you could not tell whether it was morning or noon or evening." This alternate space, indelibly linked to the environs of the mountain, was for Thoreau, "fit to entertain a traveling God."[77] Such partial, potential, and/or fantastical sheltered encounters find a more substantial example in *The Maine Woods* (1864). On what was the first of three trips into Maine's wilderness, Thoreau recounts how in traveling along the Salmon River he and his companions came across a number of houses and loggers' camps. As opposed to the private demarcations erected by standard homes, houses in these remote woods were "public houses." Although invoking a typical township's inn, Thoreau's "public" here also gestures to the permanent openness of the spaces, and, of course, in his description, no money is exchanged for lodging. In addition to the public nature of the region's homes, the logging camps themselves are shown to provide "very proper forest houses." These groups of shelters, where loggers would winter, were barely distinguishable from a "hovel for cattle." Built of logs and sealed with moss, these camps were aesthetically and practically assimilated into the forest proper, existing "as completely in the woods as a fungus at the foot of a pine in a swamp." Amid these meager and social forest spaces, loggers would establish their own domestic arrangements, and Thoreau hints at these felicitous relations by noting decks of cards left on fallen logs, evidence of whittling, and the "comfort" that must be offered by the large fireplaces at the structures' centers.[78]

The "hereish" aspects of Thoreau's para-realities include a range of places and experiences outside the domains of the so-called home. In *Walden*, Thoreau consecrates all forest spaces, lamenting that farmers of his day did not view the trees they cleared with Roman reverence, the ancients believing that they were "sacred to some god" (250). This idealized view of individuated worlds (replete with their own Big Others) takes stark material forms as well. The Romantic night-fishing scene earlier in the book has Thoreau shedding, in a Wordsworthian manner, the remains of the civilized day by immersing himself in the pond's animal nightlife. Thoreau sets up an asymmetrical encounter with part of this other world, suggesting that he was "communicating by a long flaxen line with mysterious nocturnal fishes" (175). Such communication typifies more than the Kantian notion that Beauty pleases without content.[79] For this non-signifying signal of presence literally tugs Thoreau out of his metaphysical reverie and toward the pond's ecosystem below. Although this section finds Thoreau making all sorts of anthropomorphic pronouncements (a lake as "the earth's eye," and so on [186]), he also attends to the actual physical phenomena below him. This includes ruminating how the "mysterious" fishes' "swimming impressed [him] as a kind of flight or hovering" (189). In the subsequent "The Ponds in Winter" section, he further examines this world, peering voyeuristically at the exotic "[h]eaven" below the ice where the "fabulous fishes" are as "foreign to the streets, even to the woods, foreign as Arabia to our Concord life" (284). This apparent cultural otherness soon morphs into a physical and ontological otherness, with the fish constituting "Waldenses," or, "animalized *nuclei* or crystals of the Walden water" (284).

Thoreau commonly ponders the para-realities of animals. When the locks halted his trip down the Merrimack River in *A Week*, for instance, Thoreau and his brother set off on foot through the rainy woods near Hooksett Pinnacle. The "dank forest path" they trod "now more like an otter's or a marten's trail, or where a beaver had dragged his trap, than where the wheels of travel raise a dust; where towns begin to serve as gores, only to hold the earth together" (313). This cartographic reversal, where human towns and symbolic points become like gores, or the excess empty space created when a curved map is flattened or, more accurately perhaps, the excess physical spaces that exist off (or despite) the map due to the distortion of cartographic representation, offers a playful metaphor for the alternate realities that abound in Thoreau's nature. One sees this kind of experience with plant and animal life as well. For example, just before the previous passage, Thoreau recounts how one afternoon heavy rain forced him to take cover for hours beneath a nearby tree. And he used this time "employed happily and profitably there prying with microscopic eye into the crevices of the bark or the leaves or the fungi at [his] feet" (300). This aside about micro worlds comes as Thoreau and his brother lie beneath the cover of thick bushes while light rain moved in. According to Thoreau, this space, shared with local birds, rivaled any domestic arrangement: "What were the amusements of the drawing room and the library in comparison . . . ?" (301). Earlier in *A Week*, Thoreau and John find a similar paraspace as they float beneath the "*tilia Americana*," or the linden tree, and fancy themselves entering a "strange land." In Thoreau's words, "As we sailed under this canopy of leaves we saw the sky through its chinks, and, as it were, the meaning and idea of the tree stamped in a thousand hieroglyphics on the heavens" (158–59). When one considers that while Thoreau wrote *A Week* during his stay at Walden Pond, he read books such as Melville's *Typee* (1846), this scene of pseudo plant writing dons an even more interesting cultural aspect. As I've written extensively elsewhere, *Typee* includes manifold fantasies about Polynesian tattooing practices, and, thus, here the "hieroglyphics" that the tree "stamped" on the heavens might be seen to, somewhat similarly, present an alternate signifying system and, perhaps, a distinct symbolic universe—albeit without the racial and cultural angst found in Melville's contexts.[80]

The place-based para-realities in Thoreau's work do, however, involve and implicate human socio-political forms. In *Walden*, Thoreau claims that it isn't until "we have lost the world . . . [that] we begin to find ourselves, and realize where we are and the infinite extent of our relations" (171). The world to be lost here is the standard civilized and capitalized one, as Thoreau's opening chapter makes abundantly clear. Thoreau often frames various outsides or alongsides to standard socio-political realities in a similar fashion, though perhaps with less direct political stakes. In *Walden*, he crafts something of a yeoman farmer-philosopher ideal: establishing a home and means of agricultural production without the normal hindrance of ownership or animal labor (56). Although he does not necessarily farm for substantial profits, he nonetheless compares his crops' returns to that of other Concord farmers, however ironically (55). In other passages, Thoreau departs from this flirtation with what Timothy Morton calls "agrilogistics," or the technological, economic, and ecological program that developed from its early origins into a dominating hyperobject of "global architecture."[81] In a later section of *Walden*, for instance, Thoreau visits Baker Farm, a locale he had considered adopting before choosing Walden, and found it had new owners, an Irishman named John Field and his family. Commenting on the meal he shared with the family, which included commodities such as butter and coffee, Thoreau reflects critically: "[H]e had to work hard to pay for them, and when he had worked hard he had to eat hard again to repair the waste of his system." Thoreau notes the personal discontent and loss of life that resulted from Field's consumption and labor practices, but he also links the deleterious effects of the system to broader socio-economic injunctions of the current state, which "endeavor[s] to compel you to sustain the slavery and war and other superfluous expenses which directly or indirectly result from the use of such things" (205). As opposed to this agricultural life of vicious depletion (where one spends one's time "clearing, and burning, and scratching, and harrowing, and plowing, and subsoiling" [*A Week*, 8]), Thoreau suggests that one should "[g]row wild according to thy nature, like the sedges and brakes, which will never become English hay" (207).[82]

On the level of para-places and realities, however, Thoreau's presentation of alternatives, much like his cavalier call for wildness, remain fleeting at best and unsubstantial at worst. Yet throughout his writings, we find moments and spaces of otherness that astonish him and that clearly have implications for his political and economic work. This includes a lugubrious afternoon in 1839 drifting on Walden Pond, where he "almost cease[d] to live—and began to be," an experience that made a "dallying" boatman stretched on a dock "an apt emblem of eternity."[83] Such scenes lead Thoreau to realize how the Concord River's gentle current, itself, evinced how "some flitting perspectives, and demi-experiences of the life that is in nature are . . . outside to time" (*Week*, 8). Common experiences such as these intimate, for Thoreau, ontological and material departures from the impositions of existing socio-economic systems. By way of a final example, Thoreau's discussion of fogs and clouds not only presents apt illustrations of the para-worlds I have been introducing but also hints at the way these worlds erect discontinuous material totalities. In *A Week*, Thoreau moves from the light mist he and John found along the *Merrimack* to a more substantial discussion of the fog he experienced at the top of Saddleback Mountain. He sets up the anecdote by asserting that "[m]ore extensive fogs . . . have their own limits" (180). By which he means such fogs *assert* their own limits. This is explained toward the end of his account, when he describes standing near the peak's tower observatory, "discover[ing] around [him] an ocean of mist." He was thus "left floating on this fragment of the wreck of a world, on [his] carved plank in cloudland" (188). This cloudland was, for Thoreau, nothing short of a "new world," where "[t]here was not a crevice left through which the trivial places we name Massachusetts, or Vermont, or New York, could be seen" (188). Nonetheless, this "undulating country of clouds," held for him a familiar perch (the tower as an aforementioned "wreck" from the old world) and, hence, he was able to imagine himself inhabiting these new environs ("the new terra firma perchance of my future life") (188).

Thoreau finds a very different cloudland, however, in his description of climbing Mount Katahdin in *The Maine Woods*. The clean break into a misty new realm on Saddleback Mountain is here replaced with an accumulating experience of deterritorialization. As Thoreau's group nears the elusive summit, for instance, members of the party "had not entire faith in the compass" and resort to climbing trees in order to render coordinates (58). Ascending, they front a clean mountain rill "tumbling down . . . literally from out of the clouds." Following it upward, they catch fleeting glimpses of the blue summit, but its peaks, themselves, are "almost retreating from [them][,]" and the party is once again "buried in the woods" (59). Thoreau then decides to leave his companions and climb the nearest peak alone. He describes the ascent as "scarcely less arduous than Satan's anciently through Chaos," which renders his use of Linnaean terminology directly afterward (calling the nearby black spruce trees "*Abies nigra*," for example) an ironic and faltering attempt at stability (60). Traversing a landscape of rock caverns, bear caves, and odd configurations of vegetation, Thoreau suggests that the rocks on the side of the summit were the "flocks and herds that pastured, chewing a rocky cud," and they "looked at [him] with hard gray eyes" (61). This para-natural scene brings us a long way from the comfort afforded by deep granite foundations in *Walden*. It also ushers in a more troubling version of the sublime than Shelley's "Mont Blanc" ever musters. As Thoreau ascends, the mountain itself is unhinged materially and syntactically, composed of a "vast aggregation of loose rocks, as if sometime it had rained rocks." This "undone extremity of the globe," lacking sedimented soil or a symbolic quilting point, is nothing short of the "raw materials of a planet" (63).

Thoreau's semantic swerve toward portraying this loose and high place as a potential other planet continues as he enters "the skirts of the cloud" and experiences something of a crisis in writing, employing a variety of metaphors to represent the effects of the newfound space. "It was like sitting in a chimney and waiting for the smoke to blow away," he writes. "It was, in fact, a cloud-factory,—these were the cloud-works" (63–64). Thoreau also suggests that this place has distinct effects on the human visitor: "It was vast, Titanic, and such as man never inhabits. Some part of the beholder, even some vital part, seems to escape through the loose grating of his ribs as he ascends" (64). Alas, so much for Emerson's Reason. What's more, in Thoreau's account, these effects take a sinister and antagonistic turn: "Vast, Titanic, inhuman nature has got him at disadvantage, caught him alone." In other words, within these "hostile ranks of clouds," not only are Thoreau's previous coordinates in jeopardy but so, too, is the world in toto (63). As Thoreau puts it, "It was Matter, vast, terrific,—not his Mother Earth," and "[t]here was there felt the presence of a force not bound to be kind to man" (70).

Thoreau's Mount Katahdin experience thus brings us to a seminal aspect of Thoreau's para-realities—the fact that his looping realities have stakes for real bodies and real matter in real time. Encountering the mountain's "inhuman" otherness pushes Thoreau, later in the chapter, to sound a Whitmanian note, but one infused with the fear of historical precarity.

"I stand in awe of my body," he reflects, "this matter to which I am bound has become so strange to me. I fear not spirits, ghosts, of which I am one,—*that* my body might—but I fear bodies, I tremble to meet them" (71). Let's turn now to the grounds of these meetings.

Loops 2: From Nested Loops to Loop Dialectics

If Thoreau bristles with fear at the prospect of encountering other bodies while atop Mount Katahdin, it is, perhaps, because his writings attribute significant power to different loops of reality. As such, the formation of any historical-material condition, including various para-realities, is predicated upon the ways that loops interact. Up to a point, it may be useful to think of Thoreau's "hereish" as being constituted by an infinite variety of para-realities that are, to employ the term that Morton and Sloterdijk use, "nested."[84] Nesting involves a type of braided inhabiting that allows for both monadic configurations (a modicum of discontinuity) as well as the formation of both neat and messy networks. As I've intimated, however, Thoreau's thinking, especially in the 1850s, challenges the conceptual bounds of not only his own moment's coordinates but also our own. In an effort to better understand Thoreau's structural conception of the world—along with its historical, ontological, and political stakes—I want to push us into and then out of "nested loops" and toward a less familiar modality of loop dialectics.[85]

Although we've touched on various aspects of Thoreau's para-realities, it is now important to note the sheer interactivity of these looping states. In the journal passage used as this chapter's first epigraph, Thoreau presents reality as a "concentric system of worlds." The term "system" should be emphasized, as it connotes a dynamic relation within material time. Further into the passage, Thoreau suggests that science has yet to "penetrate" this "infinite" system. Nonetheless, he hints that connections between and among these zones are possible, such as when he plays his flute "as if to leap the bounds that narrow fold where human life is penned." In addition to sound, he surmises, too, that the dispersal of seeds for some flowers may originate from bordering loops.[86] Thoreau expresses a similar sentiment in *A Week*, writing that "[i]t is easier to discover another such a new world as Columbus did, than to go within one fold of this which we appear to know" (383). And yet, as he points out, "There are perturbations in our orbits produced by the influence of outlying spheres" (386). He thus enjoins the reader to cast their life bravely toward the zones where these systems meet: "Our lives should go between the lichen and the bark" (385).

One could spend a good bit of time indexing simple examples of such "nested" realities in Thoreau's writing. Thoreau portrays consistently material relations in a manner that might strike its own chord with Haraway's aforementioned call to make "oddkin" in the Chthulucene.[87] As Thoreau notes in his journal, "There are strange affinities in this universe—strange ties stranger harmonies and relationships, what kin am I to some wildest pond among the mountains."[88] These moments and scenes, however, are often shown to be the products of wider economic and global systems. Thoreau's transcendental leanings have been well rehearsed. And with them, of course, comes a general metonymic or even metaphoric (if one follows some versions of Emerson) approach toward "nature": where particular and material aspects of reality are linked, often in a disjunctive manner (hence "transcend"), to higher ideals and laws. Thoreau's writings, though, are ever-concerned with the actual systems at work in the production and maintenance of antebellum socioeconomic arrangements. As might be expected, even on the level of historical global relations, we get a good bit of abstract deep time and planetary expanse with Thoreau. All literature, for instance, enacts an untimely schism whereby, as Thoreau puts it, "The oldest Egyptian or Hindoo philosopher raised a corner of the veil from the stature of the divinity; and still the trembling robe remains raised, and I gaze upon as fresh a glory as he did, since it was I in him that was then so bold, and it was he in me that now reviews the vision" (*Walden*, 99). As Walls notes, however, Thoreau read over six languages and, as a result, in a very material way, "to him, literature was *world* literature."[89] Hence, the global connections of his world, such as the "murmurs of many a famous river on the other side of globe" which "reach" even to placid Concord River where Thoreau drifted, include, too, cultural productions and socioeconomic networks (*A Week*, 11). In his discussion of world religion, for example, Thoreau imagines a gathering of world scriptures, a compendium of sacred greatest hits "print[ed] together" (*A Week*, 143). In Thoreau's thinking, the myopic nature of the west, with its "limited range of . . . sympathies and studies" (142), would do well to consider texts such as the Bhagavad Gita—an effort that might mitigate the master signifier of the New Testament within western society (144).

Tellingly, however, this very rumination about global cultural-religious norms is interrupted by the material emissaries of capital when a canal boat appears in the scene: "[S]uddenly a canal boat, with its sail set, glided round a point before us, like some huge river beast, and changed the scene in an instant; and then another and another glided into sight, and we found ourselves in the current of commerce once more" (*A Week*, 144). Thoreau commonly notes the local alienating effects of developing industrial capitalism, suggesting famously that "the cost of a thing is the amount of what I call life which is required to be exchanged for it" (*Walden*, 31). At the same time, Thoreau rarely loses sight of the systemic circumstances that shape local conditions. Thus, the nested loops that compose the society of his neighbors and the various para-realities about and within them are caught up in and molded by vast material loops. "Such is Commerce," he writes in *A Week*, "which shakes the cocoa-nut and bread-fruit tree in the remotest isle" (212). Although he elsewhere surmises that local food production might relieve a given community from "depend[ing] on distant and fluctuating markets" (*Walden*, 63), he also imagines, correctly it seems, that the systems and symbols of capital rivaled the natural world's ability to produce realities. Finding scraps of a newspaper while hiking Saddleback Mountain, Thoreau reflects, "These advertisements and the prices current were more closely allied to nature, and were respectable in some measure as tide and meteorological tables are" (*A Week*, 185). Notwithstanding the respectability of prices and their socio-economic worlding effects, Thoreau sees such forces producing an aimless (and hence, ethics-less) movement: "We . . . are enveloped in an invisible network of speculations—Our progress is only from one such speculation to another, and only at rare intervals do we perceive that it is no progress."[90] In this journal passage, Smith's hidden and guiding hand devolves into mysterious yet actual networks of speculation that lead nowhere. But, as Thoreau laments elsewhere, such speculations also can breed ever-anew modes of violence, slavery, and subjection.[91]

The reality of vast economic systems animating nested loops has profound effects on Thoreau's notion of history. In *Bird Relics*, Arsić portrays this concept in her discussion of Thoreau's writings about Native American mussel middens. In 1837, Thoreau begins describing these sites, such as the midden on Clamshell Hill, as "intentionally confus[ing] geology and history" by "interlacing strata of natural and artificial."[92] According to Arsić, this lesson in Native-American geo-history offers Thoreau a way of thinking of time in terms of "contemporaneous sites rather than chronologically ordered points."[93] As Walls recounts in wonderful anecdote, Thoreau's early encounters with midden sites and arrowheads—including as the famous 1837 scene where a young Thoreau magically, it seems, finds Tahatawan's arrowhead along a Concord riverbank—are a mechanism for seeing and telling alternative histories. In Walls's account, Thoreau understood that the "story told by Tahatawan's arrowhead" comprised uncomfortable local historical truths and swerving realities. This included the fact that Nashoba, the town Tahatawan worked to build, was destroyed during King Philip's war, and its fifty-eight remaining indigenous residents were sold into slavery from a prison camp in Boston Harbor. But it also included a structural sense of how the ecological-agricultural practices of the Native Americans, evidenced in the midden mounds, were being overlaid by western enclosures and regimes of agrilogistics—particularly how Native American usage rights and commons were facing appropriation and privatization.[94] The alternate synchronistic array of places found in Arsić's discussion of middens is here reformulated indirectly into discontinuous realities mediated via specific forms of violence and antagonism. Ironically perhaps, Arsić cites William Bartram's writings from the 1760s and 1770s to set up her discussion of middens. As opposed to the positive and inclusive material expanse of time that Arsić settles on, Monique Allewaert's own work on William Bartram's *Travels* (1791) reveals a dynamic and antagonistic western encounter with otherness—where, in the plantation zone, Bartram faces threatening entanglements of vegetation and fugitive bodies.[95] Following Allewaert, I want to show how Thoreau viewed historical-material reality as both dynamic and, consequently, unstable.

Even a cursory look at Thoreau's many discussions of Native American history and encounters reveals a type of uncanny closeness marked, at once, by material presence and absence—yielding a parallactic notion of chrono-ontology that, I will argue, is a component of his unique view of dialectical change. For Thoreau, both the presence of Native Americans (and their historical traces) in the present as well as their conspicuous absences are linked commonly to broader systemic and global concerns, especially those related to colonial-imperial projects. This can be seen metaphorically in *Walden* when Thoreau describes numerous laborers descending upon the pond in winter 1846–47 in order to strip the ice, or "skin" of the water, at the bidding of a local "gentleman farmer" (294). This market appropriation elicits Thoreau's light condemnation, and he rejoices quietly in moments when the undertaking stalls. In his words, "[S]ometimes Squaw Walden had her revenge, and a hired man, walking behind his team, slipped through a crack" (295). Metonymically figuring the besieged, capitalized, and, in part, relocated pond as a "squaw" is obviously odious in our own moment. But Thoreau's move is symptomatic of his wider soft critique of the historical state of Native American existence/nonexistence. However obliquely, this scene figures Native American existence as a diffuse and fading remainder after violent appropriation by global market forces. Just after fancifully noting the "squaw's" small victories, Thoreau transitions: "To speak literally, a hundred Irishmen, with Yankee overseers, came from

Cambridge every day to get out the ice" (295). The antagonism between Native Americans and market forces is here replaced with more present ethnic-class divides, and Thoreau closes the section by showing how the network of loaded relations ends with global exchanges and consumption: "Thus it appears that the sweltering inhabitants of Charlestown and New Orleans, of Madras and Bombay and Calcutta, drink at my well" (297–98).

Thoreau is here certainly caught up within period liberal sentimental rhetoric typified by at once "feeling badly" for disappearing indigenous populations and working to normalize the inevitability of their demise.[96] A similar logic is apparent in Thoreau's fraught relationship with racialized evolutionary exceptionalism, especially that of Agassiz.[97] In *Walden*, for example, he naturalizes an apparent progressive civilizing tendency in society and nature, where "[t]here is a period in the history of the individual, as of the race, when the hunters are the 'best men'" (212). According to Thoreau, these lowly, worm-like "animal" parts of the self are now "dying out" (220). Thoreau links these ideas directly to Native American culture in *The Maine Woods*. Describing a negative emotional response to moose hunting, he writes, "What a course and imperfect use Indians and hunters make of nature! No wonder that their race is so soon exterminated" (120).[98] It is the historically precarious nature of Native American life that, in part, entices Thoreau in Maine. Earlier in the book, for instance, within his descriptions of the local Native American guide Joe Aitteon, Thoreau explains that he "had employed an Indian mainly that I might have an opportunity to study his ways" (95).

In Thoreau's wider corpus, however, the disappearance of indigenous peoples is far less natural than it is a political expediency of colonial power. What's more, the very topic, which is surely overwrought in his writing, helps reveal the structural stakes of Thoreau's notion of history as well as his particular understanding of the relations in play within what I've been calling "nested loops." *A Week*, for instance, includes a number of historical asides about violent colonial encounters with local Native American tribes. To note one example, while floating near the town of Pembroke, Thoreau recounts how in 1725 Captain Lovewell's men "prevailed" over a contingent of "rebel Indians" (Thoreau includes quotes around this term) after a "bloody fight." Moving to his contemporary moment, he posits rather obliquely, "What if the Indians are exterminated, are not savages as grim prowling about the clearings to-day?" (119–20). It is not readily clear what Thoreau intends to suggest with this statement. But shortly after, he laments the violent demise and removal of the Native Americans in question: "But alas! of the crippled Indians, . . . how many balls lodged with them, . . . and finally what pension or township was granted them, there is no journal to tell" (122). He closes with an anecdote about how, before his last march, Lovewell bent an infant elm into a bow and remarked that "'he would treat the Indians in the same way.'" Thoreau rejoins, "This elm is still standing, [in Nashua] a venerable and magnificent tree" (122).

This resilient elm joins a number of other conspicuous passages in Thoreau's writings—such as Walden pond as a vengeful "squaw" or, in *A Week*, the Concord River moving with the "moccasined tread of an Indian warrior" (11)—where he figures Native American experience in the present as, on the one hand, a displaced and naturalized trace and, on the other, as a trace that remains animated by very real and specific historical antagonisms. This formulation is not necessarily new within period literature. In its admiration for continued Native American resistance, it does, however, differ ideologically from popular and earlier treatments such as Lydia Howard Huntley Sigourney's poem "The Mohegan Church" (1834), which fantasizes about exorcizing lingering Native American indignation by converting remaining "pagan" spirits, or Lydia Maria Child's notion that Christian love would eventually change the physiognomy of Native Americans by presumably shifting their very "skulls" toward that of "Caucasians."[99] As suggested, Thoreau's view of Native Americans is anything but consistent. But, like Thoreau's ambiguous description of a Native American girl sitting by a river in a small Maine town "humming or moaning a song," even in moments of ambivalence and/or ambiguity, he offers a view of history that is cut across by potential alternatives as well as by both deep and present antagonisms (*Maine*, 9).

For Thoreau, therefore, history proper is an incomplete record of events due to political domination. Yet lived and material history also includes real, though perhaps foreclosed, antagonisms within a dislocated present. In this sense, Thoreau's history is indeed a unique and expansive material collection of various temporalities—but instead of positive sedimented layers, it is comprised of active and disjunctive forces ushering *both* from uncanny banished locations/temporalities and from the everyday surface of the present.[100] Thoreau returns to this line of thinking in different terms later in *A Week*. After describing history as, literally, geological deposits and social debris (151), Thoreau moves this static spatialization of time into a more dynamic scenario, writing, "We should read history as little critically as we consider the landscape, and be more interested by the atmospheric tints and various lights and shades which the intervening spaces create" (154). He goes on: "In reality, history fluctuates as the face of the landscape from morning to evening" (154). On the one hand, one could follow Morton and read Thoreau's aestheticization of history as an example of the need to view reality (including ecological and social histories) as an expansive and complex array of material-aesthetic effects.[101] On the other, Thoreau casts the "fluctuation" of materialized time, engendered by the play of absence and presence, in terms that have sociopolitical stakes, however muted in the case of Native Americans. As we'll see, Thoreau associates this fluctuation with causalities and effects produced by the interactions among various nested loops.

This brings us to the point where we can characterize Thoreau's particular notion of the interactions among and within nested loops as his own form of dialectics. Employing the term "dialectics" risks muddying the ideological waters, as it invokes a long and variegated genealogy within western Marxism particularly that has been under siege by various liberal forms of multiplicity. It is my hope that readers sympathetic to the dialectic, and all its import, will find that Thoreau's model offers an older but perhaps nuanced form of capacious dialectics that speaks to urgent requirements of our times. Readers hesitant to engage with dialectical thought and its traditions may find that Thoreau's work provides a useful, though perhaps challenging, means to think complex networks and ontologies in terms of actual historical change and antagonism.

The structural logic of Thoreau's material-historical views comes to the surface, literally it seems, in his famous aforementioned railroad sand passage toward the close of *Walden*. Thoreau recounts the "delight" he felt while "observ[ing] the forms which thawing sand and clay assume in flowing down the sides of a deep cut on the railroad" (304). The sand itself holds unique significance for Thoreau, and he notes how the streams of earth are a "hybrid product, which obeys half way the law of currents, and half way that of vegetation." The resulting "*grotesque* vegetation" varies from resembling "leaves or vines" and lichens, to "leopards' paws or birds' feet," to the "brains or lungs or bowels, and excrements of all kinds" (305). The use of the term "grotesque" here is symptomatic of period racial anxieties. For example, in *Typee*, a book, as noted, that Thoreau read while living at Walden Pond, Melville employs the term to describe the troubling aesthetic and, ultimately, racial categorical confusion engendered by the "variety" and "infinite protrusion" of some Polynesian tattoo designs.[102] In *Walden*, the grotesque nature of the sand goes beyond the aesthetic register and implicates the "hybrid" way it is produced—occurring, in Thoreau's terms, as a "sandy rupture" that "springs into existence . . . suddenly" (306). The interference between and among the laws of physics ("currents") and the laws of vegetation thus produces an eruption of various new forms that resemble a "foliaceous mass" (306).

In typical organicist fashion, Thoreau then moves into a rumination that extrapolates from the production of sandy "lobes," as he calls them, to the "internal" and "external" production of all earthly phenomena. For Thoreau, the sandy hillside marks something of a "laboratory of the Artist who made the world," and this laboratory is "still at work" (306). The lobes of sand, therefore, "anticipate the vegetable leaf," resemble the "vitals of the animal body," and reveal the modality of becoming of all material forms—from the ear and hand to trees and the globe itself (306). To some degree, Thoreau is merely riffing on views common within period botany. In Goethe's *Italian Journey* (1816), for example, Goethe presents an organicism where "[f]rom first to last, the plant is nothing but leaf." Indeed, in 1850, as Thoreau was revising *Walden*, Emerson published an essay on Goethe that explained how "a leaf may be converted into any other organ, and any other organ into a leaf."[103] And yet, within Thoreau's display of typical transformative organicism, he depicts material reality as a process forged at the nexus of various forces in which broader material causalities shape the local manifestations of forms: "The very globe continually transcends and translates itself," he writes, "and becomes winged in its orbit" (*Walden*, 306–7). Although conditioned and perhaps contained by the laws and forces that produce it, the world's "orbit" becomes here rather "ex-orbital," with the explosion of new forms engendering multitudinous and dynamic environments.[104]

This material dynamism has important implications for Thoreau's conception of socio-political realities. If all physical forms are temporal crystallizations (a concept that long interested him) of amorphous lobe formations ("[t]he ball of the human finger is but a drop congealed"), then it follows that human institutions and inhuman economic systems are, likewise, "loitering" drops frozen over temporarily into influential historical-material forms (*Walden*, 307). As Thoreau writes:

> The earth is not a mere fragment of dead history, stratum upon stratum like the leaves of a book, to be studied by geologists and antiquarians chiefly, but living poetry like the leaves of a tree, which precede flowers and fruit, not a fossil earth, but a living earth; compared with whose great central life all animal and vegetal life is parasitic. Its throes will heave our exuviae from their graves. You may

melt your metals and cast them into the most beautiful molds you can; they will never excite me like the forms which this molten earth flows out into. And not only it, but the institutions upon it, are plastic like clay in the hands of the potter. (*Walden*, 309)

Here the earth—matter, vegetation, and human institutions alike—becomes a continual material process of change. As opposed to some variety of Deleuzian repetition and "primordial multiplicity,"[105] Thoreau's schematic presents a continuous transformation of malleable realities marked by discontinuity: Graves will be moved, metals will melt, and the earth's interior will burst into new surface formations. In other words, this perpetual transformation is not portrayed as simply an abstract truth or a purely contingent inertia-like movement. It is attributed to different causalities and potential actants. Consequently, substantive material and social reality is a changing formal landscape of historical effects and counter effects. Its material forms are "heaps" that constitute what we might call *nested totalities*. The para-realities discussed earlier in the chapter are indeed situated within nested loops, but these formations and interactions are here revealed to include contingent interactive processes where para-wholes are formed.

In pushing Thoreau's thought toward this notion of nested totalities, I am less concerned with interrogating how his writing fits within specific genealogies of dialectics than with restoring the conceptual and historical-political frameworks that shaped his work. My claims about Thoreau's worldview thus depart significantly from Jane Bennett's influential take on vital materialism, especially her notion that Thoreau offers us a "*Heteroverse*," a system where "heterogeneous elements intersect or influence one another and how this ensemble of intersections does not form a unified or self-sufficient whole."[106] At stake is the very notion of totality, a concept that is foundational within dialectical thinking. As opposed to Bennett's heteroverse or other similar contemporary models that replace elements of wholeness with liberal-pluralizing material formations (Levine's "affordances" or Morton's "mesh," for instance), a dialectical approach, according to Fredric Jameson, "begins with" totality.[107] Jameson's point is that regardless of what iteration of materialist dialectics one employs—from Marx's "historical materialism" to early twentieth-century notions of "dialectical materialism" to various formative structural approaches to the topics found in Althusser, Adorno, and others—the dialectic includes "the shift in thinking on to a new and unaccustomed plane in an effort to deal with the fact of distinct and autonomous realities that seem to offer no contact with each other."[108]

What Bennett and others may miss with regard to Thoreau, therefore, is the foundational qualitative way his expansive and dynamic world includes contact, change, influence, and, indeed, the formation of realities.[109] In related terms, the dialectic's famous practice of the "negation of the negation" is really, according to Jean Hyppolite, a "creative" process where "the posited term had been isolated and this was itself a kind of negation. From this follows that the negation of that term allows the whole to be recaptured."[110] We see this type of conceptual-material process in Thoreau's work throughout his life: from various strivings to inhabit anew classical languages and realities, to aforementioned pronouncements in *Walden* such as the claim that "not till we have lost the world, do we begin to find ourselves, and realize where we are and the infinite extent of our relations" (171), to his rumination in *A Week* about "[h]ow fortunate were [those] who did not own an acre of these shores, who had not renounced [their] title to the whole" (350). Such Romantic appeals to grander scopes and higher unities, however, obscures a potentially more formative dialectical return to historical and economic totalities within these very same works. Backing up a bit to *Walden*'s sand passage, one should remember that the sand in question is exposed by the railroad's "deep cut," thus dialectically linking the scene's horizon of possibility to capital's developing systems. Earlier in the book, Thoreau takes great pains to map the realities being formed by this system, describing how the circulation of commerce produces not only economies and outer worlds replete with slavery but also inner ones: "Up comes the cotton, down goes the woven cloth; up comes the silk, down goes the woollen; up come the books, but down goes the wit that writes them" (116). Thoreau's sandy rumination on the potentiality of all material forms, therefore, is given a specific historical frame: the actuality of antebellum American's capitalist-slave economy. According to Thoreau, the very same train whose tracks cut the earth by the pond is guided by a "planetary motion" whose "orbit does not look like a returning curve" (116). The widening path of the train's motion might recall Thoreau's claim that one's walk should take the potentially open geometric shape of a parabola. Here, though, the speculative expanse of the economic system clearly girds such potential movement and variation (ontic and ontological alike) with significant material, economic, and ideological strictures.

The point I want to make is that Thoreau's plastic "foliaceous mass" is not merely part of a massively distributed web of weaving causalities—as it surely is—but that this web affords such masses and forces the ability to produce consolidated effects. In *Walden* and Thoreau's other early writings, such effects often take the form of reverberations caused by short circuits within material-historical configurations. Much like the aforementioned dormant bug that emerges after sixty years from an apple tree table to new "winged life," Thoreau figures the present as a strange place, a "meeting of two eternities, the past and future" (*Walden*, 333, 17). And this place of new encounters and reencounters engenders a properly dialectical reorientation of the present, the future, and, indeed, the past. As Thoreau notes in his first journal, "As the least drop of wine colors the whole goblet, so the least particle of truth colors the whole of our life. It is never isolated, or simply added as dollars to our stock. When any real progress is made, we unlearn and learn anew, what we thought we knew before." In Thoreau's line of thinking, the present's "truths" not only break from the past but also literally break it into "*disjecta membra*" that one must "[pick] up and [lay] aside."[111] From this perspective, nested totalities not only embody local para-realities, local experiences of nested loops, and local dialectical sites of interaction but also afford the potential to affect breaks within such nested realities (from within and without) and to leverage wider consolations of form.

The type of dialectics Thoreau offers thus resembles key aspects of George Ciccariello-Maher's aforementioned call for a "decolonizing dialectics." In "shunning the lure of unity," Ciccariello-Maher's brand of dialectics foregrounds "the indeterminacies of political identities slamming against one another, transforming themselves and their worlds." Working to address two conspicuous foreclosures within traditional dialectics, namely the exclusion of certain types of subjects, what Frantz Fanon calls the "zone of nonbeing," and the para-space of the outside, a concept Enrique Dussel terms "exteriority," Ciccariello-Maher develops a more nuanced approach toward material and historical interaction. As Ciccariello-Maher writes, "Instead of simply loosening the bond of dialectical opposition to the point of multiplicity, . . . *colonial* difference indicates a more concrete and precise way of grasping those oppositions not visible to a traditional dialectics but whose appearance does not mark the impossibility of dialectics entirely."[112]

Although conceived within an earlier ideological milieu, Thoreau's Romantic-era take on ecological and sociopolitical change shares with Ciccariello-Maher's decolonized dialectics a conceptual inclusivity and complexity that allows it to view reality as the production of specific (hence historical) malleable realities rather than as merely contingent multiplicities. At the same time, Thoreau's views on material-historical change should be differentiated from the Darwin-inspired modes of developmental ideas, as they were popularly called, that dominated the thought of New England intelligentsia during the last years of his life. As scholars have rehearsed, although Thoreau had long been familiar with Darwin's *Voyage of the Beagle* (1839), it was his January 1860 reading of a newly arrived copy of *On the Origin of Species* (1859) that catalyzed his longstanding interest in the distribution of plants and animals as well as his rejection of Agassiz's theory of special creation.[113] With Darwin's formative theory of "descent with modification" in mind, Thoreau began a roughly two-year process of recalibrating and developing his massive journals—tirelessly listing all of the local natural phenomena by date and time and later formulating this statistical information into various charts and tables. In addition to this labor, he began working on what would become a 400-page manuscript, unpublished in his time, titled, "The Dispersion of Seeds." Taking up Darwin's work on plant dispersion, Thoreau broke aggressively with Agassiz's polemical responses to Darwin's work, a debate that played out throughout 1860 within the Boston Society of Natural History. In his manuscript, Thoreau writes that it is a "vulgar prejudice that such forests are 'spontaneously generated,' but science knows that there has not been a sudden new creation in their case but a steady progress according to existing laws, that they came from seeds—that is, are the result of causes still in operation."[114] Shifting the mechanism of and temporal register for creation, Thoreau suggests that ongoing species dispersal occurs materially at a "geologic pace."[115] Consequently, this manuscript as well as the statistical methods employed in the later journals (which include a seven-foot long map of the Concord River's flowage channels) offer distinct modifications to both the scale and method of Thoreau's intellectual work. I want to suggest, however, that we should refrain from drawing rigid demarcations between the type of dialectic seen in Thoreau's earlier work and these later reflections on biological progression. Conversely, we might see Thoreau's aforementioned dialectic expanding here to encompass geological time and, in so doing, depicting a different modality of change-in-process. As noted, in his *On the Origin of Species*, Darwin refers to what will be called, by 1866, "ecology," as an "economy of nature."[116] In this context, the type of "economy" in play for Thoreau is perhaps much more comprehensive than the received modern rubric of "ecology" may allow. For example, much hinges on the way we read the term "sudden" in Thoreau's anti-creationist line that there has not been "a sudden new creation" within the generation of tree species. If Thoreau's variety of the dialectic is dynamic enough to encompass divergent actants and realities, then it is not simply that the later Thoreau finally comes-to-science, as it were, putting away the childish Platonic roots of Transcendentalism and also, as some would have it, his temporary flings with political fanaticism. Perhaps his worldview has the remarkable ability to traverse various—often asymmetrical and discontinuous—scales and causalities. As Thoreau writes as early as 1837, "Revolutions are never sudden. Not one man, nor many men, in a few years or generations, suffice to regulate events, and dispose mankind for the revolutionary moment. The hero is but the crowning stone of the pyramid—the keystone of the arch."[117] In *A Week*, he directly links such political change to geological transformations: "As in geology, so in social institutions, we may discover the causes of all past change in the present invariable order of society. The greatest appreciable physical revolutions are the work of the light-footed air, the stealthy-paced water, and the subterranean fire." It follows that the "longer the lever the less perceptible its motion. It is the slowest pulsation which is the most vital" (128). To follow Thoreau, we too must be adept enough to follow the parallactic loops between the expanse of his late indexes of natural phenomena and the socioeconomic antagonisms that attend his earlier writings. Put differently, we should read these late passages *with* as opposed to against *Walden*, his John Brown essays, and many of his other pieces on modes of political change that invoke nothing short of a "divine violence" that Walter Benjamin would well recognize.

Read from this perspective, Thoreau's many passages about local phenomena often portray the precarious and antagonistic conditions of particular environments in terms that implicate various systems of relation. This condensation of scale tends to open up given realities to the messy networks that condition both their existence as well as their conditions of possibility—how experiences in these presents produce effects and change. Consider Thoreau's bean field as an example. As Thoreau notes, the "curious labor" of planting beans—he had, by the time of recording events, planted rows that stretched seven miles in length—both "attached [him] to the earth" as well as placed him square within dominant agricultural practices (155). In terms of the latter, Thoreau includes a tidy chart of the expenses and monetary income from his crops, and he refers to this economic data as the "result" of his "experience in raising beans" (163). What's more, maintaining the valuable bean crops yields its own type of localized "long war" against weeds of all of varieties, where these competing life forms (along with fauna such as worms and especially woodchucks) represent "enemies" to be dispatched in pseudo-bloody "weedy deed[s]" (155, 161).[118] Tellingly, Thoreau frames this warfare with a seemingly ironic appeal to national imperialism, commenting on the pride he felt at times when the village's patriotic music drifted into the woods. This strain going so far as to make him feel "as if [he] could spit a Mexican with a good relish" (161).

By acting as a connective link between "wild and cultivated fields," however, his bean labor also opens up alternate experiences and ways of seeing (158). This includes setting up a critique of large-scale farming, where he opines that the "farmer leads the meanest of lives. He knows Nature but as a robber" (165–66). Agricultural robbery extends, for Thoreau, beyond concerns of plant and animal life. Turning up arrowheads with his hoe, for example, evinces how "an extinct nation had anciently dwelt here and planted corn and beans ere white men came to clear the land" (156). Indeed, the very soil represents "the ashes of unchronicled nations" (158). Giving a keen sociopolitical spin to his aforementioned late reflections on the dispersal of seeds, Thoreau, in these earlier works, considers the colonial dispersal of plant life in terms of historical regimes of domination. In *A Week*, he describes how the advent of mills in North America led to "English grain," along with other European seeds (dandelion, burdock, catnip, etc.), being "scattered" among the "wild native ones." This process thus "plants a town" (52). In *Walden*, this historical-biological process cuts in two directions, at least speculatively. Invoking the aforementioned resistant elm that metaphorically stands in for the remaining traces of Native American life as well as the various plant and dwelling remnants of ex-slaves among the woods at Walden (Cato Ingraham's walnuts, Brister Freeman's apple trees, and so on), Thoreau suggests that the "exterminated groundnut," or as he explains, the *Apios tuberosa*, "the potato of the aborigines," might "perhaps revive and flourish . . . prove itself indigenous, and resume its ancient importance and dignity as the diet of the hunter tribe" (239). As I've intimated, Thoreau's dialectical historicism certainly includes predictable racist-colonial appeals to a becoming-naturalized historical telos.[119] But in this passage from *Walden* on the violence wrought upon Native Americans, Thoreau presents a type of untimely dislocation that yields slantwise its own material production and perhaps large-scale renewal.

The potential edge of Thoreau's fantasy about weed revolution and uncanny indigenous returns is perhaps dulled by his more congenial closing rumination about the utopic effects of the beans. As he puts it, "This broad field which I have looked at so long looks not to me as the principle cultivator, but away from me to influences more genial to it. . . . These beans have results which are not harvested by me. Do they not grow for the woodchucks partly?" (166). Moving to negate his earlier war rhetoric, he rejoices at the production of weeds, which act as a "granary of the birds," and he suggests, in turn, that the "true husbandman will cease from anxiety" (166). Although presenting localized reality in terms of dialectical effects that push into an array of para-relations, Thoreau appears to move from the specific historicity of weeds (with a defined colonial past) toward a more generalized and liberal openness to otherness. Read in the context of Thoreau's other early work, however, this openness to alterity is not necessarily without specific political import. In "The Service" (1840), for instance, Thoreau similarly applauds a "brave man" who "deals not so much in resolute action" as much as exists confidently in an open and calm "palmy state[,] . . . compelling alliance in all directions."[120] Yet this open expansion has ameliorating historical effects. "There is no ill which may not be dissipated like the dark," Thoreau writes, "if you let in a stronger light upon it." This stronger light includes, later in the essay, chivalric rhetoric about the potential need for combat: "Let not our Peace be proclaimed by the rust on our swords, or our inability to draw them from their scabbards, but let her at least have so much work on her hands, as to keep those swords bright and sharp."[121]

If considering Thoreau's fused planetary and local scales offers a means to glean his unique dialectical perspective, then by thinking together the seemingly divergent notions of a brave "palmy state" and the need for sharp and active swords provides a way to begin conceiving of his much-discussed but little understood political ontology.

Loops 3: Para-Politics, or, Militant Vegetables

This chapter ends with something of its own loop back to the image of Thoreau, amid an army of fish, wielding a crowbar against the Billerica Dam. Having passed through the previous two sections, we are now in the position to better understand this odd political scene as well as how it may relate to Thoreau's anti-slavery efforts.

Thus far, we have seen how Thoreau's universe is not a vibrant nonideational expanse, but a fabric of particular and interactive formations. Much like Timothy Morton's notion that "it's bigger on the inside than it is on the outside," implying that the worlds generated by the folds and grafts of the outside constitute discontinuous though interactive realities, for Thoreau all components of a given realty, including the very self that so occupied him, are shaped by interactive material forms.[122] Thoreau makes this point in many places, including his essay "Life Without Principle" (1863). Although the essay was published after his death, it is based upon one of his most frequent lectures, delivered for the first time in New Bedford in December 1854. After sounding familiar notes censuring the false realities generated by antebellum economic and social structures, Thoreau argues that even the most "intellectual" and "liberal" of men "come to a stand against some institution in which they appear to hold stock—that is, some particular, not universal, way of viewing things."[123] Thoreau then uses an architectural metaphor for such "particular" optics of viewing, writing, "They will continually thrust their own low roof . . . between you and the sky." This leads Thoreau to conclude that the "best men that I know are not . . . a world in themselves. For the most part, they dwell in forms."[124] This is why Thoreau is able to dismiss offhandedly public speeches and the press as mere empty repetitions, where "[s]urface meets surface."[125] The typical move here would be to cast Thoreau as a fundamental universalist peddling easy Emersonian notions of the Oversoul. Following the historical and theoretical contexts I've outlined, however, I want to suspend our own common institutions of reading and begin to think of Thoreau's claims about the universal in terms of spatial and, ultimately, historical coordinates. From this perspective, Thoreau's "universal . . . way of viewing things" is not simply a plea for some grand totality, but a move toward dialectical change and political leverage within complex sets of nested realities.

The place of ontology, where one might locate standard Romantic notions of subjectivity, has unique structural purchase for the way Thoreau describes the historical-political relations among universals and particulars, including the formations they produce. As Thoreau directs in his essay "The Last Days of John Brown" (1860), we should "[l]ook not to legislatures and churches for . . . guidance, nor to any soulless, *incorporated* bodies, but to *inspirited* or inspired ones."[126] The term "incorporated" is paramount here, invoking, as it does, a sundry of period socioeconomic relations, including the violence stemming from a slave economy and the civic debates about personhood and citizenship that attended it.[127] In other words, to be an "incorporated" body is to be a body that is fully interpellated into given forms that produce or perpetuate violence. If average men "dwell in forms," to quote Thoreau again, then what we might call revolutionary bodies are physical forms that are dwelled within ("inspirited") in ways that "inspire" historical effects in and against existing violent regimes. The place of spirit in this scenario obviously holds vast import for the possibility of para-realities, including historical and political change. One should not lose sight of the materialist implications of being inspirited. Much like Fuller's account of specific effects of nineteenth-century oppression on the shape of women's "souls" or John Keats's Romantic-era point that the world is a "vale of Soul-making," Thoreau posits a clear causal relation between the seemingly personal inside and the extra-personal historical outside.[128] At the same time, for Thoreau, only bodies holding something ("spirit") non-identical to or in excess of the coordinates of a falsely complete "incorporated" reality can offer "guidance" in the midst of historical struggles. Viewed from a formal-historical perspective, the failure of a given historical reality to totalize (despite, here, massive regimes of socio-economic violence) creates a hiccup in the looping coordinates of the present. And this hiccup becomes the very locus of the inspirited/inspired.

This same locus generates the possibility of what I have hyperbolically termed Thoreau's "militant vegetables." In a general way, militant vegetables might be thought of as active and competing constellations (or potential constellations) within the antagonistic material realities playing out in a given moment's nested loops. Therefore, to understand how Thoreau's thinking operates we must consider the specific material-historical contexts that shape these strange, expansive, and dynamic formations. If we resist separating his corpus into familiar partitions of early "nature" writing, the political essays of the 1850s, and his later Darwin-inspired work, then his political writings of the 1850s might uniquely reveal aspects about how all realities are produced and altered.

Deak Nabers offers a particularly thorough account of the ways in which Thoreau's anti-slavery essays negotiated the period's charged debates about personhood and citizenship, topics at the center the era's political and, indeed, ontological crises. Nabers considers Thoreau's 1850s antislavery essays in the context of Roger Taney's *Dred Scott* decision and the decade's sectional controversies that catalyzed a changing relationship among slavery, the law, and nature (including, loosely, natural law). Unlike the case of Lord Mansfield's *Somerset v. Stewart* decision (1772), which blamed positive law (legal statues) for engendering slavery, an "odious" practice incommensurate with natural law, in the antebellum United States positive law became seen progressively as a means for establishing and maintaining one's freedom. According to Nabers, whereas Taney's decision sought to put the breaks on this trend by naturalizing slavery as a higher law outside the emerging association between positive law and freedom, Thoreau's essays, especially his John Brown writings, aimed to legalize nature, demonstrating how "natural law is an essentially *legal* institution." Thoreau's effort thus had two primary effects: It allowed nature to "serve as a genuine source of moral authority," and, when "redeployed in terms of the American Constitution," it could act as a "forceful antislavery instrument."[129]

In Nabers's reading, however, Thoreau's move to put nature into a direct causal relationship with both natural law and civic law produces manifold logistical and practical problems. Focusing especially on "Slavery in Massachusetts" (1854), Nabers suggests that Thoreau's legal censure of slavery, where "natural law folds into the law of nature," ends up "protecting the concept of natural law, not critiquing it." Nabers asks, "How can the laws of nature (flowers growing) become natural law (purity prevailing)?" Nabers's own response is that Thoreau addresses this problematic by "binding" the zones of nature and law together into "a single organism, or ecosystem, of law."[130] This accounts, in Nabers's view, for one of the major flaws in Thoreau's approach to politics and the law—the fact that he "dwells on the production of an 'atmosphere' rather than the generation of laws."[131]

Yet, what if we replace this singular organicist ecosystem with the dynamic ecology of nested totalities? Relatedly, what if we shift our attention from Thoreau's apparent reluctance to "generate laws" to the way he views the interactions among nature, law, and natural law engendering politicized effects, including the effect of breaking or interrupting negative aspects of existing positive law?[132] Thus, in "Slavery in Massachusetts," Thoreau rails against the fact that it has been left to the Supreme Court, which, "recognizing no authority but the Constitution, . . . has decided that . . . three [million] are, and shall continue to be, slaves." In this scenario, according to Thoreau, "[t]he law will never make men free; it is men who have got to make the law free."[133] Thoreau seems cognizant of the historical and political dynamics that Judith Butler observes about the "law." In her words, the law "takes the form of a regulatory structuring of the field of appearance that establishes who can be seen, heard, and recognized. The legal domain overlaps with the political field."[134] The Thoreauvian aporia Nabers presents in the relation between laws of nature and natural law might identify the very place where Thoreau's aforementioned material dialectic operates and, consequently, where his unique political ontologies emerge. It is precisely in the blurred spaces and places and times where different realities encounter one another that things happen and change, and these events often have direct political implications, even if they may not draft ready-made laws for the distinguished sitting body of Congress.

The mere "production of an atmosphere" that Nabers censures references Thoreau's injunction at the close of "Slavery in Massachusetts" to "behave that the odor of your actions may enhance the general sweetness of the atmosphere, that when we behold or scent a flower, we may not be reminded how inconsistent your deeds are with it" (109). There is a familiar gap here between input stimulus and output action, one I discuss at length in terms of Emerson's work in Chapter 1. And yet, Thoreau clearly uses this closing reference to the fragrant water-lily as a material outside to and foil for the finite historical positive laws that allowed slavery to exist. As opposed to the "cowardice and want of principle of northern men," the flower's scent "suggests what kinds of laws have prevailed longest and widest." With this simple juxtaposition of a lacking regime of positive law and a nebulous idea of a natural one, Thoreau offers an emphatic critique of period political decision making, one that has embedded within it a clear call for immediate side-taking. Thoreau writes that the water-lily's fragrance "reminds me that Nature has been partner to no Missouri Compromise. I scent no compromise in the fragrance of the water-lily.... In it, the sweet, and pure, and innocent are wholly sundered from the obscene and baleful." Thoreau's hippy flower power thus includes a sober call for *separation* and the consolidation of political-ethical positions. He goes on: "I do not scent in this the time-serving irresolution of a Massachusetts Governor, nor of a Boston Mayor" (108–9). Liberal deliberation and its formal bureaucratic comity have little sway here, it seems.[135]

Instead of a positivist liberal dichotomy between the effectiveness of passing laws and the ineffectiveness of most other actions, Thoreau offers a wider reality of relations and effects. As Thoreau makes clear in *A Week*, one does "not avoid evil by fleeing before it, but by rising above or diving below its plane; as the worm escapes drought and frost by boring a few inches deeper" (304). Although leading off with the vague aim of "escaping" evil, Thoreau goes on to promote what he calls "fronting" the "fact" of local existence. This is a locality whose scale ranges from the gap between one and one's "neighbor" to the expanse between oneself and the "setting sun." "Let him build himself a log-house with the bark on where he is," Thoreau writes, "*fronting IT*, and wage there an old French War ... with Indians and Rangers, or whatever else may come between him and the reality, and save his scalp if he can" (304). Employing playfully a host of settler colonial tropes, Thoreau pushes the reader to negotiate material horizons in a worm-like manner, an experience that yields complications within the ideological coordinates of one's life and identity. In this specific form, such a call is surely not up to the demands imposed by the crises of antebellum slavery. But Thoreau's schematic illuminates his unique structural approach toward all such sociopolitical antagonisms. In short, he offers a reality marked by an expansive zone of causality where action and ontology exceed bourgeois and anthropomorphic registers. As with the water-lily, the worm offers an alternate means to frame and approach the real contingencies that shape material and economic life—including, here, outright war. This logic is developed in Thoreau's later essays such as "The Last Days of John Brown" (1860), where he argues that Brown and other members of the *"living* North" "went behind the human law, . . . went behind the apparent failure, and recognized eternal justice and glory." For Thoreau, however, this recognition is not merely an abstract encounter with Platonic truth. "They saw that what was called order was confusion, what was called justice, injustice," he writes. "This attitude suggested . . . the possibility . . . of a revolution in behalf of another and an oppressed people."[136]

The term "militant" in my title thus references a range of scenarios whereby an actant, or organization of actants, embedded with historically conditioned nested loops, is oriented negatively toward an existing formation of reality. Thoreau's conditions of militancy can, in this way, cross over into concrete forms of militarism. After all, it is Emerson himself who called Thoreau the latest embodiment of Napoleon.[137] But, for Thoreau, such militancy need not break into recognizable forms of physical resistance. Thoreau's militant vegetables do not just codify a prescribed identity or position, nor do they simply evince fidelity to something like abstract higher loops. Instead, the ontologies and actants that take effect and make effects align with specific forms of interactions that generate change within existing negative conditions. As Thoreau writes in his early and unpublished essay "Reform and the Reformers" (1839–1845), "I cannot bear to be told to wait for good results, I pine as much for good beginnings. We never come to final results, and it is too late to start from perennial beginnings."[138] Much like Enrique Dussel's notion of the precarity and indeterminacy of dialectics-in-motion—where, to quote Ciccariello-Maher once again, "concrete praxis . . . [is] more than simply a 'negation of the negation,' but a positive program for the abolition of ontological barriers between Being and its opposite"—Thoreau imagines forms of embodied historical critique-qua-praxis that coalesce in a process of *taking sides.*

Nowhere is this more apparent than in Thoreau's 1859 lecture "A Plea for Captain John Brown." In Thoreau's view, Brown's "meteor-like" becoming as a historical hero stems from his ability to "[stand] up serenely against the condemnation and vengeance of mankind, rising above them literally *by a whole body.*"[139] This action transforms Brown into a world-historical event, and Thoreau exclaims, "I rejoice that I live in this age— that I am his contemporary."[140] Being Brown's contemporary meant, for Thoreau, living within a moment where the injustices of antebellum reality were beginning to catalyze the creation of new and powerful counterforces. According to Thoreau, Brown's followers should be lauded because "[t]hese alone were ready to step between the oppressor and the oppressed. Surely, they were the very best men you could select to be hung. That was the greatest compliment which this country could pay them."[141] Of course, Thoreau was making similar pronouncements about the historical and ethical need for action more than ten years earlier than this. In "Resistance to Civil Government," he argues that "when a sixth of the population of a nation which has undertaken to be the refuge of liberty are slaves, . . . I think that it is not too soon for honest men to rebel and revolutionize."[142] Indeed, in another earlier essay, "The Herald of Freedom" (1844), Thoreau recounts approvingly an exchange between the abolitionist editor Nathaniel P. Rogers and a detractor who claimed that Jesus never denounced slavery. In Thoreau's retelling, Rogers answers, "[G]ranting your proposition to be true—and admitting what I deny—that Jesus Christ did not preach the abolition of slavery, then I say, '*he did'nt do his duty.*' "[143]

As we have seen, the forms of militancy just outlined range widely in Thoreau's work. The second term of my chapter's title, "vegetables," functions as a placeholder for these formations. In truth, my use of this term began as something of joke about Thoreau's aforementioned bean field at Walden. Although beans are legumes, their component plant parts (stems, and so on) are, when consumed, considered vegetables. As the OED explains, the word "vegetable" derives from Middle English notions of "growing like a plant" and the late Latin *vegetabilis*, connoting "animating." I use the word "vegetables," therefore, to signify Thoreau's understanding of biological and material formations that take on agential functions within their environments. My use of the term is far from arbitrary, for, as Arsić describes, Thoreau had an "obsessive interest in vegetal tumor" as well as a "lifelong preoccupation with vegetal decay."[144] Moreover, Thoreau often uses plants and plant metaphors to describe material functionality, including functionality within the unfolding of historical-political events.

Thoreau's thinking about plants and vegetables is, as one would expect, multidimensional. At times, he censures the sheer structural functionality of plant life and its counterparts in human bodies and sociality. As he explains in "Life Without Principles," existing institutions and "politics" are "inhuman": They are "superficial" systems produced by historical contingencies.[145] He goes on to describe politics as the "vital functions of human society," but he notes that they should be "unconsciously performed, like the corresponding functions of the physical body." In this sense, they "are *infra*-human, a kind of vegetation. I sometimes wake to a half-consciousness of them going on about me, as a man may become conscious of some of the processes of digestion" (178). In fact, Thoreau suggests that committing one's thoughts and time to this zero-level activity is a delimiting endeavor, recalling his directive in July 1850 to "[b]e not simply obedient like the vegetable."[146] These admonitions, however, may be misleading. Earlier in "Life Without," Thoreau adds an important socioeconomic qualifier to his comments about vegetation: "When we want culture more than potatoes, and illumination more than sugar-plums, then the . . . staple production, is, not slaves, nor operatives, but men,—those rare fruits called heroes, saints, poets, philosophers, and redeemers" (177). Functionality and obedience are thus not the problem; the real problem is the specific historical form these functions take within the "politics" of an antebellum society whose commodities are produced by the commodity of slave labor. Instead of slaves producing the goods that will be consumed (as in "digested") as "potatoes" and "sugarplums," we should radically shift to a society where socioeconomic vegetation produces "fruits" such as "heroes" or "redeemers."[147] As we've seen with the plane of positive law, here the historical formation of economic nested loops requires significant interventions and recalibrations. What's more, the trope of vegetation affords Thoreau a means for describing the hazy zone where elements of nature (ecologies) merge with notions of natural law (period ideals of various forms) in reaction to specific existing historical formations. "Shall I not have intelligence with the earth?" Thoreau asks in *Walden*. "Am I not partly vegetable mould myself?" (138).

Throughout his writing, Thoreau uses the notion of vegetation to make similar points about the interruptions and alterations that are required in his moment. In "Reform and the Reformer," for instance, he critiques the ineffectual methods of typical liberal reformers, imploring them to "[b]e green and flourishing plants in God's nursery, and not such complaining bleeding trees as Dante saw." He continues, "If your branches wither, send out your fibres into every kingdom of nature for its contribution . . . and make firm your trunk against the elements." In so doing, "[w]ho shall tell what blossoms, what fruits, what public and private advantage may push up through this rind we call man?" (191–92). Such green instruments, therefore, have para-effects in Thoreau's thinking. And the markedly sociopolitical nature of these effects is not lost on Thoreau.

As Thoreau notes in his early journal, "[T]here are in each the seeds of a heroic ardor, Seeds, there are seeds enough which only need to be stirred in with the soil where they lie . . . to bear fruit of a divine flavor."[148] This is why, perhaps, in *Walden*, after describing the way the icy pond in spring "has its law to which it thunders obedience when it should as surely as the buds expand," he argues man should "maintain himself in whatever attitude he find himself through obedience to the laws of his being, which will never be one of opposition to a just government, if he should chance to meet with such" (302, 323). There is surely, following Nabers, an elliptical relationship among natural laws, nature, and historical laws here. But there are also clear and imperative political stakes for the interference between nature and society. It should be noted that, in Thoreau's thinking, even these laws of one's being are historically malleable. Thoreau later notes that when one has the courage to live according to one's own "dreams," "new, universal, and more liberal laws will begin to establish themselves around and within him; or the old laws be expanded, and interpreted in his favor in a more liberal sense" (*Walden*, 323–24).[149]

It follows that Thoreau's writing about plants (which ranges from literal descriptions to Linnaean nomenclature to abstract metaphors) holds distinct historical purchase for the conditions of antebellum society. In this sense, Thoreau's vegetables, as militant vegetables, have less in common with contemporary speculative-materialist work about "plant thinking" by scholars such as Michael Marder and more affinity with the plant formations and effects found in Monique Allewaert's historical "ecological account of resistance."[150] Marder's work on vegetal life contributes productively to a wider contemporary effort by scholars such as Eduardo Kohn and Jeffrey Nealon to get outside of modernity's familiar human- and animal-focused biopolitical paradigms. In books such as *Plant-Thinking: A Philosophy of Vegetal Life* (2013) and *Grafts: Writing on Plants* (2016), Marder pushes beyond delimiting western categories of subjectivity and ontology to suggest that "vegetal life is coextensive with a distinct subjectivity with which we might engage."[151] His work argues that plants' modalities of life exceed received philosophical categories, and, in a way that is relevant for Thoreau's views, it reveals how their functions (such as "non-ideational thinking" and "non-conscious intentionality") might interface with human systems (37, 10). At the same time, Marder's perspective is thoroughly liberal in a manner consonant with many aspects of Arsić's aforementioned Deleuzian and vitalist proclivities. This includes, for example, reading the ideological divide between destructive Hegelian dialectics and benevolent Levinasian ethics into and onto vegetal life: whereby plants "resist the logic of totalization" and evince an approach to alterity that includes an "infinite relation to the other without return to oneself" (71). Marder uses this underlying logic to move from a description of "plant freedom" to what he terms "vegetable democracy," a form of non-totalizing "divisibility and participation" marked by "sharing" and "non-economic generosity" (118, 51–52).

Conversely, Allewaert offers an array of historical examples where specific material encounters and "entanglements" among humans and environments yield a condition she dubs "parahuman," a "perversion of [the] prior category" of human that "challenge[s] the hierarchal organization of life-forms... common to colonial anthropologies and natural histories."[152] By aligning animals, humans, and parahumans horizontally, Allewaert traces relations among categories without conflation. Most pertinent to Thoreau's militant vegetables, perhaps, is the way Allewaert's analysis of the "Africanized" spaces of sub-tropical zones such as swamps reveals interferences between non-white humans (such as ex-slave maroon communities) and their natural environment: creating a "militarized" ecology but also symbolic complications to the coordinates of citizen-subject that dominated, and still dominate, western notions of revolution and freedom.[153]

These two approaches thus have a divergent orientation toward political and ideological realities: with Marder seeking an outside to existing western models by speculatively arcing outward toward plants and forward toward some other future, and Allewaert finding alternative material formations that have already occurred and assessing their complications for given liberal structures. Whereas Marder, recalling Latour's speculative liberal fantasies, imagines interface between the "plant soul" and humans in terms of his understanding of plants' distinct functions, Allewaert works from the historical-material site of actual interfaces and their actual effects in time.

Somewhere between the positions offered by Marder and Allewaert, we might find a crowbar-wielding Thoreau and his "migrating nations" of shad, "armed... with innocence and a just cause." As I've mentioned, Thoreau says of the shad, "Perchance, after a few thousands of years, if the fishes will be patient,... nature will have leveled the Billerica dam" (*A Week*, 34). But Thoreau, who claims to be "with" this fishy community, also imagines the effects of an immediate and physical human blow to the dam. Taking Thoreau at his word, we might think of these patient-but-oppressed shad, working in concert with the slow revolt of nature, and this crowbar-wielding Thoreau as not just two distinct means to a shared end, but as an odd and differentiated shared means. Put differently, Thoreau's speculative-terrorist act imagines something like a political-ecological version of Elizabeth Freeman's notion of "queer temporality." In the opening of *Time Binds* (2010), Freeman uses a reading of Nguyen Tan Hoang's video *K.I.P.*

(2002), which depicts the director/writer videotaping, in the present, the screening of a gay pornographic film from the 1970s. The process of filming, however, includes Nguyen's distorted image on the screen of the video playing the older film, and Freeman uses this overlay of images and temporalities to suggest that Nguyen's film is a "queer hauntological exercise," a speculative but material means for a man to "figuratively [join] a community of past- and present-tense viewers," even if this man's own racialized identity would likely have excluded him from the actual gathering depicted in the film.[154] This sets up Freeman's aforementioned definition of erotics, which, unlike desire, "traffics less in belief than in encounter, less in damaged wholes than in intersections of body parts, less in loss than in novel possibility." Nguyen's film, therefore, presents an alternate formulation of temporal-material encounter, where "*K.I.P.*'s queer subject would thus feel an encounter with what looks like a historical index not as a restored wholeness but as a momentary reorganization or rezoning of parts, even of the part-whole relation."[155] Coviello's *Tomorrow's Parties* aptly reads Thoreau's work in terms that directly align with Freeman's model, portraying how Thoreau's approach to corporality and love present an untimely figure "who neither exemplifies his present nor anticipates the future but who, in his idiosyncratic conjugations of sexual being, suggests instead the outlines of a future that would not come to be."[156]

I want to argue that by imaginatively taking up a crowbar in the service of the shad, Thoreau erects a para-politics that shares elements of Freeman's and Coviello's notions of corporeal and temporal alterity. In Freeman's terms, the untimely and "momentary reorganization of parts" here includes a strange solidarity between fish and Thoreau: merging the future completion of an undirected historical act (how, in time, "nature" will destroy the dam) with a potential present directed act seeking the same end. It's as if Thoreau takes Fuller's cosmic material expanse of long-distance causality, discussed in the previous chapter, and levels it into an earthly temporal continuum. The apparent discontinuity between the shad/nature and the politicized Thoreau dissipates in their momentary calibration, if we might call it that, within a single "just cause" (a shared but non-identical experience of affront from the dam). In Thoreau's account, this loose alignment allows something like a gathering of force toward a point that culminates in the ability to strike out in immediate action.

Thoreau's variety of para-politics thus adds a radical twist to typical period liberal structures of sympathy. He not only sympathizes with the shad (or feels badly for them), imagining from a distance their experience of oppression, but also moves toward joining them by imagining taking up the crowbar. In one sense, the "strange affinities" Thoreau notes in his early journal between himself and material/biological others here pushes into a politicized mode of strange empathy.[157] Consequently, militant vegetables, the term I have been employing throughout, might, in the end, best name this elliptical space between the two positions (shad and Thoreau) and the two modalities of action—the very space that Thoreau's wider thinking both inhabits and seeks to retool. The logic of John Brown can be seen here, too. As Thoreau tells it, Brown had a "peculiar doctrine that a man has a perfect right to interfere by force with the slaveholder, in order to rescue the slave." Brown "loved his fellow man," he "took up his life and he laid it down for him."[158] Importantly, Thoreau could not "know" the oppression endured by the shad, just as Brown could not know the slaves he purports to save (in Thoreau's pseudo white savior scenario). And let's not forget that Thoreau *didn't* charge the dam or join ex-slaves in taking up Sharps rifles with Brown. But he did conceive, through wondrous and tortuous logic, how and why such acts could and should occur. And this is a legacy we should not take from Thoreau or banish by way of some aesthetic or scientific sleight of hand.

At the close of *Walden*, Thoreau offers a Hindu-inspired anecdote about the artist of Kouroo, who, by dedicating his life to the sole purpose of creating a staff, outlived the passage of his historical age and, in the end, "made a new system" (327).[159] Thoreau imagines not only the untimely artist of Kouroo, the patient and suffering shad of Concord, and the slow dispersion of seeds, but also the momentary leverage of a crowbar. We should not lose the point of the latter in the expansive content that the former yields. As Thorson explains, Thoreau's Billerica Dam passage in *A Week* was pulled from a journal entry dating from sometime after August 1, 1844. Unlike the book passage, which ends in the form of a question, this earlier journal closes the sentence with an exclamation mark. ("And—who knows—what may avail a crow bar against that Billerica Dam!")[160] If we are to join Thoreau or even greet his work, we must be prepared to think geologically, cosmically even, but we must also be able to keep the exclamation point and, just maybe, charge the dam.

CHAPTER 4

Unadjusted Emancipations

Best revenge is your paper.
—BEYONCÉ KNOWLES-CARTER, "Formation"

Perhaps constant escape is what we mean when we say freedom.
—FRED MOTEN, *Black and Blur*

A Miles Davis track buzzes through Harriet Jacobs's crawlspace. In Fred Moten's reading, the cramped nineteenth-century garret where Jacobs remained confined for seven years fuses with the limits Davis negotiated in his 1958 performance of the "Buzzard Song" in Gil Evans's *Porgy and Bess*. Like the crawlspace's double trajectory of restriction and escape in Jacobs's plight, Davis's placement within Evans's arrangement becomes a background confine from which he climbs an octave and "ascend[s] into the underground." Moten suggests that "Miles's . . . Jacobsean swerve in and out of the confinements of Gershwin's composition and Evans's arrangement" represents how "[f]reedom in unfreedom is flight" and, therefore, "this music could be called the most sublime in the history of escape."[1]

In Moten's reading of Davis qua Jacobs, Jacobs's mistress may "[steal] her triumph" when she buys her freedom, but, fortunately, "Miles, like Jacobs, keeps going past such emancipation."[2] The phrase "unadjusted emancipations" in my title is meant to evoke this type of furthering or othering of liberation, signaling both the para status of ex-slave emancipations as well as the irreducible horizon of economic materiality that conditions such flights. Frank B. Wilderson III uses the term "unadjusted" to speculate about the conceptual and institutional crises blackness would affect should it become unconditioned by the ideological and material limits imposed at present. Discussing black film theorists, he argues that such academics "are 'allowed' to meditate on cinema only after 'consenting' to a structural adjustment." He continues, "Such an adjustment . . . is not unlike the structural adjustment debtor nations must adhere to for the privilege of securing a loan: signing on the dotted line means feigning ontological capacity regardless of the fact that Blackness is incapacity in its most pure and unadulterated form."[3] Wilderson's comments mobilize foundational aspects of Afro-pessimism's claims about the ontological stakes of blackness, productively dislocating the traditional nexus of freedom/unfreedom and, therefore, resetting the ground for serious inquiry about the historical conditions of blackness in and out of holds.

In this chapter, I want to build on the innovative work of scholars such as Moten and Wilderson, as well as Saidiya Hartman, Christina Sharpe, and others who have rethought the historical and theoretical stakes of blackness, ontology, and resistance. Looking at three novels from the mid-nineteenth century—Harriet Beecher Stowe's *Dred; A Tale of the Great Dismal Swamp* (1856), William Wells Brown's *Clotel; or, the President's Daughter: A Narrative of Slave Life in the United States* (1853), and Martin Delany's *Blake; or, The Huts of America* (1859, 1861–62)—I trace various ways that slaves and ex-slaves negotiated and leveraged the period's systemic production of bad debts in order to distort or circumvent standard formations of emancipatory logic.

In *Black and Blur* (2017), Moten opens by recalibrating the first line of his formative *In the Break* (2003): shifting "[t]he history of blackness is testament to the fact that objects can and do resist" to "[p]erformance is the resistance of the object."[4] Moten's revised opening line to *In the Break* might also, however, provide an occasion to revisit his first book's conclusion. In those pages, Moten returns to his early rumination on Aunt Hester's scream in Douglass's narrative and suggests that this scream, as a "performance-in-objection," marks something like "a rematerialization of value."[5]

Moten's claims have significant stakes. Citing Marx's 1844 conjecture that whereas revolution necessitates dematerializations of value, anticipatory future formations will, in turn, engender modes of rematerialization, Moten casts Hester's scream as a "prefigurative working out" of a mode that might be associated with communism.[6] Following Marx's conception of communism as a "discovery procedure" rather than simply an achieved state, Moten intimates that black radicalism "might be performed in and as the arrival at becoming-social in the vexed and vexing exchange of roles."[7] Published before formative Afro-pessimist critiques of traditional Marxist formulations, Moten's schematic nevertheless sidesteps these concerns by offering formal modes that exist amid indeterminate trajectories of economic-materialist realities he elsewhere calls a "paraontology."[8] This speculative position—where it is possible for performance to effect resistance—cannot be understood using the traditional rubrics of exploitation/alienation or, for that matter, liberation/emancipation. Although Moten's work produces powerful Muñozian transports and transgressions, these moves and gestures spring from conditions very much in line with Wilderson's argument that "slavery is and connotes an ontological status for Blackness; and . . . the constituent elements of slavery are not exploitation and alienation but accumulation and fungibility" as well as Achille Mbembe's suggestion that "[t]o produce Blackness is to produce a social link of subjection and a *body of extraction*."[9]

Following Moten's lead, this chapter discerns in antebellum novels alternate and complex formations of being amid what we might call, borrowing from Jason Moore, the plantation "zone of appropriation." Moore defines zones of appropriation as "those extra-economic processes that identify, secure, and channel unpaid work outside the commodity system into the circuit of capital." Similar to Wilderson's critique of the conspicuous limits within Marxian notions of exploitation, Moore presents a structural model whereby capital functions via multiple and formally discontinuous means: exploitation of labor within the established domains of capital, on the one hand, and appropriation via seizing unpaid labor, energy, and matter, on the other. In short, Moore shows how "work/energy" can either be immediately capitalized or "appropriated via non-economic means."[10]

I am interested in revealing how, within this plantation zone of appropriation, a discontinuous and dynamically changing economic-material ground gives rise to alternate modalities of experience, particularly the experience of "emancipation" itself. The subtitle of the second part of this book, "Illiberal Ecologies," is intended to suggest these very themes. As mentioned in Chapter 3, the term "ecology" was not coined until 1866, but, at this time, the concept was associated with Charles Darwin's 1859 notion of an "economy of nature."[11] My analysis of Thoreau's conception of ecological loop dialectics demonstrated the significant stakes for how one thinks about material-ecological connections, causalities, and effects. Pushing this thinking even further by shifting our critical view away from the traditional nexus of exploitation/alienation and toward the wider realms and processes that capital uses to appropriate labor/energy, we begin to see that slavery and emancipation alike negotiated what might aptly be termed an ecology.[12] That is, the term "ecology" might offer a more capacious framework for examining the range of material and economic conditions that shaped the experiences of slaves and ex-slaves.

As black studies scholars such as Cedric Robinson and historians such as Edward E. Baptist have established, slavery's ecologies and zones of appropriation not only interfaced with familiar processes of global capitalization, but they fed and undergirded them.[13] Nineteenth-century Atlantic economies underwent a number of transitions and crises as global markets were established and commodity forms developed. The figure of the slave loomed large within the symbolic registers that sought to contain and shape modernity's emerging worlds. Stephen Best places some of the preceding schematics of economic-material indeterminacy within specific nineteenth-century legal and economic transitions, examining how "[s]lavery is not simply an antebellum institution that the United States has surpassed but a particular historical *form* of an ongoing crisis involving the subjection of personhood to property." Tracing period afterlives of slavery within changing commodity relations, Best centers the concept of fugitive personhood. Here, the fugitive "in slave law names the runaway slave who is competing parts pilfered property and indebted person, and in intellectual property law captures those emergent forms of property given occasion by new technologies of mechanical reproduction." Within an economic landscape that saw shifting modalities of money impacting aspects of contract law, Best posits the "fugitive" as "a figure for . . . [the] untethered 'inscriptions of debt and value,' for this drift of value in the marketplace."[14]

Rather than pivot on Best's use of the juridical-economic fugitive figure, charting as it does a passage from the slave commodity in the antebellum period to forms of foreclosed economic personhood in the postbellum years, I want to focus on Best's invocation of debt: a concept that, following Saidiya Hartman's work, Best presents shaping and besetting both the fugitive and the ex-slave "person."[15] As Best suggests, "The personhood enshrined in both legislative enactment and legal primer was burdened with debt, duty, and other entanglements." If, as Locke has it, every man has at least "*Property* in his own *Person*," Best shows how the fugitive (both "pilfered property and indebted person") as well as post-emancipated personhood are shot through with a number of formative transitional crises in value.[16] By focusing on debt and taking a cue from Moten, I propose to blur the diachronic, historical, and conceptual trajectories Best presents. Considering texts that appear amid mid-century crises, we find not only linear emerging formations of value and personhood, but also, as Moten gleans in Aunt Hester's scream and its afterlives, complex resonances of material-historical possibilities that are, perhaps, asymmetrical—or even queer in the aforementioned context of Muñoz's atemporal-aesthetic registers—with regard to existing realities in the making. One name for such alternate material-historical possibilities is bad debt, a concept I introduce briefly in the next section.

Ante/Bad Debts: Toward Unadjusted Emancipation

The long wake of slavery, to borrow Sharpe's figuration, extends across various eras and formations of modernity. Many contemporary scholars note the connections among the eighteenth- and nineteenth-century Atlantic slave trade and contemporary liberal and/or neoliberal formations, including that of debt.[17] If structural adjustment is the sanitized term for capital's imposition of neoliberal financial policies, where impoverished countries suffering from imposed debt receive loans from entities such as the IMF in exchange for austerity measures, then this adjustment has a longer durée and a wider scope than one might assume.[18] According to Achille Mbembe, neoliberal structural adjustment is catalyzed by "structurally insolvent debts." In this new era, the old models of exploitation give way as workers become "abandoned subjects, relegated to the role of a 'superfluous humanity.'" In this context, "the systemic risks experienced specifically by Black slaves during early capitalism have now become the norm for, or at least the lot of, all of subaltern humanity. The emergence of new imperial practices is then tied to the tendency to universalize the Black condition."[19] Within Mbembe's Afro-pessimist schematic, this condition is tantamount to a racial nothingness, a continuous historical production of modernity's discontinuous byproduct: "a kind of silt of the earth, a silt deposited at the confluence of half-worlds produced by the dual violence of race and capital."[20] In Wilderson's terms, this is why the "race of Humanism (White, Asian, South Asian, and Arab) could not have produced itself without the simultaneous production of that walking destruction which became known as the Black."[21] For both Mbembe and Wilderson, there is a long history to the production of modernity, where blackness is a functional impossibility that enables the engines of capital to produce positive coordinates of recognizable race (along with and through the very modalities of recognition per se) all the while existing as a troubling excess that is, at once, nowhere and everywhere. In Mbembe's terms, there are three specific historical nodal points for the production of what he calls the "vertiginous assemblage of blackness and race": the Atlantic slave trade; the proliferation of writing in the late eighteenth-century, when blacks began "leaving traces in a language all of their own and . . . demanded the status of full subjects"; and the instantiation of neoliberal realities in the twenty-first century.[22]

Risking our own historical vertigo, we must pass though the neoliberal present and back to the nineteenth century if we are to more fully examine the charged realities that attended slaves' movements among trajectories of "freedom" and bondage. The concept of debt offers a way to illuminate conceptually these complex constellations of relationships and realities. As Tim Armstrong explains, since the Colonial Debts Act of 1732, the North American slave credit economy was predicated upon regarding the slave as "a contracted person whose labour was due to others . . . seeing the slave as metaphorically a debtor." This rendered the fugitive slave a form of virtual property: a debt in abeyance. Consequently, for fugitive ex-slaves, freedom becomes "the refusal of a debt vested in the self."[23] In this state of deferred or denied debt, we find what I am calling unadjusted emancipations. This term brings together various registers that shape potential movements toward ex-slave existence and sociality: the forced impositions of debt (toward foreclosures), structural regimes of antiblackness (economic, material, and ideological), but also, to bring Moten back in, swerves and flights. From this perspective, debt traverses the entire ecology of slavery/freedom: including capital's command over zones of appropriation and accumulation as well as sanctioned modes of liberation-as-redemption, where slaves buy their freedom or forge selves via narratives invested in the logic of property rights and transfers. But such regimes of debt are also accompanied by the alternate modifications, contortions, and disengagements that Moten and Stefano Haney call "bad debt." This form of debt "cannot be repaid." It is "debt at a distance, the debt without creditor, the black debt, the queer debt, the criminal debt. Excessive debt, incalculable debt, debt for no reason, debt broken from credit, debt as its own principle." Calling to mind Wilderson's aforementioned notion that blackness is shaped by "accumulation and fungibility," Moten and Harney note that this form of debt is indeed "the real crisis for credit, its real crisis of accumulation. Now debt begins to accumulate without it."[24] Putting pressure on this chapter's first epigraph—the closing line from Beyoncé Knowles-Carter's "Formation," "[b]est revenge is your paper" bad debt's mode of *accumulation* might break from the term's standard association with "acquiring" and operate solely along the axis of gathering (the term's Latin root means "to heap").

In line with Moten and Harney's reading of bad debt, Richard Dienst argues that our neoliberal reality has engendered a "crisis of indebtedness": a classic debt crisis ("piling up of unserviceable obligations") as well as a more troubling systemic "breakdown in the mechanisms that maintain credit." Following Marx's suggestion that "we ought to find radical prospects in the most advanced edge of capitalistic thinking," Dienst posits indebtedness as an anticipatory aspect of emancipatory thinking. In his words, "[i]f *credit* is understood as the sweeping gesture with which capital lays claim to the present in the name of the past and the future, *debt* may be seen as a mark of the nonsynchronous." This includes, according to Dienst, nothing short of a "withdrawal from value."[25] For Dienst as well as Moten and Harney, therefore, this transmogrification within debt includes significant social and ontological effects: with indebtedness creating what Moten and Harney call a "refuge" for "the fugitive public." Here, debt becomes "fugitive from restructuring."[26]

What I am calling unadjusted emancipations are, in these varied terms, ways that nineteenth-century slaves and ex-slaves negotiated states of bondage forged by changing ecological-economic landscapes by shaping asymmetrical pathways out, around, along, and/or away from them. As Hartman and Best portray, the nineteenth century's modes of slave emancipation undoubtedly led toward a "citizenry" of or as debtors (including the post–thirteenth amendment march toward a financialized incarceral state); but this variegated march toward neoliberal policy also included complex, subtle, and not-so-subtle passages to elsewheres of bad debt. In other words, in antebellum narratives, unadjusted emancipations do certainly lead to debt (in all its formations), but also not necessarily or, at least, not yet.

The following three sections present a developing arc of antebellum unadjusted emancipations. In each, the categories of economy and ecology are, in various ways, thought within the same framework—where forms and assertions of bad debt traverse explicit economic concerns and wider networks of reality (vegetal, social, and geographic as well as the domains of the symbolic order that shape them). The first, "'Goblin Growth' in the Dismal Swamp," examines Stowe's *Dred* in light of ecological-economic hermeneutics. In my reading, the interface between humans and ecology spied by scholars who study the parahuman closes with an unsettling interface between personhood and developing models of capital, effecting new horizons for and representations of racialized emancipatory logic. The second, "William Wells Brown's Bad, Bad Debt," looks at the ways Brown's novel *Clotel* and his appended "Narrative of the Life and Escape of William Wells Brown" leverage the era's production of bad debts in order to craft points of divergence from and within standard channels of emancipation. The third, a coda titled *"Blake*'s Secret Slide," considers how the titular character and his "secret" move throughout the South's plantations in ways that radically compound. Reading this modality of secret as a blurred Moten-esque push toward a fugitive sociality of bad debt, I examine how the novel presents innovative forms of resistant collectivity.

"Goblin Growth" in the Dismal Swamp

The first word of Harriet Beecher Stowe's *Dred* is "Bills."[27] Evoking, perhaps in an uncanny way, the initial scene in Quentin Tarantino's *Django Unchained* (2012) when Stephen, the overseer of the plantation "Candyland," first appears as a pair of black hands dutifully signing his master's name on a check issued from the Bank of Mississippi, Stowe's novel opens with the white mistress of the plantation "Canema" amid a response to an implied question from her enslaved half-white bother about economic concerns. These same bills, the novel goes on to show, impose a debt that Canema's budget cannot account for, forcing Harry, who runs all aspects of the estate, to squander his own saved "freedom-money" in order to sustain the plantation (60). *Dred* goes much further than merely portraying the gradual fiduciary decline of the plantation; it also depicts the more pointed and immediate loss of capital to the nearby swamp. Through the novel's titular character, a herculean ex-slave prophet, who, following the example of his father Denmark Vesey, leads a group of fugitives within the North Carolina portion of the Great Dismal Swamp, Stowe fuses the plantation form's multi-scaled crisis (decay of domestic economy and militant threat posed by slaves and ex-slaves) into a singular economic frame. Not only does Dred threaten Canema's domestic well-being via the loss of Harry, Tiff, Milly, and other slaves but the swamp itself, which often interfaces with Dred, accounts for a massive loss of capital. As Mr. Jekyl, a hardened plantation agent aligned with Harry's antagonist half-brother Tom Gordon, explains later in the novel, "[I]t's inconceivable, the amount of property that's lost in that swamp! I have heard it estimated at something like three millions of dollars!" (437).

Jekyl's projected financial loss may be a bit high, but the period saw parties from all sides attempting to conceive of the Great Dismal Swamp in terms of economic loss and gain. Edmund Jackson's January 1852 abolitionist essay, "The Virginia Maroons," for example, estimates the number of fugitive slaves in the swamp (40,000) by dividing $1.5 million, the approximate amount, according to a Norfolk merchant, that slave owners had lost to marronage, by a slave's average worth.[28] Schemes to recover investments in slave labor and quell preemptively the possibility of future losses stretch back to the late eighteenth century. As it turns out, George Washington was the first U.S. president who wanted to "drain the swamp," as it were, proposing, among other plans, to build a canal through the expansive area as a means to divide the swampland as well as support regional trade. In 1792, the Dismal Swamp Canal Company began work on a project to connect the Chesapeake Bay and Albermarle Sound in North Carolina. Slaves and fugitive maroons alike worked on the canal project and on various lumber ventures in and around the swamp. These manifestly economic attempts to contain the space and maroons were joined by a number of civic actions. After the Nat Turner rebellion, for instance, local militias were charged with clearing the swamps, and in 1847, the North Carolina General Assembly ratified an act to apprehend fugitive slaves in the swamp by, in part, creating a registry logging all "legal" peoples entering and exiting the area.[29] In short, the swamp's "economy of nature," to cite Darwin once more, was certainly both precarious and profitable: with, according to Frederick Douglass, "uncounted numbers of fugitives" as well as manifold economic inroads seeking to appropriate natural resources via slave labor and to exploit fugitives via trade or meager wages.[30]

This backdrop offered Stowe a useful context for her attempt to pen a follow-up to *Uncle Tom's Cabin* (1852). Despite the fact that her discussions with William Wells Brown in England and the outbreak of violence in Kansas and elsewhere prompted Stowe to revise the figurations of black agency and the colonizationist views that distinguish *Uncle Tom's Cabin*, *Dred* remains a richly conflicted narrative on multiple levels. Best uses Stowe's economic anxiety about the afterlives of slavery in *Uncle Tom's Cabin* to establish the terms of his thesis about fugitive value in the long nineteenth century. I want to use it here to direct my own arguments about *Dred* and its unique orientation toward adjusted and unadjusted emancipations. According to Best, Stowe's anachronistic embrace of colonization in the early 1850s signals a broader conceptual conflation between slavery and the slave that renders it necessary for the abolition of slavery to include the abolition of slaves themselves (with "abolition" in the latter case effecting "a putting out of memory").[31] Best uses passages from *Uncle Tom's Cabin* and commentary from Stowe's husband to highlight the economic anxiety underpinning this logic. For Stowe, slavery erects an unnatural system that "takes God's original 'nontransferable' property and makes it transferable." As a result, Stowe feared that "[s]lavery threaten[ed] to live on in its commodity." That is, she worried that slavery had created a permanent "scandal of value," and citizens would henceforth "never again be able to make 'clar' the distinction between persons and property."[32]

By focusing on Stowe's presentation of Dred and his particular status as a fugitive-rebel, I hope to show how the novel's concern with a broader "scandal in value" informs both the openings toward and closures of emancipatory logic in the narrative. Amidst the declining world of the Canema plantation, *Dred*'s swamp ontology and, as I will show, swamp hermeneutics erupt as a shared mode of bad debt, in Moten and Harney's aforementioned terms. But this emerging bad debt is curtailed forcefully by the regimes of debt found within the plantation system and the liberal discourses seeking to project and protect investments in futurity. In my reading, *Dred*'s precarious ecological-economic hermeneutics portray an interface among modes of ecology, personhood, and developing models of capital. Consequently, my arguments reformulate the economic landscape that Best establishes into a singular and differentiated material-ideological ecology that merges the registers of economics proper, civics, ecology, and hermeneutics.

If Monique Allewaert's study of paraontology and the historical modes of "ecological . . . resistance" stemming from "entanglements" among black bodies and plantation-zone environments reveals manifold limits within and to Western categories (taxonomic, aesthetic, and political-civic), then I hope to here extrapolate the concept of entanglement as a critical heuristic.[33] *Dred*'s potential modes of radical alterity and revolution manifest across various registers. Following Best and Allewaert, I argue that Stowe clusters these entangled modes of being within the Great Dismal Swamp and around concerns of interpretation. Any bad debt Stowe's *Dred* may manage is, therefore, filtered through issues of his swampy hermeneutics. Reconsidering the novel in this way might necessitate a certain comfort with reading blurred realities. It is as if we need to take Gail K. Smith's notion of "cross-reading" in *Dred* (a positivist consideration of the novel's attempt to present a pluralistic expanse of reading, including "reading with the Other") and turn it sideways: considering how Dred's own localized interpretive strategies cut across material and textual realities.[34]

The claim that Stowe's supposedly radical ex-slave fugitive is ultimately hemmed in by white liberal constraints is, of course, not surprising. Scholars such as Gregg Crane, for example, have discussed how the novel and Stowe's developing abolitionist thought "[imagines] a black revolution enacting the republican and liberal principles of the Declaration of Independence." Focusing on period higher law discourses, Crane suggests that "[w]hile higher law universals, in Stowe's view, are capable of inspiring a radical transformation in black Americans, this alteration turns out to be a kind of racial imitation." According to Crane, this imitation closes down potential liberation by yoking it to whiteness.[35] Grounding this dynamic in historical contexts, Crane depicts how Stowe's thinking is complicit with the 1829 North Carolina court case *State v. Mann*, which upheld the slave holder's "absolute power" over slaves and effectively relocated higher law concerns from the juridical scene into the "private feelings of citizens." In the end, for Crane, Stowe utilizes *Dred* to establish the right of rebellion but to limit the allowed modalities available for carrying it out: "[Judge] Ruffin's *Mann* opinion is part of this recognition, an attempt to contain a nascent revolutionary force, as in Stowe's novel, which tenders the threat of revolution as support for her antislavery argument."[36]

If Moten is right that "freedom in unfreedom is flight," then there's flight here too—however awkward or temporary. I want to start my readings where accidental formations of freedom may occur, even in a white novel that sets out to liberally mobilize and contain black radical violence. Rather than simply use *Dred* as a conflicted and tempered historical ground that might afford contrasting frameworks for considering black writing from the period on similar topics, I want to speculatively consider the novel backwards from William Wells Brown and Martin Delany. Here, *Dred*'s liberal possibilities qua limits are not the symptomatic end of reading, but an envelope for other possibilities only gleaned from outsides.

Dred, himself, first appears in the novel from such an outside. As a "deep voice from the swampy thicket" near Harry on his "circuitous path" along the border of the Great Dismal Swamp, Dred emerges to reveal his "magnificent stature" and "intensely black" skin (197–98). In this scene, the novel presents Dred playing on the not-so-latent inner antagonisms that stem from Harry's condition as a mixed-race slave who identifies with his deceased master/father and indebted white half-sister. Appearing from a swamp plantation zone of both bad debt and attempted appropriation (maroon life-worlds that are, in Moten and Harney's words, constituted by "debt broken from credit" and, at the same time, precarious as a result of the literal inroads of plantation capital), Dred manipulates the indeterminacy embodied in Harry, leveraging him toward the coordinates of the swamp. Donning a "fantastic sort of turban" and invoking "old warrior prophets of the heroic ages," Dred prods Harry to break toward radical action. "How long wilt thou halt between two opinions?" Dred asks. Referencing old testament scenes, Dred succeeds in mapping for Harry a live connection among examples of biblical oppression and the contexts of the present. "Don't talk in that way!—don't!" Harry implores him. "You are raising the very devil in me!" (199). Linking his apparent freedom of focalization and movement to the swamp ("You sleep in a curtained bed.—I sleep on the ground, in the swamps! You eat the fat of the land. I have what the ravens bring me!" [199]), Dred succeeds in generating "an uprising within" Harry that manifests in something of an affective excess without present form ("the hopeless impossibility of any outlet to what was burning within him" [200]).[37] But just as Dred departs into the swamp, Milly's approach interrupts Harry's rising "spasm of emotion," and she manages to soothe his ire. Acknowledging the corrupt "business" that casts her as a servant-slave, she recalibrates these conditions via an appeal to heavenly belonging—rendering her oppressed labor here and now as secretly "for de Lord's sake." Thus, as she explains, "I don't work for Miss Loo—I works for de Lord Jesus" (202).

The tension between good debt (here Milly's appeal to heavenly compensation for worldly labor) and bad debt (Dred's swamp para-economy) plays out across Book 2 of the novel. As I've suggested, it's no secret that good debt wins out. The ground for this victory is established on several fronts throughout the first part of *Dred*, where Stowe, offering competing pathways of traditional debt, overlays incipient notions of futurity (including emancipation) with the logos of rote economics. This is seen most prominently in Stowe's presentation of Edward Clayton's and later Nina Gordon's liberal embrace of gradualist anti-slavery measures from within the context of the existing plantation system. As Clayton announces early in the novel, although supporting his own family's slave plantation "Magnolia Grove," he is an avid reader of Garrison's *The Liberator* and believes "[t]here is a wonderful and beautiful development locked up in this Ethiopian race"; as such, he plans to "educate and fit [his slaves] for freedom," which includes implementing a "graduated system of work and wages" (23–24). *Fitting* slaves for freedom ("raising *men* and *women*," in Clayton's words [24]) obviously evokes a host of liberal assumptions and socioeconomic policies that condition postbellum "relations of domination," to again borrow Hartman's terms.[38] Clayton develops these ideas later in the novel when he and Nina—now more fervidly against slavery—envision their own liberal plantation. When Nina asks, "Why don't we blow it up, right off?" Clayton tellingly responds, "The laws against emancipation are very stringent. But I think it is every owner's business to contemplate this as a future resort, and to educate his servants in reference to it" (152). For Clayton and Nina, the central white liberal actors in Stowe's drama, the ground of emancipation is thus infused with the fiduciary logic of "business" and bolstered, however precariously, by the law.

The interface among these registers comes into full relief in Clayton's epiphanous failed legal case on behalf of the Gordon slave Milly, who claimed to be unlawfully "battered" by a white man employing her. Of course, Stowe's choice to have Judge Clayton decide in favor of the master-defendant takes up aspects of the aforementioned *State v. Mann* (1829) but also *Dred Scott v. Sandford*, which was first argued in February 1856. The particular decision in the novel's fictitious case is perhaps less significant than the manner in which Edward Clayton orients himself toward the law. In taking on the case, Clayton announces, "It is a debt which we owe . . . to the character of our state, and to the purity of our institutions, to prove the efficiency of the law in behalf of that class of our population . . . under our protection" (297). Economic debt here redoubles on the plane of juridical ethics: The system of slavery, whose very existence is predicated upon an ontology of debt, creates ethical-economic paradoxes that current institutions have the obligation to address if they are to maintain themselves. After his judge-father reads the decision, finding for the defendant that the master's *"dominion is essential to the value of slaves as property,"* Edward Clayton leaves the legal profession in order to maintain his ideological fantasy that an ideal domain of the law might yet address liberal anxieties about the conditions of slavery. The close of the novel reiterates the notion that Clayton's rejection of his literal and symbolic father is merely another iteration of the underlying logic of debt. In the final pages, Clayton is shown to have bought land in Canada and "[t]o this place removed his slaves, and formed there a town-ship, which is now one of the richest and finest in the region" (543). Although Stowe does not comment on the qualitative aspects of these slaves' and ex-slaves' lives, she does manage to note that the "value of the improvements which Clayton and his tenants have made has nearly doubled the price of real estate in the vicinity" (544).

Using this legal and economic ground, Stowe encloses the conditions of possibility for the passage of slavery to ex-slavery. Although the experiences of slaves in the novel (especially Milly, Tiff, and Harry) are nuanced and differentiated, they all operate within the boundaries afforded by the logic and reality Stowe erects via Clayton and Nina. But then there's Dred. A number of scholars have noted ways in which Stowe's novel takes up period notions of black revolutionary violence, especially as it relates to religious prophecy.[39] Others have examined ways in which Dred's character and his violent potentials are thwarted, forestalled, and conditioned in the narrative.[40] Building on these readings, I want to reexamine how Dred's failed rebellion works. Ultimately, the question is: To what extent and in what ways does Stowe contain the specific modalities of fugitivity that she allows Dred? As I will suggest, Dred's experiences and agency play out across the economic and ecological borders of emerging bad debt and existing debt regimes; and Stowe attempts to capture (that is, symbolically make fungible) the divergent possibilities of this zone by coding them in terms of hermeneutics (322).

In the chapter "The Conspirators," Stowe offers context for Dred's character, which she claims to "owe" the reader. She notes that Dred was an enslaved son of Denmark Vesey born of a relationship between Vesey, then free and living in South Carolina, and a "Mandingo slave-woman" (203, 208). After noting Vesey's own use of the Bible as an "instrument of influence," where he "rendered himself perfectly familiar with all of those parts of Scripture which he thought he could pervert to his purpose," Stowe turns to Dred's childhood reading practices (205). According to Stowe, Dred was something of a prodigy, possessing an astonishing "instinctive faculty" for "the power of reading" (208). As the chapter continues, this innate faculty is tethered to the Bible—specifically his father's Bible, which he takes with him into the swamp—and given two frames. The first is Vesey and his specific community of "conspiracy": where Dred becomes, as a child, his father's "confidant" and later "heard read, in the secret meetings of conspirators, the wrathful denunciations of ancient prophets against oppression and injustice" (208, 210). This semantic lens of revolutionary "reading" offered by conspirators undoubtedly informs Dred's role of being a "herald of woe" (210).

The second frame is that of the swamp itself. Stowe first describes the swamp on the heels of a discussion of Dred's "unsuitable disposition" as a slave. According to Stowe, Dred's maladjusted orientation rendered him "like a fractious horse, . . . sold from master to master" until he kills an overseer and flees to the swamps (209). In an ambiguous jump from Dred's inner space to the space of the swamp, Stowe portrays the landscape as containing "regions of hopeless disorder, where the abundant growth and vegetation of nature, sucking up its forces from the humid soil, seems to rejoice in a savage exuberance." Conjuring Western anxieties about tropical-zone ecological "entanglements" as well as category crises period audiences associated with a "cultural grotesque," an often racialized "liminal state between human and thing," Stowe paints a swampland of troubling excesses where "[c]limbing vines, and parasitic plants, of untold splendor and boundless exuberance of growth, twine and interlace" (209).[41] The *growth* in question is a topic I will return to shortly; here, though, it is used to establish a "wild" syntactical frame for Dred's reading practice. Alone in the "vast solitude" of the swamps with his father's book, Dred is said to have "no interpreter but the silent courses of nature" (210–11). Nature nonetheless has effects within this scenario. As Stowe suggests, when the bible's "oriental seed, an exotic among us, is planted back in the fiery soil of a tropical heart, it bursts forth with an incalculable ardor of growth" (211).

The muddled blur of local semantics (slave conspiracy reading) and local syntactics (textual swamp growth) thus meet, quite literally given the previous passage, in the character of Dred. This knotted production of reading, infused with specific histories about and focalizations on oppression as well as vegetal energies and urges, engenders not only atypical biblical interpretations, but also the ability to discern "strange hieroglyphics . . . written upon the leaves" (211). Indeed, under the "nursing influence of nature," Dred is later shown to be "as perfectly *en rapport* with [nature] . . . as a tree" (273–74). As Stowe explains, Dred's connection with his surroundings is also filtered through cultural experiences. Dred's maternal grandfather was said to have been an "African sorcerer," having taught Dred "the secret of snake-charming, and had possessed his mind from childhood with expectations of prophetic and supernatural impulses" (274). Such material-cultural alignments yield remarkable abilities: from "supernatural perceptions" to escaping danger via an "instinctive discrimination which belongs to animals" (273, 275). It also yields para-collectives or, at least, para-sociality: as Dred has "a kind of fellowship" with the natural elements, rendering him "a companion of the dragons and the owls" who finds "the alligators and the snakes better neighbors than Christians" (274, 277–78). As one might expect, Stowe shrinks from the ecological-racial other that she has imagined, finding a "grotesque effect" in the way his "whole personality" was linked to his ability to "[converse] alternately in two languages" (here "the language of exaltation" and that of "common life") (275).[42]

None of these para-readings or para-realities, however, appear to preclude human sociality. In fact, at the end of "The Conspirators," Stowe recounts the ways Dred carries on a collaborative pseudo-economy with those in and around the swamp—allowing him to procure a rifle, "cultivate" a secret area of land, find a wife, and work toward his own "conspiracy against the whites" (212). Although these competing socioeconomic networks (inside and around the swamp versus outside of it) are constantly pitted against each other, ensuing antagonisms are most often portrayed in terms of religious hermeneutics. From early in the novel, Stowe presents Christianity as a central ground for leveraging power and ideological control. Chapter 14 in Part I, for example, recounts a conversation among local slave owners regarding business and the place of religion. Mr. Jekyl leads off by asserting that one of his slaves "is the more valuable because he has been religiously brought up" (159). As he explains it, "the missionaries are pretty careful; they put it in strong in the catechisms about the rights of the master." He goes on: "I can tell you ... that, in a business, practical view,—for I am used to investments,—that, since the publishing of those catechisms, and the missionaries' work among the niggers, the value of that kind of property has risen ten per cent" (160). Obviously troubled by this perspective, Stowe has Clayton step in with a thoroughgoing liberal response: "My objection is that it is all a lie," he says (160). Clayton then offers a model whereby slaves "must be taught to read the Scriptures for themselves, and be able to see that [the master's] authority accords with it. If [he] command[s] anything contrary to it, they ought to oppose it!" (162). Recalling Clayton's and Nina's economic plans to train slaves for freedom (via the civic logic of debt), his idea here clearly presents a liberal syntactical arrangement: Slaves should be free up to a certain point in order to allow them to accept what is systemically imposed on them. This liberal schematic, though, is immediately challenged due to concerns that the Bible includes passages that might catalyze insurrection. Mr. Jekyl insists upon the need to "select for [slaves] ... such portions of the word as are best fitted to keep them quiet, dutiful, and obedient" (163).

As scholars such as Gail K. Smith and Carrie Hyde have pointed out, *Dred* negotiates a number of period debates about textual and scriptural hermeneutics. In Smith's aforementioned essay on "cross-reading," for example, she notes how Stowe's presentation of competing scriptural readings is fueled by both arguments about the Bible and slavery as well as broader shifting hermeneutical paradigms, such as the advent of German "Higher Criticism" in U.S. educational institutions.[43] Smith sees the novel addressing anxieties about the indeterminacy of interpretation by offering the pluralistic model of cross-reading as an inclusive attempt to mitigate violence: teaching white Americans to "read the text with the eyes of the oppressed" as well as to "avoid the violence, injustice, and baseness that stem from distorted interpretations formed alone or in groups as a single race or gender—black men reading the Bible or Declaration of Independence alone, [or] white male mobs interpreting the law of the land."[44] Similarly, Hyde uses the novel to posit a liberal model of what she terms "theological commons," where Stowe's novel works to alter scriptural readings (especially Philippians 3:20) in order to erect a "racially inclusive" form of U.S. citizenship (linking "slaves and [white] Christians" via the experience of "estrangement").[45]

I want to show how Dred's reading and character—however fleetingly—complicate and perhaps exceed the assumptions of such contextualizations. My point is that Dred's swamp hermeneutics are not tantamount to traditional Protestant typological schemas or period debates about theological hermeneutics, though these certainly inform the action. Instead, Dred's material-interpretive practices implicate actualities of the conditions and possibilities on the ground—and mark his original, desperate, and, ultimately, ineffectual attempts at leveraging real alternatives via his own para-reality.

The themes of religious hermeneutics, Dred's para-ecology, and the heightened political landscape of the moment come together at a local camp meeting depicted near the end of the book's first part. The event draws a populous crowd from all quarters, and Stowe uses the scene to display a number of competing cross-sections of Christian discourse. Among the speakers is Father Dickinson, a figure Stowe describes as representing something of a mainstream liberal hope among other ministers, writing that he is one "who keep[s] alive our faith in Christianity, and renew[s] on earth the portrait of the old apostle" (247). Stowe juxtaposes Father Dickinson to a Father Bonnie, who is shown to enjoy a "more general and apparent popularity" due to his "rude but effective style of eloquence" and his not-so-subtle embrace of slavery. Father Dickinson confronts Bonnie's biblical defense of slavery, arguing, for example, that Abraham had "[s]ervants, perhaps[,] but not slaves!" He later consoles a dying sixteen-year-old slave by singing a hymn that was "often sung among the negroes," using the song to connect with the oppressed: "As oil will find its way into crevices where water cannot penetrate, so song will find its way where speech can no longer enter" (248, 267). On the other hand, Father Bonnie portrays the complicity between the "rude poetry" employed by the day's ministers and existing systems of power. In typical populist fashion, Bonnie uses an emotive jeremiad about sin and redemption to elicit an "electric shout [from] . . . the multitude" (258, 260). Stowe's use of Bonnie seems to reveal the conspicuous limits of the pluralistic multitudes that *both* Dickinson and Bonnie are able to shape. After Bonnie's sermon and Dickinson's displays of liberal sympathy, for example, the chapter moves to a close by mentioning that two weeks after the camp meeting, "Bonnie drove a brisk bargain with . . . [a slave] trader for three new hands." Thus, "[t]he trader had discovered that the judgment-day was not coming yet a while, and father Bonnie satisfied himself that Noah, when he awoke from his wine, said, 'Cursed be Canaan'" (269).

Dred makes his appearance in the middle of this action. Just after the aforementioned scene where Bonnie unites the crowd in "electric shout[s]," Dred's voice interrupts Bonnie's joyous heralding of Jesus's return. When the pro-slavery preacher calls out "O, brethren, let us sing glory to the Lord! The Lord is coming among us!" a "sound which seemed to come pealing down directly from the thick canopy of pines over the heads of the ministers" startles the crowd (262). Calling out from an unidentified position among the trees, Dred's physical voice effects something of a para-ecological affront: "There was deep, sonorous power in the voice that spoke, and the words fell pealing down through the air like the vibrations of some mighty bell" (262). Disrupting the previous pluralistic jubilee, Dred's words offer a militant vision of separation: "Woe unto you that desire the day of the Lord! To what end shall it be for *you*? The day of the Lord shall be darkness, and not light! Blow ye the trumpet in Zion! Sound an alarm in my holy mountain! Let all the inhabitants of the land tremble! for the day of the Lord cometh!" (262). Piercing the material fantasies sustaining the religious spectacle and disrupting an abstract and pluralist appeal to heavenly belonging with the conflicts of the present ("The Lord is against this nation!" and "I am against thee, saith the Lord, and I will make thee utterly desolate!"), Dred causes the crowd to "look confusedly on each other," "panic," and eventually disperse (262–63).

Dred's dislocating voice and message clearly develop from the broader conditions that I have been calling his para-realities (economic, ecological, hermeneutic). It is from this entangled framework that we might consider Dred's frequent appeal to wait, amid the present's messianic time, for the arrival of supernatural intervention. Of course, Dred, himself, at times expresses frustration with the delay, imploring in vain: "Wake, O, arm of the Lord! Awake, put on thy strength!" (276). This "wait," however, is not merely a metaphysical variety of Clayton's liberal pragmatic vision of gradual economic reform, nor is it just a conditioned Kantian version of freedom that, as Jared Hickman posits, operates in something like the crack or gap within a Western God.[46] Dred's impatience reveals not a heavenly but a historical-material frustration. Hickman is perhaps close here, suggesting that "the novel, like its eponymous protagonist, assumes a posture of waiting on the Lord, but with increasing . . . impatience, not merely looking for signs of God's intentions but provoking God toward justice through the production of its own signs."[47] Within Dred's swamp reality, however, it is not just new "signs" that are produced but a new ecology of alignments and material possibilities. Dred's biblical anticipatory anxiety certainly stems in part from impasses within Western, white, and/or biblical codes for the real conditions of possibility. But, due to the conditions on the ground, his modality of waiting includes a movement toward real change rather than simply a qualitative modification of symbolic schemes for and appeals to a standard god or master.

When Dred appears before Harry later in the in novel "as if he had risen from the ground" and implores him to action using various codes of natural rebellion ("Do? What does the wild horse do? Launch out our hoofs!"), we see how the novel pulls the time and act of waiting into a strange new material frame (341). Dred launches into a familiar mode of Revelations prophecy: "I tell you Harry, there's a seal been loosed—there's a vial poured out on the air; and the destroying angel standeth over Jerusalem, with his sword drawn!" (341). When a bewildered Harry asks him what he "means," Dred answers with a diatribe about how "the slain of the Lord shall be many," "his voice [sounding] like that of a person speaking from a distance." All of this is too much for Harry, who pushes Dred, begging him to "come out of this" (341–42). In this exchange, Dred's trajectory of unadjusted emancipation comes into its fullest focus. Much like his disruptive voice calling from among the trees during the camp meeting, Dred's remarks to Harry about impending righteous violence are spoken from a "distance."

In both cases, it is as if the conditions of Dred's focalization affect a radical shift within what Elizabeth Povinelli's calls *"hereish."* As I explain in Chapter 3, Povinelli uses "hereish" to offer an original way to conceive new alignments among the local and global within the modern world. According to Povinelli, the ecological catastrophes of our age alter conceptually our "object of concern . . . across competing struggles for existence, implicating how we conceptualize scale, event, circulation, and being."[48] Povinelli's concept is representative of emerging new materialist models predicated upon an experience of an actual otherness in the making that is *here* and there—where here has access (even if only affectively or aesthetically) to noumena-like conditions that exist in a larger reality (there).[49] Dred's swamp-based ex-slave status might shift the modern notion of hereish into something closer to *thereish*: a para-ontological and para-ecological condition of being in a different relation to the present (a relation to the present that, I might add, Thoreau's strange empathy aims but cannot reach). Dred's position of thereish fuses the liminal and para-ecological conditions discussed earlier into an alternate historical framework where reality is both *there* and here—where the location of ontology slides to the far side (and perhaps outside) of Western humanist "knowledge."[50] Instead of closing the vast domains of the global with the intimacy of the local/present, "thereish" allows for charged discontinuities, including antagonistically oriented or alternate locals with their own unique existing or possible recalibrations of the local-global nexus. In speculative terms, Dred's ontology unintentionally dramatizes, in a way, the aforementioned positions of Afro-pessimism by portraying how the experience of "nothing" that is indeed some*thing* dislocates standard liberal-humanist coordinates for spatial, conceptual, and political reality, however progressive then and now.[51]

Dred is there. And Harry's economy of debt and nationalist discourses of rebellion require his presence here. Despite building momentum to pull all modes of fugitivity into the ken of liberal presence, Stowe, in qualified and negative ways, gives us more of Dred's world and its political possibilities. First, she returns to the topic of ecological growth as a physical reality and symbolic metaphor for Dred's ontology and thinking-reading. In a chapter titled "*Engedi*," referencing a biblical town in the wilderness of the Dead Sea that provided sanctuary, Stowe revisits Dred's swamp "strong hold" and moves quickly from notions of strategic/political space to matters of communication and knowledge: "In all despotic countries, . . . it will be found that the oppressed party become expert in the means of secrecy" (495). After discussing again the context of Denmark Vesey and the pragmatics of conspiracy, the chapter moves to Dred's specific form of "religious enthusiasm," and Stowe comments, "It is difficult to fathom the dark recesses of a mind so powerful and active as his, placed under a pressure of ignorance and social disability so tremendous" (496). With this clear attempt to contain and curtail, Stowe jumps directly to the ecological: "In those desolate regions which he made his habitation, it is said that trees often, from the singularly unnatural and wildly stimulating properties of the slimy depths from which they spring, assume a goblin growth, entirely different from their normal habit." Expounding upon this so-called goblin growth, she writes, "All sorts of vegetal monsters stretch their weird, fantastic forms among its shadows. There is no principle so awful through all nature as the principle of *growth*" (496). The "grotesque effect" that Stowe had earlier referenced in terms of Dred's character and abilities is here planted directly within its source: unchecked and aberrant, hence, pseudo-pure growth. This "goblin growth" gives form to Stowe's own aesthetic and moral repulsions, but it also addresses the aforementioned economic anxieties that Best traces. Offering something of a representational palimpsest, Stowe's chapter struggles to cultivate (pun very much intended) the ground on which one might understand Dred's position and, in so doing, cut him down.

It should be abundantly clear by now that Dred's own "goblin growth" encompasses a number of entangled registers, and this modality is far from the period's appropriate structure for accumulation. As Jonathan Levy points out, the nineteenth century saw the emergence of an institutional shift from financial peril to "managed risk." With the development of financial corporations, including insurance markets, "risk burrowed into popular consciousness" as well as framed a wide range of narratives about personhood and freedom. In this new liberal ideal, "free and equal men must take, run, own, assume, bear, carry, and manage personal risks."[52] Dred's goblin growth, emerging and spilling over from a zone of thereish, is anything but the type of accumulation via managed risk Stowe (indirectly perhaps) and the financial class (directly) had in mind. This unbridled growth not only reproduces at uncouth rates, it also produces ways of being and seeing ("monsters") that challenge. From this vantage, Dred's waiting for divine action becomes a new mode of messianic time: not an empty period of forestalled action, but a time when his goblin growth begins to work, however circuitously, toward his unique notion of redemption and fugitivity.

As I note in Chapter 1, Giorgio Agamben develops a useful Paulinian notion of messianic time, or the "time that remains" before Jesus's return to historical reality. As Agamben explains, *Klēsis* (the Greek term for work or "calling") references, in the context of messianic time, "the particular transformation that every juridical status and worldly condition undergoes because of, and only because of, its relation to the messianic event." This means that *"messianic vocation is the revocation of every vocation"* in that each act or way of being is "undermine[d] without losing its form." That is, each way of being remains but is "pushed toward itself through the *as not*; the messianic does not simply cancel out this figure, but it makes it pass, it prepares its end."[53] Many of Dred's words may be in line with Agamben's Western schematic, but his actions and Stowe's descriptions of him are something quite different. Within what is becoming a cautionary frame, Stowe clarifies that it was specific conditions of "oppression" that led Dred to "interpret" "[a]ll things in nature and in revelation . . . by this key": that a "coming judgment" from above "shall right earth's mighty wrongs" (446–47). The historical plane and its outsides thus merge in odd ways—where the hermeneutical "key" to Dred's worldview (which is based upon specific forms of present oppression) shapes the form and aim of longed-for future divine eventual interruption.[54]

But typical eventual logic may miss certain valences of Dred's present goblin growth. In a way, Dred's goblin growth is a materialist nightmare scene where Agamben's Paulinian mode of qualitative transmogrification without quantitative change gives way to monstrous forms of distortion within present historical and biological coordinates. If there is "risk" (a conceptual-existential correlative of normative debt) here, it is risk that sheds the logic and hedged futurities of the day's market. Dred's hermeneutical bad debt anticipates a direct engagement with a perilous present, an engagement that economic managed risk and, indeed, liberal civics attempt to mitigate and forestall. Given the atypical material conditions of Dred's reality, where his ecology opens out incipiently into various material and socioeconomic registers, this coming resistance takes the form, in the present, of a shared (pre-collective) material urge—appearing as an emerging byproduct produced by goblin growth's operations within entangled material and symbolic planes.

Nonetheless, the novel soon absorbs Dred into its approved models of emancipation and progress. This conspicuous closure is carried out across several scenes and fronts: Harry's nationalist rhetoric rivaling Dred's reliance on *Revelations* (451); violence erupting only within safe frameworks, as when Harry's physical blow against Tom appears "as if a rebound" from his master's own stroke (388); Milly's *Psalms*-based readings of redemption taking hold within Dred (497, 499); and, of course, Dred's death five chapters before the end of the novel. In this penultimate scene, Stowe separates definitively the previous para-relations of Dred's ecology—with, at his death, birds singing on "unterrified by the wail of human sorrow," and Dred's body "resolv[ing] again into the eternal elements" (513).[55] And yet, the central plot device for consolidating the narrative in these ways is the eruption of a cholera outbreak. Despite all of the closures and foreclosures described here, the overwrought links between the outbreak and Dred's threatening ecology cannot be overlooked. Interestingly, cholera enters the novel directly after the above scene where Harry begs Dred to come out of "this," establishing what I have termed Dred's thereish. Playing with Dred's hermeneutical (divine redemption) and material (goblin growth) frame, the novel describes the outbreak as "spurn[ning] all laws" in its elusive destruction (342).[56] And both Harry and Dred interpret the outbreak's "meaning" as correlative with Dred's predictions (342, 447).

There is a long history of racialized anxiety about the outbreak of disease and slave rebellion, especially surrounding yellow fever and the Haitian Revolution.[57] I want to note, however, how the novel foregrounds the link between cholera and Dred's hermeneutics/material growth, where the disease turns Canema into a battlefield (the Gordon plantation becoming "a beleaguered garrison" [366]). Cholera thus becomes the only possible large-scale rebellion—something of a weaponized thereish. And it is represented perhaps the only way Stowe could imagine it: as a para-ontological viral becoming. This ecological pseudo-rebellion, if we might think of it this way, offers Stowe a convenient way to transform Dred's fugitive potential into a recognizable and acceptable form.[58] In this way, Stowe toys with the link between disease and black rebellion, divine and otherwise, in order to launch her own corrective ideological and hermeneutical warfare. Absorbing Dred's world(s) into a contained variety of physical dispersal (just as Dred's body ultimately returns to the elements) allows the liberal narrative and historical trajectory begun in Part I of the novel to again dominate, albeit in a precarious manner. In the end, one cannot help but see the cop-out Canadian landscape with which the novel closes, replete with its transplanted ex-slaves and white liberal economic hope, as the only tenable escape from not only southern slavery (and all its infections), but also, perhaps, Dred's own variety of goblin growth.

William Wells Brown's Bad, Bad Debt

Whereas Dred's swamp fugitivity maintains a precarious place within Stowe's work, William Wells Brown and his 1853 novel *Clotel* have, until recently, occupied a vexed space within the African American literary canon. According to Ann duCille, Brown's novel "has never quite walked the party line of the black experience."[59] Many later twentieth-century scholars have censured the novel's overuse of period racial stereotypes and its portrayal of what Addison Gayle calls "Blacks in white face."[60] As duCille points out, however, it is the formal methods of Brown's novel that most trouble critics. In duCille's words, "[T]he real problem with *Clotel* lies in the particular slippery nature of Brown's brand of realism, which both deploys and denies the documentary impulse that drives the reading, if not the writing, of African-American literature. Black books are expected to tell a particular black truth."[61] Put differently, it is the formal way that Brown's novel assembles and redeploys period narratives—appearing more like postmodern bricolage than antebellum "unvarnished truth"—that compromises its implied political and historical aims.[62]

In recent years, the critical landscape has shifted, and a number of scholars have turned to Brown as an underacknowledged figure through which to trace a variety of topics related to race and sociopolitical constructions.[63] I want to move from the aesthetic "edgy spirit of play" that Geoffrey Sanborn has recently spied in Brown's writing and its plagiarisms toward the serious stakes and possibilities existing beneath and alongside the realities that standard historical and formal criticism has considered.[64] As Christina Sharpe makes clear, "There is a long history and present of imaging and imagining blackness and Black selves otherwise, in excess of the containment of the long and brutal history of the violent annotations of Black being: what Spillers, for example, called the hieroglyphics of the flesh; a history that is 'the crisis of referentiality, the fictions of personhood, and the gap or incommensurability between the proper name and the form of existence that it signifies.'"[65] Following Sharpe's theorization of black textual redaction and annotation toward concerns of ontology that have been, and continue to be, subtended by infrastructures of antiblackness underwritten by white liberalisms, I turn to *Clotel* and the modified version of Brown's autobiography that served as the novel's original authorial introduction in order to trace out alternate formations of fugitivity. As Sanborn points out, Brown plagiarized roughly 87,000 words from 282 different texts, a number of which appear in the first version of *Clotel*.[66] I want to think of this apparent "theft" in terms of the aforementioned concept of bad debt and use it as a starting point for considering how Brown's rewritten and self-excerpted autobiography opens up new ways of understanding the personal and authorial conditions of possibility (and impossibility) attending the active transversals between bondage and "freedom." In lieu of "narratives" of diachronic movement toward emancipation (along any of the familiar trajectories such as literacy, recognition, and so on), we find in Brown's work something of a complex shadow ontology predicated upon precarious circulations.

The genre of ex-slave narratives obviously has a foundational place in the canon and criticism of American and African American literature, an unsurprising fact given that over one hundred former slaves published autobiographies in the nineteenth century.[67] According to Lisa Lowe, both autobiography and the novel have been formative because they "did some of the important work of mediating and resolving liberalism's contradictions." In Lowe's view, the autobiography particularly aligns with liberal political philosophy's "affirmation of the individual's passage to freedom through economic industry and political emancipation" as well as supports the "imperatives and privileges of liberal subjects, [and] . . . also its aesthetic form."[68] In the context of duCille's essay, twentieth-century dismissals of Brown's work might be said to take issue with what has been a two-part problem: Its content is not black in accepted ways and its form, notably its plagiarism and hyper-performativity, departs from the standard ideological-narrative formats and aims that Lowe notes.

The former charge is understandable from a historical perspective, as many of Brown's works, including *Clotel*, offer complex negotiations of racial and national identifications, often proffering some version of a speculative interracial compromise. In the original version of *Clotel*, for example, one sees this in the way the novel privileges the familiar "tragic mulatto" trope but also in the way it raises characters such as George, an interracial man who fought with Nat Turner but who identifies with U.S. national fantasies and modalities of freedom, over characters such as Picquillo, a "full-blooded negro" from one of the "barbarous tribes in Africa" and more recently Cuba who, with a sword fashioned from a scythe, sought "the blood of all the whites he could meet."[69] Indeed, at the novel's close, George, in Europe and passing for white, is "ashamed of his African decent," and his clerkship has him "on the road to wealth" (194–95). It's in Dunkirk that he fatefully encounters his former love interest Mary, Clotel's daughter, and learns her tale of being aided in her own escape by a gallant white Frenchman who marries her, promising to "transfer" onto her the love he had for his deceased sister (202). Now a widow, Mary soon weds George, and the two remain in a geopolitical abeyance of freedom, achieving something approaching middle-class status (including perhaps both passing as white to some degree) but being blocked from returning to the United States.

Similar themes and trajectories can be found in a number of Brown's other publications. In his 1854 lecture "St. Domingo: Its Revolutions and Its Patriots," he offers a historical defense of the violence of slave revolts, but he also works to fold these rebellions into the symbolic register of Western codes and historiography, comparing Toussaint to Napoleon before claiming that the Haitian leader "as a Christian, a statesman, and a general, will lose nothing by a comparison with that of Washington."[70] This strategy is also apparent in Brown's *The Negro in the American Rebellion: His Heroism and His Fidelity* (1867). Offering a historical compendium of black participation in American armed resistance, Brown includes chapters on the "fidelity" of African Americans such as Crispus Attucks during the American Revolution but also "The Nat Turner Insurrection" and "Slave Revolt at Sea." At points, Brown defends black violence, exclaiming: "The efforts of Denmark Vesey, Nat Turner, and Madison Washington to strike the chains of slavery from the limbs of their enslaved race will live in history, and will warn all tyrants to beware of the wrath of God and the strong arm of man."[71] In his discussion of rebellions, however, Brown often employs nationalized ethical focalizations to circumscribe events. In the very gesture of humanizing the outbreak of violence with Nat Turner, for example, Brown portrays the actions of a slave named Will as prototypically savage: "[T]hough his soul longed to be free, he evidently became of the party as much to satisfy revenge as for the liberty that he saw in the dim distance." Brown then juxtaposes the cautionary figures of

Will and Turner with the honorable slave Jim, who performs his "duty" by saving the life of his master (who was also his "half-brother") during the rebellion but then refuses to remain enslaved, offering this same master the choice of killing him on the spot or freeing him. "Putting his right hand upon his heart," Brown writes, Jim said, "'This is the spot; aim here'; the Captain fired, and the slave fell dead at his feet."[72]

From these passages, one can see why Brown may have had a vexed place within the critical tradition of African American literature. By focusing on Brown's reworked autobiography, though, I hope to, however incipiently, reformulate this critical schematic. Within Brown's atypical formal approach, we might see alternate ways of thinking about historical and ontological constructions of blackness. Brown's content might move along accepted trajectories of liberal whiteness, but, following from Lowe's logic, his formal approaches may, at times, swerve in other directions. Of course, even Frederick Douglass took issue with Brown's willingness to claim the words (and hence property) of others, writing in an 1853 issue of *Frederick Douglass' Paper* that "like some other *literary* men," Brown may have "mistaken the beautiful sentiment of another for the creation of his own fancy!"[73]

But perhaps it's Douglass who is mistaken after all. Aside from the evidence that Brown was very much aware of his practice of plagiarism, Douglass's quip about Brown may be ill-informed due to its foundational ethical assumptions about property and its conceptual assumptions about expressive subjectivity.[74] Indeed, in his original autobiography, *Narrative of William W. Brown, a Fugitive Slave* (1847), Brown recounts the odd scenario where his master, Dr. Young, charged him with going out into Saint Louis to find a new master/buyer, setting a price of 500 dollars. Soon after, when describing his plan to escape, Brown jokes that his master may soon "suspect that [he] had gone to Canada to find a purchaser."[75] Although he makes clear that attaining freedom would yield the ability to "call [his] body [his] own," Brown's playful conflation of freedom (in Canada) and continued commodification qua personhood is worth emphasizing.[76]

In the 1853 adaptation of his autobiography for *Clotel*, Brown draws on his *Three Years in Europe* (1852) to add a new scene to the narrative of this life that fills out and complicates this earlier joke about selling himself in Canada. After describing his post-escape marriage and time smuggling fugitives across Lake Erie, Brown gives an account of his "first going into business for himself" (24). He begins with opening a barbershop in the town of Monroe after he was unable to procure employment at a competing business. Renting the space, Brown bought a table and erected a sign that read, "Fashionable Hair-dresser from New York, Emperor of the West" (25). These efforts soon allow Brown to dominate the local market, and a friend encourages him to expand by "becoming a banker" (26). Brown explains at length:

> At this time, money matters in the Western States were in a sad condition. Any person who could raise a small amount of money was permitted to establish a bank, and allowed to issue notes for four times the sum raised. This being the case, many persons borrowed money merely long enough to exhibit to the bank inspectors, and the borrowed money was returned, and the bank left without a dollar in its vaults, if, indeed, it had a vault about its premises. The result was, that banks were started all over the Western States, and the country flooded with worthless paper. These were known as the "Wild Cat Banks." Silver coin being very scarce, and the banks not being allowed to issue notes for a smaller amount than one dollar, several persons put out notes of from 6 to 75 cents in value; these were called "Shinplasters." The Shinplaster was in the shape of a promissory note, made payable on demand. (25–26)

The "sad condition" of money in the United States, with "Wild Cat Banks" and their shady notes proliferating in the west, offers Brown an opportunity to develop his hair dressing business into a bank as soon as his own shinplasters are minted (26). This pivotal scene establishes the groundwork of what I call Brown's "bad, bad debt." As scholars such as Antonio Negri and Maurizio Lazzarato demonstrate, the historical modes of capitalism have produced various types of and assumptions about subjectivity. As Lazzarato explains, part of the difficulty with contemporary neoliberal formations is that the deterritorialization attending global capitalism has compromised "previous social relations and their forms of subjectivation" while, at the same time, the new "promotion of the entrepreneur" does not allow the creation of selves outside of the market's domain. The self thus has no past or present alternative and becomes trapped within the confines of constant financialized becoming—a mere "entrepreneur of the self."[77] This is the general reality to which Mbembe adds a consideration of the "subaltern" in his aforementioned assessment that contemporary neoliberalism and the Atlantic slave trade blur in conspicuous structural ways.

As we see with Brown, however, moving from slave to ex-slave status within the context of capitalism in the antebellum United States is not precisely tantamount to new forms of universalized misery found in our precarious moment of austerity, the gig economy, and geopolitical regimes of slow violence. The specific types of indebtedness experienced by antebellum ex-slaves yielded unique structural relations and different ontological possibilities, however limned by capital and modes of antiblackness. In specific terms, Brown is here negotiating three levels of bad debt: willfully denying the 500 dollars of debt he owes his owner (after Dr. Young had previously denied him the ability to purchase himself);[78] negotiating period institutional practices of profitable bad debt; and experiencing, between these first two levels of indebtedness, a strange para-position, one that twists bad debt into a precarious zone of agency and, in turn, informs Brown's writing practices as well as his constructions of self.

The second and third types of bad debts are especially important when considering the stakes of Brown's reworked autobiography. The "Wild Cat" banking scene that Brown introduces is one small horizon within a wider system of financial speculation surrounding chattel slavery. As Bonnie Martin puts it, "Slave owners worked their slaves financially as well as physically" by creating, from the colonial period onward, local networks of credit where farmers, planters, and so on raised vast sums of capital by mortgaging slaves to each other.[79] In these exchanges, investors used slaves as collateral for loans or created mortgages to access the anticipated value of young slaves. In addition, insurance polices allowed owners to offset monetary loss from slaves' untimely deaths, creating the conditions to financially work slaves past their biological lives via "ghost values" that continued to pay postmortem.[80] As Edward Baptist explains, in the early nineteenth century these local credit networks and their efforts to "leverage" the liquid capital of slaves led to new and widespread "networks of mutual indebtedness" that engendered economic crises such as the Panic of 1837.[81] These networks of debt form the root of the Wild Cat banks Brown discusses. At the center is the structural hedge afforded by enslaved bodies. With all of the debt circulating and being held in abeyance until cotton could be sold at a sufficient price, the complex networks of loans were generally maintained by purchasing more slaves to produce more anticipated cotton or by selling or mortgaging slaves to pay off portions of debt.[82] Even before Jackson finally defeated the Second Bank of the United States in 1833, which opened the floodgates to local speculative banking, large groups of merchants and planters began forming alternative credit bodies, such as the 1827 Consolidated Association of the Planters of Louisiana (CAPL). As a locally controlled bank, CAPL was established to create a "new kind of debt instrument" within the slave economy, shifting the arrangement of debt in order to allow borrowers to leverage more money under more favorable terms. Erecting a stock system, CAPL sold 2.5 million dollars in bonds that it converted into 2.5 million dollars in "sterling bills" printed in England and backed, if necessary, by the Bank of England. Soon after, CAPL leveraged this cash reserve by printing 3.5 million dollars in CAPL banknotes and creating new streams of credit out of New Orleans.[83]

Brown's own speculative bad debt, in the form of shinplasters, thus enters into a wider milieu of normalized bad debt. And yet, in the nexus of bad debts, where an ex-slave who is himself an "equivalent of a bad cheque or a counterfeit bond" produces his own variety of semi-counterfeit money, a unique set of relations emerges.[84] While these relations might be thought of as local aberrations, the exceptions yielded by this particular nineteenth-century economic landscape negotiate both period systemic arrangements as well as, even more broadly, structural aspects of capital. In Negri's reading of Marx's *Grundrisse*, a series of notebooks Marx wrote while living in England shortly after Brown's *Clotel* was first published, Negri notes the way Marx's writing intervenes critically in period economic theory by considering value from the vantage of money and all of its violent contingencies. Fittingly, Marx's chapter on money was written in response to the American economic crisis of 1857 and opens with a critique of Alfred Darimon's *De la réforme des banques* (1856), which discusses European banks' difficulties with monetary forms.[85] In Marx's analysis, Negri writes, "[W]e are not before value; we are in it; we are in that world made by money. Money represents the form of social relations; it represents, sanctions, and organizes them." By taking this analytical perspective, Marx uses money to present "immediately the lurid face of the social relation of value; it shows ... value right away as exchange, commanded and organized for exploitation."[86] According to Negri, Marx reveals money to be "*the crisis* of the law of value" in that it represents the "exclusive form" of value's actual functioning in the world, and this function occurs within social relations marked by stark antagonism.[87] It is for this reason that, in his own discussion of *Grundrisse*, Cesare Casarino notes the structural way that money, for Marx, "is above all the expression of a contradictory and potentially explosive social relation." As such, money "is precisely that *locus* where contradiction may multiply into an unco-optable surplus of contradiction, where it may saturate and exceed the subsumptive capabilities of dialectical relations."[88] Relevant for an analysis of Brown's work, Negri and Casarino show how this nexus of contradiction impacts the related topics of representation and subjectivity formation. As Casarino notes, on a formal level, the money-form is "the representation of exchange value and thus of itself"; consequently, "it no longer means anything at all. To say such a thing identifies money as an excess of signification."[89] This "realm beyond representation" is the very site of contradiction that Negri sees Marx using to develop an "antagonistic theory of capital, . . . in order to tip it toward *class composition as subjectivity of the struggle.*"[90]

Turning back to Brown's reworked autobiography, we can see how these larger collective concerns with the links among capitalist economic crises, modes of representation, and subjectivity find nuanced and differentiated modulations. In the aforementioned segment of the reworked autobiography, Brown goes out of his way to foreground how "going into business for himself" predicated something of a dynamic ruse dictated by the specific social-economic relations qua antagonisms he was forced to negotiate. Brown recounts how his turn to self-employment was catalyzed by being "cheated out of the previous summer's earnings by the captain of the steamer" which employed him (24). Wandering through Monroe, Michigan, Brown spies a crowded barbershop and, having shaved passengers on steamship cruises, he appeals for employment only to be told that the barber "did not need a hand" (25). Punning on the common economic terminology used for enslaved laborers ("hands"), Brown immediately addresses the employment scenario in terms of antagonism and underlying power dynamics, writing, "[A]fter making several offers to work cheap, I frankly told him, that if he would not employ me, I would get a room near him, and set up an opposition establishment" (25).[91] The topic of becoming a banker is thus framed by a direct marketplace antagonism with a local business owner, one that, with the vague references to stolen wages and slave terminology, implicates wider systemic economic violence. In fact, the lead-up to gaining local customers and establishing a bank pivots on Brown investing aggressively in efforts to gain leverage over this business competitor. This includes raising the aforementioned sign, "Fashionable Hair-dresser from New York, Emperor of the West," which is rife with obvious false claims, and spreading disinformation about the other owner, such as telling locals that his neighbor "did not keep clean towels, that his razors were dull, and, above all, he never had been to New York to see the fashions. Neither had I" (25). And this antagonism continues through the banking scene, where, after Brown circulates his own money, the competing owner organizes a "run" on Brown's "bank," nearly forcing him out of "business" (27).

The topic of circulation, however, threads among the themes of economic antagonism, subjectivity formation, and representation. After having a printer work up his shinplasters in a manner that would prevent counterfeiting, Brown is handed the signed bills, twenty dollars worth to begin with, "ready for circulation" (26). The transition into becoming a banker is particularly charged for Brown. He writes, "The first night I had my money, my head was so turned and dizzy, that I could not sleep. In fact, I slept but little for weeks after the issuing of my bills. This fact satisfied me, that people of wealth pass many sleepless hours" (26). The vertigo appears to attend Brown's entrance into a new pseudo class, as his seemingly playful aside about people of wealth might suggest, but also, given the contexts, into a new social-subjective position. Brown explains that once he was able to get all of his bills into circulation, "nearly all of the money received in return for [his] notes was spent in fitting up and decorating [his] shop" (26). Because his shinplasters are predicated upon systems of spurious credit and, as a result of Brown's actions, actual bad debt, Brown is clearly not "of wealth" (quantitative possession of capital); through the speculative circulation of his bills, however, he does achieve a new social and material standing. Put differently, Brown achieves new purchase on social agency and marketplace manipulation through becoming-with his minted bills.

The run on Brown's shinplasters, in which the competing barber encouraged holders of Brown's notes to demand simultaneously a return of their money, thus short circuits the precarious new reality he was in the process of creating. Until, that is, a friend educates him further about regional banking practices. The friend explains, "[W]hen your notes are brought to you, you must redeem them, and then send them out and get other money for them; and, with the latter, you can keep cashing your own Shinplasters" (27). Brown's precarious agency thus redoubles, and, by "immediately . . . putting in circulation the notes which [he] had just redeemed," all of his shinplasters were soon "again in circulation" (27–28).

Yet what kind of circulation is this? In *Grundrisse*, Marx argues that "[t]o have *circulation*, what is essential is that exchange appear as a process, a fluid whole of purchases and sales." He continues, "Circulation as the realization of exchange values implies: 1) that my product is a product only in so far as it is for others; hence suspended singularity, generality; 2) that it is a product for me only in so far as it has been alienated, become for others. . . ." As such, the "whole of this movement appears as a social process, and as much as the individual moments of this movement arise from the conscious will and particular purposes of individuals, so much does the totality of the process appear as an objective interrelation, which arises spontaneously from nature."[92] Using this period definition, Brown's bills clearly fall short of standard circulation. His shinplasters, as a commodity/money form, keep a clear connection with a particular locus and source—not just as an origin or branding mechanism, but as an essential component of their value. If these bills circulate, they do so through the manifest and continued efforts of an individual agent. In this sense, the totality of circulation itself is rendered precarious due to the subjective leveraging of bad debts and through intentional acts. Consequently, Brown's bills remain linked manifestly and continuously to specific local antagonisms and, in the process, invoke implicitly broader systemic violence.

I want to suggest that this economic context reconfigures the ontological and formal aspects of Brown's reworked autobiography and, indeed, the attached subsequent novel. According to Dienst, the nonsynchronous aspects of indebtedness (or bad debt) includes "the deferral or withdrawal of value; a way to play for a time in order to keep something alive."[93] Is this not precisely the situation depicted in Brown's shinplaster anecdote? By playing the system, Brown attempts a fraught means to "keep something alive." And this "something" is the para-ontological locus of unadjusted emancipation. As opposed to merely entering the market as a proper ex-slave individual subject (shifting from being an enslaved "unit of investment" to something like a supposedly free unit of investor), Brown erects and practices an uncertain process of liminal becoming.[94] Drawing once more from *Grundrisse*, Marx notes the way capital willfully denies that surplus value (here as profit) stems from the systems of antagonism and alienation noted above and, instead, imagines that it originates from itself. This yields an expansive process of growth that Marx describes spatially, where new profit, misrecognized as "self-realizing value," adds dimensions to existing capital, and the entire process then begins anew: "By describing its circle [capital] expands itself as the subject of the circle and thus describes a self-expanding circle, a spiral."[95] In Brown's fugitive performance of perpetual shinplaster redeployment, he produces profit and a new locus of self (evidenced materially with his shop's interior) via a surplus value that, because of the specific historical conditions in play, is not yet misrecognized by capital (or others) as capital's own. With this unique formation of bad debt, Brown becomes something of a broken or absconding piece of the spiral that, within the orbit of the broader system, begins spinning out its own coordinates.

If the recirculation of Brown's notes puts his "bank" on a "sound basis," it also puts him in a new structural position vis-à-vis sociality and agency (28). Directly after the previously mentioned paragraph referencing the perilous restoration of his bank, Brown's narrative leaps conspicuously and elliptically toward a diachronic account of his entrance into political institutions related to reform (first temperance and then abolitionism). In keeping with the bricolage approach found in the novel, this short closing account of Brown's more recent experiences is broken up and supplemented by excerpts from letters, two of which circle back indirectly to the economic-based precarity framing his experiences. The first is a January 10, 1848, letter from his last owner, Enoch Price, to one of Brown's friends in which Price describes receiving a copy of Brown's autobiography and offers to sell Brown's freedom for 350 dollars (29). The last page of Brown's reworked autobiography reproduces a subsequent letter from Price dated February 16, 1852, where, due to the passage of the Fugitive Slave Act, Price suggests he "can now take [Brown] anywhere in the United States" and raises his demand for redemption to 500 dollars (39). The closing letter's gesture to the Fugitive Slave Law sets retroactively the beginning of the narrative adrift, producing a temporal hiccup that casts the entire text into its own state of precarious movement. With these letters, Brown evidences the permanent structural fugitivity attending ex-slave status in the period and reveals the contexts of antagonism through which his own spiraling economic, formal, and, indeed, "personal" (if we can call it this) constructions emerge and re-emerge, including the note that he himself sent a copy of his original narrative to his former master.[96]

Pseudo-circulations and recirculations thus constitute the formal and structural center of Brown's reworked autobiography, and these concepts might reformulate how we think about the more typical elements of the earlier portion of the narrative. The interesting pronoun shifts and slips, where Brown uses predominantly third person to reference himself, clearly stem, in part, from the fact of re-telling portions of his previously published autobiography. Considered from the perspective of the shinplaster scenes, however, these formal moves begin to have alternate resonances and effects. In the final chapter of *In the Wake*, Sharpe turns to the topic of black orthographies, positing "Black annotation and Black redaction" as two "modes of making-sensible" in light of the fact that "so much of Black intramural life and social and political work is redacted, made invisible to the present and future, subtended by plantation logics, detached optics, and brutal architectures."[97] Offering a series of examples (from a redaction of Agassiz's photos of nineteenth-century slaves, to an account of twelve-year-old Mikia Hutchings's school wall writing, to a consideration of Michael Brown's autopsies), Sharpe uses her own version of annotation and redaction in order to move "toward reading and seeing otherwise."[98]

Following Sharpe, I want to consider how Brown's shinplaster episode and its economic-formal ramifications might *annotate* earlier passages in both versions of the autobiography pertaining to standard concerns with naming, writing, and identity. Shortly before the shinplaster scene in the reworked narrative, Brown includes an account of how he arrived at his current name. Rescued from the cold near Cincinnati during his second attempt at escaping north, Brown describes how a Quaker named Wells Brown took him into his home, offering him kindness and, ultimately, his name. Brown recounts the effects of being "regarded as a man by a white family," writing, "[A]ll this made me feel that I was not myself" (20). The transformation in question, of course, includes Brown's renaming, prompted by Wells Brown, who, when given the honor by Brown, names the ex-slave after himself. But Brown demurs slightly, adding, "I am not willing to lose my name of William. It was taken from me once against my will, and I am not willing to part with it on any terms" (21).

With this pivotal scene, Brown's reworked narrative plays with standard liberal becoming. A newly escaped ex-slave becomes a "MAN" via recognition from a white symbolic figure but only after a romantic assertion of personal courage (here coded aptly via the modality of ownership) (20). The original autobiography aggrandizes this naming scene and Wells Brown's position, framing the entire book using the logic of debt. "Base indeed should I be," Brown writes in the opening dedication, which he offers to the white Quaker, "if I ever forget what I owe to you, or do anything to disgrace that honored name!"[99] Subsequently, in the original naming scene, Brown goes as far as calling William Wells an "adopted father."[100]

But if we take the shinplaster portion of the reworked narrative as an annotation of these previous, indeed perhaps *all* previous, naming scenes, different meanings and implications come into view. The most manifest link establishing this annotation may be the juxtaposition of Brown's fence writing and the erection of the aforementioned barbershop sign advertising his services under the fictitious title "Emperor of the West." On the same page where he begins the barbershop/banking narrative, Brown recounts how, after fooling local children and citizens into helping him learn to write his name, he "marked up [a] fence for nearly a quarter of a mile, trying to copy, till [he] got so that [he] could write [his] name" (24). On the face of it, this writing might be read as a formative moment of symbolic becoming, or even as a creative act of graffiti, as Ivy Wilson describes it.[101] But if we think of this writing in light of his barbershop sign and related practices of bad debt, this writing becomes less like graffiti (a mode of public expression/spatial marking) and more like a practiced performance—where Brown advances from the earlier scene in his original autobiography when he repeatedly sounds his name (William) out loud while traveling in order to "[get] used to it" (of/for himself) toward a more radical form of public performance (of/for others).¹⁰² Indeed, because this fence writing is performed in chalk, the writing might be thought of in terms of Sharpe's notion of redaction. But the subsequent barbershop sign and shinplaster scene remaster this fence dusting even further, rendering it a kind of "unknowing," to borrow Moten's term, as much as a positive symbolic assertion of any kind.¹⁰³ The barbershop sign and Brown's related "business" as a "bank" are erected and supported by the previously discussed mode of para-circulation that launches him into a precarious economic condition, yielding not only a conspicuous form of profit but also a new social focalization evidenced by the fact that the friend who teaches him about shinplaster circulation calls him "Emperor" (26). Taken together, the barbershop sign and Brown's fence writing shift from concerns of having and being toward something like antagonistic functionality. Because Brown's writing in both scenes uses and appropriates but does not, perhaps cannot, fully take on as its own, this is a writing on and at once against the borders of individuated spaces and selves. As Alexander Weheliye notes, the nineteenth century's "juridical acknowledgement of racialized subjects as fully human often enacts a steep entry price, because inclusion hinges upon accepting the codification of personhood as property, which is, in turn, based upon the comparative distinction between groups." And these differences, seen in stark relief with the Dred Scott case, reveal "the tabula rasa of whiteness—which all groups but blacks can access— . . . as the prerequisite for the law's magical transubstantiation of a thing to be possessed into a property-owning subject."¹⁰⁴ Given this broader context, it is as if Brown forces certain modes of inclusion (pseudo circulation/exchange/entrance/agency) without full or true recognition by white subjects or infrastructures.¹⁰⁵ Using Weheliye's schematic, Brown is not fully located in or identified by his own texts or the symbolic systems that surround him. Instead, he can be seen working and spiraling within the coordinates forced upon him. This renders Brown's reworked narrative, the novel that follows, and, retroactively, his original autobiography, a ~~personal~~ narrative or even a ~~personal narrative~~, as Calvin L. Warren might put it.¹⁰⁶

Brown's spirals have ripple effects, encompassing Clotel's flight, too, and perhaps even bumping into Martin Delany's *Blake; or, The Huts of America*. The afterlives of Clotel's leap are overwrought—signaling something unfitting or conceptually discomfiting in Brown's portrayal of the scene. Scholars such as Russ Castronovo have noted the way the tragic titular character's leap into the Potomac depicts an insidious form of "necrocitizenship" common in period narratives about emancipatory possibilities.

Castronovo reads this scene, illustrated in the drawing of Clotel just after leaping from the bridge's edge and framed by an uncited appropriation of Grace Greenwald's poem "The Leap from the Long Bridge. An Incident at Washington" (1851), as portraying Clotel in the act of "leav[ing] her body" and, thus "prevail[ing] over commodification because her physical existence drops away as an encumbrance, liberating her spirit." In this sense, "Clotel flees her history" and, according to Castronovo, the broader suicide scene "secures a necrophilic fantasy of innate natural liberty by discounting history" where "[d]eath liberates the subject."[107] But what if, alongside Castronovo's important historical and ideological reading, we think of this scene in terms of Brown's spiraling formal-economic practices in the reworked autobiography?

More recently, Wilson has offered an alternate take on Clotel's suicide. Focusing on the difference between the novel's description of Clotel looking to heaven and the illustration, which depicts Clotel "maladroitly configured with her face turned to a profile position and . . . her eyes directly engaging one of her pursuers," Wilson suggests that the visual representation of Clotel's gaze "demands that her pursuers recognize her as their equivalent" and, consequently, registers an example of "black political agency."[108] Brown's own forced version of something like inclusion without recognition in the prefatory section clearly differs from the liberal coordinates that seem to undergird Wilson's description of Clotel's agency. Nonetheless, using the context of Brown's spiraling positionings, we might follow the thrust of Wilson's speculative rereading of Clotel's gaze as a fleeting assertion and think of Clotel's flight as not merely between life (slavery) and death (abstract/ahistorical heaven), but as a dramatization of a type of "irruptive placement" that Moten calls "not in between."[109] Her leap is, in these terms, not merely a desperate negation, but a spatial-material embodiment of the type of precarious spiraling out that Brown's economic and formal work in the autobiographies illuminates. Clotel's not-in-betweenness thus performs what Bryan Wagner describes as "existence without standing," a concept Moten uses to capture the inherent social reality of black existence (in apposition to Jared Sexton's claims regarding black life as social death) as prior and nonidentical to received historical and ontological models.[110] Even more directly relevant for Brown and Clotel, Moten and Harney cast this concept in the charged horizon of actual-antagonisms, twisting the notion of falling, through the example of Michael Brown, into a "refusal to stand." This refusal, for Harney and Moten, marks not only a singular act of defiance, but the foundational emergence of a type of "radical homelessness—its kinetic indigeneity, its irreducible queerness—[that] is the essence of blackness." Here, the "refusal to take place is given in what it is to occur."[111]

With these formal and physical flights, if we call them this, William Wells Brown is certainly not playing around. His serious play arises from within the movements of an impossible but actual experience of having been launched *amid* and having to work *there* to produce and sustain life as innovative fugitivity.

Blake's *Secret Slide*

By way of a coda to my discussions of *Dred* and *Clotel*, I want to offer a rumination on Martin Delany's *Blake; or, The Huts of America*, which was published serially between 1859 and 1862 in the *Anglo-African Magazine* and the *Weekly Anglo-African*. In 1970, the manuscript was presented in unified form by Beacon Press and, more recently, as a "corrected edition" by Harvard University Press. As Robert Levine explains, the history of Delany's composition and the subsequent serial publication of the novel (which may come to us incomplete, as the final six chapters purportedly appearing in the May 1862 issue of the magazine remain either lost or nonexistent) have significant stakes for how critics have approached the text.[112] Indeed, given the various post- and transnational turns in American Studies and black studies scholarship, the novel's sprawling hemispheric and transatlantic scope as well as Delany's relation to ongoing, embattled, and often antagonistic period pan-Africanist emigration efforts have rendered it newly relevant for historical critical debates.[113]

In *Blake*, the economic-ontological orbits of Brown's spirals and the ecological modes of *Dred*'s goblin growth greet one another—or, at the very least, pass furtive signs. These signs are not simply pro forma gestures ("for form's sake, by way of formality").[114] They are instead discontinuous but familiar *form*ations of fugitive worlds moving close by that are fused and set in motion by a shared ground (be it the wood of the auction block or the watery depths of M. NourbeSe Philip's documentary poem *Zong!*). It is *Blake*'s spatial and temporal terrains that first, perhaps, draw one's attention because they effect a geographic-formal distortion or even metamorphosis of the movements that Brown portrays. As Grégory Pierrot suggests, Delany's novel intervenes directly in the era's geographic and ideological landscapes. According to Pierrot, "Delany set out to break the paralyzing status of the Haitian Revolution as the absolute referent of black revolt and autonomy." Attempting to reset the established black avenger trope, a trope that had been co-opted by the West and was limiting actual large-scale efforts of black radicalism, Delany "looked for balance in referencing the unavoidable black avenger literary tradition, the related canonical representations of Haiti, channeling transnational notions of blackness intimately linked to Haitian history and offering a new, U.S.-specific model." Pierrot continues, "By writing over Haiti in *Blake*, Delany defined his novel as a cultural intervention, a renewed literary model for a new black American nation."[115] Leaving aside the question of whether Delany's aims were ultimately national or internationalist, Pierrot's assessment aptly locates the text's concerns within the nexus of world-historical crises and formal-ideological constructions.

Haiti also figures largely in Moten's concept of "not in between," which I used to consider Clotel's status vis-à-vis Brown's reworked autobiography. Discussing C. L. R. James's formal innovations in *The Black Jacobins* (1938), Moten reveals how in James's classic text on the Haitian Revolution "the Caribbean, the not in between, emerges." In Moten's reading, James's formal approach presents the emergence of actual historical-conceptual configurations that exceed traditional Western positive categories (such as revolution and the individual) as well as standard logics for absence and presence (such as aporia and rupture). Consequently, for Moten, James's writing practice effects a "complex recasting of the dialectic."[116] Moten highlights a central passage in *The Black Jacobins* where Dessalines, in his own fateful leap, jumps into a ditch outside a redoubt his forces had erected at Crête-à-Pierrot, and, with his men following behind and the French bearing down, he talks to his fellow ex-slave militants about their shared predicament.[117] According to Moten, with this encounter (the arrangement of being-with, the use of local dialect, and the historical scope of Dessalines's message), James asserts the "opposition between Toussaint and Dessalines, between (the desire for what is called) enlightenment and (the adherence to what is called) darkness, between direction to the French and direction to the slaves." Dessalines's jump into the ditch is also, in this way, a "jumping forward."[118]

Lisa Lowe offers a similar reading of James's Haiti. In her terms, "James appropriated dialectical history as a formal logic or heuristic, but the worldly material he narrated radically refuted the closures of both Hegel's liberal inclusivity and Marxian revolutionary historical method."[119] James's book, therefore, depicts how the "slaves' conditions and struggles break apart the restrictions of the received categories."[120] Of course, on a broader level, as Jeremy Matthew Glick notes, "Haiti is the generative site *par excellence* for creative work by African diasporic artist-intellectuals attempting to break free from impasses in their respective political conjunctures."[121]

What Moten's and Lowe's work shows is that this is also true, in our time, for U.S. intellectuals and artists. But, much more than this, Moten's and Lowe's readings of James raise, in startlingly keen and beautiful ways, the significant stakes of form within the negotiation, representation, and, with hope, production of historical-political reality. That is to say, Moten and Lowe reveal the sheer import of the nuanced formal textures (narrative and otherwise) involved in the conceptual coordinates of historical becoming. Returning to Pierrot's consideration of *Blake* as a means of "writing over" Haiti, I want to pivot on these formal-conceptual considerations.

Part II of *Blake* was serialized after Thomas Hamilton's *Anglo-African* came under the sway of James Redpath's Haytian Emigration Bureau. In the context of these conflicted hemispheric visions (Hamilton's magazine was anti-emigrationist, and Delany was certainly suspicious of white influence by the likes of Redpath), Delany's Cuban annexation plot represents an attempt to, as Caleb Smith explains, "develop a scheme of emigration under black leadership" distinct from those set forth by the Colonization Society or the annexationist schemes of President Pierce's ilk. Smith goes on to suggest, "But Delany's book is transnational in orientation, even in the early chapters, and its militancy is consistent from beginning to end. Page by page, it is concerned much less with emigration than with rebellion."[122]

Although concerns with specific emigration plots (or "black filibustering" as Levine dubs it) undoubtedly permeate Delany's thoughts about rebellion, I share Smith's interest in approaching *Blake* as a sustained effort to reconceive of rebellion.[123] Consequently, I want to consider Delany's novel in terms of its unique approach toward resistance, offering, as my subtitle suggests, the concept of "slide" as a way to rethink formal tactical arrangements in the novel that depict aspects of what I have been calling unadjusted emancipations. Focusing on the modalities of Henry Blake's secret in Part I of the novel, I want to show how this undisclosed stratagem for a "general insurrection of the slaves" operates via dual motions of collecting and taking in as well as spreading and scattering.[124]

As Smith notes, a key aspect of Blake's secret is the way the novel centralizes "the process of transmission." In Smith's reading, Blake thus becomes an "infrastructure of communication" that lays tracks, in a sense, establishing or "placing" semi-permanent "networks of transmission and synchronization."[125] Unlike Smith, however, I do not see Blake's secret or his modes of organizing as trafficking in standard modalities—even, and especially, through a "unifying message."[126] The secret slide I have in mind, rather, sidesteps both the positive coordinates of "message" as well as the mystical category of prophecy, invoking *avant la lettre*, something closer to the point made by Ralph Ellison's narrator in *The Invisible Man* when he claims, "This is not prophecy, but description."[127] That is, *Blake*'s secret offers an elusive structure and obscure placeholder in the novel, causing the formal operations of description and dissemination to slide within a glissando-like zone that renders the geographic, temporal, and social networks present less knowable and less operative in standard senses, but also perhaps more potent. Thinking and moving along with the novel's atypical arrangements, we might discern a new formal logic that reveals *Blake*'s approach toward conceiving a "prophetic organization," to borrow Moten and Harney's concept, one that casts disruptive waves within the liberal-national closures that cloud the second part of the novel.[128]

As Martha Schoolman notes, "*Blake*'s spatial vision . . . unfolds markedly at the level of what Michel de Certeau has famously called the 'strategic.'"[129] In recent years, scholars have traced out various historical ways of viewing the novel's unique strategic formations.[130] It is, however, Pierrot's observation of the "dreadfully pragmatic" strategy displayed early in the second part of the novel that might be most relevant for reconsidering Blake's formal-strategic concerns. In this scene, Blake works aboard the slave vessel the *Vulture* off the coast of western Africa and surreptitiously (off page) coordinates with the black sailors as well as leaders of local African groups to ensure members of the new slave cargo will act in accordance with his aims. As Pierrot explains, "The cost of this strategy is horrendous: the black crew members obey the order to throw six hundred people overboard only to ultimately let the twelve hundred remaining make it to Cuba to become soldiers for the black revolution."[131]

This secret alliance and its subsequent shipboard tactics directly catalyze the Grand Council's organized infrastructure of rebellion at the novel's close, but Blake's strategies on the *Vulture* may have their origins much earlier in the novel. In Chapter IX of Part I, Henry Blake (who is later revealed to be Carolus Henrico Blacus, the "lost" Cuban child of a "wealthy black . . . manufacturer") launches himself into fugitive status when his Natchez master sells his wife, Maggie (195). In this chapter, titled "The Shadow," Delany first lays out aspects of Blake's furtive plan. After initiating a clandestine night meeting with Andy and Charles, two local slaves, Blake tells the men, "Stop boys, till I explain. The plans are mine and you must allow me to know more about them than you. Just here, for once, the slave-holding preacher's advice to the black man is appropriate—'Stand still and see the salvation'" (39). Scholars such as Levine have noted the "elitist" nature of Blake's plan, where "intelligent slaves" might affect a revolution that carries out Delany's Masonic pan-African goal of "redeeming" his race.[132] Without disputing these claims, we might shift focus instead to the actual formal relations presented in this and other scenes. Levine offers the useful note that the Exodus 14:13 passage referenced by Blake pertains to the "emancipatory moment . . . when Moses at the Red Sea convinces the fleeing Israelites not to return to slavery."[133] In the novel, however, the injunction to "stand still and see" does not just evoke a messianic temporal register, it also implicates the material and collective foundation of the secret plan.

One should take seriously Blake's rhetorical plea for his fellow slaves to "allow" him to "know more" at present. This becomes elitist only if one privileges the assumptions of a proprietary individuation that is the luxury of the white *homo economicus*. Here, rather, the strategic withholding of information is more a tactical caretaking, a holding-for, whereby, as Blake states at the outset, the three men are themselves materially linked in both condition and consequence ("you can only be true to me by being true to yourselves" [39]). In other words, it is as if Blake is asking his fellow slaves not to step on the strategy, not to move too quickly, not to try to own or know a plan that is composed of and by more than them. This can be seen, too, in the fact that there is a preponderance of socially distributed furtive efforts that allow this night meeting to occur in the first place (such as the slave Ailcey passing along stones as a means of communication and Daddy Joe and Mammy Judy distracting the Franks). If Moses is a textual referent here, then it seems as if Delany's novel is attempting to recast this subplot more in line with David Walker's earlier agenda. As Chris Apap notes, "Instead of a community of slaves, passively waiting for deliverance, Walker suggests that African Americans become a community of rebels."[134]

During this first night meeting, Blake soon shares his plan with Andy and Charles: "I now impart to you the secret—it is this: I have laid a scheme, and matured a plan for a general insurrection of the slaves in every state, and the successful overthrow of slavery!" (40). Here and now, it is perhaps difficult to read this declaration and not think of W. E. B. Du Bois's 1935 description of the efforts of slaves and ex-slaves before and during the Civil War as a "general strike of slaves."[135] As David Roediger explains, "The massive defection from slavery that Du Bois gave such an apt name took myriad forms, involving the flight of perhaps half a million slaves and daily mutiny by a far greater number who stayed but resisted plantation labor."[136] While the language of Blake's plan, coupled with his injunction for waiting in some form, suggests a synchronic revolt, the diffuse and diverse constituent elements of Du Bois's singular general strike might usefully reset assumptions about the scope and temporality of Blake's agenda. This is especially true given that the means of this general insurrection remain the secret aspect of Blake's plan. When Andy asks, "[H]ow's dis to be carried out?" Blake expresses concern over sharing immediately the strategic details and, ultimately, the reader is left in the dark. But Blake does note that the plan "is so simple that the most stupid among the slaves will understand it. . . ." He then launches into a series of ecological scenarios: "So simple is it that the trees of the forest or an orchard illustrate it; flocks of birds or domestic cattle, fields of corn hemp or sugar cane . . . all keep it constantly before their eyes and in their memory" (40–41).

Blake's decision to place the actual strategies of the plan in abeyance may be simply practical—much like Douglass's decision not to publish in his original autobiography the means he used to escape to the north fearing the information might stymie its effectiveness for current and future slaves. But barring direct knowledge of a plan that is so natural, if you will, that it hides in plain sight draws attention to the surrounding aspects of its operations. This may be why Blake says that he approaches the plan with "religious fear" (40). Unlike Dred, Blake figures religion as a purely tactical and ideological concept, telling Andy and Charles, "You must make your religion subserve your interests, as your oppressors do theirs!" (43). Blake's religious fear, in this context, becomes less trepidation concerning the metaphysical and more anxious reverence regarding the import of the material scenario. Unlike Dred's hermeneutical relation to ecological phenomena, which linked ecology at once to biblical passages and an active Big Other, here the ecological scenarios harken directly to the plan itself *as* existing reality. As Blake tells his collaborators, "such is the character of this organization, that punishment and misery are made instruments for its propagation. . . ." Blake goes on: "Every blow you receive from the oppressor impresses the organization upon your mind" (41). Here the negative realities of oppression, in all of their perverse intimacies and immense systemic networks, shape the possible formations (both conceptual and tactical means) that any resistance might take. Just as Blake moves toward disclosing the secret strategy by offering a "prayer," telling the men the idea while they are still on their knees and thus occupying and distorting a standard form of devotion, the greater plan appears to be "simple" because it derives from the tortured ground slaves are forced to live upon.[137]

Although the reader does not learn the details of the plan, Blake does tell Andy and Charles that they must "go on and organize continually." Blake explains, "It makes no difference when, nor where you are, so that the slaves are true and trustworthy, as the scheme is adapted to all times and places." When the men ask for additional direction, Blake clarifies, "All you have to do, is find one good man or woman . . . on a single plantation, and hold a seclusion and impart the secret to them, and make them the organizers for their own plantation, and they in like manner impart it to some other next to them, and so on. In this way it will spread like smallpox" (42). Whereas Dred's specific historical agency may be diminished when transmogrified abstractly into the spread of cholera, Blake harnesses directly the modality of viral dispersion as a way to describe how the plan for revolt will be implemented. Later in the novel, Blake uses the term "scatter" in the negative context of spreading "red ruin" (129). But the term is apt for understanding the foundation of Blake's plan as well. Recently, the concept of "scatter" has been taken up by Western philosophers such as Geoffrey Bennington, who posit scattering as a way for politics to think against the limits imposed by teleology. This materialist (anti-metaphysical) approach to redefining and, in fact, defending politics as a category is quite welcome. Yet one cannot read today such remobilizations of Derrida and others without feeling an implicit appeal, however unintentional, to the aforementioned dominant liberal Deleuzian paradigms of multiplicity without dialectical synthesis (that is, more options for all without a "violent" reordering the systemic ground we live on).

In *Blake*, scattering the plan does indeed work toward such radical change, but it does so in a manner that is conceptually tight at the same time that it is formally and spatially loose. This leads to chronotopic distortions, as seen in the aforementioned passage when Blake tries to describe the temporal logic of his scheme. When Charles asks Blake when they will "hear" from him, Blake responds, "Not until you shall see me again; when that will be, I don't know. You may see me in six months, and might not in eighteen. I am determined, now that I am driven to it, to complete an organization in every slave state before I return, and have fixed two years as my utmost limit" (43). From hearing to seeing, from six months to an oddly imposed limit of two years, the scattering of the plan, composed by so many moving parts, takes on an aspect of atemporality. This distortion includes an aspect of condensation in the way Blake's geographic movement, seen in the novel's map of his "generalized route," is fused ambiguously with his desire to rescue his wife from her current enslavement, so that the family revenge plot, via necessity, melds with broader systemic socio-economic concerns (46). As Blake recognizes from the start, the only way for this Orpheus to free Eurydice is to level completely the kingdom of the underworld. As we will see when we turn to the novel's close, however, there's still the question of what would happen to the "peaceful" surface above.

Orpheus and his lyre are clearly lacking stand-ins for Blake's reality, but I do want to return to the musical metaphor of the glissando's slide that I introduced earlier to describe the formal-material relationships engendered by Blake's secret plan. Returning to this metaphor via the preceding scene where Blake introduces his plan, we get a sense of how he conceives structurally of this vast effort. Blake's secret is not, formally speaking, a rest—what Susan Howe, in a very different context, describes as a wish that has yet to betray itself—because the secret's positive effects condition the formal trajectories of the plot and the content of the narrative.[138] These same formal trajectories and effects are what constitute a glissando movement. As opposed to a standard glissando, however, which is composed of diachronic progress up or down a scale, the novel's secret plan generates formal effects and strategies that operate as a supplemented glissando, one whose movement takes the form of a chiasmus-like "V" trajectory. In other words, as an absent cause, the secret plan forms a redoubled glissando that links and sets in motion via indeterminate circuits (hence sliding) the processes of both dissemination and description: scattering *and* collecting-reporting.

Although I have already discussed the mode and significance of how Blake intends to scatter the secret plan, it is worth noting how the novel repeatedly uses the term "sow" to capture this operation. Time and again, Blake is said to be "sowing seeds from which in due season, he anticipated an abundant harvest" (74). This harvest includes necessary violence, where Blake, as a "messenger," is "sowing the seeds of future devastation" as well as having to kill in the present in order to continue his movement across the south (84). But this devastation is shown to be part of a new iteration of longstanding utopic and liberatory efforts. As Blake enters the Dismal Swamp, Gamby Gholar, a former companion of Nat Turner and a high conjurer, recognizes him as someone he had anticipated arriving. Even in this fertile ecology of fugitivity with its own rich history, Blake is said to have "continued . . . scattering to the winds and sowing the seeds of a future crop, only to take root in the thick black waters which cover it" (113).

On a manifest level, Blake scatters these seeds of revolt in order to reap them subsequently with the material effects of large-scale revolution. The novel, however, performs its own type of intermediate reaping in the way its first part is composed largely by collecting anecdotes and descriptions from various sites along the circuit that Blake travels. As Britt Rusert aptly notes, "Henry's meticulous empirical observations aid him in concealing his identity, allowing him to pose as a local slave from a neighboring plantation 'when accosted by a white,' but they are also part of Henry's larger project of collecting data on the status and conditions of enslavement."[139] This "data" includes a varied record of atrocities and oppressions, from the Crane plantation on the Red River where female slaves worked nearly in the nude to the violence used to quell a slave rebellion plot in New Orleans. In the second part of the novel, this charged mode of reporting becomes a means for folding together—another sliding, if you will—the personal motivations that fire Blake and the larger systemic contexts that define the conditions of oppression and resistance to them. Newly in Cuba, Blake is "determin[ed] to witness all that he could pertaining to Cuban slavery. He had come in search of his poor lost wife, and was anxiously desirous of having some idea of her true condition" (171). In the same scene, Blake is forced to witness quietly plantation owner Madame Garcia whipping a slave child while the boy's mother pleads for mercy. Having to check his immediate desire to halt the violence, Blake becomes, in Delany's words, a "serious spectator" (172). I would like to suggest that the position of a serious spectator might stand in for the place where the two modes of dissemination and description meet—occupying, in a sense, the range of movements constituted by the novel's formal trajectories. In coming back around to Pierrot's discussion of Blake's "dreadfully pragmatic" strategy aboard the *Vulture*, we might now see that the modes of reporting and actively sowing the groundwork for revolt are, in fact, structurally joined and have an ongoing relation in the novel.

The slide between dissemination and description thus effects a loose dialectic, one that is nearby and in motion but that remains undefined from the reader's limited vantage. The modality of Blake's secret plan as it is presented, therefore, formally offsets the very ground of what might become politics and praxis: operating in a looming haze of Dred-like thereish but churning out effects as it approaches. It acts, that is, like a distant unlit train nearing from somewhere in the dark and jarring the ground beneath for miles. The para-ecological loop dialectics we saw with Thoreau are here contracted into the pulsing horizon of the present. In a way, it is as if Brown's fugitive and expansive spirals are militarized and sent recruiting— to tactically reinforce but also, as in the Latin root of the term recruit, *crescere*, "to grow."

Part II of *Blake* moves into more complex ideological and historical terrain, with Blake organizing in Cuba, helping to form a Grand Council composed of elite revolutionaries from the island, and, as mentioned, traveling to Africa in order to surreptitiously assemble an army. The nascent

Grand Council's use of bureaucratic positions and acceptance of moneyed-class influence (meeting in Madame Cordora's mansion, elite members voting on major decisions that impact masses of slaves and distant free people of color) hint at an "adjusted" emancipation in the making. Given the aforementioned contexts of Haiti (mentioned twice in the novel) and active U.S. Cuban annexation plots, however, one might ask if a second black revolution in the Caribbean, no matter how liberal, would be, by default, unadjusted in conspicuous ways. Nonetheless, the prevalent tensions in the last available chapters (the council voting for war, the Spanish authorities cracking down on U.S. nationals due to fear of filibustering efforts, and, in the final line, Gofer Gondolier, a member of the council, running into the streets to spread "[w]oe . . . unto those devils of whites") complicate any definitive narrative or political trajectories in the novel (313).

There is, however, at least one consistency that remains: the structural logic we glean about Blake's original secret plan. (After all, Blake tells his cousin Placido, "I have come to Cuba to help to free my race; and that which I desire here to do, I've done in another place" [197].) In the early scene where Blake shares the details of his plan with Andy and Charles, he closes by encouraging them to teach slaves to "take all the money they can get from their masters, to enable them to make the strike without a failure." As he explains, having money is "an important part of the scheme of organization." Blake then goes on: "Bear this in mind; it [money] is your certain passport through the white gap" (44). Much like religion, Blake figures money as a tactical means—in this case a means to literally move into and out of geographic and symbolic spaces. More than this, however, and perhaps via a distant nod to Brown's shinplaster episode, money becomes a means to break into modes of circulation: providing a way to effect agency, to manipulate, and, therefore, to transform.

Earlier, when Blake tells Mammy Judy he is running away, he recounts, "I'm incapable of stealing from any one, but I have from time to time, taken by littles, some of the earnings due me for more than eighteen years' service to this man Franks." Using an estimate of 200 dollars a year, Blake suggests that he was actually due 1,600 dollars more than the 200 guineas he had secured. "'Steal' indeed!" Blake reflects. "I would that when I had an opportunity, I had taken fifty thousand instead of two" (32–33). Beginning with a delimited ethical position hemmed by the logic of indebtedness (inability to steal), Blake moves quickly toward an ambiguous position that at least extols the economic fairness of reparations (leveraging the logic of fair wages and debt to argue for back pay, in a sense) and at the extreme presents something approaching the workings of a general strike or general re-appropriation. Instead of an individual spinning out fugitive constellations as with Brown, Blake appears to offer a large-scale vision whereby slaves and ex-slaves might pass to the other side of economic-agential relations—to not merely gain the authority to pass through a given border (passport) into new varieties of present and future "relations of domination," but to somehow flip, pass over, turn inside out the logic and circulations that have given rise to the negative conditions of their present. In the novel, the pro-slavery northern Judge Ballard at one point cites the Compromise of 1850 to dub all free blacks in the north and south "slaves at large" (63). This systemic economic logic, quite familiar by now, may be another way of thinking through Blake's earlier ecological metaphors for the ease and naturalness of the secret revolt plan. The slaves will "strike," in Blake's terms, from the outside, through the "white gap," because the conditions of oppression that define their lives (and, as mentioned, their means of resistance) double as the conditions whereby capital generates dominant modes of profit. The existing "web of life," to borrow Jason Moore's term—the complex network of material, economic, and social relations otherwise known as antebellum America—is, in this sense, up for a rude awakening.

Among the competing codes and formations of emancipation included in the second part of *Blake*, the diffuse logic of Blake's original plan remains in play. Although liberal coordinates of emancipation frame the closing chapters, among and beneath them the secret continues its work.[140] Most notably, this includes Blake's aforementioned *Vulture* endeavor (which, in addition to secret plots, utilized the rumor of slave revolt to manipulate slave-market values) and Gondolier's plan to exploit his position as head of the colonial culinary department in order to introduce "into general use, his patent Cuban Carver, to give to every black the opportunity of having in their possession a formidable deadly weapon, without the violation of law, suspicion, or even objection of the whites" (271). Gondolier's plan may reveal how Blake's claim about *money* offering a "passport through the white gap" is slyly misleading. When the category of money is embodied and dispersed within living slave labor, it is everywhere; it constitutes and shapes reality itself. As discussed in the context of Marx's *Grundrisse* and Brown's shinplasters, however, money also constitutes the locus through which the true antagonisms and contradictions of a given reality might be discerned and come to a head. In Gondolier's plan, Blake's previously mentioned large-scale logic of secret revolt takes concrete form: where the omnipresent (there but overlooked and, hence, unseen) locus of embodied money might suddenly raise knives. As it turns out, the secret will not emerge as a passage to Canada and the opportunity to work in a liberal white man's town (where *Dred* closes). Heidegger's broken tools have sharp edges, it seems.[141]

In the end, Delany's incomplete novel doesn't portray a state of historical reality moving along a singular path toward action or anything approaching resolution. Perhaps this is best. Perhaps, after all, it's supposed to slide.

EPILOGUE

Care, *There and Now*

The original and abandoned preface to this book, written some time in 2015, opened with an epigraph from Joshua Clover and Juliana Spahr's *#Misanthropocene: 24 Theses*: "First of all. Fuck all y'all."[1] At the time, I sought to harness this affront so as to begin *Xenocitizens* with an honest break from what I viewed as conspicuous liberal limits within dominant trends in literary scholarship. (I wrote, "Let's calm down. Let's repair this. Let's reassemble this social. But collegiality's association with 'shared responsibility,' indeed, with its root in *collegium*, even 'partnership,' asserts, not so implicitly, a multitude of limits.") This negative gesture of calling out and clearing away was intended to serve the broader positive move of laying some ground, any ground, for glimpsing what *is* possible by looking again at what *was* possible in the nineteenth century. The development of the book and the changing ideological ground of the intervening years, however, took me away from this original approach.[2] I've learned that what I really want to say, have wanted to say, is that we need to be serious now. That we need to move together in new ways. And that part of this is beginning to care anew.

Even a concept such as care is embattled, and, as such, it can easily turn out to be a problem in its own right. As Judith Butler notes, care today often exists in modes shaped by neoliberal privatization and nongovernmental philanthropic organizations that "understand their task as repairing and ameliorating . . . conditions between bouts of destruction." In the case of Palestine, such care paradoxically "supports the normalization of the occupation" and conveniently "often [opens] up temporary market potential."[3] The neocolonial roots of this brand of care extend to modalities of nineteenth-century liberal sympathy, where, as I mention in my third chapter, teary-eyed U.S. whites registered "feeling badly" for the plight of Native Americans during the removal era.[4] Such liberal emotion was both progressive *and* predicated upon racist discourses, allowing lament and calls for acts of mercy to grease the wheels of lucrative ongoing extraction zones.

The same liberal structures that helped simultaneously birth (build) and decry (bleak half-measured protests) the transatlantic slave trade shaped western "aid" to the victims of the 2010 Haitian earthquake. In her poignant reflections about finding and living with an image of a suffering Haitian girl lying on the ground after the earthquake with the word "ship" taped to her forehead, Christina Sharpe writes:

> I marked the violence of the quake that deposited that little girl there, injured, in this archive, and the violence in the name of care of the placement of that taped word on her forehead, and then I kept looking because that could not be all there was to see or say. *I had to take care.* (A different kind of care and a different optic than the ones employed in the wake of the *Zorgue*, that ship called Care.)[5]

The violence with the name "Care" is here the eighteenth-century slave ship originally named *Zorgue* (sometimes shortened to *Zorg*, the word translates from Dutch as "care"), which was changed to *Zong* after being seized and purchased by the British before its crew's infamous insurance money-driven massacre of over one hundred slaves in 1781. As Sharpe portrays in stark relief, the wake of care's violence is both long and wide— imbricating the physical and financial engines of the Atlantic slave trade as well as distant twenty-first-century "humanitarian" efforts.

I want to harness Sharpe's call for a "different type of care," one she describes as beginning with thinking and rethinking care "laterally." Such a modality of care does not attenuate into pluralities and differences; it gathers and pushes back materially in a "care as force."[6] Others have called for new types of care amid the changing conditions of the present. María Puig de la Bellacasa, for instance, suggests that care in a "more than human world" requires "affective, ethical, and hands-on agencies of practical and material consequence," but also "the right distance."[7] In the context of Sharpe's and Puig de la Bellacasa's timely comments on care, I hope my chapters may begin to show how the "right distance" is perhaps less of a matter of tolerant spacing (offered by the proper friend, proper global citizen, or proper historian) and more of an alternate and charged relation of and to. The latter portion of my epilogue's title, "there and now," is intended to evoke such possible arrangements—and to pull my fourth chapter's conception of "thereish" into the frame of care. In that chapter, I suggested that Dred's fugitive status was thereish (as opposed to Elizabeth Povinelli's notion of "hereish") due to its para-ontological and para-ecological condition of being in a different relation to what one might call the present.[8] Instead of closing the vast domains of the global with the intimacy of the local/present, "thereish" allows for charged discontinuities, including antagonistically oriented para- or alternate locals with their own possible recalibrations of the local-global nexus. In other words, thereish offers the possibility for outsides or, to borrow from Fred Moten and Stefano Harney, "surrounds" with their own stakes regarding the status of "reality."[9] If we are to think of present realities along with their distant pasts, we must do so with care. But with a care that may be quite unfamiliar.

For all of Emerson's idealistic and cultural shortcomings, he may be on to something with his counterintuitive point that in order to "follow" the "sublime Vision of the Right," you need only "[p]lace yourself in the middle of the stream, the stream of power and wisdom which flows into you." He continues, "[P]lace yourself in the full centre of that flood; then you are without effort impelled to truth, to right, and a perfect contentment."[10] Emily Dickinson offers something of her own more practical, and perhaps more poignant, materialist version of this hopeful becoming-as-abandonment, writing in an 1862 letter to Thomas Wentworth Higginson, "The Sailor cannot see the North—but knows the Needle can—."[11] Taking cues from Emerson and Dickinson, caring *there* and now might abandon the individuated and mediating modes of emotion (sanctioned faux organic responses conditioned by ideological fantasies) so often employed in politics and lived ethics and break out from the affective realm. It might begin as simply, in a sense, as an unthinking hand moving to an injured elbow or knee, but then amplifying and accelerating as this relay extends outward toward wider realities and universes. This amplification must yield both quantitative and qualitative changes in our current critical and political paradigms, producing a type of care that somehow affords the ability to think and/or perform *preservation* (of the immediate, the precarious, the fragile, and the precious) along with *annihilation* (the future of slow violences already afoot and the possible consequences of forcing change within the systemic violences of existing realities). Distinct from familiar philosophical quandaries such as conceiving of the particular along with the universal or political impasses such as leftist utopianism versus center-left practicality, care, for xenocitizens, might bridge, quite literally, that and this, there and here, in a dynamic and dialectical manner.

It is my sincere hope that my chapters offer useful structural models or loose formations that might be employed, if not tactically, at least imaginatively, within our dire predicament. In this regard, the type of care I am hinting at becomes something of an accompaniment to serious study, thinking, planning, fighting, and building. From Emerson's joyous operative moods to Fuller's sistrumatic agitation, from Thoreau's wondrous looping universes and armies of shad to Brown's bad debts and Delany's fugitive movements across the Antebellum South—perhaps wherever and whenever we find ourselves we can attempt to push our vibrancies and our new materialisms into new actualities. In order to do so, caring there and now will require not only the ability to think ecologically in the vein of weak- or non-correlationalism, as Timothy Morton and others would have it, but also the willingness and the ability to somehow pass over into material action—whether it be along with (as with Dickinson's needle) or by joining with (as in Emerson's Romantic vision).[12] As Fred Moten notes in his discussion of C. L. R. James's formal approach to "not-in-betweenness," James's writing gives form to "some kind of syncopated but nonhesitational phrasing."[13] There is perhaps no better way of capturing syntactically what we may need to jolt scholarly, artistic, and, with hope, political thinking toward its present outsides. Indeed, caring there and now feels along with thinkers such as José Esteban Muñoz, for whom queerness is a "rejection of a here and now" in favor of "a doing for and toward the future."[14] But, by necessity and lessons learned, it conceives of this future other place/time as part of the present (despite itself), and also the past.

We might find this, find each other (even Whitman, whom I've heard tell is loafing in wait for a good fight) in the loops of time somewhere amid the nineteenth-through-twenty-first centuries.[15] Moving forward-as-back, sideways, and, yes, sliding, we might begin the work it will take

NOTES

INTRODUCTION: XENOCITIZENS

1. For the former, see especially Carrie Hyde's *Civic Longing: The Speculative Origins of U.S. Citizenship* (2018); for the latter, see studies such as Eva Cherniavsky's *Neocitizenship: Political Culture After Democracy* (2017).

2. Lauren Berlant and Lee Edleman, *Sex, or the Unbearable* (Durham, N.C.: Duke University Press, 2014), 40–41.

3. By suggesting that the national model of citizenship is anachronistic, I am in no way disregarding the very real benefits that this model offers at foundational levels or the strategic roles it can play in efforts to forge social, political, and/or economic change. What is more, the long and ongoing civil rights and citizenship battles fought in the United States, especially in relation to race, should be foregrounded as both relevant and important for any discussion of citizenship as a critical or political category. See, for example, Martha S. Jones's *Birthright Citizens: A History of Race and Rights in Antebellum America* (2018) for a recent historical study of this topic in terms of the nineteenth century. Nonetheless, and with all caveats included, V. I. Lenin's 1917 thoughts in *The State and Revolution* are perhaps still relevant here. Lenin asserts Marx's claim that, in Lenin's terms, "the state is an organ of class rule, an organ for the *oppression* of one class by another; it is the creation of 'order,' legalizing and perpetuating this oppression by moderating the clashes among the classes." Moreover, Lenin argues, "That the state is an organ of the rule of a definitive class which *cannot* be reconciled with its antipode (the class opposite to it) is something the petty-bourgeois democrats can never understand." Consequently, the "liberation of the oppressed" requires not only revolution, but also "*the destruction* of the apparatus of state power which was created by the ruling class" (9). Against misreadings of Engels's notion that the bourgeois state "withers away" after revolution, however, Lenin goes on to suggest that the proletarian revolution will need the state's apparatus, strategically and logistically, in order to carry out the changes required to combat bourgeois counter-measures. To quote Lenin one last time: "The proletariat needs state power, the centralized organization of force, the organization of violence both to crush the

resistance of the exploiters and to *lead* the enormous mass of the population ... in the work of 'establishing' a socialist economy" (24–25). See Lenin's *The State and Revolution*, trans. Robert Service (New York: Penguin, 1992). My point is not to assert naively Lenin's embattled call for some dictatorship of the proletariat. Instead, I want to draw attention to the contextual stakes that attend any appeal to traditional democratic state structures when addressing historical or emerging forms of oppression/liberation.

4. Lisa Lowe, *The Intimacies of Four Continents* (Durham, N.C.: Duke University Press, 2015), 39, 3. This is perhaps why Tariq Ali argues: "It is revolutions that make history happen. Liberals of every sort, with rare exceptions, are found on the other side" (*The Dilemmas of Lenin: Terrorism, War, Empire, Love, Revolution* [New York: Verso Books, 2017], 3).

5. Gregg Crane, *Race, Citizenship, and Law in American Literature* (Cambridge: Cambridge University Press, 2002), 2.

6. Crane, *Race*, 2. As Isabelle Stengers notes, Aristotle thought of citizens as "political animals." As such, the traditional western category is predicated upon manifold foreclosures. "When political animals gather and discuss what is good or bad for the city," Stenger writes, "neither gods nor mountains nor forests have a voice in the process" ("The Challenge of Ontological Politics," in *A World of Many Worlds*, ed. Marisol de la Cadena and Mario Blaser [Durham, N.C.: Duke University Press, 2018], 84).

7. According to Puar, "'[D]ebilitation' is distinct from the term 'disablement' because it foregrounds the slow wearing down of populations instead of the event of becoming disabled. . . . [T]he former [term] comprehends those bodies that are sustained in a perpetual state of debilitation precisely through foreclosing the social, cultural, and political translation to debility" (*The Right to Maim: Debility, Capacity, and Disability* [Durham, N.C.: Duke University Press, 2017], xiii–xiv).

8. Qtd. in Ivy Wilson, *Specters of Democracy: Blackness and the Aesthetic of Politics in the Antebellum U.S.* (New York: Oxford University Press, 2011), 6.

9. Charles W. Mills, *Black Rights/White Wrongs: The Critique of Racial Liberalism* (New York: Oxford University Press, 2017), xiv.

10. Mills, *Black Rights*, xvi, 201.

11. Chantal Mouffe, *For a Left Populism* (New York: Verso, 2018), 5.

12. In addition to offering something of a defense and recontextualization of her and Ernesto Laclau's 1985 *Hegemony and Socialist Strategy: Toward a Radical Democratic Politics*, Mouffe argues that, in our current moment, traditional left discourses are inadequate. In her words, "The fundamental mistake of the 'extreme left' has always been . . . not engag[ing] with how people are in reality, but with how they should be according to their

theories. As a result, they see their role as making them realize the 'truth' about their situation. Instead of designating the adversaries in ways that people can identify, they use abstract categories ... thereby failing to mobilize the affective dimension necessary to motivate people to act politically" (*For a Left*, 50).

13. Mouffe, *For a Left*, 6, 24.

14. For example, I hope to build on hopeful work such as Dana D. Nelson's conception of early-American "commons democracy," which she describes as "the political power not just of the 'many,' some abstract 'majority,' but specifically of ordinary, poor—*common*—folk: the people" and Carrie Hyde's aforementioned speculative study of the origins of U.S. citizenship, which ultimately ends up pondering if, in light of current immigration debates, the Declaration of Independence's use of "persons" rather than "citizens" (given the Fourteenth Amendment's use of birthright) might be a move worth revisiting (Nelson, *Commons Democracy: Reading the Politics of Participation in the Early United States* [New York: Fordham University Press, 2016], 9–10, and Hyde, *Civic Longing: The Speculative Origins of U.S. Citizenship* [Cambridge: Harvard University Press, 2018], 185).

15. Cary Wolfe, *What Is Posthumanism* (Minneapolis: University of Minnesota Press, 2010), xv. As Wolfe notes, his phrase derives from Jean-François Lyotard's comments on postmodernism.

16. Darwin qtd. in John Bellamy Foster and Paul Burkett, *Marx and the Earth: An Anti-Critique* (Chicago: Haymarket Books, 2016), vii. As Jesse Oak Taylor notes, the term "Ecology" derives from the Greek "'*oikos*,' meaning 'house' or 'dwelling,'" and, as Juliana Chow explains, it was formulated within institutional science in the mid-nineteenth century by scholars such as Ernst Haeckel. During the period, Haeckel defined the term as "the study of all those complex interrelations referred to by Darwin as the conditions of the struggle for existence." See Jesse Oak Taylor, *Sky of Our Manufacture: The London Fog in British Fiction From Dickens to Woolf* (Charlottesville: University of Virginia Press, 2016), 5, and Juliana Chow, "Partial Readings: Thoreau's Studies as Natural History's Causalities," in *Anthropocene Reading: Literary History in Geologic Times*, ed. Tobias Menely and Jesse Oak Taylor (University Park: Pennsylvania State University Press, 2017), 119.

17. Louis Althusser, "From *Capital* to Marx's Philosophy," in *Reading Capital*, trans. Ben Brewster (New York: Verso, 2009), 14.

18. Althusser, "From *Capital* to Marx's Philosophy," 15.

19. Bruno Bosteels, *The Actuality of Communism* (New York: Verso, 2011), 223.

20. Bosteels, *The Actuality of Communism*, 29.

21. Bruno Bosteels, *Marx and Freud in Latin America: Politics, Psychoanalysis, and Religion in Times of Terror* (New York: Verso, 2012), 5.

22. Karl Marx, "Speech on the Anniversary of the *People's Paper*," in *Karl Marx: Selected Writings*, ed. David McLellan (New York: Oxford University Press, 2000), 369. Henry David Thoreau, *Walden* (Princeton: Princeton University Press, 2004), 98. Taking up this theme in the context of the Oceti Sakowin's long struggle against U.S. settler colonialism, Nick Estes notes how Crazy Horse gathered dirt from mole mounds in order to wash his body—because he knew this dirt included "medicine" from the roots beneath. According to Estes, "Hidden from view to outsiders, this constant tunneling, plotting, planning, harvesting, remembering, and conspiring for freedom—the collective faith that another world is possible—is the most important aspect of revolutionary work" (*Our History Is the Future* [New York: Verso, 2019], 19).

23. Étienne Balibar, *Citizenship*, trans. Thomas Scott-Railton (New York: Polity, 2015), 3.

24. Balibar, *Citizenship*, 29.

25. Balibar, *Citizenship*, 30–31. As Raúl Coronado notes using the example of eighteenth-century Spanish America, even in historical contexts shaped by European modes of political rhetoric, there existed "alternate model[s] of modernity." In the case of Spanish-American revolutions of this era, he suggests, "[W]hile on the surface all ostensibly yearned for liberty and equality," there was often "incommensurable understandings of those very terms, liberty and equality" (*A World Not to Come: A History of Latino Writing and Print Culture* [Cambridge: Harvard University Press, 2013], 8–9).

26. Álvaro García Linera, *Plebeian Power: Collective Action and Indigenous Working-Class, and Popular Identities in Bolivia*, trans. Shana Yael Shubs et al. (Chicago: Haymarket Books, 2014), 89–90.

27. Linera, *Plebeian Power*, 91. Using similar terms, Mouffe argues that "[w]hile being a central category in a pluralist liberal democracy, citizenship can be understood in a variety of ways that command very different conceptions of politics" (*For a Left*, 65).

28. Alyosha Goldstein, *Poverty in Common: The Politics of Community Action During the American Century* (Durham, N.C.: Duke University Press, 2012), 28–29. Goldstein references Jean-Luc Nancy's *The Inoperative Community* (1991) and *The Truth of Democracy* (2010).

29. George Ciccariello Maher, *Decolonizing Dialectics* (Durham, N.C.: Duke University Press, 2017), 170. Ciccariello-Maher goes on to write, "If we can loosen our conception of 'the state' to its broadest sense—as status, the status quo, the existing state of things—we might be able to grasp

decolonization as truly constituting, as [Maia Ramnath] puts it, 'the highest form of anarchism'" (170).

30. Contemporary scholars have begun to illuminate any number of these modern foreclosures, building from and, at their best, complicating traditional notions of biopolitical power. Judith Butler and Athena Athanasiou's "dispossessed," Jasbir Puar's "Terrorist Assemblages," Giorgio Agamben's "camp," and Saskia Sassen's "expulsions" are notable examples. See Judith Butler and Athena Athanasiou, *Dispossession: The Performative in the Political* (2013); Jasbir Puar, *Terrorist Assemblages: Homonationalism in Queer Times* (2007); Giorgio Agamben, *Means Without Ends: Notes on Politics* (2000); and Saskia Sassen, *Expulsions: Brutality and Complexity in the Global Economy* (2014).

31. Timothy Mitchell, *Carbon Democracy: Political Power in the Age of Oil* (New York: Verso, 2013), 3. For a study of nineteenth-century democracy's negative production of citizen-subjects, see Caleb Smith's *The Prison and the American Imagination* (New Haven: Yale University Press, 2011). Smith builds on Foucault and others to offer a nuanced account of how "the prisoner represent[s] the perfect subjectivity of the modern citizen and, at the same time, the abject body outcast from the circle of rights-bearing humanity" (6). For commentary on the long lineages of contemporary democratic un-freedoms, especially as they pertain to race, see books such as Eddie S. Glaude Jr.'s *Democracy in Black: How Race Still Enslaves the American Soul* (2016) and Neil Roberts's *Freedom as Marronage* (2015).

32. Coronado, *A World Not to Come*, 8.

33. Monique Allewaert, *Ariel's Ecology: Plantations, Personhood, and Colonialism in the American Tropics* (Minneapolis: University of Minnesota Press, 2013), 30, 50.

34. Balibar, *Citizenship*, 31.

35. Qtd. in Orlando Patterson, *Slavery and Social Death: A Comparative Study* (Cambridge: Harvard University Press, 1985), 4.

36. See Heidegger's *Being in Time*, trans. Joan Stambaugh (Albany: SUNY Press, 1996), 325.

37. W. E. B. Du Bois, *Black Reconstruction in America: An Essay Toward a History of the Part Which Black Folk Played in the Attempt to Reconstruct Democracy in America, 1860–1880* (New York: Oxford University Press, 2007), 119.

38. Nicole M. Guidotti-Hernández, *Unspeakable Violence: Remapping U.S. and Mexican National Imaginaries* (Durham, N.C.: Duke University Press, 2011), 7–8.

39. Qtd in Deak Nabers, *Victory of Law: The Fourteenth Amendment, the Civil War, and American Literature, 1852–1867* (Baltimore: Johns Hopkins University Press, 2006), 99.

40. Fred Moten, *Stolen Life* (Durham, N.C.: Duke University Press, 2018), 75–77.

41. Allewaert, *Ariel's Ecology*, 14.

42. Achille Mbembe, "Necropolitics," *Public Culture* 15, no. 1 (2003): 11–40; Russ Castronovo, *Necro Citizenship: Death, Eroticism, and the Public Sphere in the Nineteenth-Century United States* (Durham, N.C.: Duke University Press, 2007), 10.

43. Kerry Larson, "Illiberal Emerson," *Nineteenth-Century Prose* 33, no. 1 (Spring 2006): 42.

44. Frederick Douglass, "What to the Slave is the Fourth of July?," in *The Oxford Frederick Douglass Reader*, ed. William L. Andrews (New York: Oxford University Press, 1996), 118.

45. David Harvey, *A Brief History of Neoliberalism* (New York: Oxford University Press, 2007), 2. For more on the role of the Chicago School, see Philip Mirowski and Dieter Plehwe's *The Road from Mont Pèlerin: The Making of the Neoliberal Thought Collective* (2015).

46. In Ciccariello-Maher's terms, neoliberal structural adjustment entails "cutting wages, laying off teachers and other pubic-sector workers, cutting social-welfare spending, and privatizing public goods by selling off natural resources and services like water and gas—not to the highest bidder, but often to the highest briber. Under duress from international lenders, governments handed over their sovereignty by restructuring entire economies according to the dictates of the global market" (*Building the Commune: Radical Democracy in Venezuela* [New York: Verso, 2016], 3).

47. Qtd. in P. K. Rao, *Development Finance* (New York: Springer, 2003), 79.

48. Amanda Anderson, *Bleak Liberalism* (Chicago: University of Chicago Press, 2016), 2.

49. Eva Cherniavsky, *Neocitizenship: Political Culture After Democracy* (New York: NYU Press, 2017), 1; Dawson Barrett, *The Defiant: Protest Movements in Post-Liberal America* (New York: NYU Press, 2018), 17; Mouffe, *For a Left*, 49. Mouffe's call to distinguish between political liberalism and economic liberalism is a response to the way neoliberal policy has resignified "democracy" as "freedom," where "a defense of economic liberty and private property replaces a defense of equality as the privileged value in a liberal society" (31). Calling for a return and/or commencement of "agonistic confrontation," Mouffe hopes that the traditional democratic and political sides of the liberal tradition might yet be asserted (93). This push for a stark confrontation seems to modify Mouffe's earlier focus on agonistic pluralism, where she suggests that the "crucial issue . . . is how to establish [the] us/them distinction, which is constitutive of politics, in a way that is compatible with the recognition of pluralism" (*Agonistics: Thinking The*

World Politically [New York: Verso, 2013], 7). Mouffe's assertion of the radical potential in political liberalism departs drastically from Lionel Trilling's *The Liberal Imagination* (1950), which censured the dangers and shortcomings of the "impulse to organization" within political liberalism and promoted a return to more idealistic and aesthetic fantasies about liberalism (*The Liberal Imagination: Essays on Literature and Society* [New York: New York Review of Books, 2008], xxi). Mouffe's approach also differs from contemporary historical approaches such as Christopher Taylor's *Empire of Neglect: The West Indies in the Wake of British Liberalism* (Durham, N.C.: Duke University Press, 2018). Taylor highlights with nuance the violence of British economic liberal policies (where "liberal freedom *became* a form of liberal neglect"). At the same time, he focuses explicitly on "how the discourse of liberalism was practically *enacted* and trace[s] the looping consequences of those enactments" rather than considering the broader ideological discourses of liberalism at play (presumably the ones that Mouffe would like to radicalize and the ones scholars such as Lowe choose to examine). In Taylor's view, the term "liberal" has become "vague" in its modern circulations, and, as such, "liberalism is not a transhistorical philosopheme with an inbuilt tendency toward fashioning self-possessive subjects or excluding infantilized others" (3). Taylor goes on to say that his decision to focus on "enactments" of liberal policy is catalyzed by an attempt to "push back against scholarship that attempts to save Enlightenment or liberalism from itself by stressing the anticolonial, anti-imperial, or antiracist fundaments of these varied traditions." He continues, "[W]e cannot fuse our postcolonial political horizons with those of the eighteenth and nineteenth centuries" (4).

50. A number of other contemporary scholars recalibrate the relation between our neoliberal present and liberalism's long history of slavery by asserting forms of continuity and connection. See, for example, Christina Sharpe's *In the Wake: On Blackness and Being* (2016), Kathryn Yusoff's *A Billion Black Anthropocenes or None* (2018), and the Revolutionary Abolitionist Movement's *Burn Down the American Plantation: Call for a Revolutionary Abolitionist Movement* (2017).

51. Achille Mbembe, *Critique of Black Reason* (Durham, N.C.: Duke University Press, 2017), 13, 2–3; Cedric Robinson, *Black Marxism: The Making of the Black Radical Tradition* (Chapel Hill: University of North Carolina Press, 2005), 2; Fred Moten, *Stolen Life*, 82. By privileging left scholars such as Mbembe who acknowledge the links between neoliberalism and earlier regimes of liberalism, I am not at all denying the political foreclosures that attended the Cold War and the subsequent advent of neoliberal policies. For example, Eddie S. Glaude, Jr. notes that in the 1930s and early 1940s "black liberals struggled alongside black nationalists and

Communists." With the late forties push toward consensus, "any hint of communism or socialism shaping black politics had to be purged, and the radical elements of black political life marginalized. Black liberalism had to stand alone." According to Glaude, a similar purge occurred with regard to the black radicalisms of the 1960s and 1970s, where reestablishing black liberalism as "the only acceptable form of black politics" required "an all-out assault on . . . radical political imaginations" (*Democracy in Black: How Race Still Enslaves the American Soul* [New York: Crown Publishers, 2016], 148–49). For a study of race and the development of institutional liberal regimes, see Jodi Melamed's *Represent and Destroy: Rationalizing Violence in the New Racial Capitalism* (2011).

52. Jethro K. Lieberman, *Liberalism Undressed* (New York: Oxford University Press, 2012), 3.

53. Stephen Holmes, *The Anatomy of Antiliberalism* (Cambridge: Harvard University Press, 1996), 3–4. Qtd. in Lieberman, *Liberalism Undressed*, 4. In *Intimacies of Four Continents*, Lowe offers a similar overview of liberalism. In her view, the concept encompasses "the branches of European political philosophy that include the narration of political emancipation through citizenship in the state, the promise of economic freedom in the development of wage labor and exchange markets, and the conferring of civilization to human persons educated in aesthetic and national culture—in each case unifying particularity, difference, or locality through universal concepts of reason and community" (3–4).

54. Domenico Losurdo, *Liberalism: A Counter-History* (New York: Verso, 2014), 59.

55. Losurdo, *Liberalism*, 35.

56. Smith qtd. in Losurdo, *Liberalism*, 60. Scholars such as W. E. B. DuBois (*Black Reconstruction in America* [1935]) and, more recently, Edward Baptist (*The Half Has Never Been Told: Slavery and the Making of American Capitalism* [2014]) have disproved emphatically this longstanding fantasy about historical and economic progress.

57. See Losurdo, 60, 154–55.

58. Antonio Negri, *Marx Beyond Marx: Lessons on the* Grundrisse, trans. Harry Cleaver et al. (Massachusetts: Bergin and Garvey Publishers, 1984), 12. Negri uses the terms "plural universe" to describe Marx's method, writing, "The dialectic research-presentation is . . . open on all sides: every conclusion that takes the form of presentation of the research opens spaces to new research and new presentation." Here, "each determination of a new subject immediately reveals a new antagonism and sets in motion, through this, a process in which the determination of new subjects emerges" (12). More recently, Marisol de la Cadena and Mario Blaser use "pluriverse" to

describe to a similar concept, where "heterogeneous worldings [come] together as a political ecology of practices, negotiating their difficult being together in heterogeneity" ("Pluriverse: Proposals for a World of Many Worlds," in *A World of Many Worlds*, 4).

59. Christopher Nealon, "Infinity for Marxists," *Mediations* 28, no. 2 (Spring 2015): 48.

60. Bosteels, *Actuality of Communism*, 42–43.

61. Bosteels, *Actuality of Communism*, 44, 43. The first of these approaches works in the lineages of Heidegger's "destruction of metaphysics of being as presence and Lacan's subversion of the ideology of the subject of ego" (including scholars such as Jacques Derrida, Giorgio Agamben, Alain Badiou, and Slavoj Žižek) and the other takes up a "neo-Spinozist or Deleuzian ontology of substance as pure immanence" (including the likes of Antonio Negri and Michael Hardt on the left and, as I will argue, a variety of new materialisms at the liberal center) (*Actuality*, 46).

62. Adrian Johnston, *Prolegomena to Any Future Materialism. Volume I: The Outcome of Contemporary French Philosophy* (Evanston, Ill.: Northwestern University Press, 2013), 82.

63. Johnston, *Prolegomena to Any Future Materialism*, 23.

64. Fred Moten and Stefano Harney, *The Undercommons: Fugitive Planning and Black Study* (New York: Minor Compositions, 2013), 17.

65. For the reasons outlined, I dispense with the term "subject." There are, however, theoretical uses of the concept that remain relevant for the arguments I will make in the following chapters. To note one example, Alain Badiou's conception of "subject" is anything but the familiar notion of the subject of state or simply a figure formed by the cut of symbolic castration. Instead, it is a "militant of truth," a singular or collective "operant disposition of the traces of the event and of what they deploy in the world" (*Being and Event*, trans. Oliver Feltham [New York: Bloomsbury, 2007], xvi; *Logics of Worlds: Being and Event II*, trans. Alberto Toscano [New York: Bloomsbury, 2013], 33). This is why the function of a "truth procedure" lies at the core of Badiou's theory of the event, for it is only via the "militant subjective composition of a truth" yielded by the experience of a historical evental site that can push given ideological and political coordinates toward transformation. The conflict Johnston locates at the core of ontology might be seen to manifest on the historical/political plane as a militant push for change, or what Badiou calls "forcing."

66. Allewaert, *Ariel's Ecology*, 10. Allewaert offers a useful account of the development the term *person* in liberal thought (from Hobbes to Blackstone and Locke). In arguing for a new category of personhood, she invokes Nancy Ruttenburg's earlier call for a similar terminological shift, which

could be used within the formation of a "genealogy of nonliberal democracy" (10).

67. Michael Snediker, *Queer Optimism: Lyric Personhood and Other Felicitous Persuasions* (Minneapolis: University of Minnesota Press, 2009), 3.

68. Alexander G. Weheliye, *Habeas Viscus: Racializing Assemblages, Biopolitics, and Black Feminist Theories of the Human* (Durham, N.C.: Duke University Press, 2014), 1–2; Lowe, *The Intimacies of Four Continents*, 34.

69. Maurizio Lazzarato, *Signs and Machines: Capitalism and the Production of Subjectivity*, trans. Joshua David Jordan (Los Angeles: Semiotext(e), 2014), 8–9.

70. Wendy Brown, *Undoing the Demos: Neoliberalism's Stealth Revolution* (New York: Zone Books, 2015), 44.

71. Mbembe, *Critique of Black Reason*, 3–4.

72. Building on the work of Deleuze and Luhmann, Massumi replaces the longstanding notion of the self-interested subject in western liberal thought (á la Adam Smith) with a self that is "internally differentiated, containing its own population of 'minority practices' of contrasting affective tone and tenor, in a zone of indistinction between rational calculation and affectivity." He goes on to suggest that the self constitutes "an *infra-individual* complexity quasi-chaotically agitating within the smallest unit [of society]" (*The Power at the End of the Economy* [Durham, N.C.: Duke University Press, 2015], 20, 8). Massumi views the very same "infra-individual" as something of a limit to the economy, the location where the economy "ends." As such, this site is crucial for economic regeneration (crisis as profit) but also for the production of alternate, perhaps radical, affective modulations and effects (110).

73. Christopher Castiglia, *Interior States: Institutional Consciousness and the Inner Life of Democracy in the Antebellum United States* (Durham, N.C.: Duke University Press, 2008), 1–3.

74. Castiglia, *Interior States*, 10–11, 102.

75. Castiglia, *Interior States*, 294.

76. Such studies include Monique Allewaert's *Ariel's Ecology*, which provides a new optic for thinking the "parahuman" (including varieties of "creolized ontology") via specific sites of minoritarian personhood in the eighteenth-century plantation zone; Colleen Glenney Boggs's *Animalia Americana: Animal Representations and Biopolitical Subjectivity* (2013), which considers how animal representations in American literature "are an interface where the literal and the figurative meet and unsettle the terrains of modern taxonimization" and, in the process, unsettle assumptions about liberal subjectivity by revealing its status as both "the battleground as well as the byproduct of biopolitics" ([New York: Columbia University Press,

2013], 189, 187); and Alexander G. Weheliye's *Habeas Viscus: Racializing Assemblages, Biopolitics, and Black Feminist Theories of the Human* (2014), which uses the titular concept of habeas viscus ("You shall have the flesh") to "investigate the breaks, crevices, movements, languages, and such found in zones between flesh and law" and, consequently, reveals significant foreclosures within the dominant categories of bare life (Agamben) and biopolitics (Foucault, et al.) (2, 11).

77. My call to rethink the category of "biopolitical" by focusing on the political side of the term thus shares with Jason W. Moore's suggestion to replace the popular term "Anthropocene ('Age of Man')" with "Capitalocene ('Age of Capital')" a concern with the foreclosures produced by criticism in our era of posthuman and/or nonhuman turns (*Capitalism in the Web of Life: Ecology and the Accumulation of Capital* [New York: Verso, 2015], 77).

78. Lauren Berlant, *Cruel Optimism* (Durham, N.C.: Duke University Press, 2011), 297.

79. Jared Sexton, "Afro-Pessimism: The Unclear Word," *Rhizomes* 29 (2016): para. 6.

80. Qtd. in Sexton, "Afro-Pessimism," para. 12.

81. Fred Moten, "Blackness and Nothingness (Mysticism in the Flesh)," *South Atlantic Quarterly* 112, no. 4 (Fall 2013): 739.

82. In "Blackness and Nothingness," Moten acknowledges the limitations of the term "wretchedness" and notes a preference for the related term "damnation"—the latter word constituting a perhaps better translation of Fanon's text (738).

83. Moten, "Blackness and Nothingness," 737–38. In Achille Mbembe's Afro-pessimist reading, the condition of blackness is tantamount to a racial nothingness, a continuous historical production of "a kind of silt of the earth, a silt deposited at the confluence of half-worlds produced by the dual violence of race and capital" (*Critique*, 37). In Wilderson's terms, the "race of Humanism (White, Asian, South Asian, and Arab) could not have produced itself without the simultaneous production of that walking destruction which became known as the Black" (*Red, White, Black: Cinema and the Structure of U.S. Antagonisms* [Durham, N.C.: Duke University Press, 2010], 20). Taking these positions one step further, Calvin L. Warren offers a position of "black nihilism," where, in an antiblack world, "Blacks . . . have function but not Being," rendering "black being" a terrifying "metaphysical nothing" (*Ontological Terror: Blackness, Nihilism, and Emancipation* [Durham, N.C.: Duke University Press, 2018], 5).

84. Moten, "Blackness and Nothingness," 739, 749. Moten's formulation of paraontology thus shares with Warren's more recent suggestion that because blackness lacks being within the antiblack coordinates of western

ontology, then blacks have an "existence" rather than "ontology" per se (*Ontological Terror*, 12).

85. Nahum Dimitri Chandler, *X—The Problem of the Negro as a Problem for Thought* (New York: Fordham University Press, 2014), 11–14.

86. Chandler, *X*, 16.

87. Chandler, *X*, 17.

88. It is important to note how Wilderson's work, especially, illuminates a foundational asymmetry between blackness and all other racial and ontological formations. Discussing the specific case of indigenous identity in relation to white settler colonialism, Wilderson suggests that the "Settler and the 'Savage' share . . . a capacity for time and space coherence." He continues, "This capacity for cartographic coherence is the thing itself, that which secures subjectivity for both the Settler and the 'Savage' and articulates them to one another in a network of connections, transfers, and displacements" (*Red, White, Black*, 181). Although my book's focus on what I am calling illiberal ontologies at times dovetails structurally with aspects of Moten's and Chandler's conception of paraontology (and directly takes it up in Chapter 4), I do want to underline the distinct non-/para-ontological status of blackness as it is presented by black studies scholars such as Wilderson and Moten.

89. Robert Warrior, "Home / Not Home: Centering American Studies Where We Are," *American Quarterly* 69, no. 2 (June 2017): 197.

90. Estes, *Our History Is the Future*, 14–15.

91. Estes, *Our History Is the Future*, 47. In terms of what might be called indigenous para-politics, Estes discusses the Oceti Sakowin notion of Pte Ska Win, or the White Buffalo Woman, who "formalized the first treaty with the human and other-than-human worlds" (66).

92. De la Cadena and Blaser, "Pluriverse," 5–6. In *Earth Beings: Ecologies of Practice Across Andean Worlds* (Durham, N.C.: Duke University Press, 2015), de la Cadena discusses her encounter with notions of Andean *tirakuna*, or "other-than-human beings who participate in the lives of those who call themselves *runakuna*, people" (xxiii–xxiv). She notes how her interactions with indigenous peoples of the region and their worlds yielded "conversations across different onto-epistemic formations" (xxv).

93. Levi Bryant, Nick Srnicek, and Graham Harman, eds., *The Speculative Turn: Continental Materialism and Realism* (Melbourne: re.press, 2011), 1, 3.

94. *The Speculative Turn* is not at all dogmatic about its borders: including the likes of Žižek and Badiou—two philosophers who are very much part of the post-Lacanian tradition of Marxism and that have had much to say about the modern western obsession with "reality." Furthermore, contemporary noncorrelationists such as Quentin Meillassoux have offered innovative,

though embattled, philosophical positions. Žižek, for example, suggests that Meillassoux "transposes what appears to transcendental partisans of finitude as the limitation of our knowledge (the insight that we can be totally wrong about our knowledge, that reality can in itself can be totally different from our notion of it) into the most basic positive ontological property of reality itself" (*Disparities* [New York: Bloomsbury, 2016], 56).

95. In *Absolute Recoil*, for example, Žižek argues that Fredric Jameson "was correct to claim that Deleuzianism is today the predominant form of idealism: as did Deleuze, New Materialism relies on the implicit equation: matter = life = stream of agential self-awareness." According to Žižek, "New Materialism takes a step back into (what can only appear to us moderns as) premodern naivety, covering up the gap that defines modernity and reasserting the purposeful vitality of nature" ([New York: Verso, 2014], 8, 12).

96. Adrian Johnston, *Adventures in Transcendental Materialism: Dialogues with Contemporary Thinkers* (Edinburgh: Edinburgh University Press, 2014), 299, 314.

97. Johnston, *Adventures in Transcendental Materialism*, 319.

98. This includes works such as Anna Tsing, Heather Swanson, Elaine Gan, and Nils Bubandt's *Arts of Living on a Damaged Planet* (2017), Elizabeth Povinelli's *Geontologies: A Requiem to Late Liberalism* (2016), Donna Haraway's *Staying With the Trouble: Making Kin in the Chthulucene* (2016), Jeffrey Nealon's *Plant Theory: Biopower and Vegetable Life* (2016), Jason Moore's *Anthropocene or Capitalocene? Nature, History, and the Crisis of Capitalism* (2016) and *Capitalism in the Web of Life: Ecology and the Accumulation of Capital* (2015), Stacy Alaimo's *Exposed: Environmental Politics and Pleasures in Posthuman Times* (2016), T. J. Demos's *Decolonizing Nature: Contemporary Art and the Politics of Ecology* (2016), John Bellamy Foster and Paul Burkett's *Marx and the Earth: An Anti-Critique* (2016), and Anna Tsing's *The Mushroom at the End of the World: On Possibility of Life in Capitalist Ruins* (2015).

99. A number of scholars working in the wake of the nonhuman turn emphasize the expansive aspects of an ontological focus. In *How Forests Think: Toward an Anthropology Beyond the Human*, for example, Eduardo Kohn argues that "an anthropology beyond the human is perforce an ontological one. That is, taking nonhumans seriously makes it impossible to confine our anthropological inquiries to . . . epistemological concern[s]" ([Berkeley and Los Angeles: University of California Press, 2013], 10).

100. Elizabeth A. Povinelli, *Geontologies: A Requiem to Late Liberalism* (Durham, N.C.: Duke University Press, 2016), 14.

101. Povinelli, *Geontologies*, 4–5.

102. Margaret Ronda, "Anthrogenic Poetics," *The Minnesota Review* 83 (2014): 103.

103. In Dana Luciano's "The Inhuman Anthropocene" (*Avidly* [March 22, 2015]), she cites recent studies positing both 1610 CE and 1492 CE as alternate origin dates for the Anthropocene. As mentioned, my arguments tend to follow Jason Moore's suggestion in *Capitalism in the Web of Life* that "Capitalocene" may be a more useful category than the ubiquitous "Anthropocene." For a useful overview of discourses surrounding the scholarly understanding of the Anthropocene, see especially Christophe Bonneuil and Jean-Baptiste Fressoz's *The Shock of the Anthropocene* (2016). For a critique of racial foreclosures within approaches to the Anthropocene, see Kathryn Yusoff's *A Billion Black Anthropocenes or None* (2018).

104. Bruno Latour, *Reassembling the Social: An Introduction to Actor-Network-Theory* (New York: Oxford University Press, 2005), 5.

105. Latour, *Reassembling the Social*, 5.

106. Bruno Latour, *An Inquiry Into Modes of Existence: An Anthropology of the Moderns* (Cambridge: Harvard University Press, 2013), xxvi, 182, 13. Critiquing indirectly Latour's political logic, Isabelle Stengers suggests that all "cosmopolitics is badly limited." In her words, "The cry 'you will destroy us,' even if it may cause fright in the political assembly, even if, as amplified by diplomats, it may effectively disrupt the collective deliberation and maybe reorient it toward new horizons, is still defined as a disruption, political deliberation being now defined as what must accept disruption. Accept or tolerate? What is lurking is nothing other than the curse of tolerance, a tolerance that would have 'us' accept the crucial importance of 'causes' for 'others' while, except for very special cases, 'we' would be 'free'" ("The Challenge of Ontological Politics," 95).

107. Latour's liberal assumptions take stark relief in pieces such as his introduction ("From Realpolitik to Dingpolitik") to *Making Things Public: Atmospheres of Democracy* (2005). In Latour's more recent work, these liberal positions yield problematic gestures of leveling and universalization. In *Down to Earth: Politics in the New Climatic Regime*, trans. Catherine Porter (Medford, Mass.: Polity, 2018), Latour envisions a "wicked universality" where climate crises produce a scenario where "all find themselves facing a universal lack of shareable space and inhabitable land" (9). Within this new reality, "the migratory crisis has been generalized" (6). To illustrate this situation, Latour imagines ironically a colonizer addressing a "postcolonial" subject—asking them how they survived and playfully suggesting that the two antagonists are now, on another level, linked within a horizon of shared vulnerability (7–8). As scholars such as Rob Nixon (*Slow Violence*) have rehearsed convincingly, however, the emerging material and ecological crises humans face are by no means experienced "in common" as Latour suggests (9). Furthermore, these emerging material and ecological crises

generate new horizons of antagonism and oppression. (For example, one can easily re-narrate Latour's ironic and imaginary dialogue by placing the colonizer/bourgeois subject upon an armed yacht.) In a fashion similar to Latour, Timothy Morton's *Humankind: Solidarity with Nonhuman People* offers the wonderful aim of "[reimagining] what 'to have in common' means" ([New York: Verso, 2017], 13). But, in so doing, Morton levels material-historical reality and conceives of "solidarity" as a foundational "reliance between discrete yet deeply interrelated beings." As such, solidarity is "very cheap because it is default to the biosphere and very widely available" (2, 14). From Latour's nonhuman diplomacy to Morton's universalized always-already solidarity, we see evidence of a liberal move whereby specific historical antagonisms and worldviews are negated or, at least, curtailed by manifestly material (universalist) appeals to broader horizons of relation. By citing the liberal undercurrents of Latour's work, however, I am not counting out radical and emancipatory potentials found within them. For example, Patricia Yaeger's "Sea Trash: Dark Pools, and the Tragedy of the Commons" uses the very "imaginary" diplomacy scene I mention to leverage an inquiry about who/what is entitled to "rights" (and, therefore, how we conceive of political capabilities) (*PMLA* 125, no. 3 [May 2010]: 523–45).

108. Peter Wolfendale, *Object-Oriented Philosophy: The Noumenon's New Clothes* (Falmouth, UK: Urbanomic, 2014), 211.

109. Moore, *Capitalism in the Web of Life*, 39.

110. See Bosteels, *Actuality of Communism*, 62–63 and Rachel Greenwald Smith, *Affect and American Literature in the Age of Neoliberalism* (Cambridge: Cambridge University Press, 2015); a similar critique can be made against contemporary work such as Brian Massumi's *What Animals Teach Us About Politics*, where his appeal for "mutual inclusion" shares conspicuously with the contemporary development of "inclusive capitalism" ([Durham, N.C.: Duke University Press, 2014], 4).

111. In *Geontologies*, Povinelli levels a similar criticism against Jane Bennett's mode of materialist vitalism, pointing out that "new vitalisms take advantage of the longstanding Western shadow imposition of the qualities of one of its categories (Life, Leben) onto the key dynamics of its concept of existence (Being, Dasein)" (18).

112. As I hope my chapters will reveal, my project's historical stakes are very much allied with the sprit of the Frankfurt School idea that Marx often located future possibilities within the past itself. To quote Adorno and Horkheimer: "What is at stake is not conservation of the past but the fulfillment of past hopes" (*Dialectic of Enlightenment: Philosophical Fragments*, ed. Gunzelin Schmid Noerr, trans. Edmund Jephcott [Stanford: Stanford

University Press, 2002], xvii). A similar logic can be found in contemporary projects such as José Esteban Muñoz's notion of "queer futurity," where "a backward glance enacts a future vision" (*Cruising Utopia: The Then and There of Queer Futurity* [New York: NYU Press, 2009], 4).

113. For studies of eighteenth- and nineteenth-century slavery and/or abolitionism, see especially Marisa J. Fuentes's *Dispossessed Lives: Enslaved Women, Violence, and the Archive* (2018), Julius S. Scott's *The Common Wind: Afro-American Currents in the Age of the Haitian Revolution* (2018), Britt Rusert's *Fugitive Science: Empiricism and Freedom in Early African American Culture* (2017), Simone Browne's *Dark Matters: On the Surveillance of Blackness* (2015), Chad Luck's *The Body of Property: Antebellum American Fiction and the Body of Property* (2015), Martha Schoolman's *Abolitionist Geographies* (2014), Hoang G. Phan's *Bonds of Citizenship: Law and the Labors of Emancipation* (2013), Caleb Smith's *The Oracle and the Curse: A Poetics of Justice From the Revolution to the Civil War* (2013), Ivy G. Wilson's *Specters of Democracy: Blackness and the Aesthetic of Politics in the Antebellum U.S.* (2011), and Daphne A. Brook's *Bodies in Dissent: Spectacular Performances of Race and Freedom, 1850–1910* (2006). For criticism on aspects of nineteenth-century liberal society, see Peter Coviello's *Tomorrow's Parties: Sex and the Untimely in Nineteenth-Century America* (2013), Dana Luciano's *Arranging Grief: Sacred Time and the Body in Nineteenth-Century America* (2007), Russ Castronovo's *Beautiful Democracy: Aesthetics and Anarchy in a Global Age* (2007), and Elizabeth Maddock Dillon's *The Gender of Freedom: Fictions of Liberalism and the Literary Public Sphere* (2004).

114. Edward Said, *Humanism and Democratic Criticism* (New York: Columbia University Press, 2004), 2, 10.

115. Wolfe, *What Is Posthumanism?*, 99.

116. Thoreau, *Walden*, 333.

1. EMERSON'S OPERATIVE MOOD

1. See the February 6, 1849 *New-York Daily Tribune* issue. F.O. Matthiessen, *American Renaissance: Art and Expression in the Age of Emerson and Whitman* (New York: Oxford University Press, 1968), 3.

2. Qtd. in Larry J. Reynolds, *Righteous Violence: Revolution, Slavery, and The American Renaissance* (Athens: University of Georgia Press, 2011), 46.

3. Branka Arsić and Cary Wolfe, Introduction to *The Other Emerson* (Minneapolis: University of Minnesota Press, 2010), ix.

4. Scholars who, to various degrees, portray a definitive political turn in Emerson's thought abound. See, for instance, Len Gougeon's *Virtue's Hero* (1990), Michael Ziser's "Emersonian Terrorism: John Brown, Islam, and Postsecular Violence" (2010), Donald Pease's "'Experience,' Antislavery, and

the Crisis of Emersonianism" (2010), and Larry Reynolds's *Righteous Violence* (2011). For studies that link Emerson's later radicalism to his early works, see especially Michael Lopez's "*The Conduct of Life*: Emerson's Anatomy of Power" (1999) and Martha Schoolman's "Emerson's Doctrine of Hatred" (2007).

5. This prevalent view of discontinuity in Emerson's thought often follows Len Gougeon's formula where Emerson shifted from "silent years" of philosophical rumination to abolitionist activism in August 1844 (*Virtue's Hero: Emerson, Antislavery, and Reform* [Athens: University of Georgia Press, 1990], 41).

6. My concept of an "operative mood" is based loosely on Alain Badiou's assertion that "a subject is an operative disposition of the traces of the event and of what they deploy in the world" (*Logics of Worlds: Being and Event II*, trans. Alberto Toscano [New York: Continuum, 2009], 33). Ralph Waldo Emerson, "The Over-Soul," in *The Collected Works of Ralph Waldo Emerson*, vol. 2, ed. Joseph Slater, Alfred R. Ferguson, and Jean Ferguson Carr (Cambridge: Belknap/Harvard University Press, 1980), 164.

7. Branka Arsić, "Brain Walks: Emerson on Thinking" in *The Other Emerson* (Minneapolis: University of Minnesota Press, 2010), 60, 64. See also Arsić's *On Leaving: A Reading in Emerson* (2010).

8. Arsić, "Brain Walks," 59–60. In her analysis of the constructive impersonality of moods, Arsić departs from the portrayal of moods in Sharon Cameron's "The Way of Life by Abandonment: Emerson's Impersonal" (1998) and Russell Goodman's *American Philosophy and the Romantic Tradition* (1990). Arsić's broader project attends to the productive nuances in Cameron's rich work on the topic of impersonality. In her more recent collection *American Impersonal: Essays with Sharon Cameron* (2014), Arsić gathers a number of essays that seek to, as the title suggests, work with the critical perspectives Cameron has offered. Within this collection, see especially essays by Paul Grimstad and Johannes Voelz, which begin to offer innovative approaches for furthering and tweaking Cameron's original reading of Emerson. Although I will discuss briefly Cameron's arguments, suffice it to say that while I am indebted to the line of thinking that continues to follow her rhetorical and critical lead, my chapter breaks indirectly with the ideological assumptions about personhood found within Cameron's model.

9. Christopher Newfield, *The Emerson Effect: Individualism and Submission in America* (Chicago: University of Chicago Press, 1996), 2.

10. Johannes Voelz, *Transcendental Resistance: The New Americanists and Emerson's Challenge* (Hanover, N.H.: Dartmouth College Press, 2010), 4.

11. Kerry Larson, "Illiberal Emerson," *Nineteenth Century Prose* 33, no. 1 (Spring 2006): 67, 62.

12. Ralph Waldo Emerson, "Courage," in *The Collected Works of Ralph Waldo Emerson*, vol. 7, *Society and Solitude*, ed. Ronald A. Bosco and Douglas Emory Wilson (Cambridge: Belknap/Harvard University Press, 2007), 140.

13. Qtd. in Reynolds, *Righteous Violence*, 80.

14. Ralph Waldo Emerson, *The Journals and Miscellaneous Notebooks of Ralph Waldo Emerson*, vol. 4, ed. Alfred R. Ferguson (Cambridge: Harvard University Press, 1964), 27.

15. I reference "theoretical knowledge" in the sprit of Jacques Lacan's concept of the "university discourse." According to Lacan, in the modern world the classical social arrangement found in the master-slave dialectic shifts, producing "a modification in the place of knowledge" (Jacques Lacan, *The Seminar of Jacques Lacan, Book XVII: The Other Side of Psychoanalysis*, ed. Jacques-Alain Miller, trans. Russell Grigg [New York: Norton, 2007], 31). In this new alignment, institutional knowledge is in the position of agency.

16. Mary Kupiec Cayton, *Emerson's Emergence: Self and Society in the Transformation of New England, 1800–1845* (Chapel Hill: University of North Carolina Press, 1989), 114–15. For more on Unitarianism's institutional contexts, see especially Philip F. Gura's *American Transcendentalism: A History* (2007) and Richard A. Grusin's *Transcendental Hermeneutics: Institutional Authority and the Higher Criticism of the Bible* (1991).

17. Barbara L. Packer, *The Transcendentalists* (Athens: University of Georgia Press, 2007), 14.

18. Packer, *Transcendentalists*, 11.

19. Ralph Waldo Emerson, "To the Proprietors of the Second Church," September 11, 1832, in *The Letters of Ralph Waldo Emerson*, vol. 2, ed. Ralph L. Lusk (New York: Columbia University Press, 1939), 357.

20. Emerson, "To the Proprietors of the Second Church," 24, 27.

21. Ralph Waldo Emerson, "The Divinity School Address," in *The Collected Works of Ralph Waldo Emerson*, vol. 1, ed. Alfred R. Ferguson (Cambridge: Belknap/Harvard University Press, 1971), 77, 79. Subsequent page references will appear parenthetically in the text.

22. Wesley T. Mott, "'The Power of Recurring to the Sublime at Pleasure': Emerson and Feeling," in *Emerson Bicentennial* Essays, ed. Joel Myerson and Ronald Bosco (Boston: Massachusetts Historical Society, 2006), 379.

23. Ralph Waldo Emerson, "Religion," in *The Early Lectures of Ralph Waldo Emerson*, vol. 2, ed. Stephen E. Whicher, Robert E. Spiller, and Wallace E. Williams (Cambridge: Harvard University Press, 1964), 83. Subsequent page references will appear parenthetically in the text.

24. Ralph Waldo Emerson, "Compensation," in *Collected Works of Ralph Waldo Emerson*, vol. 2, ed. Joseph Slater, Alfred R. Ferguson, and Jean Ferguson Carr (Cambridge: Belknap/Harvard University Press, 1979), 60.

25. Ralph Waldo Emerson, *Nature*, in *The Collected Works of Ralph Waldo Emerson*, vol. 1, ed. Alfred R. Ferguson (Cambridge: Belknap/Harvard University Press, 1971), 45, 43. Subsequent page references will appear parenthetically in the text.

26. Ralph Waldo Emerson, *The Journals and Miscellaneous Notebooks of Ralph Waldo Emerson*, vol. 3, ed. William H. Gilman and Alfred R. Ferguson (Cambridge: Harvard University Press, 1963), 139.

27. Giorgio Agamben, *The Time that Remains: A Commentary on the Letter to the Romans*, trans. Patricia Dailey (Stanford: Stanford University Press, 2005), 25.

28. Stephen E. Whicher and Robert E. Spiller, Introduction to *The Early Lectures of Ralph Waldo Emerson*, vol. 2, ed. Stephen E. Whicher, Robert E. Spiller, and Wallace E. Williams (Cambridge: Harvard University Press, 1964), xiii–xxvii, quotation on xx. See especially Johannes Voelz's *Transcendental Resistance* for a consideration of how the lyceum system shaped Emerson's rhetoric.

29. Laura Dassow Walls, *Emerson's Life in Science: The Culture of Truth* (Ithaca, N.Y.: Cornell University Press, 2003), 15.

30. Laura Dassow Walls, "The Anatomy of Truth: Emerson's Poetic Science," *Configurations* 5, no. 3 (1997): 425–61, quotation on 423.

31. For a traditional view on how Romanticism was a defensive reaction to the rise of science, see Hans Eichner's "The Rise of Modern Science and the Genesis of Romanticism" *PMLA* 97, no. 1 (1982): 8–30. Alternately, Morse Peckham's "Toward a Theory of Romanticism" *PMLA* 66, no. 2 (1951): 5–23 identifies "organicism" as an originary element of all Romanticism. As mentioned, a bloom of studies has focused on tracing either science's influence on Romanticism or vice versa. In terms of the former, in addition to work by Lee Rust Brown and Laura Dassow Walls, see especially Mark Noble's "Emerson's Atom and the Matter of Suffering," *Nineteenth-Century Literature* 64, no. 1 (2009): 16–47; David M. Robinson's *Natural Life: Thoreau's Worldly Transcendentalism* (2004); and Elizabeth A. Dant's "Composing the World: Emerson and the Cabinet of Natural History," *Nineteenth-Century Literature* 44 (1989): 18–44. For the latter, see Noah Heringman's collection *Romantic Science: The Literary Forms of Natural History* (2003), Robert J. Richards's *The Romantic Conception of Life: Science and Philosophy in the Age of Goethe* (2002), and Trevor H. Levere's "Romanticism, Natural Philosophy, and the Sciences: A Review and Bibliographic Essay," *Perspectives on Science* 4, no. 4 (1996): 464–88.

32. In terms of Emerson's relation to Science, I am forwarding a view that falls more in line with Michael Lopez's contention that the "Emersonian universe is . . . a 'stupendous antagonism'" (*Emerson and Power*

[DeKalb: Northern Illinois University Press, 1996], 4) rather than with Laura Dassow Walls's argument that Emerson "successfully merged science with poetry and religion," albeit with a "precarious balance" ("The Anatomy of Truth," 425).

33. Ralph Waldo Emerson, "The Relation of Man to the Globe," in *The Early Lectures of Ralph Waldo Emerson*, vol. 1, ed. Stephen E. Whicher and Robert E. Spiller (Cambridge: Harvard University Press, 1959), 27–49, quotation on 28–29; subsequent page references will appear parenthetically in the text.

34. Ralph Waldo Emerson, "Humanity of Science," in *The Early Lectures of Ralph Waldo Emerson*, vol. 2, ed. Stephen E. Whicher, Robert E. Spiller, and Wallace E. Williams (Cambridge: Harvard University Press, 1964), 69–83, quotation on 25.

35. Jennifer J. Baker, "Natural Science and the Romantics," *ESQ* 53 (2007): 387–412, quotation on 389.

36. Ralph Waldo Emerson, "The Naturalist," in *The Early Lectures of Ralph Waldo Emerson*, vol. 1, ed. Stephen E. Whicher and Robert E. Spiller (Cambridge: Harvard University Press, 1959), 27–49, quotation on 76.

37. Emerson, *The Journals and Miscellaneous Notebooks*, vol. 4, 288.

38. Emerson, *The Journals and Miscellaneous Notebooks*, vol. 4, 200; Emerson, "The Uses of Natural History," in *The Early Lectures of Ralph Waldo Emerson*, vol. 1, ed. Stephen E. Whicher and Robert E. Spiller (Cambridge: Harvard University Press, 1959), 10. Subsequent page references will appear parenthetically in the text.

39. Samson Reed, *Observations on the Growth of the Mind* (Boston: Hilliard and Metcalf, 1826), 24.

40. Ralph Waldo Emerson, "Prospects," in *The Early Lectures of Ralph Waldo Emerson*, vol. 3, ed. Robert E. Spiller and Wallace E. Williams (Cambridge: Harvard University Press, 1972), 366–82, quotation on 381–82.

41. Lawrence Buell notes that Emerson was fascinated with the notion that "'ideas' or 'intellect' should be impersonal yet thoughts must be personal" (*Emerson* [Cambridge: Belknap/Harvard University Press, 2003], 228). Cary Wolfe illuminates this relation by considering Cavell's arguments about Emersonian perfectionism via Niklas Luhmann's work, suggesting that the Emersonian self should be seen to "move in 'abandonment' beyond the self" ("'The Eye Is the First Circle': Emerson's 'Romanticism,' Cavell's Skepticism, Luhmann's Modernity," in *The Other Emerson*, 294). Similarly, Branka Arsić portrays an Emersonian ontology where "impersonal thinking . . . constitutes the interiority of the 'I'" (*On Leaving: A Reading in Emerson* [Cambridge: Harvard University Press, 2010], 14, 134). In terms of political subjectivity, Donald E. Pease asserts that there is a link between an

Emersonian subjectivity marked by a "constitutive division" without recourse to "any unified identity" and the figure of the "anti-slave," a figure that exists "at the limit" of historical/personal "trauma and the order of Emersonian provocation" ("'Experience,' Antislavery, and the Crisis of Emersonianism," in *The Other Emerson*, 137, 163). As my chapter's final section will make clear, I am not only joining with scholars such as Cavell, Arsić, Wolfe, and Pease who view the impersonal as a positive constitutive aspect of the Emersonian self; I am also suggesting that these same critics sometimes overlook radical elements in Emerson's early work related to this division within the self.

42. Stanley Cavell, "Thinking of Emerson," in *Emerson's Transcendental Etudes*, ed. Mieke Bal and Hent de Vries (Stanford: Stanford University Press, 2003), 17.

43. Sharon Cameron, "The Way of Life by Abandonment: Emerson's Impersonal," in *Impersonality: Seven Essays* (Chicago: University of Chicago Press, 2007), 81, 102, 106–7. Earlier in her chapter, and elsewhere in her writings on Emerson, Cameron carefully traces the ways that Emerson's portrayal of the impersonal productively complicates and recalibrates traditional notions of the self. Along these lines, in her preface to *Impersonality: Seven Essays* (2007), Cameron suggests that personality and impersonality "do not stand in a binary relation." And her careful work in the essays collected reveals exquisite layers of how "[i]mpersonality disrupts elementary categories" (ix). As I suggest earlier, however, Cameron's innovative work on Emerson tends to reinscribe standard liberal parameters of the self when it evaluates the social implications of Emerson's thought. Instead of approaching the precarious Emersonian self via the "moment of its disintegration," a postulate that clearly grounds the self within assumed parameters of a fully formed western subject, I offer an alternate take on his conception of personhood. In so doing, I present a drastically divergent ethical and political Emersonian landscape (*Impersonality*, viii).

44. Christopher Newfield, *The Emerson Effect*, 5.

45. Ralph Waldo Emerson, "Love," in *The Collected Works of Ralph Waldo Emerson*, vol. 2, ed. Joseph Slater, Alfred R. Ferguson, and Jean Ferguson Carr (Cambridge: Belknap/Harvard University Press, 1979), 99.

46. Germaine de Staël, "The Influence of the Passions on the Happiness of Individuals and Nations," in *Major Writings of Germaine de Staël*, trans. Vivian Folkenflik (New York: Columbia University Press, 1987), 153. It should be noted that at the close of *Germany* (1813), de Staël embraces the type of religious enjoyment that Emerson promotes.

47. These relations are apparent in Emerson's 1839 lecture "Comedy," where he claims, "it is in comparing fractions with essential integers or

wholes, that laughter begins" (*The Early Lectures of Ralph Waldo Emerson*, vol. 3, ed. Robert E. Spiller and Wallace E. Williams [Cambridge: Harvard University Press, 1972], 366–82, quotation on 121–22).

48. Qtd. in Joel Porte, *Consciousness and Culture: Emerson and Thoreau Reviewed* (New Haven: Yale University Press, 2004), xi.

49. Ralph Waldo Emerson, "Spiritual Laws," in *The Collected Works of Ralph Waldo Emerson*, vol. 2, ed. Alfred R. Ferguson, Joseph Slater, and Douglas Emory Wilson (Cambridge: Harvard University Press, 1979), 81.

50. Stanley Cavell, *Conditions Handsome and Unhandsome: The Construction of Emersonian Perfectionism* (La Salle: Open Court, 1990), 3.

51. Cavell, *Conditions Handsome and Unhandsome*, 12.

52. Stanley Cavell, "What Is the Emersonian Event? A Comment on Kateb's Emerson," in *Emerson's Transcendental Etudes*, ed. Mieke Bal and Hent de Vries (Stanford: Stanford University Press, 2003), 189.

53. Cavell, "What Is the Emersonian Event?," 184, 188–89.

54. Emerson, "Courage," 140. As noted, Emerson's essay "Courage" is based on a lecture he delivered in November 1859. As Ronald A. Bosco points out, however, Edward Waldo Emerson's editorial commentary references how this later essay "underwent many changes" (qtd. in "Courage," 250n7).

55. Michael Ziser, "Emersonian Terrorism: John Brown, Islam, and Postsecular Violence," *American Literature* 82, no. 2 (June 2010): 337.

56. Ralph Waldo Emerson, *The Journals and Miscellaneous Notebooks of Ralph Waldo Emerson*, vol. 7, ed. A. W. Plumstead and Harrison Hayford (Cambridge: Harvard University Press, 1969), 25. In this context, Emerson's line from an 1839 lecture, "I am to fire what skill I can the artillery of sympathy & emotion," becomes prophetic (*JMN* 7:270).

57. Emerson, "Courage," 138.

58. Larry Reynolds argues that Emerson's turn to activism in the 1850s "ran counter to his peace principles" (*Righteous Violence*, 56). Furthermore, he suggests that Emerson's early work promoted "peaceful means to achieve social justice" and elided or omitted direct commentary on specific acts of violence (57–58). While historically accurate, Reynolds's overview may overlook the way Emerson's early thought, such as his formulations of religious sentiment, directly links to potential modes of active political agency and resulting violence.

59. Qtd. in Reynolds, *Righteous Violence*, 62.

60. Ralph Waldo Emerson, "Fate," in *The Collected Works of Ralph Waldo Emerson*, vol. 6, ed. Douglas Emory Wilson, Joseph Slater, et al. (Cambridge: Belknap/Harvard University Press, 2003), 16. Subsequent page references will appear parenthetically in the text.

61. Ralph Waldo Emerson, "Politics," in *The Early Lectures of Ralph Waldo Emerson*, vol. 3, ed. Robert E. Spiller and Wallace E. Williams (Cambridge: Harvard University Press, 1972), 238–47, quotation on 240. Subsequent page references will appear parenthetically in the text.

62. Orestes Brownson, "Mr. Emerson's Address. An address delivered before the Senior Class in Divinity College, Cambridge, Sunday Evening, 15 July, 1838," *The Boston Quarterly Review*, vol. 1 (Boston: 1838), 507.

63. Ralph Waldo Emerson, "Napoleon, or the Man of the World," in *The Collected Works of Ralph Waldo Emerson*, vol. 4, ed. Joseph Slater, Douglas Emory Wilson, and Wallace E. Williams (Cambridge: Belknap/Harvard University Press, 1987), 131.

64. Emerson, "Napoleon," 130, 148.

65. Ralph Waldo Emerson, "Demonology," in *The Early Lectures of Ralph Waldo Emerson*, vol. 3, ed. Robert E. Spiller and Wallace E. Williams (Cambridge: Harvard University Press, 1972), 151–71, quotation on 156.

66. Ralph Waldo Emerson, "Introductory Lecture," in *The Collected Works of Ralph Waldo Emerson: Nature, Addresses, and Lectures*, ed. Robert Spiller, et al. (Cambridge: Harvard University Press, 1971), 178.

67. Ralph Waldo Emerson, "Duty," in *The Early Lectures of Ralph Waldo Emerson*, vol. 3, ed. Robert E. Spiller and Wallace E. Williams (Cambridge: Harvard University Press, 1972), 138–50, quotation on 139. Subsequent page references will appear parenthetically in the text.

68. Qtd. in Allison Giffen, "'Let no man know': Negotiating the Gendered Discourse of Affliction in Anne Bradstreet's 'Here Follows Some Verses Upon the Burning of Our House, July 10th, 1666,'" *Legacy* 27, no. 1 (2010): 6.

69. According to Robert D. Richardson Jr., Emerson was familiar with Kant, reading F. A. Nitsch's *A general and introductory view of Professor Kant's principles* (1796) (*Emerson: The Mind On Fire* [Berkeley: University of California Press, 1995], 121).

70. Immanuel Kant, *The Conflict of the Faculties*, trans. M. J. Gregor (New York: Abaris Books, 1979), 153.

71. Slavoj Žižek, *In Defense of Lost Causes* (New York: Verso, 2008), 225.

72. Slavoj Žižek, "Robespierre, or, the 'Divine Violence' of Terror," in *Virtue and Terror*, trans. John Howe (New York: Verso, 2007), xxvi.

73. Alenka Zupančič, *Ethics of the Real: Kant and Lacan* (New York: Verso, 2000), 28.

74. Immanuel Kant, *Critique of Practical Reason*, qtd. in Zupančič, *Ethics of the Real*, 19.

75. Immanuel Kant, *Critique of Practical Reason*, qtd. in Slavoj Žižek, *The Parallax View* (Cambridge: MIT Press, 2006), 22.

76. For obvious historical reasons, readings of Emerson as an exponent of liberal-democracy and its values abound. Neal Dolan's *Emerson's Liberalism* (Madison: University of Wisconsin Press, 2009) is perhaps the most apt recent example of this ideological presentation of Emerson. As his title suggests, Dolan posits unabashedly that "Emerson was a liberal" (5), casting Emerson's thought in a rather predictable space of post-feudal openness: "transmitting countertraditional liberal values without creating another . . . repressive tradition" (4–5). It might not be surprising that, in order to sustain this perspective, Dolan relies on Emerson's concept of "moral law" and "moral sentiment" (14–15). Privileging these terms allows him to read "Fate" as an example of "moderate, gradualist, and generous-spirited historical optimism" (286). My focus on Emerson's foundational and hybrid concept of religious sentiment thus runs directly counter to Dolan's narrative. In addition, my reading of Emerson departs from Larry Reynolds's aforementioned *Righteous Violence: Revolution, Slavery, and The American Renaissance*, where Emerson's embrace of radical abolitionism is considered a case of bloodlust. It also diverges significantly from George Kateb's assertion that there is a "sharp distinction between mental self-reliance and active self-reliance" (*Emerson and Self-Reliance* [Oxford: Rowman and Littlefield, 2002], 17). Moreover, it differs from Christopher Newfield's thesis that the Emersonian political subject evinces a "corporate individualism" marked by "submission" to "decentralized, diffused, and multidirectional modes of power" (*Emerson Effect*, 2, 5).

77. Ziser, "Emersonian Terrorism," 336, 334.
78. Pease, "'Experience,' Antislavery, and the Crisis of Emersonianism," 150.
79. Pease, "'Experience,'" 156–57.
80. Pease, "'Experience,'" 162.
81. Pease, "'Experience,'" 163.
82. See Russ Castronovo's *Nerco Citizenship: Death, Eroticism, and the Public Sphere in the Nineteenth-Century United States* (Durham, N.C.: Duke University Press, 2007), particularly Chapter 1, "Political Necrophilia: Freedom and the Longing for Dead Citizenship." My reading clearly differs from Castronovo's contention that Emerson largely promotes a broader conservative move to make "freedom the property of a disembodied and historically impoverished subject" (27). It should be noted that Castronovo later rescues Emerson, in a sense, suggesting that his poem "On Freedom" "breaks with a theory of freedom, and instead offers a strategy responsive to context, emerging from passions of the local and momentary" (51). Gregg Crane offers an alternate take on Emerson's political ethics that is more optimistic about the democratic efficacy of abstractions, where "[r]ejecting the determinisms of race and history but being a creature formed of race

and history, Emerson turns to abstraction for a vision of justice that does not simply reiterate prior articulations." This overtly liberal reading of Emerson's relation to the law clearly seeks to toe the mainstream line regarding the value supposedly imbued within federal documents such as the constitution. Crane goes on to write: "Severing justice from identity enacts human agency in such a way as to leave future generations a tangible legacy—the example of change. Indeed, the Constitution creates the possibility of change through the abstractness of its language" (*Race, Citizenship, and Law in American Literature* [Cambridge: Cambridge University Press, 2002], 99–100).

83. Pease, "'Experience,'" 156.

84. Rei Terada, *Feeling in Theory: Emotion After the Death of the Subject* (Cambridge: Harvard University Press, 2003), 4.

85. I borrow the term "disjunctive synthesis" from Alain Badiou's *Logics of Worlds*, 32.

2. AGITATING MARGARET FULLER

1. Margaret Fuller, undated manuscript of "Fuller's Western Journal. A trip to Niagara Falls," Margaret Fuller family papers, 1662–1970, Houghton Library, Harvard University.

2. Margaret Fuller, *Summer on the Lakes, in 1843* (Urbana: University of Illinois Press, 1991), 4. In the earlier journal entry, Fuller hints that she, herself, might be the victim of the imagined attack, writing, "It eventually seemed as if some evil being had stolen behind me, as I sat talking. I would start and turn around. The figures of Indians came continually before my fancy stealing upon a foe with uplifted tomahawk" (HL, Box 1). But the closing line includes an ambiguous reference to this foe. Although it is possible that she is the foe in question, the surrounding syntax suggests that that Indians are, perhaps, attacking an imagined third party.

3. To cite just one example, at the close of Lydia Maria Child's 1843 *National Anti-Slavery Standard* column, "The Indians," she describes her unease while watching a visiting contingent of "Sacs, Fox, and Iowas" leaders perform a war dance. After spending pages censuring biological racial essentialism and lamenting the country's crimes against Indians, Child describes the "terrific" dance and her inclination to look "to the door" of P. T. Barnum's lecture hall "to see if escape were easy, in case they really worked themselves up to the scalping point" (*Letters From New-York* [London: 1843], 278, 287).

4. In an April 20, 1836 letter to Sam Ward, Fuller describes a scene that is similar to the one at Niagara. Here, however, the energy of the moving water tempts *her* to act violently (via suicide). Fuller writes, "This morning I

felt a sort of timidity about standing quite at that point to which the undulating motions . . . seemed to tend. I felt that, unless I had an arm of flesh and blood to cling to, I should be too much seduced from humanity" (*The Letters of Margaret Fuller*, vol. 1, ed. Robert N. Hudspeth [Ithaca, N.Y.: Cornell University Press, 1983], 249). This theme also occurs in her translation of Bettina von Arnim's novel *Die Günderode*, where Günderode commits suicide along the Rhine.

5. Margaret Fuller, *The Letters of Margaret Fuller*, vol. 5, ed. Robert N. Hudspeth (Ithaca, N.Y.: Cornell University Press, 1988), 295.

6. Margaret Fuller, "Bombardment and Defeat," Dispatch 34, in *"These Sad But Glorious Days": Dispatches from Europe, 1846–1850*, ed. Larry Reynolds and Susan Belasco Smith (New Haven: Yale University Press, 1991), 308–9.

7. Margaret Fuller, "New and Old World Democracy," Dispatch 18, in *"These Sad But Glorious Days": Dispatches from Europe*, 166.

8. Margaret Fuller, "The Next Revolution," in *"These Sad But Glorious Days*,*"* 321.

9. Fuller, "New and Old World Democracy," 165.

10. Fuller, "The Next Revolution," 323.

11. Qtd. in John Carlos Rowe, *The New American Studies* (Minneapolis: University of Minnesota Press, 2002), 84.

12. See Larry Reynolds's *Righteous Violence: Revolution, Slavery, and the American Renaissance* (Athens: University of Georgia Press, 2011), where he claims that Fuller "transformed" and "had a change of heart" while in Europe in the late 1840s (40–41). Other scholars have noted earlier transformations in Fuller's thought. For example, in Jeffrey Steele's *Transfiguring America: Myth, Mythology, and Mourning in Margaret Fuller's Writing* (Columbia: University of Missouri Press, 2001), he suggests that in 1840 Fuller noted a "radical realignment of her being," resulting in the composition of a series of "mystical essays" in October and November (71).

13. Reynolds goes as far as to suggest that "Fuller's example" of revolutionary fervor in the 1840s "may have indirectly" led to the Civil War and, more broadly, that her "support of political violence in Europe prefigured a major change in antislavery thinking in the United States" (*Righteous Violence*, 39).

14. As Fuller notes in a letter from her 1846 departure for Europe, she saw herself acting in the capacity of a journalist now: "But it must be in the capacity of a journalist, and for that I need this new field of observation" (qtd. in Paula Blanchard, *Margaret Fuller: From Transcendentalism to Revolution* [New York: Delacorte Press/Seymour Lawrence, 1978], 244).

15. For example, Mickiewicz wrote to Fuller after their first encounter in 1846, urging her to become more politically engaged: "You have pleaded the

liberty of woman in a masculine and frank style. Live and act, as you write" (qtd. in Blanchard, *Margaret Fuller*, 263).

16. Even amid Fuller's revolutionary fervor, she laments the physical destruction of Roman architecture and art. Writing to Emerson in June 1849, she praises the "heroic spirit that animates" the revolutionaries and notes the "pleasure" she received from her daily visits to the rebels' hospitals. Yet, she describes remorsefully the way the war was destroying Rome (its "sacred beauty" "that seemed the possession of the world forever"): "O, Rome, *my* country! could I imagine that the triumph of what I held dear was to heap such desolation on thy head" (Fuller, *The Letters of Margaret Fuller*, vol. 5, 239–40).

17. Fuller, *The Letters of Margaret Fuller*, vol. 5, 146–47.

18. Fuller, *The Letters of Margaret Fuller*, vol. 5, 58–59. Fuller's idealization of political action can be seen in her February 16, 1850 letter to Arthur Hugh Clough, where she laments that the citizens of Florence do not share the courage of those in Rome: "I care least for these cowed and coward Florentines; they are getting only what they deserve" (*The Letters of Margaret Fuller*, vol. 6., ed. Robert N. Hudspeth [Ithaca, N.Y.: Cornell University Press: 1994], 64).

19. Fuller, "New and Old World Democracy," 164.

20. Fuller, *The Letters of Margaret Fuller*, vol. 5, 294–95.

21. Margaret Fuller, "The Springtime Revolutions of '48," Dispatch 23, in "*These Sad But Glorious Days*," 211.

22. Steele argues, "Although Zwarg's analysis has the great merit of highlighting the intellectual mobility of Fuller's mature political writings, it does not sufficiently theorize the ways in which her critique of existing social structures also stabilized new pathways of political action" (*Transfiguring America*, 229–30).

23. Steele, *Transfiguring America*, ix.

24. Steele, *Transfiguring America*, 21.

25. Steele, *Transfiguring America*, 21.

26. For contemporary critiques of liberal multiculturalism, see especially Jodi Melamed's *Represent and Destroy: Rationalizing Violence in the New Racial Capitalism* (2011) and Jared Sexton's *Amalgamation Schemes: Antiblackness and the Critique of Multiculturalism* (2008).

27. Wai Chee Dimock, *Through Other Continents: American Literature Across Deep Time* (Princeton: Princeton University Press, 2006), 52–53. Dimock's "planetary" horizon thus productively pushes the conceptual bounds of the transnational paradigms that have dominated contemporary Americanist discourses. For useful examples of the latter that consider Fuller, see especially William Stowe's "Transatlantic Subjects" *American*

Literary History 22, no. 1 (Spring 2010): 159–70, and Charles Capper and Cristina Giorcelli's (eds.) *Margaret Fuller: Transatlantic Crossings in a Revolutionary Age* (Madison: University of Wisconsin Press, 2007).

28. Dimock, *Through Other Continents*, 64.
29. Dimock, *Through Other Continents*, 66.
30. Dimock, *Through Other Continents*, 68.
31. Dimock, *Through Other Continents*, 69.
32. Karl Marx, *The Eighteenth Brumaire of Louis Bonaparte*, in *The Marx-Engels Reader*, second edition, ed. Robert C. Tucker (New York: Norton, 1978), 595.
33. Marx, *The Eighteenth Brumaire*, 596.
34. Marx, *The Eighteenth Brumaire*, 597.
35. Theodor Adorno and Max Horkheimer, *Dialectic of Enlightenment: Philosophical Fragments*, ed. Gunzelin Schmid Noerr, trans. Edmund Jephcott (Stanford: Stanford University Press, 2002), xvii.
36. Karl Marx, Letter to Arnold Ruge, September 1843, in *German Socialist Philosophy: Ludwig Feuerbach, Karl Marx, and Friedrich Engels*, ed. Wolfgang Schirmacher (New York: The Continuum Publishing Company, 1997), 87–89.
37. In this sense, it seems Dimock supports a reading of Marx that would be consonant with Jacques Derrida's arguments in *Specters of Marx: The State of the Debt, the Work of Mourning, and the New International* (2006). But Dimock does not explicitly or fully articulate the type of ethics of responsibility toward the past that Derrida had in mind—where the past calls for a different future even if the present is unable to immediately or effectively implement it.
38. Fuller, "The Next Revolution," 323.
39. Ralph Waldo Emerson, "Visits to Concord," in *Memoirs of Margaret Fuller Ossoli*, vol. 1 (London: 1852), 295.
40. Margaret Fuller, *Woman in the Nineteenth Century*, in *The Essential Margaret Fuller*, ed. Jeffrey Steele (New Brunswick: Rutgers University Press, 1995), 350–51. Subsequent page references will appear parenthetically in the text.
41. See especially Jeffrey Steele's *Transfiguring America* (2001), Annette Kolodny's "Inventing a Feminist Discourse: Rhetoric and Resistance in Margaret Fuller's *Woman in the Nineteenth Century*" (1994), and Robert D. Richardson Jr.'s "Margaret Fuller and Myth" (1979).
42. Margaret Fuller, "Sistrum," in *The Essential Margaret Fuller*, 235.
43. Margaret Fuller, Untitled poem, in *The Essential Margaret Fuller*, 233.
44. Margaret Fuller, "A Dream," in *The Essential Margaret Fuller*, 6.
45. Fuller, "A Dream," 6.

46. Fuller, "Self-Definitions," 9.
47. Fuller, Untitled poem, in *The Essential Margaret Fuller*, 233.
48. Margaret Fuller, undated manuscript. Margaret Fuller family papers, 1662–1970, Houghton Library, Harvard University.
49. Qtd in Timothy Morton, *Hyperobjects: Philosophy and Ecology After the End of the World* (Minneapolis: University of Minnesota Press, 2013), 30.
50. Elizabeth Eva Leach, "Gendering the Semitone, Sexing the Leading Tone: Fourteenth-Century Music Theory and the Directed Progression," *Music Theory Spectrum* 28, no. 1 (Spring 2006): 1–2. Timothy Morton's discussion of sixth-century musical anxiety pushes concerns of materiality even further, revealing their sociopolitical subtexts. As Morton explains, in this era, Pope Gregory banned the augmented fourth chord, the infamous *diabolus in musica* (the devil in music). This chord, known as the tritone (*tritonus*), is composed of an interval of three entire tones, which essentially divides the octave in half. Consequently, the chord produces a troubling dissonance because it can act as its own inversion, where "the sound itself may function in two different ways that depend on context" (qtd. in *The Harvard Dictionary of Music*, ed. Don Michael Randel [Cambridge: Harvard University Press, 2003], 911). According to Morton, Gregory banned the chord in part because "it allows the ear to access a vast range of harmonics, a range that evokes a hugely expanded sense of what in musical language is called timbre: the material that generates sound." Thus, in Morton's view, the chord engenders a troubling and "profound range of materiality" (*Hyperobjects*, 169).
51. Margaret Fuller, untitled manuscript from journal dated 1833. Margaret Fuller family papers, 1662–1970, Houghton Library, Harvard University.
52. Slavoj Žižek, *The Parallax View* (Cambridge: MIT Press, 2006), 229.
53. Žižek, *The Parallax View*, 229. Žižek goes on to qualify this claim by suggesting that music itself often *"lies in a fundamental way as to its own status"* (230). Using a reading of Wagner's *Tristan*, he notes the complex way it negotiates meaning and feeling—not simply or directly delivering the goods of metaphysical or narrative "truth." In his subsequent *In Defense of Lost Causes* (New York: Verso, 2008), he historicizes this, writing: "[I]f Mozart was *the* supreme musical genius, perhaps the last composer with whom the musical Thing transposed itself into musical notes in a spontaneous flow, and if in Beethoven, a piece only achieved in its definitive form after a long heroic struggle with the musical material, Prokofiev's greatest pieces are monuments to the defeat of this struggle" (238).
54. Žižek, *The Parallax View*, 230.
55. Sigmund Freud, *Beyond the Pleasure Principle*, ed. James Strachey, trans. James Strachey (New York: Norton, 1989), 46–47, 61. In the book,

Freud describes the path that led him to speculations about the death drive, writing, "In the first instance the analysis of the transference neuroses forced upon our notice the opposition between the 'sexual instincts,' which are directed towards and object, and certain other instincts, which we were very insufficiently acquainted and which we described provisionally as the 'ego-instincts'" (61).

56. Lee Edelman, *No Future: Queer Theory and the Death Drive* (Durham, N.C.: Duke University Press, 2004), 22.

57. Todd McGowan, *The Real Gaze: Film Theory After Lacan* (New York: SUNY Press, 2008), 222. It is in this context that Edelman writes, "The structural mandate of the drive, therefore, could be seen to call forth its object or end, indeed, the whole register of sexuality itself, as a displacement of its own formal energies" (*No Future*, 22–23).

58. Emerson, "Visits to Concord," 310.

59. Žižek, *In Defense of Lost Causes*, 238.

60. Fuller, *Memoirs of Margaret Fuller Ossoli*, vol. 1, 301–2.

61. Margaret Fuller, undated manuscript titled "Extract made by Taylor from Plutarch's Isis and Osiris with regard to the Sistrum," Margaret Fuller family papers, 1662–1970, Houghton Library, Harvard University.

62. Edelman, *No Future*, 9.

63. Todd McGowan, *The Impossible David Lynch* (New York: Columbia University Press, 2007), 146.

64. McGowan, *The Impossible David Lynch*, 146.

65. Fuller, *Memoirs of Margaret Fuller Ossoli*, vol. 1, 302–3.

66. Fuller, *Memoirs of Margaret Fuller Ossoli*, vol. 1, 303.

67. Fuller, *Memoirs of Margaret Fuller Ossoli*, vol. 1, 308.

68. Fuller, *Summer on the Lakes*, 82.

69. Fuller, *Summer on the Lakes*, 91.

70. I use this phrase in the spirit of Jacques Derrida's claim in *Specters of Marx* that deconstruction is something of a "structural messianism, a messianism without religion, even a messianic without messianism" (New York: Routledge, 1994), 74. John D. Caputo puts this in his own terms: "To pray is not only to say 'Yes, Yes' and 'Come' to justice but it is also to open one's mouth and say 'Yes.' To pray is to open one's mouth and say 'Come.' Let the Other come. Let something Other, something In-Coming, come" (qtd. in James Olthuis, *Religions With/Out Religion: The Prayers and Tears of John D. Caputo* [New York: Routledge, 2012], 298).

71. Fuller, *Memoirs of Margaret Fuller Ossoli*, vol. 1, 178.

72. Qtd. in John Matteson, *The Lives of Margaret Fuller* (New York: Norton, 2012), 143.

73. Fuller, *Memoirs of Margaret Fuller Ossoli*, vol. 1, 164.

74. As I will show in the last section of this chapter, this meantime is quite distinct from the notion messianic time, or the "time that remains." For more on the latter, see especially Giorgio Agamben, *The Time that Remains: A Commentary on the Letter to the Romans* (2005).

75. Elizabeth Freeman, *Time Binds: Queer Temporalities, Queer Histories* (Durham, N.C.: Duke University Press, 2010), 13–14.

76. William Wordsworth, *The Prelude*, in *Selected Poems*, ed. Stephen Gill (New York: Penguin, 2004), 258–59.

77. Margaret Fuller, "Review of Anton Schindler, *The Life of Beethoven*," in *Margaret Fuller, Critic: Writings from the New-York Tribune, 1844–1846*, ed. Judith Mattson Bean and Joel Myerson (New York: Columbia University Press, 2000), 72–73.

78. Fuller, "Review of Anton Schindler," 71–72.

79. Qtd. in Laura Saltz, "The Magnetism of a Photograph: Daguerreotype and Margaret Fuller's Conceptions of Gender and Sexuality," *ESQ* 56, no. 2 (2010): 112.

80. Adam Crabtree, *From Mesmer to Freud: Magnetic Sleep and the Roots of Psychoanalytic Healing* (New Haven: Yale University Press, 1993), 5.

81. Deborah Manson, "'The Trance of the Ecstasia': Margaret Fuller, Animal Magnetism, and the Transcendent Female Body," *Literature and Medicine* 25, no. 2 (Fall 2006): 298–99.

82. Ora Frishberg Saloman, *Listening Well: On Beethoven, Berlioz, and Other Music Criticism in Paris, Boston, and New York, 1764–1890* (New York: Peter Lang, 2009), 127. I am also indebted to Saloman's work for its comprehensive review of Fuller's encounters with the music in the 1830s and 1840s.

83. Justine S. Murison, *The Politics of Anxiety in Nineteenth-Century American Literature* (New York: Cambridge University Press, 2011), 82–83. As Murison points out, the discourse of the electrical body made its way into the halls of Congress when, in 1850, at the request of Henry Clay and Daniel Webster, John Bovee Dods offered a lecture on "electrical psychology" (83).

84. Gilles Deleuze and Félix Guattari, *A Thousand Plateaus: Capitalism and Schizophrenia*, trans. Brian Massumi (New York: Continuum, 2004), 27.

85. Murison, *The Politics of Anxiety*, 2–4, 77.

86. Qtd. in Murison, *The Politics of Anxiety*, 84. In addition to medical rhetoric proper, Fuller's thought on electricity indirectly takes up various period notions of scientific vitalism. See Monique Allewaert's *Ariel's Ecology: Plantations, Personhood, and Colonialism in the American Tropics*, especially 52–63, for a review of this historical trend.

87. See, for example, Fuller's 1845 *Tribune* review of *Etherology; or, The Philosophy of Mesmerism and Phrenology* or her 1846 review of *Animal Magnetism; or, Psychodunamy*.

88. Margaret Fuller, "Autobiographical Romance," in *The Essential Margaret Fuller*, 24, 31.

89. Margaret Fuller, undated manuscript of "Unlabeled Journal." Margaret Fuller family papers, 1662–1970, Houghton Library, Harvard University.

90. John Keats, "To George and Georgiana Keats, 14 February–3 May 1819," in *John Keats: Selected Letters*, ed. Robert Gittings (New York: Oxford University Press, 2002), 232–33.

91. When Fuller briefly mentions Frederica Hauffe in *Woman in the Nineteenth Century*, she is far less subtle about the cause of her ailments, claiming that Hauffe was "jarred into disease by an unsuitable marriage" (304).

92. Steele, *Transfiguring America*, 21.

93. C. Michael Hurst, "Bodies in Transition: Transcendental Feminism in Margaret Fuller's *Woman in the Nineteenth Century*," *Arizona Quarterly* 66, no. 4 (Winter 2010), 26. Of course, Mesmer held that "the harmonious flow of animal magnetism in the body produces health, and the disharmonious flow its opposite," and this belief had broader, although vague, social implications, evidenced by Mesmer's establishment of the "society of Harmony" (*The Occult in Nineteenth-Century America*, ed. Cathy Gutierrez [Aurora, Co.: The Davies Group, 2005], 89).

94. James Delbourgo, *A Most Amazing Scene of Wonders: Electricity and Enlightenment in Early America* (Cambridge: Harvard University Press, 2006), 200. For the social implications of mesmeric concerns, see Russ Castronovo's *Necro Citizenship: Death, Eroticism, and the Public Sphere in the Nineteenth-Century United States*, especially Chapter 3, "'That Half-Living Corpse': Female Mediums, Séances, and the Occult Public Sphere."

95. Lora Romero, *Home Fronts: Domesticity and Its Critics in the Antebellum United States* (Durham, N.C.: Duke University Press, 1997), 76, 81, 84.

96. Delbourgo, *A Most Amazing Scene of Wonders*, 132.

97. Fuller's concept of electrical dynamics not only departs in important ways from medical discourses of the era, it also differs from predominant nineteenth-century thoughts on polarity. For example, Laura Saltz uses Fuller's obsession with the daguerreotype portrait of her friend Anna Loring to suggest that the image opens up a way of understanding the radical power that magnetism afforded Fuller. According to Saltz, the image of Loring "might finally be said to embody and project light's polar, hermaphroditic, bisexual forces—the push and pull caused by that universal magnetic fluid that surrounds and structures every human body." This thesis is predicated upon a reading of Fuller's personal idolization of the Carbuncle, a red crystallization that, because of its ability to attract and disperse various forms of light, supposedly embodied the dual and hence "bisexual" forces of masculine and feminine ("The Magnetism of a Photograph," 128). Saltz

grounds this logic in the era's notion of polarity, citing Julia Ward Howe's "Polarity II," a long commentary on gender that in many ways recalls Fuller's own contention that people are a mixture of masculine and feminine traits. Howe's work here, as well as her unpublished novel *The Hermaphrodite*, takes up widely held notions about polarity, or "the law that explained the existence of paired opposites in the natural world" (Saltz, 126). In Howe's novel, this topic of polarity plays out across a varying landscape of events. For Laurence, the intersexed main character, however, the experience of transgender reality was far less utopian and materialist than Fuller's thought proves to be. For example, in an epiphanic moment in the plot, they experience a religious vision that includes the "harmonious" chorus of angels' voices—where "the modulation of their voices was so changeful and melodious that it seemed . . . a rainbow of sound." But Laurence is soon severed from this sonic-spiritual reality by a dark angel at the gate of heaven wielding a sword with the word "madness" written upon it (*The Hermaphrodite*, ed. Gary Williams [Lincoln: University of Nebraska Press, 2004], 48).

98. Megan Marshall, *Margaret Fuller: A New American Life* (New York: Mariner Books, 2013), 231.

99. Marshall, *Margaret Fuller*, 231.

100. Viewing Fuller's thoughts on magnetism and electrical dynamics in terms of a dialectical model of "ravishing harmony" also complicates formative readings of Fuller's thought by scholars such as Cynthia Davis ("Margaret Fuller, Body and Soul," *American Literature* 71 [1999]: 31–56) and Deborah Manson ("'The Trance of the Ecstatica'"), that suggest Fuller's experience of physical pain engendered metaphysical insight. I argue that, for Fuller, the body and its excesses (pain, movement, desire, and so on) are also radically aligned with foreign forces that stem from the ideal (forces I earlier associated with the drive and which I will subsequently link to reverberations of distant harmony).

101. Fuller, "Review of Anton Schindler," 72–73.

102. Margaret Fuller, "Music" in *Margaret Fuller, Critic*, CD-ROM; Fuller, "Music in New York," in *Margaret Fuller, Critic*, CD-ROM.

103. Saloman, *Listening Well*, 114.

104. Irving Lowens, "Writings About Music in the Periodicals of American Transcendentalism," *Journal of the American Musicological Society* 10, no. 2 (Summer 1957): 72–73.

105. Saloman, *Listening Well*, 144.

106. Lorraine Byrne, "Goethe and Zelter: An Exchange of Musical Letters," in *Goethe: Musical Poet, Musical Catalyst, Proceedings of the Conference Hosted by the Department of Music, National University of Ireland, Maynooth, 26 & 27 March 2004*, ed. Lorraine Byrne (New York: Peter Lang, 2004), 45.

107. As Saloman notes, Fuller pushed concert organizations such as the Boston Academy of Music and the Philharmonic Society of New York to offer repeat performances and public rehearsals, which would allow people to have a better chance to hear and understand complex works. She also lobbied to end the common practice of breaking up symphonies with operatic interludes, which, in her view, compromised the original intended effects of the works (*Listening*, 143).

108. Margaret Fuller, "Ole Bull" in *Margaret Fuller, Critic*, 241–42.

109. Fuller, "Ole Bull," 243.

110. Margaret Fuller, "Music in New York," CD-ROM. Emphasis in original.

111. Thomas Crawford, *Description of the Orpheus and Other Works of Sculpture by Thomas G. Crawford of Rome: Now Exhibiting at the Athenaeum* (Boston Athenaeum leaflet, 1844), 5.

112. There are many texts that shape Fuller's use of the Orpheus myth. According to Gary Williams, Fuller's reading journals reveal that she considered George Sand's philosophical play *Le Sept Cordes de la Lyre* (*The Seven Strings of the Lyre*) in 1839 (see Williams, "What Did Margaret Think of George?" in *Toward a Female Genealogy of Transcendentalism*, ed. Jana L. Argersinger and Phyllis Cole [Athens: University of Georgia Press, 2014], 125). The play includes a magic lyre that, along with Hélène's heroism, rescues Albertus from Méphistophélès's designs.

113. Fuller, "Review of Anton Schindler," 73. Fuller has many passages extoling the virtues of Beethoven's music, often in the context of articulating a divide between the present state of society/music and the higher truths Beethoven is able to access. For example, in "The Grand Festival Concert at Castle Garden," Fuller replicates the logic presented in her review of Schindler, suggesting that Beethoven's symphony "overshadowed like a tower the wandering mind; we could only feel it . . . ." (in *Margaret Fuller, Critic*, 427). In an 1829 journal entry, Fuller writes a letter to Beethoven, asking why he is able to achieve "genius" while she struggles to do so. Is it, she wonders, "because, as a woman, I am bound by a physical law, which prevents the soul from manifesting itself? Sometimes the moon seems mockingly to say so.—To say that I, too, shall not shine until I can find a sun. O, cold and barren moon, tell a different tale, and give me a sun of my own. But thou, Oh blessed Master, don't answer all of my questions and make it my privilege to be, like a humble wife to the sage . . . , it is my triumph that I can understand, can receive thee wholly" (Margaret Fuller, November 29, 1829 manuscript of "Letter to Beethoven," Margaret Fuller family papers, 1662–1970, Houghton Library, Harvard University).

114. Margaret Fuller, "The Magnolia of Lake Pontchartrain," in *The Essential Margaret Fuller*, 45–46.

115. Margaret Fuller, "The Celestial Empire," in *Margaret Fuller, Critic*, 261; similarly, in "The Beethoven Monument," Fuller suggests that Goethe was no longer "in harmony with the great national movement" the way Beethoven was ("The Beethoven Monument," in *Margaret Fuller, Critic*, CD-ROM). In the quoted passage from "The Celestial Empire," Fuller presents the "narrowest monotony" and "repetition" of Chinese music as implicitly different from the welcome repetition found with the sistrum. Fuller thus appears to create an ethnic and national boundary whereby the Egyptian rattle can access elements of distant harmony while Chinese music is, to again quote the passage, "like nothing else in the heavens or on the earth."

116. Margaret Fuller, undated manuscript of "Moonlight & other reflections," Margaret Fuller family papers, 1662–1970, Houghton Library, Harvard University.

117. Fuller, "Self-Definitions," 8.

118. Ralph Waldo Emerson, *Nature* in *The Collected Works of Ralph Waldo Emerson*, vol. 1, ed. Alfred R. Ferguson (Cambridge: Belknap/Harvard University Press, 1971), 45, 43.

119. Emerson, "Visits to Concord," 310–11.

120. Theodor Adorno, *Night Music: Essays on Music, 1928–1962*, ed. Rolf Tiedman, trans. Wieland Hoban (New York: Seagull Books, 2009), 11–12.

121. The structural model that Fuller presents thus differs from Emerson's own telescoping expanse. As seen in texts such as *Nature*, the Emersonian universe is indeed "one vast picture," but this picture, which unites the particular (body, world, and so on) and a distant universal is conceived via a distinct form of phenomenological idealism (36). See Chapter 1 for a detailed account of Emerson's own brand of transcendental materialism.

122. Margaret Fuller, "Yuca Filamentosa," in *The Essential Margaret Fuller*, 50.

123. Fuller, "Self-Definitions," 15–17.

124. The type of transcendental-materialist fantasy Fuller is using here might be seen to replicate aspects of the experience of capital's own newly instituted modes of circulation. In describing Marx's comments on circulation in *Grundrisse*, Cesare Casarino suggests that circulation within capitalism "appears as a transcendent social form that is apprehensible and operative only as an immanence in the singular moment of social relation, only as the structuring and enabling principle in that epiphenomenal moment of relation. Circulation appears as its own material condition of possibility, as the absent effect of its own just-as-absent cause" (*Modernity at Sea: Melville, Marx, Conrad in Crisis* [Minneapolis: University of Minnesota

Press, 2002], 85). In this sense, Fuller's presentation of the experience of imperfect or partial earthly harmonics (effects of distant divine harmony) has a similar, to borrow again from Casarino, "modality of appearance" as the experience of the circulation of capital in Marx's work. With the movement or appearance of capital, of course, the goal is for circulation to continue—for the social antagonisms produced by capital to generate new profit, and so on and for significant crises (including the halt or disruption of circulation) to be perpetually deferred. In Fuller's transcendental model, true and complete harmony does not yet exist in earthly time; thus, social coordinates must be altered (via agitation) in order to produce a new historical reality.

125. My use of the concept of transversal shares aspects of David Kazanjian's use of the term in *The Brink of Freedom: Improvising Life in the Nineteenth-Century Atlantic World*. Here, Kazanjian establishes the transversal as a means to reveal "overlooked connections" between nineteenth-century Liberia and Yucatán. As Kazanjian explains, "From the Latin *transvertere* (*trans* meaning 'across' and *vertere* meaning 'to turn'), the verb *transverse* means to turn across or athwart, to turn into something else, to turn about, or to overturn. A transverse is thus not simply a line that cuts across, but also an unruly action that undoes what is expected" ([Durham, N.C.: Duke University Press, 2016], 7). Much like Kazanjian, I am interested in examining how the two realms of Fuller's cosmic model cut across each other—producing a strange and dynamic appositional structure of material relation. Slavoj Žižek's discussion of Romantic-era conceptions of the absolute might be useful for formulating Fuller's particular transcendentalist model. He writes, "The question here is whether the transcendental horizon is the ultimate horizon of our thinking. If we reject (as we should) any naturalist or other return to naïve realism, then there are only two ways to get over (or behind/beneath) the transcendental dimension. The first form of this third attitude of thought toward objectivity is an immediate or intuitive knowing which posits a direct access to the Absolute. . . . The second form . . . is Hegel's dialectics, which does exactly the opposite with regard to intuitive knowing: instead of asserting a direct intuitive access to the Absolute, it transposes into the Thing (the Absolute) itself the gap that separates our subjectivity from it" (*Absolute Recoil: Towards a New Foundation of Dialectical Materialism* [New York: Verso, 2014], 16). While we might lump Emerson, Fichte, Schelling, et al. into the first category (with significant caveats), Fuller's notion of harmony certainly is anything but immediate intuitive knowledge. Yet it is also quite distinct from the Hegelian model mentioned here. Instead, we might say that Fuller offers an odd compromise (here a forth form within Žižek's schematic): accounting for the gap be-

tween self and the absolute via an expansive material/temporal divide, one that is, from the perspective of the absolute, already closed, and, from the perspective of historical humanity, in the inevitable process of closing (existing because of the very condition of historical reality itself). In other words, Fuller's transcendental model transposes into historical reality the gap that separates our reality from the absolute.

126. Qtd. in Branka Arsić, "What Music Shall We Have? Thoreau on the Aesthetics and Politics of Listening," in *American Impersonal: Essays With Sharon Cameron*, ed. Branka Arsić (New York: Bloomsbury, 2014), 175.

127. During this era, Fuller and other writers within the American Transcendentalist scene were adding a more nuanced element of materiality to a widely held view that the private aesthetic sphere might afford an "independent starting point" for reform, a position that approximates elements of Kant's arguments about the faculty of judgment's a priori laws in *The Critique of Judgment* (1790). But many of these other U.S. writers reinstate a Coleridgean bifurcation between harmony and discord. Albert Brisbane, for instance, who was among one of the most adamant promoters of Fourierist thought in America, argued, "Establish true social institutions . . . institutions in harmony with the laws of organization in creation (and consequently in harmony with the spiritual forces which are in harmony with the creation)[,] and we shall see them produce as high a degree of harmony as they now produce discord" (Qtd. in Lowens, "Writings," 76). Similarly, in his *Aesthetic Papers* (1849), Timothy Dwight saw the beauty of music resulting from the "marriage of spiritual fact with a material form," a position, no doubt, heavily influenced by Emerson's work. For Dwight, the "native impulses of the soul" are shaped and called by "harmony." In his words: "To meet, to unite, to blend by methods intricate as swift, is their whole business and effort through eternity." He contrasts this natural attraction with various negative movements within society: "not to collision, not to excess followed by exhaustion; not to discord." Ultimately, for Dwight, music is sent to us in our current "long winter of disharmony and strife" as an "actual foretaste . . . of that harmony which must yet come" (qtd. in Lowens, "Writings," 77–79).

128. My reading here should be seen to implicitly break from contemporary readings of Fuller that employ traditional and reified categories, such as materialism and idealism. See especially Larry J. Reynolds's "Subjective Vision, Romantic History, and the Return of the 'Real': The Case of Margaret Fuller and the Roman Republic" *South Central Review* 21, no. 1 (2004): 1–17, and Dennis Berthod's "Response to Larry Reynolds, 'Subjective Vision, Romantic History, and the Return of the 'Real': The Case of Margaret Fuller and the Roman Republic'" in the same issue. A sociopolitical paradox

might also be noted here. As many scholars have pointed out, the development of capitalism has commenced in part via what Todd McGowan calls the "spatialization of time." Quoting Georg Lukács, McGowan writes, "[T]ime sheds its qualitative, variable, flowing nature; it freezes into an exactly delimited, quantifiable continuum filled with quantifiable 'things'" (*Out of Time: Desire in Atemporal Cinema* [Minneapolis: University of Minnesota Press, 2011], 20–21). In her own historical moment, Fuller in effect *adds* a horizon of speculative spatialization to time (with the supposition of distance between historical reality and the ideal realm of harmony) in order to return elements of its, to quote Lukács once more, "qualitative, variable, flowing nature."

129. Morton, *Hyperobjects*, 159, 127, 165, 126. By drawing this superficial comparison between Fuller and Morton, I am in no way challenging the soundness (if I may pun here) of Morton's claims. Instead, I intend to underscore the historical differences that give shape to their varying models. On the one hand, Morton's more sophisticated materialist approach might cast Fuller's nineteenth-century fantasies as being motivated structurally by a facile idealism. On the other, Fuller's dialectical material utopianism might illuminate some of the political and social limits of Morton's arguments—even if these limits may stem from our very real historical conditions.

130. Jane Bennett, *Vibrant Matter: A Political Ecology of Things* (Durham, N.C.: Duke University Press, 2010), 21, 23, 32, 122.

131. Arsić, "What Music," 169, 173, emphasis mine.

132. Arsić, "What Music," 177. As Arsić notes, her reading departs drastically from "theological interpretation[s]" of Thoreau's notion of music, such as Alan D. Hodder's *Thoreau's Ecstatic Witness* (New Haven: Yale University Press, 2001) (191). My own reading of Fuller's conception of harmony shares this desire to move past traditional views on Romantic-era fantasies of divine harmony and ontological accord.

133. Arsić, "What Music," 187, 186. Arsić transitions into her claims about Thoreau's musical-political thought, where she ultimately claims that it breaks from totalizing structures and politics, by invoking directly Lacoue-Labarthe and Adorno. Arsić cites, loosely, Adorno's view that "the magic of romantic music would thus be its transubstantiation of the empirical into an idealized or 'second reality'" and Lacoue-Labarthe's criticism of Romanticism's tendency to shift the category of the human into that of "superhumanness," a move best exemplified by the "masses stimulated by a Wagner opera" (182–83). Although it is outside the scope of this chapter to engage Arsić's nuanced consideration of Thoreau, it should be noted that scholars such as Alain Badiou have questioned the ideological motivations and formal concerns of Lacoue-Labarthe's and Adorno's readings of Wagner. See

especially Badiou's *Five Lessons on Wagner* (New York: Verso, 2010), which contests point-by-point Lacoue-Labarthe's analysis of Wagner and situates Adorno's anti-Hegelianism (its fear that Hegel's dialectic "engulfs difference in sameness") as a post–World War II attack on "the identity principle in Western rationalism" (18, 31). Given my chapter's aim to reveal political and social aspects of Fuller's thought that have been foreclosed by longstanding liberal paradigms, it might be worth pointing out how significantly Arsić's claims about Thoreau (for example, the way he "cancels the aesthetic strategies of musica ficta and, in so doing, resists complicity in its political programs") are informed by Lacoue-Labarthe's more contemporary liberal positions on musical and artistic ideals ("What Music," 190).

134. As I intimate earlier in the chapter, Fuller's concept of social harmony exceeds and/or differs from predominant aesthetic/musical views of the era. It also differs from other utopian social fantasies in the era, such as Charles Fourier's notion of "Harmony" as an ideal society of unalienated labor or Frédéric Bastiat's *Harmonies Économiques* (1851), which Marx cites as an idealist approach to socio-economic relations based upon a fantasy of *locus communis* (Karl Marx, *Grundrisse*, trans. Martin Nicolaus [New York: Penguin, 1993], 85), as well as psychological or medical beliefs about the topic (in Jeffrey Steele's view, Fuller "adds a psychological dimension to [Fourier's] . . . concept by using the term [harmony] to refer to an ideal state in which the different facets of a person's being are in balance" [*The Essential Margaret Fuller*, 452]).

135. Margaret Fuller, Untitled poem, in *The Essential Margaret Fuller*, 227. A similar form of easy idealism can be found in Fuller's *Tribune* piece "Music," where she describes how a reform-minded speech at a concert in Liverpool aimed at giving "advantage" to "the working classes" might be a model for those in the United States: "Come we and do likewise, and we shall think more and love more in our country, and the Capitalist and Laborer may yet be bound in a harmony cheerful as the music of Haydn, prophetic as that of Beethoven" ("Music," in *Margaret Fuller, Critic*, CD-ROM). Although this move toward harmony occurs from the ground up—with political speeches and so on—it ends with an idealistic unity of classes without (apparently) any social strife or substantial reform.

136. Margaret Fuller, undated manuscript, Margaret Fuller family papers, 1662–1970, Houghton Library, Harvard University.

137. Fuller, "Self-Definitions," 14, 12.

138. José Esteban Muñoz, *Cruising Utopia* (New York: NYU Press, 2009), 1.

139. Muñoz, *Cruising Utopia*, 12. According to Lauren Berlant, affect "registers the conditions of life that move across persons and worlds." This includes the "noise" of society that exists below and within forms of filtering

mediation, or what might be thought of as symbolic structures such as ideological fantasies. In Berlant's reading, this noise often relates to forms of "affective binding" that, as in her reading of George W. Bush, can be used to constitute and mobilize conservative political movements. Yet, as she demonstrates, many forms of art also "remobilize and redirect the normative noise that binds the affective public of the political to normative politics as such" (*Cruel Optimism* [Durham, N.C.: Duke University Press, 2001], 16, 224, 228). I am arguing that Fuller offers something of a materialist-utopic inverse of Berlant's example of Bush. While Bush desired to rid politics of all filters (historical knowledge, political ratiocination, and so on) in order to capitalize (pun intended) on raw affect, Fuller believed that the noise of her moment was both a misrecognized filter (as we lacked an appropriate hermeneutics) as well as a material link to a potential utopian political future.

140. Fuller, *Autobiographical Romance*, 30.

141. See Steele's notes on Minerva in *The Essential Margaret Fuller*, no. 19 (xlviii) and no. 131 (461).

142. Margaret Fuller, "The Great Lawsuit. Man Versus Men. Woman Versus Women," *The Dial*, no. XIII (1843), 47.

143. For an interesting historical perspective on Fuller's notions of heroism, see especially Robert Hudspeth's "Margaret Fuller and the Ideal of Heroism" in *Margaret Fuller: Transatlantic Crossings in a Revolutionary Age*, ed. Charles Capper and Cristina Giorcelli (Madison: University of Wisconsin Press, 2007), 45–65.

144. In terms of slavery, Fuller does indeed seem to privilege the cause of women, writ large, over the specific sufferings of slaves. Nonetheless, the issue of slavery is clearly on her mind across the 1840s, as seen in an 1848 *Tribune* dispatch where she admits: "How it pleases me here to think of the Abolitionists! I could never endure to be with them at home, they were so tedious, often so narrow, always so rabid and exaggerated in their tone. But, after all, they had a high motive, something eternal in their desire and life; and, if it was not the only thing worth thinking of it was really something worth living and dying for to free a great nation from such a terrible blot, such a threatening plague" ("Things and Thoughts in Europe," in *The Essential Margaret Fuller*, 409–10).

145. This very constitution, however, was predicated upon typical liberal foreclosures: declaring Spain and Spanish-America a single country, but denying Americans equal representation, and slavery, of course, remained in place. This is not to suggest that such contexts negate potential radical innovation within Fuller's adaptation of the term; yet, if we are to understand Fuller's political thought, the discursive liberal ideological frameworks

with which she works, with all of their imposed limits, should be highlighted instead of diminished. For more on "Los Exaltados," see Charles Wentz Fehrenbach's "Moderados and Exaltados: The Liberal Opposition to Ferdinand VII, 1814–1823," *The Hispanic Historical Review* 50, no. 1 (February 1970): 52–69. Phyllis Cole and Jana Argersinger borrow this politically inflected term from Fuller within their 2011 introduction to an *ESQ* special issue titled "Exaltadas: A Female Genealogy of Transcendentalism." Their description of Fuller's personal and political efficacy, however, tends to fall within the traditional bounds of political ontology that this chapter has been pushing against. They write, "'Exaltadas' exemplifies Fuller's claim *for women* as possessors of a high, quasi-divine consciousness and truth-telling power 'within'" (*ESQ* 57 [2011]: 2).

146. Fuller, "The Next Revolution," 323. For the Isaiah passage, see *Isaiah* 7:14.

3. THOREAU'S MILITANT VEGETABLES

1. Henry David Thoreau, *Journal*, vol. 1, 1837–1844, general editor, John C. Broderick, *The Writings of Henry David Thoreau* (Princeton: Princeton University Press, 1981), 55.

2. Henry David Thoreau, *Journal*, vol. 5, 1852–1853, editor-in-chief, Elizabeth Witherell, *The Writings of Henry David Thoreau* (Princeton: Princeton University Press, 1997), 424.

3. Jason Moore, *Capitalism in the Web of Life: Ecology and the Accumulation of Capital* (New York: Verso, 2015), 35.

4. Qtd. in Foster and Burkett's *Marx and the Earth: An Anti-Critique* (Chicago: Haymarket Books, 2016), vii.

5. Moore, *Capitalism in the Web of Life*, 158.

6. Henry David Thoreau, *Journal*, vol. 3, 1848–1851, editor-in-chief, Elizabeth Witherell, *The Writings of Henry David Thoreau* (Princeton: Princeton University Press, 1990), 94–95.

7. Thoreau, *Journal*, vol. 3, 95.

8. Qtd. in Robert D. Richardson, Jr., *Henry David Thoreau: A Life of the Mind* (Berkeley and Los Angeles: University of California Press, 1986), 213.

9. Thoreau, *Journal*, vol. 3, 95.

10. Henry David Thoreau, *Cape Cod*, ed. Joseph J. Moldenhauer, *The Writings of Henry D. Thoreau* (Princeton: Princeton University Press, 2004), 5.

11. Thoreau, *Cape Cod*, 7, 9.

12. Richardson, *Henry David Thoreau*, 203.

13. Branka Arsić, *Bird Relics: Grief and Vitalism in Thoreau* (Cambridge: Harvard University Press, 2016), 51. Subsequent page references will appear parenthetically in the text.

14. See Wai Chee Dimock, *Through Other Continents: American Literature Across Deep Time* (Princeton: Princeton University Press, 2006), 52–53, and Elizabeth Freeman, *Time Binds: Queer Temporalities, Queer Histories* (Durham, N.C.: Duke University Press, 2010), 14.

15. Thoreau, *Journal*, vol. 3, 95.

16. Later in the same section, Arsić discusses explicitly her strategic approach toward Thoreau, writing: "Thoreau's politics are typically discussed in light of his civil disobedience and the John Brown essays. And although such an approach is, of course, valid, in what follows I suggest that the centrally important site of Thoreau's politics is in fact his philosophy of life. The question one should ask about Thoreau's understanding of life is not only whether it is scientifically grounded or even rationally possible, but also what idea of justice and democracy it outlines" (*Bird Relics*, 129). Although this passage ends by positing democracy as an open variable, it does so after predicating an initial bifurcation within Thoreau's corpus that conditions the seemingly neutral categories of "justice" and "democracy."

17. George Ciccariello-Maher, *Decolonizing Dialectics* (Durham, N.C.: Duke University Press, 2017), 6. According to Ciccariello-Maher, decolonization is not a simple outgrowth of class struggle, just as "a decolonized (and decolonizing) dialectics . . . predates, exceeds, and exists independently of even Hegel's own formulations." In these terms, Frederick Douglass "preemptively radicalizes" Hegel's own standard formulations (153). It should be noted that Ciccariello-Maher moves in important ways past the Hegel-based historical analysis found in works such as Susan Buck-Morss's *Hegel, Haiti and Universal History* (2005).

18. Gayatri Chakravoty Spivak, *A Critique of Postcolonial Reason: Toward a History of the Vanishing Present* (Cambridge: Harvard University Press, 1999), 208.

19. In his later work, Fredric Jameson posits a similar notion of historical and ontological discontinuity at the heart of dialectics. In counterpointing dialectics to deconstruction, he writes: "[W]here the dialectic pauses, waiting for the 'new' dialectical solution to freeze over in its turn and become an idea or an ideology to which the dialectic can again be 'applied' . . . , deconstruction races forward, undoing the very incoherence it has just been denouncing and showing that seeming analytic result to be itself a new incoherence and a new 'contradiction' to be unraveled in its turn" (*Valences of the Dialectic* [New York: Verso, 2009], 27). Jameson's account of the dialectic's asymmetrical movement across and among interruptions as well as the logic that informs his censure of deconstruction's perpetual action is relevant for thinking about Arsić's type of vitalism. As I mention, Arsić's thought is itself part of a wide constellation of con-

temporary perspectives (inheritors of Deleuze but also Spinoza) that prefer a positive, singular but manifold reality. Following Jameson, can't we view this approach as a constructive inversion of deconstruction? Here Deleuzian proponents of positive multiplicity erect their worlds by perpetually adding without synthesis—as if the buoyancy and inertia of perpetual positive movement along various axes is in itself valuable (à la the modality of accumulation) and natural.

20. In *The Senses of Walden* (Chicago: University of Chicago Press, 1992), Cavell notes how *Walden* evinces a "power of dialectic, of self-comment and self-placement, in the portion and in the whole of it." But this dialectical modality is relegated almost exclusively to the plane of language and narrative. "Once in [*Walden*]," Cavell writes, "there seems no end; as soon as you have one word to cling to, it fractions or expands into others" (13). Moving toward historical and political concerns, Sharron Mariotti's *Thoreau's Democratic Withdrawal: Alienation, Participation, and Modernity* (Madison: University of Wisconsin Press, 2010) uses Theodor Adorno's conception of negative dialectics to consider the "democratically valuable" aspects of Thoreau's "withdrawal" and "excursions" (29).

21. See Buell's *The Future of Environmental Criticism: Environmental Crisis and Literary Imagination* (2005) and *The Environmental Imagination: Thoreau, Nature Writing, and the Formation of American Culture* (1995); Robinson's *Natural Life: Thoreau's Worldly Transcendentalism* (2004); Walls's *Seeing New Worlds: Henry David Thoreau and Nineteenth-Century Natural Science* (1995); Thorson's *Walden's Shore: Henry David Thoreau and Nineteenth-Century Science* (2014) and *The Boatman: Henry David Thoreau's River Years* (2017); Cavell's *The Senses of* Walden (1972); Cameron's *Writing Nature: Henry Thoreau's Journal* (1985); Davis's *Ornamental Aesthetics: The Poetry of Attending to Thoreau, Dickinson, and Whitman* (2016); Nabers's *Victory of Law: The Fourteenth Amendment, the Civil War, and American Literature, 1852–1867* (2006); Mariotti's *Thoreau's Democratic Withdrawal* (2010); and Larry Reynolds's *Righteous Violence: Revolution, Slavery, and The American Renaissance* (2011).

22. Robert M. Thorson, *Walden's Shore: Henry David Thoreau and Nineteenth-Century Science* (Cambridge: Harvard University Press, 2014), 9; Thorson, *The Boatman: Henry David Thoreau's River Years* (Cambridge: Harvard University Press, 2017), xiii.

23. Thorson, *The Boatman*, xvi.

24. See *Thoreau at Two Hundred (Essays and Reassessments)*, ed. Kristen Case and K. P. Van Anglen (Cambridge: Cambridge University Press, 2016).

25. Qtd. in Peter Coviello, *Tomorrow's Parties: Sex and the Untimely in Nineteenth-Century America* (New York: NYU Press, 2013), 214.

26. Coviello, *Tomorrow's Parties*, 33.

27. Thoreau, *Journal*, vol. 3, 96.

28. 1 Samuel 7:12 (King James Version).

29. Henry David Thoreau, *A Week on the Concord and Merrimack Rivers*, ed. Carl F. Hovde et al., *The Writings of Henry D. Thoreau* (Princeton: Princeton University Press, 2004), 70. Subsequent page references will appear parenthetically in the text.

30. Henry David Thoreau, *Walden* (Princeton: Princeton University Press, 2004), 10. Subsequent page references will appear parenthetically in the text.

31. I reference obliquely Rob Nixon's *Slow Violence and the Environmentalism of the Poor* (Cambridge: Harvard University Press, 2011). According to Nixon, "slow violence . . . occurs gradually and out of sight, a violence of delayed destruction that is dispersed across time and space" (2). In Thoreau's case, I am invoking the negative connotation that Nixon establishes as well as adding a positive potential to this dispersed mode of violence.

32. By employing the term "viscous," I reference loosely Timothy Morton's *Hyperobjects: Philosophy and Ecology After the End of the World* (Minneapolis: University of Minnesota Press, 2013). Morton suggests that "hyperobjects," such as global warming, are both "nonlocal" and withdrawing as well as up close and "viscous," "which means that they 'stick' to beings that are involved with them" (1).

33. Henry David Thoreau, "Slavery in Massachusetts," in *Reform Papers*, ed. Wendell Glick, *The Writings of Henry D. Thoreau* (Princeton: Princeton University Press, 1973), 108.

34. Henry David Thoreau, "Resistance to Civil Government," in *Reform Papers*, 74.

35. In *Utopia, Limited: Romanticism and Adjustment* (Cambridge: Harvard University Press, 2015), Anahid Nersessian forwards the claim that Romantic-era political and material realities engendered "Romantic attentiveness to precarity" and a new form of pseudo-utopian orientation that she calls "the possibility of adjustment" (2). She defines adjustment as "a formal as well as an ethical operation that allows human beings to accommodate themselves to the world by minimizing the demands they place upon it." Nersessian counterpoints this mode of "utopian doing-with-less" with the type of Leftist "political desire" found in scholars such as Judith Butler (and her injunction to "demand the impossible") and then, in a familiar move among contemporary liberal scholars, attempts to link Butler's logic with both Hegelian fundamentalism and neoliberalism's own functions (3–4). For most readers, it should be quite apparent how Nersessian's own model of adjustment fits every-so-nicely with liberalism's/neoliberalism's developing fantasies of tolerance and presents its own version of what Rachel Greenwald

Smith calls "compromise aesthetics" (see Smith's *Affect and American Literature in the Age of Neoliberalism* [Cambridge: Cambridge University Press, 2015]). In her closing chapter, Nersessian, perhaps defensively, claims her work is not liberal ("this book is not pro-liberal"), but then promptly posits a specious historical and functional distance between "liberal attitudes and capitalist systems" (176). Against Nersessian's notion of adjustment, I posit Dr. Martin Luther King's rather illiberal notion in December 1957 that "[t]he world is in desperate need of . . . maladjustment. And through such courageous maladjustment, we will be able to emerge from the bleak and desolate midnight of man's inhumanity" (*The Papers of Martin Luther King, Jr. Volume VI: Advocate of the Social Gospel, September 1948–March 1963*, ed. Clayborne Carson and Susan Carson [Berkeley and Los Angeles: University of California Press, 2007], 327–28).

36. Henry David Thoreau, *Journal*, vol. 4, 1851–1852, general editor, Robert Sattelmeyer, *The Writings of Henry David Thoreau* (Princeton: Princeton University Press, 1992), 468.

37. Richardson, Jr., *Henry David Thoreau*, 194.

38. Thoreau, *Journal*, vol. 4, 468.

39. Caroline Levine, *Forms: Whole, Rhythm, Hierarchy, Network* (Princeton: Princeton University Press, 2015), 2–3. I will return to Levine's notion of form subsequently.

40. Patrick Jagoda, *Network Aesthetics* (Chicago: University of Chicago Press, 2016), 3.

41. See especially Mary Louise Pratt's *Imperial Eyes: Travel Writing and Transculturation* (New York: Routledge, 1992); for Romantic notions of the visual, see Jonathan Crary's *Techniques of the Observer: On Vision and Modernity in the Nineteenth Century* (Cambridge: MIT Press, 1991).

42. Emerson, *Nature*, in *The Collected Works of Ralph Waldo Emerson*, vol. 1, ed. Alfred R. Ferguson (Cambridge: Belknap/Harvard University Press, 1971, 31.

43. Henry David Thoreau, *Journal*, vol. 1, 87.

44. In *A Week*, Thoreau writes, "If we look into the heavens they are concave, and if we were to look into a gulf as bottomless, it would be concave also" (331).

45. Peter Sloterdijk, *Bubbles: Spheres I*, trans. Wieland Hoban (Los Angeles: Semiotext(e), 2011), 27. One should not miss the Deleuzian resonances here, and Sloterdijk indeed moves to consider Deleuze's well-known claim that the subject is a "fold" of the outside (90).

46. Sloterdijk, *Bubbles*, 25.

47. Peter Sloterdijk, *Globes: Spheres II*, trans. Wieland Hoban (Los Angeles: Semiotext(e), 2014), 444 and 452.

48. Peter Sloterdijk, *Foams: Spheres III*, trans. Wieland Hoban (Los Angeles: Semiotext(e), 2016), 23.
49. Sloterdijk, *Foams*, 25, 38.
50. Sloterdijk, *Foams*, 54, 564.
51. Laura Dassow Walls, *Seeing New Worlds: Henry David Thoreau and Nineteenth-Century Natural Science* (Madison: University of Wisconsin Press, 1995), 4.
52. Walls, *Seeing New Worlds*, 4–5.
53. Qtd. in Kevin Dann, *Expect Great Things: The Life and Search of Henry David Thoreau* (New York: Penguin, 2017), 267.
54. See Thorson, *Walden's Shore*, 123.
55. Thorson, *Walden's Shore*, 4–5.
56. Sloterdijk, *Globes*, 780–82.
57. Sloterdijk, *Globes*, 782–83.
58. Thorson, *Walden's Shore*, 5.
59. The term "worlding" relates to Heidegger's three famous theses: "[1.] The stone is worldless; [2.] The animal is poor in word; [3.] Man is world-forming" (*World, Finitude, Solitude*, 184. Qtd. in Jeffrey Nealon, *Plant Theory: Biopower and Vegetable Life* [Stanford: Stanford University Press, 2016], 38.) More recently, Marisol de la Cadena and Mario Blaser cite John Law's discussion of the western "colonial ontological occupation of territories" resulting in a "one-world world: a world that has granted itself the right to assimilate all other worlds and, by presenting itself as exclusive, cancels possibilities for what lies beyond its limits." Working against this colonial reality, de la Cadena and Blaser offer their notion of a "pluriverse": "heterogeneous worldings coming together as a political ecology of practices, negotiating their difficult being together in heterogeneity" (*A World of Many Worlds*, ed. Marisol de la Cadena and Mario Blaser [Durham, N.C.: Duke University Press, 2018], 3–4). In the context of contemporary thought, I am suggesting that Thoreau's own Romantic-era "pluriverse" should be seen as distinct from liberal forms of and assumptions about pluralism (whose work of inclusion-via-multiplicity offers, paradoxically, its own variety of "one" world in the making).
60. Elizabeth A. Povinelli, *Geontologies: A Requiem to Late Liberalism* (Durham, N.C.: Duke University Press, 2016), 13.
61. Scholarship on various historical and conceptual definitions of the Anthropocene abounds. I employ here a basic historical schematic that has the period, which combines the Greek terms *anthropos* (human being) and *kainos* (new), beginning around the late eighteenth century when coal and later hydrocarbons and uranium began shifting ecosystems away from previous configurations found in the Holocene. For an overview of this

narrative, see especially Christophe Bonneuil and Jean-Baptiste Fressoz's *The Shock of the Anthropocene* (New York: Verso, 2015). For a useful and brief account of varying historical notions of the Anthropocene as well as their political stakes, see Dana Luciano's "The Inhuman Anthropocene," *Avidly* (March 22, 2015).

62. Morton, *Dark Ecology: For a Logic of Future Coexistence* (New York: Columbia University Press, 2016), 6.

63. Morton, *Dark Ecology*, 7.

64. Donna Haraway, *Staying with the Trouble: Making Kin in the Chthulucene* (Durham, N.C.: Duke University Press, 2016), 2.

65. Haraway, *Staying with the Trouble*, 13.

66. Haraway, *Staying with the Trouble*, 61.

67. Haraway, *Staying with the Trouble*, 32.

68. Henry David Thoreau, "Walking," in *Excursions*, ed. Joseph J. Moldenhauer, *The Writings of Henry D. Thoreau* (Princeton: Princeton University Press, 2007), 195–96.

69. Thoreau, "Walking," 186. Thoreau makes a similar point toward the end of *A Week*, writing: "The traveler must be born again on the road, and earn a passport from the elements" (306).

70. Henry David Thoreau, *Journal*, vol. 8, 1854, ed. Sandra Harbert Petrulionis, *The Writings of Henry David Thoreau* (Princeton: Princeton University Press, 2002), 13.

71. Coviello, *Tomorrow's Parties*, 30.

72. Levine, *Forms*, 3.

73. Lace Newman, *Our Common Dwelling: Henry David Thoreau, Transcendentalism, and the Class Politics of Nature* (New York: Palgrave, 2005), 136–37.

74. Soon after discussing the topic of domestic space, Arsić describes "Thoreau's walker" as a new type of subject along the lines of a Bejaminian "artist of becoming." Invoking Baudelaire, she asserts that this Thoreauvian form of self "generates and embodies no less than a Parisian flâneur" (*Bird Relics*, 322). Of course, in *The Arcades Project*, Benjamin does indeed portray the flâneur as a harbinger of the new, but this new figure is wholly subsumed by the market. According Benjamin, the flâneur is both the "subject of lyric poetry" and the "scout in the marketplace"—in fact, this subject "surrenders itself to the market" (*The Arcades Project*, trans. Howard Eiland and Kevin McLaughlin [Cambridge: Harvard University Press, 1999], 21).

75. I here reference correlationism, a long tradition within Western thought (via Descartes, Locke, Kant, and so on) where humans have access to only the correlation between thinking *and* being—never each on its own. In such modes of "strong correlationism," as it's sometimes called, "there are

things in themselves … but … they aren't 'realized' until they are correlated by a correlator," here via forms of human reason (Timothy Morton, *Humankind: Solidarity with Nonhuman People* [New York: Verso, 2017]), 7. For a contemporary review of this tradition as well as an innovative and perhaps embattled attempt to move past it, see Quentin Meillassoux's *After Finitude* (2008) and *Time Without Becoming* (2014).

76. Henry David Thoreau, "The Dispersion of Seeds," in *Faith in a Seed: The Dispersion of Seeds and Other Late Natural History Writings*, ed. Bradley P. Dean (Washington, D.C.: Island Press, 1993), 39.

77. Thoreau, *Journal*, vol. 2, 155.

78. Henry David Thoreau, *The Maine Woods*, ed. Joseph J. Modenhauer (Princeton: Princeton University Press, 2004), 18–20. Subsequent page references will appear parenthetically in the text.

79. See Alain Badiou, *The Rebirth of History: Times of Riots and Uprising*, trans. Gregory Elliott (New York: Verso, 2012), 21.

80. For information on Thoreau's reading of Melville, see Robert Sattelmeyer's "Thoreau and Melville's *Typee*," *American Literature* 52, no. 3 (November 1980): 462–68. For my analysis of tattooing in *Typee*, see *Antebellum at Sea: Maritime Fantasies in Nineteenth-Century America* (2012).

81. Morton, *Dark Ecology*, 42.

82. As Thoreau writes in his journal, "Men have become the tools of their tools—the man who independently plucked the fruits when he was hungry—is become a *farmer*" (*Journal*, vol. 2, 162).

83. Thoreau, *Journal*, vol. 1, 69–70.

84. See Morton, *Dark Ecologies*, 59, 69; Sloterdijk, *Foams*, 23; *Globes*, 778.

85. I borrow the term "nested loops" from Morton, *Dark Ecologies*, 59.

86. Thoreau, *Journal*, vol. 2, 167.

87. Haraway, *Staying with the Trouble*, 4.

88. Thoreau, *Journal*, vol. 2, 158.

89. Laura Dassow Walls, *Henry David Thoreau: A Life* (Chicago: Chicago University Press, 2017), xiii.

90. Thoreau, *Journal*, vol. 1, 58.

91. For more on period notions of economic aspects of "speculation," see especially Jonathan Levy's *Freaks of Fortune: The Emerging World of Capitalism and Risk in America* (2012). Although Thoreau's journal passage ends with reference to thought (juxtaposing wondering "without reference or inference" with speculation's aimless flitting), the term "speculation" clearly has economic resonances in the period. Furthermore, the passage opens with reference to Adam's fall, which connotes the deleterious effects of knowledge as well as the unwelcome imposition of labor.

92. Arsić, *Bird Relics*, 204.

93. Arsić, *Bird Relics*, 206.
94. Walls, *Henry David Thoreau*, 4–15.
95. Arsić, *Bird Relics*, 203. Allewaert notes, "As Bartram's meditation on vines makes clear, the tropical ecology was an animate force whose combinatory power could provide strength, and was imagined to do just that for African agents, but could also consume—and was imagined to do just that to Anglo-European agents" (*Ariel's Ecology: Plantations, Personhood, and Colonialism in the American Tropics* [Minneapolis: University of Minnesota Press, 2013], 44).
96. As Maureen Konkle avers, in the nineteenth century "the two discursive means of denying Native peoples' political autonomy and squaring the fact of history of treaty-making with U.S. (and white) authority . . . [were] the difference of Indians on the one hand and whites' sympathy for the Indians on the other" (*Writing Indian Nations: Native Intellectuals and the Politics of Historiography, 1827–1863* [Chapel Hill: University of North Carolina Press, 2004], 28).
97. In his *Principles of Zoölogy* (1848), Agassiz sets out to locate animal and plant life according to "their rank in the scale of being," a scale determined by God's "plan" (qtd. in Walls, *Seeing New Worlds*, 145).
98. In the book, Thoreau does partake in an uneventful moose hunt before swearing off the practice—more comfortable "looking for flowers" (*Maine*, 122). It should be noted, however, that he ate moose meat throughout his journey.
99. See Sigourney's "The Mohegan Church," in *Poems* (1834) and Lydia Maria Child's "The Indians," in *Letters From New-York* [London: 1843], 247–57.
100. Scholars such as Meredith McGill have productively stressed the "illocality" and "temporal dislocation" in Thoreau's work, particularly in *A Week*. At the same time, McGill's strict focus on poetic commonplace books may limit her analysis. See McGill, "Common Places: Poetry, Illocality, and Temporal Dislocation in Thoreau's *A Week on the Concord and Merrimack Rivers*," *American Literary History* 19, no. 2 (Summer 2007): 357–74.
101. In *Hyperobjects*, for example, Morton suggests, "The present does not truly exist. We experience a crisscrossing set of force fields, the aesthetic-casual fields emanated by a host of objects" (93).
102. Herman Melville, *Typee: A Peep at Polynesian Life*, ed. Harrison Hayford et al. (Evanston, Ill.: Northwestern University Press, 2003), 78.
103. Qtd. in Richardson, Jr., *Henry David Thoreau*, 30.
104. In Baudrillard's "Global Debt and Parallel Universe" (1996), he describes the way modern debt circulates in a manner that is "ex-orbital, ex-centered, ex-centric, with only a very faint probability that, one day, it

might rejoins ours" (qtd. in Franco "Bifo" Berardi's *The Uprising: On Poetry and Finance* [South Pasadena, Calif.: Semiotext(s)], 25).

105. See Slavoj Žižek, *Less Than Nothing: Hegel and the Shadow of Dialectical Materialism* (New York: Verso, 2012), 227.

106. Jane Bennett, *Thoreau's Nature: Ethics, Politics, and the Wild* (Lanham, Md.: Rowman & Littlefield, 2002), 53. In *Humankind: Solidarity with Nonhuman People*, Timothy Morton uses the notion of "implosive whole" to offer a similar notion, where "entities are related in a non-total, raggedy way" (New York: Verso, 2017), 1.

107. Fredric Jameson, *Valences of the Dialectic* (New York: Verso, 2009), 15. A number of contemporary liberal-inflected approaches toward systems, networks, and scale evince an aversion toward a traditional dialectical notion of synthesis, unification, or "deep causes." These include Caroline Levine's *Forms* (with its pluralizing approach to material formations) and Timothy Morton's developing theses in books such as *Hyperobjects* and *Dark Ecology* (with "mesh" constituting "a sprawling network of interconnection without center or edge" [*Dark Ecology*, 81]). If Levine's move to bracket deep causes in favor of dispersed networks of causality is a typical and valued conceptual materialist compromise of our era, my reading of Thoreau both requires and supports something of an about face toward totality. What Thoreau offers, I argue, is a multitudinous reality that nonetheless includes dialectical-material change. Here history proper is composed as an unfinished, indeed precarious, formation(s)-in-process. The type of totality Thoreau offers might, in this way, be thought of along with Fred Moten's conception of "ensemble": a type of "nonexclusionary" and "improvisatory whole" (*Stolen Life* [Durham, N.C.: Duke University Press, 2018], 44–45).

108. Jameson, *Valences of the Dialectic*, 24. Jameson's *Valences* and his *The Hegel Variations: On the Phenomenology of Spirit* (2010) offer detailed summaries of the dialectic's semantic and systemic genealogy in Western thought.

109. Although Engels's famous triumvirate definition of dialectics in *Dialectics of Nature* ("The law of the transformation of quantity into quality and *vice versa*; The law of the interpenetration of opposites; The law of the negation of the negation") is beyond embattled even on the left, its basic notion that dialectics is a "science of interconnectivity" that replaces "metaphysics" with material "natural" history is relevant for thinking about Thoreau's work (*Dialectics of Nature*, trans. and ed. Clemens Dutt [New York: International Publishers, 1940], 26). In Engels's words, "The mistake lies in the fact that these laws are foisted on nature and history as laws of thought, and not deduced from them" (26). Ironically, Jameson notes the way Engel's own use of the term "law" is symptomatic of his moment's emerging science (esp. Helmholtz) and legal associations (a Hegelian leftover

in which the "'casus' is supposed to adjust the empirical contingency of the facts to the abstract universality of law") (*Valences*, 14). Nonetheless, and with all due caveats, I want to suggest that Bennett and others who break up the dialectic into multiplicities effect something of a metaphysical interjection of liberal relation into what is for Thoreau, somewhat like Engels, a material approach toward becoming and historical change.

110. Jean Hyppolite, *Genesis and Structure of Hegel's* Phenomenology of Spirit, trans. Samuel Cherniak and John Heckman (Evanston, Ill.: Northwestern University Press, 1974), 15.

111. Henry David Thoreau, *Journal*, vol. 1, 24–25.

112. Ciccariello-Maher, *Decolonizing Dialectics*, 6, 158–59.

113. As Robert Thorson notes, as early as 1852 Thoreau had started to depart from Agassiz's misguided creationist views regarding the geological formation of New England (found in texts such as *Etudes sur les Glaciers*), embracing glacial terminology and considering James Forbes's physics of ice (*Walden's Shore*, 7).

114. Henry David Thoreau, *The Dispersion of Seeds*, in *Faith in a Seed*, 36.

115. In "Low-Tech Thoreau; or, Remediations of the Human in *The Dispersal of Seeds*," Jason Gladstone suggests that Thoreau's focus on the modalities of seed dispersal effectively results in a *"modification of the human that makes it natural*: a conversion of the human-writing into nature's recording function" (*Criticism* 57, no. 3 [Summer 2015], 349). Similarly, Juliana Chow's "Partial Readings: Thoreau's Studies as Natural History's Casualties" considers the way Thoreau's *The Dispersal of Seeds* presents "a concurrence of biological, literary, and historical forms based on ecological relations of partialities rather than organic wholes" (in *Anthropocene Reading: Literary History in Geologic Times*, ed. Tobias Menely and Jesse Oak Taylor [University Park: Pennsylvania State University Press, 2017], 118).

116. Qtd., in John Bellamy Foster and Paul Burkett, *Marx and the Earth*, vii. The term "ecology" was coined by the German zoologist Ernst Haechel.

117. Thoreau, *Journal*, vol. 1, 23.

118. In the journal passage used to form the "The Bean-Field" chapter, Thoreau refers to his antagonism with weeds as a "small warfare" (*Journal*, vol. 2, 158).

119. In *A Week*, for example, he moves from the "scar[s]" in the landscape at sites of colonial violence to images of "crumbling" indigenous bones to abstract notions of a continuing "metamorphosis" where, presumably, one day "what was the Indian's will ere long be the white man's sinew" (237).

120. Henry David Thoreau, "The Service," in *Reform Papers*, 3.

121. Thoreau, "The Service," 7, 13.

122. Morton, *Dark Ecology*, 12.

123. Henry David Thoreau, "Life Without Principle," in *Reform Papers*, 167–68.
124. Thoreau, "Life Without Principle," 168.
125. Thoreau, "Life Without Principle," 169.
126. Henry David Thoreau, "The Last Days of John Brown," in *Reform Papers*, 150.
127. According to Allen Trachtenberg, in the nineteenth century, "incorporation" referenced "an emergent form of ownership in which power is distributed inwardly along hierarchical lines and outwardly in new social configurations" ("Preface to the Twenty-fifth-Anniversary Edition," in *The Incorporation of America: Culture and Society in the Gilded Age* [New York: Macmillan, 2007], x). For more on the topic of early American property, ownership, and personhood, see especially Chad Luck, *The Body of Property: Antebellum American Fiction and the Phenomenology of Possession* (2014), and Michelle Burnham, *Folded Selves: Colonial New England Writing in the World System* (2014).
128. John Keats, "To the George Keats's," February 14–May 3, 1819, in *John Keats: Selected Letters*, ed. Robert Gittings (New York: Oxford University Press, 2002), 232. Keats's point is that suffering in the world renders possible the existence of the soul. See my second chapter for a discussion of Fuller's notion of femality and historical oppression.
129. Deak Nabers, *Victory of Law: The Fourteenth Amendment, the Civil War, and American Literature, 1852–1867* (Baltimore: Johns Hopkins University Press, 2006), 93.
130. Nabers, *Victory of Law*, 121.
131. Nabers, *Victory of Law*, 122.
132. To be clear, I am not disputing Nabers's historical claims about the place of positive law within abolitionist discourses of the period—including Thoreau's. I am, however, suggesting that Thoreau's work negotiates these views in nuanced and non-identical ways.
133. Thoreau, "Slavery in Massachusetts," 98. Subsequent page references will appear parenthetically in the text. Thoreau is here making an argument that shares many aspects with Walter Benjamin's aforementioned notion of "divine violence," where an act suspends or breaks the law in order to recalibrate it. See Benjamin's "Critique of Violence," in *Selected Writings*, vol. I, 1913–1926, ed. Marcus Bullock and Michael W. Jennings (Cambridge: Harvard University Press, 2004). In "Robespierre, Or, the 'Divine Violence' of Terror" (in *Virtue and Terror: Maximilien Robespierre*, ed. Jean Ducange, trans. John Howe [New York: Verso, 2007]), Slavoj Žižek suggests that the "divine" nature of divine violence is not metaphysical in nature, but a material force springing from the foreclosed realms of a given reality/

society. My point in shifting from Nabers's focus on the positive production of laws to the positive interruption of laws also corresponds with Ciccariello-Maher's previously discussed call for a decolonized dialectics that foregrounds rupture rather than a rush to unity or consolidation. For Thoreau and for Ciccariello-Maher, both the means and the ends of unity remain a charged and open question.

134. Judith Butler, *Notes Toward a Performative Theory of Assembly* (Cambridge: Harvard University Press, 2015), 40–41.

135. Thoreau caustically recounts in "A Plea for Captain John Brown": "The slave-ship is on her way, crowded with its dying victims; new cargoes are being added in mid ocean; a small crew of slaveholders . . . is smothering four millions under the hatches, and yet the politician asserts that the only proper way by which deliverance is to be obtained, is by 'the quiet diffusion of the sentiments of humanity,' without any 'outbreak'" (in in *Reform Papers*, 124).

136. Thoreau, "The Last Days of John Brown," 147.

137. See Nancy Rosenblum's "Thoreau's Militant Conscience," *Political Theory* 9, no. 1 (February 1981), 82. Rosenblum defines "militancy" as "close but not identical to militarism and organized aggression; it is a way of characterizing the spiritual qualities of individuals, and it designates a distinctive psychological appetite for opposition" (81). My own point about the way Thoreau's ontologies and actants are oriented negatively toward existing conditions foregoes the dated pathologizing found in Rosenblum's definition. The term "negative" that I employ signals a historical situatedness whereby militancy passes from a strictly interior or symbolic orientation and into a material one. In one sense, my use of "negative" follows the path of Adorno's *Negative Dialectics*, which attempts to avoid the "positive" and consolidated identity-based aims of western dialectics (trans. E. B. Ashton [New York: Continuum, 2007], xix). At the same time, it allows for various standard and para (new/other) positive formations to emerge and assert historical effects. See Shannon Mariotti's *Thoreau's Democratic Withdrawal* for more on connections between Thoreau's thinking and Adorno's negative dialectics. In terms of historical contexts, recent studies that offer useful historical approaches to abolitionist protest and militancy include Martha Schoolman's *Abolitionist Geographies* (2014), David Roediger's *Seizing Freedom* (2014), Hoang G. Phan's *Bonds of Citizenship* (2013), Caleb Smith's *The Oracle and the Curse* (2013), Robin Blackburn's *The American Crucible* (2011), and Daphne A. Brook's *Bodies in Dissent* (2006).

138. Henry David Thoreau, "Reform and the Reformers," in in *Reform Papers*, 184. Subsequent page references will appear parenthetically in the text.

139. Thoreau, "The Last Days of John Brown," 145; and "A Plea for Captain John Brown," 125.

140. Thoreau, "A Plea for Captain John Brown," 126.

141. Thoreau, "A Plea for Captain John Brown," 132.

142. Thoreau, "Resistance to Civil Government," 67.

143. Henry David Thoreau, "Herald of Freedom," in *Reform Papers*, 56.

144. Arsić, *Bird Relics*, 21.

145. Thoreau, "Life Without Principles," in *Reform Papers*, 177. Subsequent page references will appear parenthetically in the text.

146. Thoreau, *Journal*, vol. 3, 96.

147. It should be noted that those supporting slavery in this era made concerted efforts to stymie all other (para-political) possible forms of directed functionality and behavior—hence Thomas Ruffin's 1829 court ruling, which found the slave to be merely an "animated instrument" of the master.

148. Thoreau, *Journal*, vol. 1, 49.

149. The adjective "liberal" here clearly connotes general period notions of tolerant and accommodating, or avoiding petty doctrinal intransience (see Kerry Larson, "Illiberal Emerson"); as I've noted, Thoreau commonly criticizes the specific socioeconomic policies and practices associated with the term.

150. Allewaert, *Ariel's Ecology*, 49.

151. Michael Marder, *Plant-Thinking: A Philosophy of Vegetal Life* (New York: Columbia University Press, 2013), 8. Subsequent page references will appear parenthetically in the text.

152. Allewaert, *Ariel's Ecology*, 86.

153. Allewaert, *Ariel's Ecology*, 33, 45.

154. Elizabeth Freeman, *Time Binds*, 13.

155. Freeman, *Time Binds*, 14.

156. Peter Coviello, *Tomorrow's Parties*, 32.

157. Thoreau, *Journal*, vol. 2, 158. It is important to consider Saidiya Hartman and Frank Wilderson III's argument that "[t]here's a structural prohibition (rather than merely a willful refusal) against whites being the allies of blacks due to this . . . 'species' division between what it means to be a subject and what it means to be an object: a structural antagonism" (qtd. in Christina Sharpe, *In the Wake: On Blackness and Being* [Durham, N.C.: Duke University Press, 2016], 57). I want to suggest that Thoreau's pseudo strange empathy is a potential supplemental-retroactive empathy: borne not from an original shared position of oppression or knowledge, but via the praxis of joining the other in a shared material resistance (a resistance that carries its own formative existential and symbolic limits and dangers). In this sense,

Thoreau's mode of strange empathy might anticipate aspects of Keeanga-Yamahtta Taylor's contemporary point that "[s]olidarity is standing in unity with people even when you have not personally experienced their particular oppression" (*From #BlackLivesMatter to Black Liberation* [Chicago: Haymarket Books, 2016], 215).

158. Thoreau, "A Plea for Captain John Brown," 132–33.

159. For a contextual discussion of Thoreau's narrative of the artist of Kouroo, including his appropriation of the Bhagavad Gita's tenets, see especially Alan D. Hodder's *Thoreau's Ecstatic Witness* (2001).

160. Thorson, *The Boatman*, 83.

4. UNADJUSTED EMANCIPATIONS

1. Fred Moten, *Black and Blur* (Durham, N.C.: Duke University Press, 2017), 85.

2. Moten, *Black and Blur*, 85.

3. Frank B. Wilderson III, *Red, White & Black: Cinema and the Structure of U.S. Antagonisms* (Durham, N.C.: Duke University Press, 2010), 40, 38.

4. Fred Moten, *In the Break: The Aesthetics of the Black Radical Tradition* (Minneapolis: University of Minnesota Press, 2003), 1; and Moten, *Black and Blur*, vii.

5. Moten, *In the Break*, 251.

6. Moten, *In the Break*, 251–53.

7. Moten, *In the Break*, 253.

8. In "Blackness and Nothingness (Mysticism in the Flesh)," *South Atlantic Quarterly* 112, no. 4 (Fall 2013): 737–80, Moten argues that "blackness is ontologically prior to . . . logistic and regulative power." Consequently, "blackness is prior to ontology" (739). Moten's work offers a rich and variegated engagement with Marx. For commentary on Marx relevant to the arguments he makes in *In the Break*, see especially Moten's *Stolen Life* (Durham, N.C.: Duke University Press, 2018), 82, 87.

9. Wilderson, *Red, White & Black*, 14; Achille Mbembe, *Critique of Black Reason* (Durham, N.C.: Duke University Press, 2017), 18. For Moten's discussion of Muñoz, see especially *Black and Blur*, 192–94. For an account of how Moten's work negotiates aspects of Afro-pessimism, see Moten, "Blackness and Nothingness," 738–39.

10. Jason Moore, *Capitalism in the Web of Life: Ecology and the Accumulation of Capital* (New York: Verso, 2015), 17, 14–15. Macarena Gómez-Barris refers to this same process, in a different context, as a "zone of extraction," where the longue durée of colonial capitalism "converted natural resources . . . into global commodities" (*The Extractive Zone: Social Ecologies and Decolonial Perspectives* [Durham, N.C.: Duke University Press, 2017], xvi).

11. Qtd. in John Bellamy Foster and Paul Burkett's *Marx and the Earth: An Anti-Critique* (Chicago: Haymarket Books, 2016), vii.

12. Monique Allewaert defines her use of the term "ecology" as "an assemblage of interpenetrating forces" (*Ariel's Ecology: Plantations, Personhood, and Colonialism in the American Tropics* [Minneapolis: University of Minnesota Press, 2013], 30). Along these lines, Jason Moore asserts that capitalism is an "ecological regime" (*Capitalism*, 158). François Vergès's chapter "Racial Capitalocene" builds on Moore's notion of the Capitalocene in ways that push sterile assessments of the ubiquitous term "Anthropocene" toward contexts related to race (see *Futures of Black Radicalism*, ed. Gaye Theresa Johnson and Alex Luben [New York: Verso, 2017]). Kathryn Yusoff takes up this topic as well, arguing that the dominant geological logics used to conceive of the Anthropocene are themselves part of an antiblack regulatory system (*A Billion Black Anthropocenes or None* [Minneapolis: University of Minnesota Press, 2018], 2). Even closer to the themes I will examine, Christina Sharpe uses the notion of "the weather" to describe "the totality of our environments; the weather is the total climate; and that climate is antiblack." Consequently, after the passage of the Fugitive Slave Act, "[S]lavery undeniably became the total environment" (*In the Wake: On Blackness and Being* [Durham, N.C.: Duke University Press, 2016], 104).

13. See especially Cedric J. Robinson's *Black Marxism: The Making of the Black Radical Tradition* (2005), and Edward E. Baptist's *The Half Has Never Been Told: Slavery and the Making of American Capitalism* (2014).

14. Stephen Best, *The Fugitive's Properties: Law and the Poetics of Possession* (Chicago: University of Chicago Press, 2004), 16–17.

15. In *Scenes of Subjections: Terror, Slavery, and Self-Making in Nineteenth-Century America* (New York: Oxford University Press, 1997), Hartman studies the "exclusions constitutive of liberalism, and the blameworthiness of the freed individual." The postbellum movements toward twentieth-century Civil Rights battles are, according to Hartman, laid with and foreclosed by various systemic limitations. Hartman's book goes on interrogate "the role of rights in facilitating relations of domination, the new forms of bondage enabled by proprietorial notions of the self, and the pedagogical and legislative efforts aimed at transforming the formerly enslaved into rational, acquisitive, and responsible individuals" (6).

16. Best, *Fugitive's Properties*, 13, 8–9.

17. In Sharpe's view, slavery is not a contained "singular" historical phenomenon but a "singularity": an expansive, continuing, and evolving condition (*Wake*, 106). For additional studies that link slavery with neoliberal realities, see especially Lisa Lowe's *The Intimacies of Four Continents*, Jared Sexton's *Amalgamation Schemes: Antiblackness and the Critique of*

Multiracialism, the anonymous *Burn Down the American Plantation: Call for a Revolutionary Abolitionist Movement*, Katherine McKittrick's "Plantation Futures," *Small Axe* 42 (November 2013): 1–15, and George Beckford's varied research on what is now termed the "plantation thesis," including *Persistent Poverty: Underdevelopment in Plantation Economies of the Third World* (1972). For a study of how liberal/neoliberal regimes produce acceptable modes of racial equality (through various "race-liberal orders") see Jodi Melamed's *Represent and Destroy: Rationalizing Violence in the New Racial Capitalism* (Minneapolis: University of Minnesota Press, 2011), x.

18. In George Ciccariello-Maher's terms, neoliberal structural adjustment entails "cutting wages, laying off teachers and other pubic-sector workers, cutting social-welfare spending, and privatizing public goods by selling off natural resources and services like water and gas—not to the highest bidder, but often to the highest briber. Under duress from international lenders, governments handed over their sovereignty by restructuring entire economies according tot the dictates of the global market" (*Building the Commune: Radical Democracy in Venezuela* [New York: Verso, 2016], 3).

19. Mbembe, *Critique of Black Reason*, 3–4.
20. Mbembe, *Critique of Black Reason*, 2, 37.
21. Wilderson, *Red, White & Black*, 20.
22. Mbembe, *Critique of Black Reason*, 2–3.
23. Tim Armstrong, *The Logic of Slavery: Debt, Technology, and Pain in American Literature* (New York: Cambridge University Press, 2012), 39. 41. See also Chad Luck's chapter "Anxieties of Ownership: Debt, Entitlement, and the Plantation Romance" in *The Body of Property: Antebellum American Fiction and the Phenomenology of Possession*.
24. Fred Moten and Stefano Harney, *Undercommons: Fugitive Planning & Black Study* (Brooklyn, N.Y.: Minor Compositions, 2013), 61–62.
25. Richard Dienst, *The Bonds of Debt: Borrowing Against the Common Good* (New York: Verso, 2011), 13, 151–52. The Marxist school of autonomism, represented most recently by the work of Franco "Bifo" Bernardi and others such as Christian Marazzi, has also written extensively about debt and its relation to modes of complication/resistance. See Moten and Harney's *The Undercommons* 64–65 for a critique of Bernardi's brand of autonomism. For other recent studies of debt, see Strike Debt's *The Debt Resistor's Operations Manual* and David Graeber's *Debt: The First 5,000 Years*.
26. Moten and Harney, *Undercommons*, 61, 66.
27. Harriet Beecher Stowe, *Dred: A Tale of the Great Dismal Swamp* (Chapel Hill: University of North Carolina Press, 200), 7. Subsequent page references will appear parenthetically in the text.

28. Edmund Jackson, "The Virginia Maroons," *Liberty Bell*, January 1, 1852. Qtd in Sylviane A. Diouf's *Slavery's Exiles: The Story of the American Maroons* (New York: New York University Press, 2014), 211.

29. See Diouf, *Slavery's Exiles*, 215.

30. Frederick Douglass, "Inhumanity of Slavery: Extract from a Lecture on Slavery, at Rochester, December 8, 1850." In *Frederick Douglass: Autobiographies*, ed. Henry Louis Gates, Jr. (New York: Library of America, 1994), 425. As Herbert Aptheker notes, maroons "carried on a regular, if illegal, trade with white people living on the borders of the swamp" (qtd. in Martha Schoolman, *Abolitionist Geographies* [Minneapolis: University of Minnesota Press, 2014], 161). According to Diouf, when landscape architect Frederick Olmsted visited the swamp in 1854, he was told that the fugitive slaves obtained "enough to eat, and some clothes, and perhaps two dollars a month in money" from local industry in and around the swamp. But the line between appropriation and exploitation was clearly blurred. In his 1895 "The Great Dismal Swamp," Alexander Hunter recounts that "especially the runaways were the hardest workers of this gang [of 'shingle-getters' and timber laborers]; and, as [the overseer] . . . was supposed to be unaware of their existence, he never paid them anything" (*Slavery's Exiles*, 213).

31. Best, *Fugitive's Properties*, 2.

32. Best, *Fugitive's Properties*, 2–3. As Best explains subsequently, Stowe's anxiety stems from her fear that "the fugitive is implicated in broader transformations in commercial law and culture," including "the relation between alienable (property) and inalienable (the self)" (17). As Crane points out, other prominent white abolitionists shared this view. Lydia Maria Child, for example, believed that "slavery was immoral . . . because it defied the contractual principle legitimating property." According to Child, while "[a]ll ideas of property are properly founded upon the mutual agreement of the human race," "[i]n slavery here is no *mutual* agreement" (*Race, Citizenship, and Law in American Literature* [Cambridge: Cambridge University Press, 2002], 56). For more on the broader relation between the changing status of property and personhood in the era, see especially Coviello's "Intimate Property: Race and the Civics of Self-Relation" (in *Intimacy in America: Dreams of Affiliation in Antebellum America*) and Luck's *The Body of Property: Antebellum American Fiction and the Phenomenology of Possession*.

33. Allewaert, *Ariel's Ecology*, 49, 30. I discuss Allewaert's notion of "paraontology" in my Introduction and ecological "entanglements" in Chapter 3.

34. Gail K. Smith, "Reading with the Other: Hermeneutics and the Politics of Difference in Stowe's *Dred*," *American Literature* 69, no. 2 (June 1997): 290.

35. Crane, *Race*, 70–72.

36. Crane, *Race*, 72, 74. According to Martha Schoolman's *Abolitionist Geographies*, "[W]hite radical abolitionists discovered in the maroon an object of imaginative identification to guide their increasingly counternationalist and revolutionary conception of what would have to be done to end slavery. . . . For them, the mountains and swamps associated with the maroons became invested imaginatively as spaces of resistance from which white radicals could rewrite the racial roles assigned by Garrisonian disunion by imagining a new mixed-race radical abolitionism as itself emerging from the swamp" (163). Schoolman concludes that white abolitionist appeals to black violence were "pragmatic" attempts to push existing legislative processes "toward a politically desirable end" (188). In a similar vein, Carrie Hyde's reading of *Dred* in *Civic Longing: The Speculative Origins of U.S. Citizenship* (Cambridge: Harvard University Press, 2018) is concerned with showing how the novel's theological innovations and unique presentation of "heavenly citizenship" reveal Stowe's vision of a "transracial community of estranged Christians" (69). Although Hyde acknowledges the political limitations of Stowe's Christian abolitionism (using Martin Delany and Frederick Douglass as counterpoints) (84), her reading of the novel is located within the parameters of Christian liberalism. This includes considering the prospective nature of Dred's revolutionary failure and precipitous death as "strategic" from the vantage of the white Christian marketplace (as the plot itself caused "dread" within white readers and, consequently, "the novelistic fulfillment of Dred's insurrectionary plot . . . almost certainly would have diminished its political efficacy in the 1850s") (71). Hyde claims that Dred's "insurrectional energies" remain "unrealized and yet immanent" and, as such, they "continue to loom for readers in historical time" (72). For Hyde, this "spectral agency" includes the projection of "new political futures" (73). One might ask, though, whose futures and what agencies live on. These matters are clarified in Hyde's closing arguments about Stowe's "abolitionist rehabilitation of the tradition of Christian estrangement," whereby "*Dred* moves away from the sentimental terrain of interracial sympathy and Christian domesticity and toward an estranged, theological commons" (80). In Hyde's reading, what "joins slaves and Christians in *Dred* is not the charitable sympathy of white abolitionists, but the sense that, theologically speaking, estrangement is endemic to life." Thus, Hyde presents a "heavenly citizenship" that is "a racially inclusive model of political citizenship" (81). Hyde notes that such "heavenly citizenship" might depict a Jamesonian "imaginary 'solution' to a real problem" (84). But perhaps the "imaginary" scenario Hyde discerns in *Dred* is, in actuality, part of the real historical problem itself—an example of the common liberal ruse of appealing to a

perceived shared structural lack or a shared positive status as a means to incorporate black/other realities. (In nineteenth-century contexts, one might think of the ideological role of death and mourning; in contemporary contexts, one might think of Latour's aforementioned claim that our climate crisis universalizes the migrant condition or the move from "Black Lives Matter" to "All Lives Matter" made by some misinformed liberals and conservatives alike.) For other readings of *Dred* that remain primarily within the ideological horizons of liberalism, see especially Maria Karafilis's "Spaces of Democracy in Harriet Beecher Stowe's *Dred*," *Arizona Quarterly* 55, no. 3 (1999): 23–49, and John Carlos Rowe's "Stowe's Rainbow Sign: Violence and Community in *Dred: A Tale of the Great Dismal Swamp* (1856)," *Arizona Quarterly* 58, no. 1 (Spring 2002), 37–55.

37. Stowe's novel shows how Harry's racial hybridity not only catalyzes conflict but also acts as a framework for the possible ways such conflicts might manifest. This is especially apparent in the way Harry orients himself toward his master-father. Although Harry feels "just like the bat in the fable . . . neither bird nor beast," he identifies as "Colonel Gordon's oldest son," and this same father-master had "charged" him with care of Nina and the plantation upon his death (62–63). Thus, Harry feels anxiety about the estate falling into "debt," as his "one pride in life . . . is to give it up to Miss Nina's husband in good order" (63). Stowe presents Harry's constitutional whiteness (adherence to debt, father, law, and so on) pervading even his affective-emotive rebellions toward injustice, portraying the way Harry's anger at Tom turned him "deadly pale; even his lips were of ashy whiteness." And, at this moment, both Nina and Tom notice "on the rigid lines of [Harry's] face . . . a resemblance to Col. Gordon" (144–45). The point here is that the rebellion Dred inspires in Harry is not a simple bifurcation—but plays out on the very ground of debt/whiteness.

38. According to Edward Clayton's sister, his plan envisions that the slaves "may be emancipated on the soil, just as the serfs were in England" (*Dred*, 310).

39. See especially Rowe's "Stowe's Rainbow Sign: Violence and Community in *Dred: A Tale of the Great Dismal Swamp*," where he suggests that Stowe "invokes the millenarian rhetoric and political activism of the African American Church as a potential resource for renewing religious credibility in the U.S." (39). See also Samuel Otter's "Stowe and Race" (in *The Cambridge Companion to Harriet Beecher Stowe*) and Robert S. Levine's *Martin Delany, Frederick Douglass, and the Politics of Representative Identity*.

40. According to Jacob Stratman, "Dred's insurrection . . . never really begins" ("Harriet Beecher Stowe's Preachers of the Swamp: Dred and the Jeremiad," *Christianity and Literature* 57, no. 3 [2008]: 380). See also Schoolman's *Abolitionist Geographies* and Hyde's *Civic Longing*.

41. See Allewaert's *Ariel's Ecology* and Leonard Cassuto's *The Inhuman Race: The Racial Grotesque in American Literature and Culture* (New York: Columbia University Press, 1997), 7.

42. The grotesque effect Stowe notes in this doubled linguistic reality, where Dred speaks both in terms of "exaltation" (ideal/whole) and "common life" (quotidian/particular), shares a structural resonance with the aforementioned economic anxiety Best sees in Stowe, in which she fears that slavery has compromised the commodity form. Here, emancipated black bodies would "speak" simultaneously of/from the vantage of particular person and universal exchange.

43. See Smith's "Reading with the Other," 303. For more on period debates about religious hermeneutics and Higher Criticism, see especially Richard A. Grusin's *Transcendentalist Hermeneutics: Institutional Authority and the Higher Criticism of the Bible.* For studies of black experience and Christianity, see James H. Cone's *God of the Oppressed* and *Black Theology & Black Power* as well as Cornel West's *Prophesy Deliverance!*.

44. Smith, "Reading," 299–300.

45. Hyde, *Civic Longing*, 81. See previous note on Hyde's reading of Stowe's pluralistic "heavenly citizenship."

46. In *Black Prometheus: Race and Radicalism in the Age of Atlantic Slavery*, Hickman argues that "*Dred* asks of the Euro-Christian God—'the God of *their* fathers' as Dred pointedly puts it—when, if ever, He is going to provide a more satisfying conclusion to the cosmic story of racial slavery than the novel itself, as of 1856, can provide" ([New York: Oxford University Press, 2017], 368).

47. Hickman, *Black Prometheus*, 368.

48. Elizabeth Povinelli, *Geontologies: A Requiem to Late Liberalism* (Durham, N.C.: Duke University Press, 2016), 13.

49. Povinelli's concept thus shares some aspects with Timothy Morton's notion of "hyperobjects," which posits that vast material "objects" such as global warming are both "viscous" (all over/in us) and withdrawing (too massive in scale for humans to fully conceive). See Morton, *Hyperobjects*.

50. *Dred*'s thereish is certainly over there, in a positive geo-spatial sense, for *Dred*'s fugitive coordinates and constitution are shaped by the real conditions that establish his swamp existence. Yet his fugitive status exceeds the simple register of physical/spatial difference. As Nahum Dimitri Chandler writes of the "African American problematic," "Its development, that is of the situation specific to African Americans, and there is always such specificity, comes about only by way of social processes that are excessive to any locality, no matter how locality is defined." Chandler continues: "Thus, the very particularity of the African American situation is

what sets in motion, or calls for, a form of suprainhabitation of thought or demands that a certain meta-perspective take shape right in the midst of experience, self-consciousness, or the particularities of existence. It solicits the development of a paraontological discourse" (qtd. in Moten, *Stolen Life*, 11). Following Chandler, I am suggesting that *Dred*'s specific and localized modes of fugitivity distort standard models for here and there, inside and outside.

51. As Mr. Jekyl explains to Harry, "[A] slave, not being a person in the eye of the law, cannot have a contract made with him. The law, which is based on the old Roman code, holds him, *pro nullis, pro mortuis*; which means . . . that he's held as nothing—as dead, inert substance" (385).

52. Jonathan Levy, *Freaks of Fortune: The Emerging World of Capitalism and Risk in America* (Cambridge: Harvard University Press, 2012), 5–6.

53. Giorgio Agamben, *The Time: A Commentary on the Letter to the Romans*, trans. Patricia Dailey (Stanford: Stanford University Press, 2005), 22–25.

54. I use the adjective "evental" in reference to Alain Badiou's concept of a revolutionary "event"; see especially *Being and Event* and *Logics of Worlds*.

55. Some scholars have been more optimistic about the ideological work of Dred's death. In John Carlos Rowe's account, "Stowe seems to resolve the difference between Dred's revolutionary aims and Milly's pacifism by treating them as two parts of the same emancipatory project. Perhaps Stowe stages Dred's sacrificial death in order to argue such revolutionary zeal might still be achieved through challenges to legal rhetoric and rhetorical exhortation, including the work of the abolitionist novel" ("Stowe's Rainbow Sign," 51).

56. The spread of cholera is thus reminiscent of pro-slavery characters' anxiety, earlier in the novel, about the spread of slave literacy, where it would "blaze" and "catch on" (313). The link between Dred (qua swamp ontology) and the cholera outbreak is also supported by the period's miasma theory, a notion that diseases such as cholera were transmitted by "fumes of decomposing organic matter" common to swampland (Jesse Oak Taylor, *Sky of Our Manufacture: The London Fog in British Fiction From Dickens to Woolf* [Charlottesville: University of Virginia Press, 2016]), 35.

57. See especially Kelly Wisecup's "'The Progress of the Heat Within': The West Indies, Yellow Fever, and Citizenship in William Wells Brown's *Clotel*," *Southern Literary Journal* 41, no. 1 (2008): 1–19.

58. Stowe's transition from a conflict defined by racial oppression to a disease caused by an infectious agent thus mirrors the way some contemporary "green" groups (what Ramachandra Guha and Joan Martinez-Alier call "full-stomach" environmentalisms) choose to protest ecological devastation without attending to underlying human (racial, class, regional,

and so on) oppression. For more on this topic, see especially Rob Nixon's *Slow Violence and the Environmentalism of the Poor*. Fred Moten writes that if blackness is indeed a "pathogen," then he "bear[s] the hope that blackness bears or is the potential to end the world" ("Blackness and Nothingness," *South Atlantic Quarterly* 112, no. 4 [Fall 2013], 739). My point is that Stowe's variety of black pathogen is, in effect, a type of violent liberal antidote or inoculation. Dred's cholera is a small disaster: a containable contagion.

59. Ann duCille, "Where in the World Is William Wells Brown? Thomas Jefferson, Sally Hemings, and the DNA of African-American Literary History," *American Literary History* 12, no. 3 (October 2000): 453.

60. Qtd. in duCille, "Where in the World," 454.

61. duCille, "Where in the World," 458.

62. I reference Ann Fabian's *The Unvarnished Truth: Personal Narratives in Nineteenth-Century America* (2002).

63. Such studies include Glenda R. Carpio's *Laughing Fit to Kill: Black Humor in the Fictions of Slavery* (New York: Oxford, 2008), which argues that Brown's humorous appropriation of stereotypes rhetorically effected "social change" (35); Ivy Wilson's *Specters of Democracy: Blackness and the Aesthetics of Politics in the Antebellum U.S.* (New York: Oxford, 2011), which claims that *Clotel* and its formal approaches represent a "mid-nineteenth century African American theorization of democracy" (39); Martha Schoolman's *Abolitionist Geographies*, which resituates Brown's writing within the context of transnational "critical cosmopolitanism" (99); and Geoffrey Sanborn's *Plagiarama!: William Wells Brown and the Aesthetic of Attractions* (New York: Columbia University Press, 2016), which considers Brown's "highly performative understanding of the self and its signifiers" within the context of the era's exhibitive economy (8).

64. Sanborn, *Plagiarama!*, 9. Somewhat in the vein of contemporary anti-critique, Sanborn's book pivots toward an aesthetic-historical rumination. As Sanborn explains, "The aim . . . is to contribute to the developing discussion of the more-than-necessary and other-than-purposive aspects of early African American writing and to argue for the centrality . . . of Brown" (5). While Sanborn offers a careful consideration of Brown's textual adaptations and plagiarism, his self-proclaimed Barthesian focus on textual enjoyment and use of liberal historical frameworks are somewhat limiting. These themes come together in moments when Sanborn makes central claims, such as his suggestion that "[i]n the final analysis, blackness is, for Brown, both a brogue, a rich inflection of a common tongue, and a flag whose colors can and should be rallied around. Understood in those terms, it is capable of being an object of enjoyment without being, for that reason, an

object of contempt" (85). Considering ways in which Brown's textual manipulations of racial constructions shift the presentation and consumption of blackness in the period is certainly a worthy line of discussion. The problem is that within Sanborn's reading, this "enjoyment" is borne primarily of and experienced by a white marketplace. Hemmed in by the stated desire to portray "a more-than-necessary and other-than-purposive" black aesthetic, Sanborn employs liberal platitudes and aesthetic framing devices instead of examining the nuanced ways Brown's formal approaches negotiate and produce a developing black aesthetic. In his reading, for example, Brown's use of a "variety-show aesthetic" "held out, for him, the prospect of a democratically non-narrative space, a stage on which various discourses and subjectivities might intermittently, clashingly appear." Consequently, Brown offered his white audience "what a culture based on the pleasurableness of difference might feel like" (10). And at the end of his book, Sanborn closes by suggesting that Brown "means to be multitonal, to cast overlooked objects in a new light, to exist by sympathy, to communicate clearly—to be, in short, relational, versatile, inclusive, and responsive" (126). Instead of reading black performance toward recognizable (and consumable) modes of aesthetic democratic inclusivity, scholars such as Daphne Brooks portray in nuanced historical ways how, across the nineteenth and twentieth centuries, "African Americans rehearsed methods to transform the notion of ontological dislocation into resistant performance so as to become the agents of their own liberation" (*Bodies in Dissent: Spectacular Performances of Race and Freedom, 1850–1910* [Durham, N.C.: Duke University Press, 2006], 3). For more on the radical black aesthetic and its potentials, see also Moten's aforementioned texts.

65. Sharpe, *In the Wake*, 115.

66. Sanborn, *Plagiarama!*, 8.

67. See Edward E. Baptist, *The Half Has Never Been Told: Slavery and the Making of American Capitalism* (New York: Basic Books, 2014), xxvii.

68. Lisa Lowe, *Intimacies of Four Continents* (Durham, N.C.: Duke University Press, 2015), 46–47.

69. William Wells Brown, *Clotel; Or, The President's Daughter* (New York: Modern Library, 2000), 177. Subsequent page references will appear parenthetically in the text.

70. William Wells Brown, "St. Domingo: Its Revolutions and Its Patriots. A Lecture Delivered Before the Metropolitan Athenaeum, London, May 16, And St. Thomas Church, Philadelphia, December 20, 1854" (Boston: Bela Marsh, 1855), 37.

71. William Wells Brown, *The Negro in the American Revolution: His Heroism and His Fidelity* (Athens: Ohio University Press, 2003), 20.

72. Brown, *The Negro in the American Revolution*, 12, 14.

73. Qtd. in Sanborn, *Plagiarama!*, 36.

74. As Sanborn points out, in *The Black Man* (1863), Brown goes as far as playfully, it appears, plagiarizing a defense of Alexandre Dumas's own practice of plagiarism (lifted from Wilson Armistead's *God's Image in Ebony* [1854]) (39).

75. William Wells Brown, *Narrative of William W. Brown, a Fugitive Slave. Written by Himself*. In *William Wells Brown: A Reader*, ed. Ezra Greenspan (Athens: University of Georgia Press, 2008), 38, 40.

76. Brown, *Narrative of William W. Brown*, 41.

77. Maurizio Lazzarato, *Signs and Machines: Capitalism and the Production of Subjectivity*, trans. Joshua David Jordan (Los Angeles: Semiotext(e), 2014), 8–9.

78. Brown includes a February 16, 1852, letter from Price in his reworked autobiography that resets Brown's value at $500 (*Clotel*, 39). In 1854, shortly after *Clotel* was published, Brown's English friends purchased his freedom from Enoch Price, allowing Brown to return to the United States.

79. Bonnie Martin, "Neighbor-to-Neighbor Capitalism: Local Credit Networks and the Mortgaging of Slaves," in *Slavery's Capitalism: A New History of American Economic Development*, ed. Sven Beckert and Seth Rockman (Philadelphia: University of Pennsylvania Press, 2016), 108.

80. Sven Beckert and Seth Rockman, "Introduction: Slavery's Capitalism," in *Slavery's Capitalism: A New History of American Economic Development*, ed. Sven Beckert and Seth Rockman (Philadelphia: University of Pennsylvania Press, 2016), 18.

81. Edward E. Baptist, "Toxic Debt, Liar Loans, Collateralized and Securitized Human Beings, and the Panic of 1837," in *Capitalism Takes Command: The Social Transformation of Nineteenth-Century America*, ed. Michael Zakim and Gary J. Kornblith (Chicago: University of Chicago Press, 2012), 73. For a comprehensive study of the relation between nineteenth-century capitalism and slavery, see especially Baptist's *The Half Has Never Been Told*.

82. Baptist, "Toxic Debt," 79.

83. Baptist, "Toxic Debt," 80–81.

84. Tim Armstrong uses this language to reference Douglass's fugitive economic status. See Armstrong, *The Logic of Slavery*, 46.

85. Karl Marx, *Grundrisse: Introduction to the Critique of Political Economy*, trans. Martin Nicolaus (New York: Vintage, 1973), 115. Discussing the *Grundrisse* in a December 12, 1857 letter to Engels, Marx writes, "The American crisis—which we foresaw . . . would break out in New York is fantastic. . . . I am working like a madman for whole nights in order to

coordinate my work on economics, and to get together the *Grundrisse* before the deluge" (qtd. in Antonio Negri, *Marx Beyond Marx: Lessons on the Grundrisse*, trans. Harry Cleaver, Michael Ryan, and Maurizio Viano [Brooklyn: Autonomedia, 1991], 2).

86. Antonio Negri, *Marx Beyond Marx*, 23.
87. Negri, *Marx Beyond Marx*, 24.
88. Cesare Casarino, *Modernity at Sea: Melville, Marx, Conrad, in Crisis* (Minneapolis: University of Minnesota Press, 2002), 89.
89. Casarino, *Modernity at Sea*, 90.
90. Negri, *Marx Beyond Marx*, 9.
91. For more on the terminology of "hands" in relation to slavery, see especially Edward Baptist, *The Half Has Never Been Told*, 102.
92. Marx, *Grundrisse*, 196.
93. Dienst, *The Bonds of Debt*, 151.
94. The term "unit of investment" is from historian Sharon Ann Murphy and quoted in Armstrong, *The Logic of Slavery*, 42.
95. Marx, *Grundrisse*, 746.
96. In addition to noting that he sent a copy of his autobiography to Price, Brown explains, after reproducing this first letter, that "he could not conscientiously purchase his own liberty, because, by so doing, he would be putting money into the pockets of the manstealer which did not justly belong to him" (29–30).
97. Sharpe, *In the Wake*, 113–14.
98. Sharpe, *In the Wake*, 117.
99. Brown, *Narrative of William W. Brown*, 5.
100. Brown, *Narrative of William W. Brown*, 59.
101. According to Wilson, "it . . . seems . . . important to note that it is precisely fences upon which Brown scribbles his name, pieces that, taken together, might approximate a form of outsider art displayed in the public domain. If this scene is emblematic of what Stepto has called liberation through literacy, it is one that is engendered by a graffiti aesthetic" (*Specters*, 38).
102. Brown, *Narrative of William W. Brown*, 55. Brown gestures toward this performative and pragmatic function of naming in his original autobiography's discussion of an Uncle Frank who made a living peddling fortunes. He writes, "Whether true or not, he had the *name*, and this is about half of what one needs in this gullible age" (*Narrative of William W. Brown*, 51).
103. Moten, "Blackness and Nothingness," 742.
104. Weheliye, *Habeas Viscus*, 77–78.
105. It is unclear from the narrative how much Brown or his various textual positions desire something like recognition. Contemporary scholars

of Indigenous Studies such as Glen Sean Coulthard have discussed a long and differentiated tradition of indigenous rejection of liberal pluralist projects of recognition-as-incorporation (see *Red Skin, White Masks: Rejecting the Colonial Politics of Recognition*); Audra Simpson makes a similar move in her book *Mohawk Interruptus: Political Life Across the Borders of Settler States* (Durham, N.C.: Duke University Press, 2014), positing "refusal" as a political alternative to multicultural recognition (2). For a useful historical overview of the "era of assimilation," see Beth H. Piatote's *Domestic Subjects: Gender, Citizenship, and Law in Native American Literature.* David Kazanjian has studied the related themes of period biopolitical foreclosures, such as the juridical state of exception used by article nine of the Treaty of Guadalupe Hidalgo to appropriate and incorporate Mexican peoples and property without full citizenship rights (see *The Colonizing Trick: National Culture and Imperial Citizenship in Early America*). My point about Brown's unique mode of spiraling agency lies somewhere amid and among these specific historical coordinates.

106. In *Ontological Terror*, Warren bars the term "being" within the term "black being" in order to signal how "blackness lacks Being" and, consequently, opens up "the abyss of ontology" ([Durham, N.C.: Duke University Press, 2018], 12).

107. Russ Castronovo, *Necro Citizenship: Death, Eroticism, and the Public Sphere in the Nineteenth-Century United States* (Durham, N.C.: Duke University Press, 2007), 40–42.

108. Wilson, *Specters of Democracy*, 55.

109. Moten, *Black and Blur*, 2.

110. Bryan Wagner, quoted in Moten, "Blackness and Nothingness," 739.

111. Stefano Harney and Fred Moten, "Michael Brown," *boundary 2* 42, no. 4 (2015): 82–83.

112. Robert S. Levine, *Martin Delany, Frederick Douglass, and the Politics of Representative Identity* (Chapel Hill: University of North Carolina Press, 1997), 175–76. For more on the textual history of *Blake*, see Jerome McGann's "Editor's Note" in Martin R. Delany's *Blake; or the Huts of America*, ed. Jerome McGann (Cambridge: Harvard University Press, 2017), xxxiii–xxxviii.

113. Long considered a founding figure of black nationalism, Delany has been portrayed by scholars such as Eric Sundquist and Paul Gilroy as a progenitor of strategic transnational and transatlantic black radicalism (see Sundquist's *To Wake the Nations: Race in the Making of American Literature* and Gilroy's *The Black Atlantic*). For a useful consideration of Delany's various emigration and pan-Africanist efforts and their relation to his evolving domestic racial/political positions, especially vis-à-vis those of Douglass, see

Levine's *Martin Delany, Frederick Douglass, and the Politics of Representative Identity*; for Delany's scientific thought and its influence within his writing, see Britt Rusert's *Fugitive Science: Empiricism and Freedom in Early African American Culture*. Born free in Virginia, Delany studied with black leaders in Pittsburgh and, by the early 1840s, apprenticed as a doctor and began editing the black newspaper *Mystery*. After a short stint co-editing the *North Star* with Douglass and being expelled from Harvard Law School on racial grounds, Delany published *The Condition, Elevation, Emigration, and Destiny of the Colored People of the United States* (1852). After moving to Canada in 1856, Delany focused attention on his various emigration efforts, especially a plan to help African Americans emigrate to West Africa. In 1859, while composing and publishing parts of *Blake*, Delany toured the Niger Valley, eventually signing a treaty with the Abeokuta for land, and these experiences led to Delany's *Official Report of the Niger Valley Exploring Party* (1861). During the war, when his emigration plans fell through, Delany worked to recruit black troops and was eventually commissioned as a Major. Later in life, after working in the Freeman's Bureau in South Carolina, Delany returned to his African emigration efforts and published *Principia of Ethnography: The Origin of Race and Color* (1879).

114. "Pro forma," *Online Etymology Dictionary*, https://www.etymonline.com/search?q=pro+forma.

115. Grégory Pierrot, "Writing Over Haiti: Black Avengers in Martin Delany's *Blake*." *Studies in American Fiction* 41, no. 2 (Fall 2014), 177.

116. Moten, *Black and Blur*, 2.

117. James's account of Dessalines's message to his men is as follows: "Take courage, I tell you, take courage. The French will not be able to remain long in San Domingo. They will do well at first, but soon they will fall ill and die like flies. Listen! If Dessalines surrenders to them a hundred times he will deceive them a hundred times. I repeat, take courage and you will see that when the French are few we shall harass them, we shall beat them, we shall burn the harvests and retire to the mountains. They will not be able to guard the country and they will have to leave. Then I shall make you *independent*. There will be no more whites among us.' Independence. It was the first time that a leader had put it before his men. Here was not only the programme, but tactics" (qtd. in Moten, *Black and Blur*, 6).

118. Moten, *Black and Blur*, 7.

119. Unlike Lowe, Moten allows for such dialectical dissonance and refutation within aspects of Marxism. See especially *Black and Blur*, 9.

120. Lowe, *Intimacies of Four Continents*, 156.

121. Jeremy Matthew Glick, *The Black Radical Tragic: Performance, Aesthetics, and the Unfinished Haitian Revolution* (New York: New York University Press, 2016), 5.

122. Caleb Smith, *The Oracle and the Curse: A Poetics of Justice from the Revolution to the Civil War* (Cambridge: Harvard University Press, 2013), 195.

123. Levine, *Martin Delany*, 203

124. Martin R. Delany, *Blake; or, The Huts of America*, ed. Jerome McGann (Cambridge: Harvard University Press, 2017), 40. Subsequent page references will appear parenthetically in the text.

125. Smith, *Oracle and the Curse*, 204–6.

126. Smith, *Oracle and the Curse*, 202.

127. Ralph Ellison, *The Invisible Man* (New York: Vintage, 1995), 577. For discussions of this Ellison passage, see Moten's *In the Break*, 73, and *Stolen Life*, 43.

128. Moten and Harney, *The Undercommons*, 27.

129. Schoolman, *Abolitionist Geographies*, 2.

130. For example, Schoolman uses the cartographic to consider Brown's work and Rusert traces aspects of "fugitive science" in Brown's writing. It is outside the scope of this chapter to engage with Rusert's rich historical claims about black fugitive science. I do, however, want to point out the way her nuanced historical discussion is predicated upon on an implied equivalence between Jane Bennett's liberal model of vibrant matter and Fred Moten's work on what Rusert calls the "'dispossessive force' of objects" (*Fugitive Science: Empiricism and Freedom in Early African American Culture* [New York: NYU Press], 173). It should be noted that Moten's most recent trilogy starts out by reformulating his earlier statements about blackness and object-ness. But even within *In the Break*, the text Rusert cites, the "irruption" that is/constitutes blackness is a far cry from (indeed, is perhaps structurally antithetical to) the type of positive animated material Bennett is after.

131. Pierrot, "Writing Over Haiti," 190. Here Pierrot is referencing the scene where, with a British ship in pursuit, the American captain of the *Vulture* orders his crew to throw all sick and dying slaves overboard in order to lighten the load and increase speed.

132. Levine, *Martin Delany*, 193–95.

133. Levine, *Martin Delany*, 194.

134. Chris Apap, "'Let no man of us budge one step': David Walker and the Rhetoric of African American Emplacement," *Early American Literature* 46, no. 2 (2011): 330.

135. W. E. B. Du Bois, *Black Reconstruction in America: An Essay Toward a History of the Part Which Black Folk Played in the Attempt to Reconstruct Democracy in America, 1860–1880* (New York: Oxford University Press, 2007), 119.

136. David Roediger, *Seizing Freedom: Slave Emancipation and Liberty for All* (New York: Verso, 2014), 5.

137. Blake's secret plan is religious, therefore, in the sense that Walter Benjamin's concept of "divine violence" is religious. As I note in Chapter 3, Slavoj Žižek suggests that the "divine" nature of divine violence is not metaphysical in nature but a material force springing from the foreclosed realms of a given reality or society.

138. Susan Howe, *This That* (New York: New Directions, 2010), 28. In *The America Play*, Suzan-Lori Parks defines "(rest)" as to "[t]ake a little time, a pause, a breather; make a transition" (qtd. in Anthony Reed, *Freedom Time: The Poetics and Politics of Black Experimental Writing* [Baltimore: Johns Hopkins University Press, 2014], 155).

139. Rusert, *Fugitive Science*, 166–67.

140. Such liberal mechanisms abound, including Maggie using the Spanish law *coartación* to purchase her freedom and the council's proper declaration of war.

141. I reference Heidegger's notion that the broken tool illuminates the way a systemically normalized and ignored object/function appears only when it ceases to operate smoothly. See *Being in Time*, trans. Joan Stambaugh (Albany: SUNY Press, 1996), 325. Following Henri Wallon's notion that the state of slavery renders one an "animated instrument," the slaves/ex-slaves here become a locus for the irruption of a new assertion of agency (qtd. in Orlando Patterson, *Slavery and Social Death: A Comparative Study* [Cambridge: Harvard University Press, 1985], 4).

EPILOGUE: CARE, *THERE AND NOW*

1. Joshua Clover and Juliana Spahr, *#Misanthropocene: 24 Theses* (Oakland: Commune Editions, 2014), 3.

2. As I suggest in my introduction, the results of the 2016 election and its subsequent impacts have undoubtedly had ripple effects within humanities scholarship, disrupting the sanitized and aesthetic trends that dominated fields in literary studies during the years of the Obama administration.

3. Judith Butler, *Notes Toward a Performative Theory of Assembly* (Cambridge: Harvard University Press, 2015), 12–13.

4. Maureen Konkle, *Writing Indian Nations: Native Intellectuals and the Politics of Historiography, 1827–1863* (Chapel Hill: University of North Caroline Press, 2004), 28, 43.

5. Christina Sharpe, *In the Wake: On Blackness and Being* (Durham, N.C.: Duke University Press, 2016), 120.

6. Sharpe, *In the Wake*, 20, 123.

7. María Puig de la Bellacasa, *Matters of Care: Speculative Ethics in More Than Human Worlds* (Minneapolis: University of Minnesota Press, 2017), 4–5.

8. As I explain in earlier chapters, Povinelli's conception of "hereish" offers an original way of thinking about the compromised relation between local and global in the modern world. For Povinelli, the geological catastrophes of the present force us to inhabit a new space/time and, in so doing, they shift conceptually our "object of concern . . . across competing struggles for existence, implicating how we conceptualize scale, event, circulation, and being" (*Geontologies: A Requiem to Late Liberalism* [Durham, N.C.: Duke University Press, 2016]), 13.

9. Moten and Harney, *Undercommons: Fugitive Planning and Black Study* (Brooklyn, N.Y.: Minor Compositions, 2013), 17.

10. Ralph Waldo Emerson, "Duty," in *The Early Lectures of Ralph Waldo Emerson*, vol. 3, ed. Robert E. Spiller and Wallace E. Williams (Cambridge: Harvard University Press, 1972), 138–50, quotation on 139.

11. Emily Dickinson, L265, qtd. in Susan Howe, *My Emily Dickinson* (New York: New Directions, 2007), 132.

12. A foundational aspect of Morton's work, and that of the speculative realism crowd, has been to attack what they deem as the anthropocentric "strong correlationism" of Western philosophical traditions, especially the post-Kantian lineages of Hegel (a form of thinking where "there are things in themselves . . . but . . . they aren't 'realized' until they are correlated by a correlator," here via forms of human reason) (Morton, *Humankind: Solidarity with Nonhuman People* [New York: Verso, 2017], 7). Morton's wide-ranging work offers compelling examples of how embracing weak correlationism, or moving past correlationism altogether, may have positive effects. At the same time, within Morton's work, the theoretical and political ramifications of this position are often underdeveloped, especially within his various brief attempts to critique or influence Marxist analysis. On the one hand, as my third chapter suggests, Morton's modes of weak correlationism provide original theoretical schemas that might aid directly the political modality of care I am discussing. On the other hand, Morton's frequent recourse to pluralistic and flattened relations renders these models susceptible to the type of syntactical liberalism (or worse) I discuss in my introduction. To quote just one passage from Morton's *Dark Ecology*: "Future coexistence . . . accepts contradiction and ambiguity. It is neither a progression nor a regression from contemporary consumerist agrilogistics. It has accepted the fact that we Mesopotamians never killed the loopy Hydra. Humans should act to change their material conditions, but those conditions aren't an Easy Think Substance. Those conditions might be wasps, mycelium, spores, and leopards. . . . Consider how we might recover from agrilogistics. The point would not be to dismantle global agriculture and replace it with yet another top-down solution. Instead, we need many

toy structures, many temporalities." Invoking Jane Bennett's brand of vibrant materialism, Morton goes on to conclude that "[t]he exit from modernity is somewhere in the craft store with its gaudy, sparkly Christmas ornaments for trees full of light, pagan consumerism" (143, 146–47). In this attempt to push past constituent limits of traditional dialectics as well as the left's political imagining, Morton leaves us in a more familiar place than he may think—with stylized irony and ever anew modes of consumerism. Many of these problematics are also apparent in his newest book's attempt to level "solidarity" into a zero-level of material relation. Here, he claims that reality exists in a biosphere he calls "the symbiotic real" (a "weird 'implosive whole' in which entities are related in a non-total, ragged way"). Solidarity, therefore, describes a type of "reliance between discrete yet deeply interrelated beings" that is mediated at every level by the "incompleteness of the symbiotic real." As such, solidarity becomes *"the phenomenology of the symbiotic real"* and "only works when it is thought at this scale" (*Humankind*, 1–2). There is not room here to parse the ways this partial appropriation of Lacan may dilute potential formations of specific collectives and their interventions. It's worth noting, though, how Morton's move returns paradoxically to the ground his first major ecological study, *Ecology Without Nature*, seeks to disband—where he, in effect, dismisses solidarity along agonistic or antagonistic axial lines by naturalizing it as a byproduct of biospheric operations.

13. Fred Moten, *Black and Blur* (Durham, N.C.: Duke University Press, 2017), 10.
14. José Esteban Muñoz, *Cruising Utopia: The Then and There of Queer Futurity* (New York: NYU Press, 2009), 1.
15. As Whitman writes at the close of "Song of Myself," "Failing to fetch me at first keep encouraged, / Missing me one place search another, / I stop somewhere waiting for you" (*Leaves Of Grass* [Brooklyn, N.Y.: 1855], reproduced in *The Walt Whitman Archive*, ed. Ed Folsom and Kenneth M. Price, 57.) The type of presentism I am suggesting is anything but idealist or magical in nature. Instead of merely constituting part of our present's prehistory (after a definitive or assumed break), the nineteenth century might be thought of as part of a longer constellation of "now" (albeit a now composed of a "series of discontinuous interruptions," to borrow Spivak's phrase from a different context) (*A Critique of Postcolonial Reason: Toward a History of the Vanishing Present* [Cambridge: Harvard University Press, 1999], 208). Using various historical frames, the nineteenth-through-twenty-first centuries might be seen as existing within a differentiated and multi-horizoned reality of Capital (economic/material), or the Anthropocene (geological/material), or liberalism/neoliberalism (ideological/material), and so on. Historical events and causalities might still be contingent and "aleatory" in the sense

that Althusser argues for with his nonteleological notion of "materialism of the encounter," for instance, but they should be seen to occur within long, multitudinous planes or fronts (*Philosophy of the Encounter: Later Writings, 1978–1978*, ed. François Matheron and Oliver Corpet, trans. G. M. Goshgarian [New York: Verso, 2006], 167). This is different from the common notion of a *longue durée*, which is positive in nature and tends to travel along a two-dimensional and diachronic trajectory (forward and back). I am thinking more along the lines of Anna Tsing's conception of "third nature," where "[l]ike virtual particles in a quantum field, multiple futures pop in and out of possibility; third nature emerges within such temporal polyphony" (*The Mushroom Cloud at the End of the World: On the Possibility of Life in Capitalist Ruin* [Princeton: Princeton University Press, 2015], viii). The emergence of such realities, however, might circuit through or spring from any part of the thickened now I am suggesting. In *Our History Is the Future* (New York: Verso, 2019), Nick Estes argues that "[t]here is no separation between the past and present, meaning that an alternative future is also determined by our understanding of our past" (14). In the context of the Oceti Sakowin, this distended notion of the present means, on the one hand, that processes of domination are "never complete." Although "[t]he colonial state's methods for gaining access to new territories change over time," "[t]oday's state violence and surveillance against Water Protectors is a continuation of the Indian Wars of the nineteenth century" (89–90). This logic can be seen, in a different context, in Christina Sharpe's aforementioned notion of the long wake of slavery. Here, one must assert the foundational role of loss—both in terms of the obliteration of bodies and worlds via modes of genocide and in terms of the implicit and explicit silences and refusals found in the past and present alike. Stephen Best's arguments against what he terms "melancholy historicism," for example, and the need to shift away from an archive and aesthetics of historical loss and toward one that "accepts the past's turning away" illuminates, in its own way, the stakes for how one might orient toward such manifold presents and un-presents (*None Like Us: Blackness, Belonging, Aesthetic Life* [Durham, N.C.: Duke University Press, 2018], 20–21). This being said, the realities produced by the continued and connected conditions of the past and present offer ongoing ways to resist and leverage alternatives. Both Sharpe and Katherine McKittrick intimate, in poignant ways, such present and future potentialities (see Sharpe's *In the Wake* and McKittrick's "Plantation Futures," *Small Axe* 42 [November 2013]: 1–15). In his own work, Estes describes an elder who, in the aftermath of a 2016 government raid on a Water Protector camp, donned regalia with copper pennies that "had holes drilled into Lincoln's ears with red ribbon threaded through." This elder explained that Lincoln "didn't listen" when he signed the execution orders of thirty-eight Dakota people in 1862 (the same week Lincoln signed the Emancipation Proclamation), "so we opened his ears" (130). As this woman danced, the "pennies swayed with the flickering fire and billowing smoke. Behind her, armed police were perched on a hill half mile away" (131). In my own rumination, caring there and now includes negotiating layers of history in ways that see and use the connections among pasts, presents, and futures. It is not just about producing gradual positivist reform or historical "knowledge" (telos), but about imagining and generating specific interventions from within or across horizons of now/then/here/there—and, sometimes, nowhere. In this sense, new conceptual pivots and bands of relation can and will spring even from the deep realities of a hole in a copper ear.

INDEX

abolition movements. *See* slavery and abolition movements
The Actuality of Communism (Bosteels), 5–6, 16
Adorno, Theodor, 65, 91, 94
Adventures in Transcendental Materialism (Johnston), 23
Afro-pessimism, 19–20, 154–55, 157–58, 172, 215–16nn83–84
Agamben, Giorgio, 39, 173–74
Agassiz, Jean Louis Rodolphe, 115, 131, 138, 185
Allewaert, Monique: on ecological accounts of resistance, 8, 28, 120, 130, 149, 150, 162, 260n12; on parahumans, 214–15n76; on personhood, 17, 213–14n66
Althusser, Louis, 1, 5, 277n15
Anderson, Amanda, 12
Anglo-African Magazine, 189, 191
Ansichten der Natur (Humboldt), 115
Antebellum Posthuman (Ellis), 26
Anthropocene, 24, 117, 118, 215n77, 218n103, 250n61, 260n12
Apap, Chris, 193
Aptheker, Herbert, 262n30
Apuleius, 66
Arcades Project (Benjamin), 114
Argersinger, Jana, 245n145
Armstrong, Tim, 158
Arsić, Branka: on biopolitics, 107; *Bird Relics*, 106–7, 120, 129–30; on Emerson, 33–34, 224–25n41; Marder and, 149; *The Other Emerson*, 33–34; on Thoreau, 28, 94, 105–8, 112, 147, 242–43n133, 246n16
Attucks, Crispus, 177
"Autobiographical Romance" (Fuller), 78–79

bad debts: in *Clotel*, 29, 157–59, 163–64, 180–84, 204; collective resistance and, 29; defined, 158; in *Dred*, 161–62, 164–65, 172–73
Badiou, Alain, 27, 34, 83, 213n65, 216n94
Baker, Jennifer, 41–42
Balibar, Étienne, 6–7, 8–9
Baptist, Edward E., 156, 180
Bartram, William, 130
Bastiat, Frédéric, 243n134
Beecher, Catharine, 81, 82
Beethoven, Ludwig van, 75, 84, 90–91, 238n113, 239n115
Benjamin, Walter, 68, 114, 139, 251n74, 256n133, 274n137
Bennett, Jane, 23–25, 28, 93–94, 106, 135
Bennington, Geoffrey, 195
Benvenuto Cellini (Berlioz), 85
Berlant, Lauren, 1, 19, 244–45n139
Berlioz, Hector, 85
Berardi, Franco, 253–54n104, 261n25
Best, Stephen, 156, 159, 161–62, 277n15
Billerica dam, 108, 110–11, 114, 150, 152
biopolitics: alternatives to, 17, 19, 23–24, 25–26, 149–51, 215n77; Arsić on, 107; liberal subjectivity and, 214–15n76; necropolitics and, 10
The Biopolitics of Feeling (Schuller), 26
Black and Blur (Moten), 153, 154–55, 156–57
The Black Jacobins (James), 190
Black Rights/White Wrongs (Mills), 3–4
Blake; or, The Huts of America (Delany), 189–200; comparison to *Clotel*, 187, 189, 199; comparison to *Dred*, 189, 194–95; landscapes of, 189–90; overview, 5, 29, 154, 160; prophet organization within, 191–92; serial publication of, 189, 191

279

Blaser, Mario, 22, 212–13n58, 250n59
The Boatman (Thorson), 108
Boen, Johannes, 68
Boggs, Colleen Glenney, 120, 214–15n76
Bonaparte, Napoleon, 50
Bosteels, Bruno, 5–6, 16, 23, 25
Boston Quarterly Review, 49
bourgeois, 6–9, 65, 114–16, 120–21, 145–46, 205–6n3
Briante, Susan, 101
Brisbane, Albert, 85
Brown, John: Emerson on, 36, 47; Thoreau on, 111, 139, 142–43, 146–47, 152
Brown, Wells, 186
Brown, Wendy, 17–18
Brown, William Wells, writings of: "Narrative of the Life and Escape of William Wells Brown," 29, 159–60, 178–79, 182–83, 185–86; *Narrative of William*, 178, 186, 270n102; *The Negro in the American Rebellion*, 176–77; plagiarism and, 175–76, 178–79; "St. Domingo," 176; *Three Years in Europe*, 178–79. See also *Clotel*
Brownson, Orestes, 48–49
Bryant, Levi, 23
Bubbles (Sloterdijk), 113–14
Buell, Lawrence, 224–25n41
Bull, Ole, 85–87, 90
Burke, Edmond, 14
Burns, Anthony, 55
Bush, George W., 244n139
Butler, Judith, 144, 202, 209n30, 248n35

Cambridge Platonists, 37
Cameron, Sharon, 34, 45, 108, 109, 221n8, 225n43
Cape Cod (Thoreau), 104
capitalism: liberalism and, 11–12; neoliberalism and, 11–12, 210n46; personhood and, 22, 29, 45; subjectivity and, 178–84
Caputo, John, 234n70
care, 201–4
Casarino, Cesare, 181–82, 239–40n124
Castiglia, Christopher, 18–19, 29
Castronovo, Russ, 10, 56, 187–88, 228n82
Cavell, Stanley, 45, 46–47, 107–8, 224–25n41
"The Celestial Empire" (Fuller), 90, 239n115

Chandler, Nahum Dimitri, 20–21, 265–66n50
Channing, William, 46, 62, 104
Chartist movement, 61
Cherokee Nation v. Georgia (1831), 3
Chicago School of Economics, 11
Child, Lydia Maria, 132
Chow, Juliana, 207n16
Ciccariello-Maher, George, 8, 107, 137, 146, 208–9n29, 210n46, 246n17, 257n133, 261n18
"Circles" (Emerson), 46
citizens and citizenship: defined, 1–3; necro citizenship, 10; origin, 207n14; race-based, 3, 9–11; rethinking, 6–8, 208n27, 208–9n29 (see also xenocitizens); violence sanctioned through, 9–11, 14. See also personhood
Citizenship (Balibar), 6–7
Clotel; or, the President's Daughter (Brown): bad debt in, 29, 157–59, 180–84, 204; comparison to *Blake*, 187, 189, 199; criticisms of, 175–78, 267–68n64, 269n74; naming and identity in, 185–86; overview, 5, 29, 154, 159–60; plagiarism and, 175–76, 178–79; shinplasters of, 179, 181–87, 198–99; spiraling positionings in, 187–89; symbolism of writing in, 186–87; *Three Years in Europe* as source for, 178–79
Clover, Joshua, 201
Cole, Phyllis, 245n145
Coleridge, Samuel Taylor, 91
Collins, James, 120–21
Colonial Debts Act (1732), 158
communism, 5–6, 154, 212n51
conflict ontology, 16
Congregationalism, 36–37
Connolly, William, 23
Consolidated Association of the Planters of Louisiana (CAPL), 180–81
Constant, Benjamin, 37
Coronado, Raúl, 8, 208n25
correlationism, 23, 121, 204, 251–52n75, 275n12
Coulthard, Glen Sean, 22
"Courage" (Emerson), 36, 47, 226n54
Cousin, Victor, 41
Coviello, Peter, 109, 119, 151, 220n113, 262n32

Crabtree, Adam, 74
Cranch, Christopher P., 85
Crane, Gregg, 2, 3, 162–63, 228–29n82
Crawford, Thomas, 87, 88
Crutzen, Paul, 24
Curtis, George W., 85
Cushing, Caleb, 78

Dana, Charles A., 85
Darimon, Alfred, 181
Darwin, Charles: on ecology, 5, 102, 155, 207n16; *On the Origin of Species*, 138; Thoreau on, 115, 137–38, 143; *Voyage of the Beagle*, 138
Dean, Jodi, 5
death drive, 69–72, 233–34n55, 234n57
debt, 156–59, 164–66, 180, 198, 261n25. *See also* bad debts
de Certeau, Michel, 192
Decolonizing Dialectics (Ciccariello-Maher), 8, 107, 137, 208n29, 246n17
de la Cadena, Marisol, 22, 212–13n58, 216n92, 250n59
Delany, Martin R., 189–91, 193, 271–72n113. *See also Blake*
De la réforme des banques (Darimon), 181
Delbourgo, James, 81
Deleuze, Gilles, 5, 23, 28, 106, 135, 214n72, 217n95
"Demonology" (Emerson), 50
Dempster, M. Beth, 118
Derrida, Jacques, 195, 232n37, 234n70
de Staël, Germaine, 46
The Dial (journal), 75, 85
Dickinson, Emily, 203
Dienst, Richard, 159, 184
Dimock, Wai Chee, 63–65, 95, 105, 231n27
Diouf, Sylviane A., 262n30
Dismal Swamp Canal Company, 161
"The Dispersion of Seeds" (Thoreau), 138
Disraeli, Benjamin, 14
divested prayer, 72–73, 234n70
Divinity School Address (Emerson), 37, 38, 49
Django Unchained (film), 160
Douglass, Frederick: autobiography of, 194; on blacks as less-than-citizens, 3, 11; on Brown (W. W.), 178; on Dismal Swamp fugitives, 161; on liberalism, 11; Moten on, 154–55; "What to the Slave Is the Fourth of July," 11, 13

Dred: A Tale of the Great Dismal Swamp (Stowe), 160–75; bad debts in, 161–62, 164–65, 172–73; comparison to *Blake*, 189, 194–95; ecological-economic hermeneutics in, 158, 162, 167, 174–75; goblin growth in, 172–74; overview, 29, 154, 159; on passage from slave to ex-slave, 162–63, 165–66; plantation zone of appropriation in, 160, 162; plot of, 163–70, 174–75; religion in, 167–71; setting of, 160–61, 166–67, 169, 262n30
Dred Scott v. Sandford (1856), 143–44, 164, 165, 187
Du Bois, W. E. B., 9, 193–94
duCille, Ann, 175, 176
Dussel, Enrique, 8, 137, 146
"Duty" (Emerson), 48, 51–52, 53, 57
Dwight, John Sullivan, 85, 241n127

ecology: Darwin on, 5, 102, 155, 207n16; defined, 5, 102, 155, 207n16, 260n12; ecological accounts of resistance, 8, 28, 120, 130, 149, 150, 162, 260n12; para-ecological loop dialects of Thoreau, 101–5, 110–27, 155–56, 197. *See also Dred*
economic crisis (2008), 4, 11
economy of nature, 5, 102, 138–39, 155–56, 161, 207n16
Edelman, Lee, 1, 69, 71, 95
The Eighteenth Brumaire of Louis Bonaparte (Marx), 64–65
Elective Affinities (Goethe), 82–83
electrical energy: of Fuller's sistrum, 75–76; gender differences and, 76–78, 79–81, 236–37n97; harmony of, 80–84; historical context, 73–76; polarity of, 82–84, 86, 236–37n97; soul formation and, 79
electrical humanitarianism, 81
Elizabeth I (queen), 97
Ellis, Cristin, 26
Ellison, Ralph, 192
Emerson, Ralph Waldo: on caring, 203; duality of, 27, 33–35; on electrical energy, 75; on Fuller, 58, 60, 65–66, 70; on Goethe, 134; on impersonality, 5, 26–27, 34–35, 45, 57, 224–25n41, 225n43; on incompleteness of the self, 46–47, 52–53; on mesmerism, 74; on moral sentiment, 37–38, 49, 52–53; on natural

Emerson, Ralph Waldo (*continued*)
sciences, 39–45, 223–24n32; optimism of, 33–35, 46, 57, 204, 225–26n47; on peace, 47–48, 226n58; on political personhood, 27, 34–35, 36, 49, 53–55, 57; political radicalism of, 27, 33–35, 47–57, 226n58, 228–29n82; positivism and, 55; on Reason, 34, 38–41, 44, 46, 53–54, 75; on religious sentiment, 34–42, 45–51, 52, 54, 56, 86; on Thoreau, 146

Emerson, Ralph Waldo, writings of: "Circles," 46; "Comedy," 225–26n47; "Compensation," 38; "Courage," 36, 47, 226n54; "Demonology," 50; Divinity School Address, 37, 38, 49; "Duty," 48, 51–52, 53, 57; "Experience," 55–56; "Fate," 36, 48, 52, 54–55; "Humanity of Science," 41; "Introductory Lecture," 51; *Journals and Miscellaneous Notebooks*, Volume 3, 39; *Journals and Miscellaneous Notebooks*, Volume 4, 36, 42, 43; *Journals and Miscellaneous Notebooks*, Volume 7, 47; "The Lord's Supper," 36, 37, 48; "Love," 46; *Memoirs of Margaret Fuller Ossoli*, 58, 65; "Napoleon, or the Man of the World," 50; "The Naturalist," 45; *Nature*, 33, 38, 40–45, 91; "Politics," 48, 49–51; "Prospects," 45; "On the Relation of Man to the Globe," 40–41; "Religion," 37–38, 46; "Self-Reliance," 48, 55; "Spiritual Laws," 46; "War," 47–48; "Uses of Natural History," 43–44; "War," 47–48; Waterville College speech, 36

"Emersonian Terrorism" (Ziser), 55, 56
Empire of Neglect (Taylor), 211n49
equality, 7–11, 208n25, 261n17
Estes, Nick, 22, 208n22, 216n91, 277n15
Evans, Gil, 153
"Experience" (Emerson), 55–56
"'Experience,' Antislavery, and the Crisis of Emersonianism" (Pease), 55–57

Fanon, Frantz, 8, 20, 137
"Fate" (Emerson), 36, 48, 52, 54–55
femality, 77–79, 83
Feminist Conversations (Zwarg), 63
Ferdinand VII (king), 98
flat ontology, 25
Foams (Sloterdijk), 114
For a Left Populism (Mouffe), 4, 12, 206–7n12, 208n27, 210–11n49

Fourier, Charles, 243n134
Frederick Douglass' Paper, 178
Freeman, Elizabeth, 105, 150–51
Freud, Sigmund, 69
Fugitive Slave Act, 185, 260n12
Fuller, Margaret, 58–98; on attunement, 68–69; comparison to Emerson, 91; comparison to Thoreau, 94, 142–43, 151; death of, 59, 103; on dissonant energy, 58, 59, 68–73, 89, 92; Emerson on, 58, 60, 65–66, 70; on femality, 77–79, 83; on gender differences, 76–78, 79–81; on impersonality, 5, 98; Isis portrayal by, 64, 66–67, 70, 72, 96; as journalist (see *New-York Daily Tribune*); materialistic idealism of, 89–95, 239n124; musical tropes of, 58–60, 64–73; on music as a medium, 73–75, 84–90, 238n113, 239n115; mythology references by, 63–64, 66–67, 70, 72, 87–89, 96, 238n112; on polarity, 82–84, 86, 236–37n97; on political personhood, 27, 28, 60, 63; political radicalism of, 58–65, 95–98, 230–31nn12–18, 231n22, 243–44n139; positivism and, 59–60, 64, 73–74, 93, 95–96, 98; sistrum symbolism and, 65–73, 75–76, 86–87, 89, 96, 98, 204. *See also* electrical energy; harmony

Fuller, Margaret, writings of: "Autobiographical Romance," 78–79; "Bombardment and Defeat," 59; "The Celestial Empire," 90, 239n115; "A Dream," 67; "The Great Lawsuit," 96–97; *The Letters*, Volume 5, 59, 62, 231n16; *The Letters*, Volume 6, 231n18; "The Magnolia of Lake Pontchartrain," 90; "Music in New York," 86–87; "Mystical Experiences" reflections, 91; "New and Old World Democracy," 59, 62; "The Next Revolution," 59, 65, 98; "Ole Bull," 86; Orpheus poem, 87–88; reviews, 73, 75, 84, 85–87, 89; "Sistrum," 66–69, 72–73, 75–77, 86–89; "The Springtime Revolutions of '48," 62; *Summer on the Lakes*, 58, 71–72, 80; "Western Journal," 58; *Woman in the Nineteenth Century*, 64, 66, 76–80, 81–84, 87–89, 96–98; "Yuca Filamentosa," 91

Gayle, Addison, 175
Geontologies (Povinelli), 23–24
German Higher Criticism, 37, 168, 265n43

Glick, Jeremy Matthew, 190
Globes (Sloterdijk), 114
Goethe, Johan Wolfgang von, 72, 82–83, 85, 134
Goldstein, Alyosha, 8
Grafts (Marder), 149
"The Great Lawsuit" (Fuller), 96–97
Great Recession (2008), 4, 11
Greenwald, Grace, 188
Grundrisse (Marx), 181–82, 183–84, 199, 239–40n124
Guidotti-Hernández, Nicole M., 9–10
Gupta, Akhil, 9

Haeckel, Ernst, 207n16
Haitian earthquake (2010), 202
Haitian Revolution, 174, 189–90
Hamilton, Thomas, 191
Haraway, Donna, 118–19, 128
The Harbinger (journal), 85
Hardt, Michael, 7
Harman, Graham, 23
harmony: distributive harmonies, 89–95, 240–41n125, 241n127; of electrical bodies, 81–82; Fuller's social conception of, 89; material-idealist model of, 94–95, 243n134; music and, 84–89, 90–92; of opposites, 85; political agency as unharmonious, 59, 60, 63; promise of future harmony, 67; ravishing harmony, 82–84, 88–89, 92; Thoreau on, 94; traditional notion of, 80–81
Harney, Stefano: on bad debt, 158, 162, 163; on "existence without standing," 188–89; on "prophetic organization," 192; on "surrounds" concept, 17, 203
Hartman, Saidiya, 9, 154, 156, 159, 164, 258n157, 260n15
Harvard Divinity School, 36–37
Harvey, David, 11
Hauffe, Frederica, 72, 80, 83–84
Haytian Emigration Bureau, 191
Heidegger, Martin, 9, 116–17, 200, 250n59
"The Herald of Freedom" (Thoreau), 147
"hereish," 117–18, 122–23, 127, 171–72, 203, 275n8
Hickman, Jared, 170
Holbrook, Josiah, 39
Holmes, Stephen, 13–14
Horkheimer, Max, 65, 219n112
Howe, Julia Ward, 82, 237n97
Howe, Susan, 196

Hugo, Victor, 85
humanism, 2, 4, 13, 19, 27, 94–95
Humankind (Morton), 219n107, 254n106
Humboldt, Alexander von, 115–16, 117
Hunter, Alexander, 262n30
Hurst, C. Michael, 80–81, 190
Hyde, Carrie, 168, 207n14, 263n36
Hyperobjects (Morton), 93, 248n32, 253n101, 265n49
Hyppolite, Jean, 136

"Illiberal Emerson" (Larson), 11, 35
illiberalism, 2, 3, 4–5, 22, 216n88
impersonality: Emerson on, 5, 26–27, 34–35, 45, 224–25n41, 225n43; Fuller on, 5, 98; Thoreau on, 121
indigenous peoples: Fuller on, 58–59; Thoreau on, 129–33, 140, 202
Indigenous studies scholarship, 21–22, 216n88, 216nn91–92
An Inquiry into Modes of Existence (Latour), 25
interiority, 18–19, 29. *See also* personhood
Interior States (Castiglia), 18–19
In the Break (Moten), 20, 154–55, 273n130
In the Wake (Sharpe), 175–76, 185, 202, 258n157, 260n12
Intimacies of Four Continents (Lowe), 2, 176, 190–91, 212n53
The Invisible Man (Ellison), 192
Isis (goddess), 64, 66–67, 70, 72, 96
Italian Journey (Goethe), 134
Italian Revolution, 59, 60–62, 65
Ives, Elam, 85

Jackson, Edmund, 160–61
Jacobs, Harriet, 153
Jagoda, Patrick, 112–13
James, C. L. R., 190–91, 204, 272n117
James, Henry, 60
Jameson, Fredric, 107, 135, 217, 246–47n19
Jardin des Plantes (Paris), 43–44
Jesus, 110, 147
Johnston, Adrian, 16, 23–25

Kant, Immanuel, 53–54, 68, 69, 93, 241n127
Kazanjian, David, 10, 240n125, 271n105
Keats, John, 79, 142–43

K.I.P. (Nguyen), 150–51
King, Martin Luther, Jr., 111, 249n35
Kohn, Eduardo, 149
Kosmos (Humboldt), 115

Lacan, Jacques, 16, 93
Lacoue-Labarthe, Philippe, 94, 242–43n133
Larson, Kerry, 11, 35
Las Exaltadas, 98, 245n145
Latour, Bruno, 24–26, 93, 150, 218–19nn106–107
Law, John, 250n59
Lazzarato, Maurizio, 179
Leach, Elizabeth Eva, 68
"The Leap from the Long Bridge" (Greenwald), 188
left populism, 4, 206–7n12
Letters to the People on Health and Happiness (Beecher), 81
Levine, Caroline, 112, 119–20, 192–93, 254n107
Levine, Robert, 189, 191–93
Levy, Jonathan, 173
liberal humanism, 2–3, 13, 94–95
liberalism: abandonment of, 1–2; abolition movements and, 3–4, 9–11, 13, 14–15; in antebellum America, 11; as bourgeois political realities, 6–9; caring and, 202; challenges to, 12–13; collective black resistance against, 9; economic practice of, 11–13; equal rights and, 7; historical use of term, 14, 35; oppression of, 3–4, 9–11, 13–15, 19–20, 214–15n76; on personhood, 17–18, 20; political practice of, 11–14, 212n53; racial liberalism, 3–4, 9–11, 13, 19–20; scholarship trends influenced by, 5–6; subjectivity and, 18, 35, 45, 53–55, 176
Lieberman, Jethro, 13
The Life of Beethoven (Schindler), 73, 84
"Life Without Principle" (Thoreau), 141–42, 147–48
Linera, Álvaro García, 5, 7–8
Locke, John, 37
Lopez, Michael, 223n32
"The Lord's Supper" (Emerson), 36, 37, 48
Loring, Anna, 236n97
Los Exaltados, 98, 244–45n145
Losurdo, Domenico, 3, 14

Lowe, Lisa: *Intimacies of Four Continents*, 212n53; on James's writing style, 190–91; on liberal humanism, 2, 3; on political practice of liberalism, 17, 212n53; on slave narratives, 176, 178
Lowens, Irving, 85
Luhmann, Niklas, 214n72
Luther, Martin, 52

Madison, James, 10
"The Magnolia of Lake Pontchartrain" (Fuller), 90
The Maine Woods (Thoreau), 122, 125–27, 131, 132, 253n98
Manson, Deborah, 74
Marder, Michael, 28, 149–50
Mariotti, Shannon, 107–8
The Market Wonders (Briante), 101
Martin, Bonnie, 180
Marx, Karl, 154–55, 159, 243n134; *The Eighteenth Brumaire of Louis Bonaparte*, 64–65; *Grundrisse*, 181–82, 183–84, 199, 239–40n124
Marxism, 5–6, 13, 155, 190, 261n25
Massumi, Brian, 18, 214n72
Matthiessen, F. O., 33, 34
Mazzini, Giuseppe, 61
Mbembe, Achille, 10, 13, 18, 155, 157–58, 179, 211n51, 215n83
McGowan, Todd, 69, 71, 234n57
Meillassoux, Quentin, 216–17n94
Melamed, Jodi, 212n51, 261n17
Melville, Herman, 123–24, 133
Memoirs of Margaret Fuller Ossoli (Emerson), 58, 65
Mesmer, Franz Anton, 74, 81
mesmerism, 74, 78
The Metamorphosis, or Golden Ass (Apuleius), 66
Mickiewicz, Adam, 61, 230–31n15
middens, 129–30
Mills, Charles W., 3–4, 14
#Misanthropocene: 24 Theses (Clover & Spahr), 201
Mitchell, Timothy, 8
Mont Pèlerin Society, 11
Moore, Jason, 25, 102, 155, 199, 215n77, 218n103, 260n12
Morton, Timothy: correlationism and, 204, 275–76n12; *Dark Ecology*, 117–18, 124, 141, 254n107, 275–76n12; on human experience, 93–94, 242n129;

Humankind, 219n107, 254n106;
Hyperobjects, 93, 242n129, 248n32, 253n101, 265n49; on loops, 117–18, 124, 127, 141; on new materialism, 219n107; on Thoreau, 133
Moten, Fred: *Black and Blur*, 153, 154–55, 156–57, 204, 272n119; on black existence as a paraontology, 19–21, 22, 119, 215–16n84; on "existence without standing," 188–89; *In the Break*, 20, 154–55, 273n130; on James's writing style, 190, 191, 204; on "not-in-between," 190, 204; on "prophetic organization," 192; on racial state capitalism, 13; on "surrounds" concept, 17, 203; on unadjusted emancipations, 153, 157, 158–59, 162–63; on "unknowing," 186; on U.S. national policy in eighteenth century, 10
Mott, Wesley T., 37
Mouffe, Chantal, 4, 12, 206–7n12, 208n27, 210–11n49
Muñoz, José Esteban, 95, 155, 157, 204, 219n112
Murison, Justine, 75, 78
music: Fuller's musical-social ideal, 87–89; Fuller's musical troupes, 58–60, 64–73; Fuller's reviews on, 85–87; Fuller's use of music as a medium, 73–75, 84–90, 238n113, 239n115; harmony and, 84–89, 90–92; of nineteenth century, 84–85; sistrum's symbolism, 65–73, 75–77, 86–89, 96, 98, 204; Thoreau's music boxes, 105
"Music in New York" (Fuller), 86–87
"Mystical Experiences" reflections (Fuller), 91

Nabers, Deak, 143–44, 149
Nancy, Jean-Luc, 8
"Napoleon, or the Man of the World" (Emerson), 50
Napoleon I, 50
National Magazine and Republican Review, 78
Native Americans: Fuller on, 58–59; Thoreau on, 129–33, 140, 202
Natural History Society, 44
"The Naturalist" (Emerson), 45
Nature (Emerson), 33, 38, 41, 40–45, 91
Nealon, Christopher, 16
Nealon, Jeffrey, 149

necro citizenship, 10, 187–88
necropolitics, 10
Negri, Antonio, 7, 15, 179, 181–82, 212–13n58
Nelson, Dana D., 207n14
neoliberalism: abandonment of, 1–2; capitalism and, 13, 210n46; challenges to, 12–13; contradictions of, 4; defined, 11–12; economic practice of, 17–18; on personhood, 17–18, 214n72; structural adjustment and, 12, 154, 157, 210n46
Nersessian, Anahid, 111, 248–49n35
New Americanism, 26
New England Congregationalism, 36–37
Newfield, Christopher, 35, 45
Newman, Lance, 120
new materialism, 4, 16, 22–26, 106, 217n95, 218–19n107
New-York Daily Tribune: Fuller's employment at, 61, 62, 84, 230n14; Fuller's musical reviews in, 75; Fuller's review of Bull in, 85–87, 89; Fuller's review on Schindler in, 73, 84; Marx's employment at, 64
New-York Pathfinder, 77, 83
"The Next Revolution" (Fuller), 98
Nguyen, Tan Hoang, 150–51
Niagara Falls, 58, 59, 70
Nixon, Rob, 218n107, 248n31

Obama administration, 19
Observations on the Growth of the Mind (Reed), 44–45
Oceti Sakowin, 22, 208n22, 216n91
Olmsted, Frederick, 262n30
On the Origin of Species (Darwin), 138
"On the Relation of Man to the Globe" (Emerson), 40–41
ontology, 5, 15–16, 20–26, 142, 171, 176. *See also* impersonality; paraontology; personhood
Orpheus, 87–89, 238n112
Orpheus and Cerberus (Crawford), 87, 88
Orpheus poem (Fuller), 87–88
Ossoli, Giovanni Angelo, 61, 103, 104, 109
Ossoli, Margaret Fuller. *See* Fuller, Margaret
The Other Emerson (Arsić & Wolfe), 33–34

Packer, Barbara, 36–37
Palestine, 202

parahuman, 29, 150, 159–60, 162, 214–15n76
paraontology: black existence as, 19–22, 119, 215–16nn83–84; overview, 16, 19–21, 216n88; relation to existing paradigms, 22
Pease, Donald, 55–57, 224–25n41
personhood: citizenship and, 8; democracy without, 29; federal affect and, 18–19; liberalism and, 17–18, 20; neoliberalism and, 17–18, 214n72; overview, 5, 17, 213–14nn65–66; place and location considerations, 21–22; political (*see* political personhood)
Pierrot, Grégory, 189–90, 191, 192, 197
plantation zone of appropriation, 8, 130, 155–56, 162–63
Plant-Thinking (Marder), 149
Plater, Emily, 97
Plebeian Power (Linera), 7–8
pluralsim, 11, 15, 25, 27, 210–11n49
plural universe, 15, 212–13n58
Plutarch, 70–71, 96
political personhood: Emerson on, 27, 34–35, 49, 53–55, 57; Fuller on, 27–28, 60
political radicalism: of Emerson, 27, 33–35, 47–57, 226n58, 228–29n82; of Fuller, 58–65, 95–98, 230–31nn12–18, 231n22, 243–44n139; of Thoreau, 107–11, 119–20, 141–52, 246n16
"Politics" (Emerson), 48, 49–51
populist moment, 4
Porgy and Bess (Gershwin & Evans), 153
Porte, Joel, 46
positivism: Emerson and, 55; Fuller and, 59–60, 64, 73–74, 93, 95–96, 98; Kant and, 54; suggested abandonment of, 6, 15; Thoreau and, 105, 107–8, 115–18, 143–48
posthumanism, 4, 19, 27
Povinelli, Elizabeth, 23–24, 117, 171, 203, 275n8
Price, Enoch, 185, 269n78
Prolegomena to Any Future Materialism (Johnston), 16, 23
Puar, Jasbir, 3, 206n7
Puig de la Bellacasa, María, 202–3

racial liberalism, 3–4, 9–11, 13, 19–20
racism. *See* Native Americans; slavery and abolition movements; violence

Rancière, Jacques, 19, 119–20
Reading Capital (Althusser), 1, 5
Reason: Emerson on, 34, 38–41, 44, 46, 53–54, 75; Fuller on, 91; personhood and, 27
Reassembling the Social (Latour), 24–25
Redpath, James, 191
Reed, Samson, 44–45
"Reform and the Reformers" (Thoreau), 146, 148
"Religion" (Emerson), 37–38, 46
religious sentiment: Emerson on, 27, 34–42, 45–51, 52, 54, 56, 86; Fuller on, 86; theory of, 27
resistance: collective resistance, 9, 29; ecological accounts of, 8, 28, 120, 130, 149, 150, 162, 260n12
"Resistance to Civil Government" (Thoreau), 111, 147
Reynolds, Larry, 226n58, 230nn12–13
Richardson, Robert D., Jr., 107
Robinson, Cedric, 13, 156
Roediger, David, 193
Rogers, Nathaniel, 147
Romero, Lora, 81
Ronda, Margaret, 24
Rossi, Pellegrino, 62
Ruffin, Thomas, 9, 163
Rusert, Britt, 196–97, 273n130
Ruttenburg, Nancy, 213–14n66

Said, Edward, 27
Saint-Martin, Louis Claude de, 96
Saloman, Ora Frishberg, 75, 84–85, 238n107
Saltz, Laura, 236n97
Samuel (*Old Testament*), 109, 110
Sanborn, Geoffrey, 175, 176, 267–68n64, 269n74
Schindler, Anton, 73, 84
Schleiermacher, Friedrich, 37
Schoolman, Martha, 192, 263n36, 267n63, 273n130
Schuller, Kyla, 26
Second Church of Boston, 36, 37
Sedgwick, Eve Kosofsky, 1
"Self-Reliance" (Emerson), 48, 55
"The Service" (Thoreau), 141
Sexton, Jared, 20, 188
Sharpe, Christina, 175–76, 185, 187, 202–3, 260n12, 277n15
Sigourney, Lydia Howard Huntley, 132

Index

"Sistrum" (Fuller), 66–69, 72–73, 75–77, 86–89
sistrum symbolism, 65–73, 75–77, 86–89, 96, 98, 204
slavery and abolition movements: collective black resistance and, 9, 29; ecology of, 155–56 (see also *Blake*; *Dred*; plantation zone of appropriation); emancipation and, 28–29, 157–60 (*see also* unadjusted emancipations); foreclosed economic personhood and, 156–57 (see also *Blake*; *Clotel*); Fuller on, 60–61, 97, 244n144; liberalism and, 3–4, 9–11, 13, 14–15; Stowe (H. B.) on, 161–62; Thoreau on, 143–52
"Slavery in Massachusetts" (Thoreau), 111, 144–45
Sloterdijk, Peter, 113–17, 127
Smith, Adam, 14
Smith, Caleb, 191, 209n31
Smith, Gail K., 162, 168
Smith, Rachel Greenwald, 25, 249n35
Snediker, Michael, 17
Somerset v. Stewart (1772), 143
Spahr, Juliana, 201
Spanish revolutions, 61, 98, 198, 208n25, 244–45n145
Specimens of the Table-Talk (Coleridge), 91
The Speculative Turn (Bryant, Srnicek, & Harman), 23
speculative turn counterpoint, 23, 216–17n94
Spiller, Robert, 39, 104
Spinoza, Baruch, 23, 28, 78, 93
"Spiritual Laws" (Emerson), 46
Spivak, Gayatri Chakravorty, 107, 276n15
Spring, Marcus, 61, 62
Spring, Rebecca, 61, 62
Srnicek, Nick, 23
State v. Mann (1829), 163, 164
Staying with the Trouble (Haraway), 118–19
Steele, Jeffrey, 62–63, 64, 80, 230n12, 231n22
Stengers, Isabelle, 206n6, 218n106
Stoler, Ann Laura, 95
Story, William Wetmore, 85
Stowe, Harriet Beecher, 81, 160–64. See also *Dred*

subjectivity: blackness and, 20–21, 155–56, 157–58, 187–88; bourgeois and, 116, 121; capitalism and, 178–84; Cartesian, 53–54, 57, 69; citizen-subjects (*see* citizens and citizenship; xenocitizens); communism and, 6; dialectics and, 137; duty and, 53–55, 57; ecological loop dialectics of, 149–50; economics and, 18; liberalism and, 18, 35, 45, 53–55, 176; not-quite-subjects, 23; Romanticism and, 142–43; structures of, 120–21; subject, defined, 17, 213n65 (*see also* personhood); violence and, 51, 53, 129
Summer on the Lakes (Fuller), 58, 71–72, 80
Swammerdam (Dutch biologist), 42
Swedenborg, Emanuel, 41
syntactical anthropomorphism, 26
syntactical liberalism, 26

Taney, Roger, 10, 143
Tarantino, Quentin, 160
Taylor, Christopher, 211n49
Taylor, Jesse Oak, 207n16, 266n56
Taylor, Matthew A., 26
Taylor, Thomas, 66, 70
Terada, Rei, 57
Thatcher, Margaret, 25
"thereish," 171–72, 173–74, 203, 265–66n50
Thoreau, Henry David: Arsić on, 28, 94, 105–8, 112, 147; comparison to Fuller, 94, 142–43, 151; on habitation, 120–24; on harmony, 94; "hereish" notion of, 117–18, 122–23, 127; on impersonality, 121; on Native Americans, 129–33, 140, 202; nested loop dialectics of, 105–8, 127–41, 155–56, 204; overview, 5, 28; para-ecological loop dialects of, 101–5, 110–27, 149–50, 155–56, 197; political radicalism of, 107–11, 119–20, 141–52, 246n16; positivism and, 105, 107–8, 115–18, 143–48; scientific thought of, 108–9, 115–16; on sexuality, 109; shipwreck scenes described by, 103–4; on slavery, 143–52; sonic materiality theory of, 104–5; visions of nature, 101–2, 108, 121, 125–26, 133–41, 147–48; worldview, 101, 135–41

Thoreau, Henry David, writings of: *Cape Cod*, 104; "The Dispersion of Seeds," 138; "The Herald of Freedom," 147; John Brown essays, 139, 142–43, 146–47, 152, 257n135; *Journal*, Volume 1, 101, 113, 125, 129, 137, 139, 148; *Journal*, Volume 2, 101, 122, 127, 128, 252n82, 255n118; *Journal*, Volume 3, 103–5; *Journal*, Volume 4, 112; *Journal*, Volume 5, 102; *Journal*, Volume 8, 119; "Life Without Principle," 141–42, 147–48; *The Maine Woods*, 122, 125–27, 131, 132, 253n98; "Reform and the Reformers," 146, 148; "Resistance to Civil Government," 111, 147; "The Service," 141; "Slavery in Massachusetts," 111, 144–45; *Walden*, 108–10, 117, 120–24, 128–31, 133–37, 139–40, 148–49, 152; "Walking," 118–19; *A Week on the Concord and Merrimack Rivers*, 110–11, 113, 123–25, 127–29, 131–33, 136, 139–40, 145–46, 150, 152, 249n44, 255n119
Thorson, Robert, 108, 115, 116, 117
Time Binds (Freeman), 150–51
Tocqueville, Alexis de, 14–15
Tomorrow's Parties (Coviello), 109, 151
transcendentalism: Emerson and, 27, 50–51, 56–57; Fuller and, 27, 69; overview, 27; Thoreau and, 116–17, 128
Transcendentalist movement, 85
Transcendental Resistance (Voelz), 35
Transfiguring America (Steele), 62–63
Travels (Bartram), 130
Trump administration, 19
Turner, Nat, 161, 177–78
Typee (Melville), 123–24, 133

unadjusted emancipations, 28–29, 153–54, 157–60. *See also* bad debt; *Blake*; *Clotel*; *Dred*
Uncle Tom's Cabin (Stowe), 161
Unitarian church, 36–37
Universes Without Us (Taylor), 26

Vesey, Denmark, 166, 172, 177
vibrant materialism, 93, 94, 111, 273n130, 276n12
violence: black radical violence, 163, 165–66; of capitalism, 180–84; caring and, 202–4; citizenship and, 9–11, 14; Emerson on, 34–35; of race, 130–31, 140–43, 157–58, 161, 168, 176–77, 196–97; subjectivity and, 51, 53, 129. *See also* political radicalism
"The Virginia Maroons" (Jackson), 160–61
Virno, Paolo, 95
vitalism, 23, 28, 106–7
Voelz, Johannes, 35
Voyage of the Beagle (Darwin), 138

Waggoner, Josephine, 22
Wagner, Bryan, 188
Walden (Thoreau), 108–10, 117, 120–24, 128–31, 133–37, 139–40, 148–49, 152
Walker, David, 193
"Walking" (Thoreau), 118–19
Wallon, Henri, 9
Walls, Laura Dassow, 40, 114–16, 117, 128, 129–30, 224n32
"War" (Emerson), 47–48
Warren, Calvin L., 187, 215–16nn83–84
Warrior, Robert, 21–22
Washington, George, 161
Washington, Madison, 177
Washington Consensus, 12
Watt, James, 24
Wealth of Nations (Smith), 14
Weekly Anglo-African, 189
A Week on the Concord and Merrimack Rivers (Thoreau), 110–11, 113, 123–25, 127–29, 131–33, 136, 139–40, 145–46, 150, 152, 249n44, 255n119
Weheliye, Alexander, 17, 187, 215n76
"Western Journal" (Fuller), 58
Whicher, Stephen, 39
Whitman, Walt, 75, 204, 276n15
Wilderson, Frank B., III, 20, 153–55, 157–58, 215n83, 216n88
Williams, Gary, 238n112
Williamson, John, 12
Wilson, Ivy, 186, 188, 267n63
Wolfe, Cary, 4, 17, 33–34, 224–25n41
Wolfendale, Peter, 25
Woman in the Nineteenth Century (Fuller), 64, 66, 76–80, 81–84, 87–89, 96–98

worlding, 22, 110–11, 116–18, 129, 250n59
A World of Many Worlds (de la Cadena & Blaser), 22, 212–13n58

xenocitizens: black resistance and, 9, 29; caring and, 201–4; defined, 1–5, 7–8; illiberalism and, 2, 3
X—The Problem of the Negro as a Problem for Thought (Chandler), 20–21, 265–66n50

Young Italy movement, 61–62
"Yuca Filamentosa" (Fuller), 91

Ziser, Michael, 55, 56
Žižek, Slavoj, 23, 53, 69, 70, 216–17nn94–95, 240n125
Zorgue (slave ship), 202
Zupancic, Alenka, 53
Zuzeca Sapa, 22
Zwarg, Christina, 63, 231n22

JASON BERGER is Associate Professor of English at the University of Houston. He is the author of *Antebellum at Sea: Maritime Fantasies in Nineteenth-Century America* (2012).

www.ingramcontent.com/pod-product-compliance
Lightning Source LLC
Chambersburg PA
CBHW030435300426
44112CB00009B/1016